State/Space

State/Space

A Reader

Edited by

Neil Brenner, Bob Jessop,
Martin Jones, and Gordon MacLeod

Blackwell
Publishing

350 Main Street, Malden, MA 02148-5018, USA
108 Cowley Road, Oxford OX4 1JF, UK
550 Swanston Street, Carlton, Victoria 3053, Australia
Kurfürstendamm 57, 10707 Berlin, Germany

First published 2003 by Blackwell Publishers Ltd, a Blackwell Publishing company

Library of Congress Cataloging-in-Publication Data

State/space : a reader / edited by Neil Brenner... [et al.].
    p. cm.
  Includes bibliographical references and index.
  ISBN 0-631-23033-5 (alk. paper) – ISBN 0-631-23034-3 (pbk.: alk. paper)
    1. State, The. 2. Globalization. 3. Local government. 4. Regionalism. I. Brenner, Neil.

JC11 .S77 2003
320.1–dc21   2002071227

ISBN 0-631-23033-5 (hardback); ISBN 0-631-23034-3 (paperback)

A catalogue record for this title is available from the British Library.

Set in 10/12pt Plantin
by Kolam Information Services Pvt. Ltd, Pondicherry, India

For further information on
Blackwell Publishing, visit our website:
http://www.blackwellpublishing.com

Contents

Acknowledgments

The idea for this book originated in a series of discussions among the editors inspired by two sets of panels on the political economy of scale at geography conferences in 2000. Gordon MacLeod and Jane Pollard co-organized some panels on "Political and economic geographies of scale" at the Joint Annual Meeting of the Royal Geographical Society and Institute for British Geographers, held in January 2000 at the University of Sussex. These panels revealed some of the basic theoretical problems involved in theorizing the changing political economy of scale and its implications for state space. Comments by Jamie Gough and Erik Swyngedouw were especially helpful in this regard. An opportunity for further inspiration and discussion came from a series of panels on "State space in transformation: new approaches to political geography and state theory," which were co-organized by Neil Brenner and Martin Jones at the Annual Meeting of the Association of American Geographers, April 2000, in Pittsburgh, Pennsylvania. All four editors presented papers here and we received some very useful feedback from our co-panelists and other participants. Neil Brenner would like to thank the Economic Geography Research Group of the RGS-IBG for providing a Young Researchers Travel Grant that enabled him to attend the Sussex conference. Bob Jessop would like to thank *Antipode* and Blackwell Publishing for supporting his travel to the same meeting. The editors also gratefully acknowledge the comments provided by three anonymous reviewers, which proved extremely helpful as we worked to complete the project.

This book provides no more than a first cut into a large, multidisciplinary, and rapidly growing research field. It makes no claim to provide a comprehensive survey of recent work on state space. Many difficult, even painful, editorial decisions were required in order to meet some very strict length requirements imposed by the publisher. We do hope, however, that this volume will provide readers with a broad overview of this exciting new field of theory and research. We also anticipate, in future work, the further development of our own research agenda on the production and transformation of state space under modern capitalism.

Apeldoorn, B. van (2001) "The Struggle over European Order: Transnational Class Agency in the Making of 'Embedded Neo-Liberalism,'" in Andreas Bieler and Adam David Morton, eds, *Social Forces in the Making of the New Europe: The*

Restructuring of European Social Relations in the Global Political Economy. Basingstoke: Palgrave, pp. 70–89 (copyright © Palgrave, Houndmills, Basingstoke, Hampshire, reproduced with permission of Palgrave).

Arrighi, Giovanni (1996) "The Rise of East Asia and the Withering Away of the Interstate System," *Journal of World Systems Research*, vol. 2 (15). University of Colorado. Originally published in *Journal of World-Systems Research*, II, 15, 1996. This revised version first published in N. Lazarus and C. Bartolovich, eds, *Marxism, Modernity and Postcolonial Studies*. Cambridge: Cambridge University Press, 2002.

Blatter, J. (2002) "Debordering the World of States. Towards a Multi-Level System in Europe and a Multi-Polity System in North America? Insights from Border Regions." Reprinted by permission of Sage Publications Ltd from *European Journal of International Relations*, 7 (2). (© Sage Publications Ltd and European Consortium for Political Research, 2001.)

Cameron, A. and Palan, R. "The Imagined Economy: Mapping Transformations in the Contemporary State," in Millennium: *Journal of International Studies*, vol. 28, no. 2 1999, pp. 267–89.

Escolar, M. (1997) "Exploration, Cartography and the Modernization of State Power," *International Social Science Journal*, issue 151. (Copyright © Blackwell Publishers.)

Holston, James and Appadurai, Arjun. Introduction, *Cities and Citizenship*, pp. 1–17, ed. James Holston. Copyright 1999, Duke University Press. All rights reserved. Reprinted with permission.

Keating, Michael (1996) "The Invention of Regions: Political Restructuring and Territorial Government in Western Europe," a working paper for ARENA (Advanced Research on the Europeanisation of the Nation-state). Copyright © ARENA and Michael Keating.

Keil, R. (2001) "Globalization Makes States: Perspectives on Local Governance in the Age of the World City," *Review of International Political Economy*, 5 (4), copyright © Routledge, Taylor and Francis.

Lefebvre, H. (1977) *De L'Etat: le mode de production etatique*. Paris: Union Generale d'Editions.

Lipietz, Alain. Excerpted from "The National and the Regional: Their Autonomy Vis-à-Vis the Capitalist World Crisis" by Alain Lipietz, as published in *From Transcending the State–Global Divide: A Neostructuralist Agenda in International Relations*, edited by Ronan P. Palan and Barry Gills. Copyright © 1995 by Lynne Reinner Publishers, Inc. Used with permission of the publisher.

Mann, Michael (1988) *States, War and Capitalism: Studies in Political Sociology*, pp. 1–32, copyright © *Archives Europeennes De Sociologie*.

Nordstrom, C. (2000) "Shadows and Sovereigns." Reprinted by permission of Sage Publications Ltd from *Theory, Culture & Society*, 17 (4), pp. 35–54. (© Sage Publications Ltd and Theory, Culture & Society Ltd, 2000.)

Poulantzas, N. (1978) *State, Power, Socialism*. Copyright © Verso, London.

Shaw, M. (1997): "The State of Globalization: Towards a Theory of State Trans-formation," *Review of International Political Economy*, 4 (3), pp. 497–513, copyright © Routledge, Taylor and Francis.

Smith, N. "Remaking Scale: Competition and Cooperation in Prenational and Postnational Europe," in H. Eskelinen and F. Snickars (eds), *Competitive European Peripheries*. Berlin: Springer, pp. 59–74. Copyright © Springer Verlag Heidelberg, Germany.

Sum, N.-L. (1999) "Rethinking Globalisation: Re-articulating Spatial Scale and Temporal Horizons of Trans-border Spaces," in K. Olds et al., eds, *Globalisation and the Asia Pacific*, London: Routledge, pp. 129–45. Copyright © Routledge, Taylor and Francis.

Taylor, P. J. (1994) "The State as Container: Territoriality in the Modern World-System," *Progress in Human Geography*, 18 (3), pp. 151–62 (Copyright © Arnold, member of Hodder Headline Group, London.)

Yuval-Davis, N. (2000) "Citizenship, Territoriality and the Gendered Construction of Difference," in E. F. Isin, ed., *Democracy, Citizenship and the Global City*, pp. 171–88. Copyright © Routledge Journal, Taylor and Francis.

Every effort has been made to trace the copyright holders of the above material.

Introduction: State Space in Question

Neil Brenner, Bob Jessop, Martin Jones, and Gordon MacLeod

The contributions to this book explore the spatiality of state power in historical and contemporary capitalist social formations. The observation that states are spatial entities may seem self-evident to many readers. Modern states are demarcated from each other by territorial boundaries that they patrol and regulate for military, police, economic, political, demographic, and many other reasons. Likewise, modern states are internally divided into diverse territorial jurisdictions and administrative subdivisions. The most cursory glance at a contemporary world political map seems to confirm the self-evident character of these spatial properties of the modern state. For such maps depict a plethora of distinct state territories, large and small, separated from one another by a global grid of boundaries, and generally demarcated as color-coded "blocks" of space on a flat surface. Thus each individual state is represented as a kind of container that separates an "inside" of domestic political interactions from an "outside" of international or inter-state relations (Walker 1993). This container metaphor also underpins conventional depictions of intra-national political spaces. Thus each regional or local jurisdiction is viewed as a self-enclosed political territory within a nested hierarchy of geographical arenas contained within each other like so many Russian dolls.

Our introduction identifies and comments on an emergent research agenda that is concerned with the production and transformation of state space. This agenda is particularly focused on the restructuring of territorially demarcated forms of state power and the recent decentering of nationally scaled forms of state activity. It also highlights the differential effects of newly emergent political and state spaces on the structural and strategic capacities of the state, the mobilization of social forces, and the dynamics and effectivity of political struggles. Taken together, as we explore below, these complementary research agendas are systematically challenging the entrenched geographical assumptions of mainstream approaches to state space.

Recent Challenges to the Naturalization of State Space

Images of state spatiality as a pre-given and relatively unchanging feature of modernity are epitomized in Max Weber's famous definition of the modern state as "a human community that (successfully) claims the monopoly of the legitimate use of physical force within a given territory" (Weber 1946: 78). This definition also illustrates the pervasive taken-for-grantedness of territoriality among most twentieth-century social theorists and social scientists. Indeed, while Weber invested much effort in defining the concepts of legitimacy and force, he did not attempt to problematize or analyze territoriality. Instead he simply accepted it as the necessary condition for the definition of the subjects of state power (*Staatsvolk*) and for the internal exercise of organized violence. Typically, the issue was reduced, in his major theoretical writings, to one point on a definitional checklist that could simply be presupposed in any discussion of modern bureaucratic states. Apart from a few innovative political geographers (e.g., Gottmann 1973), most social scientists have followed Weber's example in neglecting state territoriality as an object of serious intellectual inquiry.

This naturalization of state space in modern societies is associated with a range of implicit geographical assumptions that political geographer John Agnew has aptly summarized as the "territorial trap" (1994). This "geographical unconscious" has haunted much of postwar state theory, international relations, and political sociology, silently pervading theory construction and empirical research. It comprises three core assumptions. First, the state is said to possess sovereign control over its territorial borders. This implies that mutually exclusive, territorially self-enclosed, and unitary state actors constitute the basic units of the global political system. Second, and consequently, the binary opposition between the "domestic" and the "foreign" is regarded as a fixed feature of the modern inter-state system. This establishes the national scale as the ontologically necessary foundation for modern political life. And, third, the state is conceived as a static, timeless territorial "container" that encloses economic and political processes. This conception shapes analyses of the geographies of all other social relations – this is especially evident in the assumption that state, society, and economy are contained by congruent, more or less perfectly overlapping geographical borders.

The inter-state system instituted by the Treaty of Westphalia in 1648 is generally presented as the dominant form of geopolitical organization from its inception until the late twentieth century. This Westphalian system was premised on the "bundling" of sovereignty (the notion that each state commands a monopoly of legitimate power within its own domain and is entitled to exercise it without external interference) and territoriality (the delineation of that domain around self-enclosed, mutually exclusive borders) (see Ruggie 1993; for an alternative interpretation, see Osiander 2001). In this context, the geographical assumptions associated with Agnew's "territorial trap" appear to have a certain material – but imperfect and partial – foundation as products of state interaction within the Westphalian system. But failure to relativize these assumptions in relation to the history of state formation in a particular period is bound to produce a limited and somewhat static approach to the relations between state power and social space.

As if in confirmation of Hegel's remark that the owl of Minerva takes flight at dusk, social scientists since the mid- to late 1980s have begun to develop new and creative approaches to the study of state space that offer diverse escape routes from the (Westphalian) territorial trap. Initially they questioned how far, under the rapidly changing geopolitical conditions of the late twentieth century, conventional territorialist mappings of the inter-state system still provided an adequate framework for understanding political life. In a rapidly expanding set of literatures, social scientists have also decentered the hitherto entrenched role of the national scale as the predominant locus for state activities; in so doing, they have also questioned the internal coherence of national economies and national civil societies as real and/ or imagined targets for state policies (Radice 1984; Keating 1998; Scott 1998). Such concerns have prompted many scholars to study the historical origins and eventual consolidation of the Westphalian geopolitical system, with its apparently self-enclosed, directly contiguous, mutually exclusive, and sovereign territorial units (see, e.g., Spruyt 1994; Kratochwil 1986). This in turn has prompted increasing critical attention to the changing spatialities of state power and political life and to the development of new methodologies for their study.

This emergent research agenda has been consolidated in recent years through a number of closely related, albeit analytically distinct, approaches to theorizing and investigating state space. Together these have generated several distinct research perspectives, four of which are especially relevant here:

1 *Society and space*. Inspired by Henri Lefebvre (1974) among others, there has been a wide-ranging "reassertion of a critical spatial perspective in social theory" (Soja 1989: 1). As well as human geographers, whose work has long been concerned with the spatiality of social life, numerous social theorists and historical sociologists have explicitly integrated sociospatial considerations into their research (see, e.g., Harvey 1982, 1989a, 1989b; Castells 1983; Scott and Storper 1986; Gregory and Urry 1985; Giddens 1985; Mann 1986, 1993; Wallerstein 1988). These scholars were joined in the 1990s by an emergent school of "critical international relations theory" that questions the unreflexive methodological territorialism of both realist and liberal approaches to world politics and emphasizes the historical-geographical specificity of the territory–sovereignty nexus as a mode of geopolitical and geoeconomic organization (Macmillan and Linklater 1995; Walker 1993). At the same time, anthropologists began to develop explicitly spatialized conceptual vocabularies to grasp emergent forms of "diasporic" cultural identity and political mobilization that appear to escape direct territorialization in allegedly self-enclosed geographical arenas (see, e.g., Appadurai 1996; Gupta 1993). The overall impact of these different bodies of work has been to break the taken-for-granted link between state territoriality and society and, indeed, for some, to destabilize, if not completely undermine, the very notion of society (cf. Anderson 1996; Mann 1986).

2 *The "globalization" debates*. Since the early 1970s, debates have raged over the nature, extent, and significance of globalization. These have prompted social scientists to rethink issues of space, highlighting its social production and historical transformation in and through many emergent, interconnected geographical scales. Consequently, space no longer appears as a static platform or surface on which social relations are constructed, but rather as one of their constitutive dimensions. In particular the state's role as "power container" appears to have been perforated; it seems to be leaking, and thus the inherited model of territorially self-enclosed, state-defined societies, economies, or cultures is becoming highly problematic. In response to this, globalization researchers have constructed a variety of heterodox, interdisciplinary, and even

postdisciplinary methodologies to challenge the "iron grip of the nation-state on the social imagination" (Taylor 1996: 1923) and its associated, Cartesian image of space as a static, bounded block. Indeed, spatialized approaches to state restructuring have played a key role in facilitating the growing intellectual backlash among globalization researchers against naïve forecasts of the national state's imminent demise (see, e.g., Cox 1997; Jessop 1999; Brenner 1997).

3   *The crisis of the Keynesian welfare state.* The Keynesian welfare states that developed in most advanced capitalist economies during the postwar boom were instituted primarily at the national scale. This involved a socially constructed correspondence between the national economy as the primary object of economic management, the national state as the primary political scale on which economic management was conducted and social welfare was delivered, and the treatment of political subjects as national citizens (Jessop 2002; Peck 2001). This coincidence of couplings at the national scale was disrupted in various ways from the early 1970s onwards by the crisis of North Atlantic Fordism, the increasing internationalization of economic relations, the resurgence of regional and local economies with their own distinctive economic and social problems, the growing rejection of overloaded "big government," the crisis of US hegemony in the international order, and the increasing mobility of very large numbers of people across national borders. These developments have prompted a decentering of the national scale and the proliferation of new institutions, projects, and struggles at both subnational and supranational scales and this has complicated the articulation of different scales. In response to this "relativization of scale" (Collinge 1996: 1 and *passim*), recent work has introduced more dynamic and self-reflexive approaches to state spatiality. Moving beyond vertically nested representations of state space, it has explored the tangled, contested, and rapidly changing scalar hierarchies involved in the political regulation of social life under modern capitalism.

4   *New localisms and new regionalisms.* Since the late 1980s economic and political geographers have sought to connect the emerging institutions and policies of local/regional economic development with transitions in the territorial govern-ance of contemporary capitalism in response to the crisis of Fordism (MacLeod 2001). This not only involves the emphasis on specific local, urban, and regional problems that require specially tailored solutions rather than a one-size-fits-all national strategy, but has also opened a space for the resurgence of the urban and regional scales in their own right. This (re)discovery of the local and regional is also associated with the development of new forms of governance that give more emphasis to multi-scalar networks and partnerships rather than relying on nationally coordinated bureaucratic hierarchies (Goodwin and Painter 1996; Jessop 1998). Whereas the new localism involves the reassertion of the importance of the local in economic regeneration, political participation, and community building, the new regionalism tends to involve the emergence of broader and strategically more competitive regions than those characteristic of North Atlantic Fordism. Nonetheless both involve the (re-)emergence of new types of regulatory experiments, strategies, and struggles at subnational scales – albeit often promoted by national states or, indeed, supranational state bodies and international inter-governmental or non-governmental bodies (Lovering

1999; Jones 2001). A closely related phenomenon is the increased importance attached to global cities, but this differs from the new localism and new regionalism owing to the horizontally articulated relationships that obtain among global cities in the global city hierarchy. Indeed, studies of world cities have contributed to the turn away from territorialist models of political-economic life by underscoring the key role of transversal inter-urban networks in coordinating socioeconomic relations under global capitalism (on global cities, see Knox and Taylor 1995; Sassen 2001).

A critical theme running through these four sets of emerging issues is the "political economy of scale." This refers to the ways in which the scalar organization of political-economic life under capitalism is socially produced and periodically transformed (Swyngedouw 1997; Smith 1993; Brenner 1998; McMaster and Sheppard 2002). From this viewpoint, the scalar organization of state space – from the global level of the inter-state system and the national level of state territoriality to subnational tiers of governance such as regional, local, and neighborhood-level institutions – is never fixed forever. Instead, in conjunction with broader socioeconomic pressures, constraints, and transformations, it is liable to recurrent redesign, restructuring, and reorientation (see Smith, this volume). The political economy of scale is pivotal to this volume insofar as the contributors (1) call into question the taken-for-grantedness of national state space as the necessary arena of political life; (2) suggest that a relativization of scale is currently unfolding as subnational and supranational levels of state space acquire increasing importance; and (3) analyze ongoing struggles to establish new scales as sites of state regulatory activity under conditions of rapid geoeconomic change.

The articles included in this anthology have been chosen on several grounds. First, we have sought to include chapters that challenge the entrenched assumptions associated with the "territorial trap," as outlined above, and which, on this basis, open up useful methodological perspectives for the investigation of currently unfolding transformations of state space. Second, and relatedly, we have looked for articles that implicitly or explicitly adopt a broadly postdisciplinary perspective rather than operating within only one disciplinary paradigm (on post-disciplinarity, see Jessop and Sum 2001). Third, we have sought to include contributions that represent cutting-edge contributions from one or more of the major theoretical traditions concerned with state space (including, among others, historical sociology, Marxism, world systems theory, the new institutionalism, critical international political economy, feminist state theory, the regulation approach, and contemporary urban and regional political economy).

The organization of this volume reflects three key thematic questions, which we consider important in the study of state space:

1 What are the appropriate theoretical categories and methods through which to explore the geographies of state space? Thus part I contains contributions that elaborate some of the theoretical foundations for the investigation of state space under modern capitalism.
2 In what ways are inherited formations of state territoriality being transformed under contemporary conditions? Thus part II examines the remaking of state

territoriality since the early 1970s, focusing on the apparent demise of the Westphalian geopolitical order and the ensuing "relativization of scales."

3　How have the geographies of sociopolitical struggle and conflict been transformed under contemporary conditions? Thus part III explores the reshaping of political space more generally in the current period, focusing in particular on the crystallization of new forms of sociopolitical mobilization at a variety of scales and their reciprocal implications for the character of state activity.

Theoretical Foundations: Dimensions and Dynamics of State Space

The contributions to this anthology indicate convincingly the need to move beyond the prevalent notion of state space as a pre-given, static container within which social relations happen to occur. In so doing, they explore one or more of three crucial dimensions of what we term "state space" (see box 1):

1　They examine changes in the state's distinctive form of spatiality, namely, the territorialization of political power. This dimension includes, among other issues, the changing meaning and organization of state territoriality; the evolving role of borders, boundaries, and frontiers; and the changing intra-national geographies of state territorial organization and administrative differentiation. We refer to this aspect as state space in the "narrow" sense.

2　They also systematically explore the geographies of the territorial state's changing forms of intervention into social and economic processes at various spatial scales, whether territorially defined or not. For, as several authors

Box I　Dimensions of state space considered in this book

State space in the narrow sense	Refers to the state's distinctive form of spatiality. This comprises the changing organization of state territoriality in the modern inter-state system; the evolving role of borders, boundaries, and frontiers; and the changing intra-national geographies of state territorial organization and internal administrative differentiation.
State space in the integral sense	Refers to the territory-, place-, and scale-specific ways in which state institutions are mobilized strategically to regulate and reorganize social and economic relations and, more generally, to the changing geographies of state intervention into social and economic processes. This includes non-territorial as well as territorial modes of state intervention.
State space in the representational sense	Refers to competing spatial imaginaries that represent state and political spaces in different ways as a basis for demarcating states from each other, demarcating the state from the wider political system, and demarcating the wider political system from the rest of society. These spatial imaginaries also provide an important basis for the politics of representation, for the mobilization of territory-, scale-, and place-specific forms of state intervention and for territorial politics within (and against) the state.

Note: most of the chapters consider each of the three dimensions.

indicate, the geographies of state space are not limited to the state's territorially bounded configuration as a self-contained "apparatus" but also encompass the territory-, place-, and scale-specific ways in which state institutions are mobilized to reorganize and regulate (albeit temporarily) the social and economic relations of capitalist society. In short, state spatiality must be viewed as a complex expression of ongoing processes and practices of sociospatial regulation at various scales. We refer to this latter, and more general, aspect as state space in the "integral" sense. As such it extends beyond the territorial and the juridico-political features of state institutions to include their contested imprints and effects upon the geographies of socioeconomic relations within and beyond state boundaries.

3 Finally, several contributions explore the role of different forms of discourse and representational practices in constituting state space as an "imagined" (rather than natural or pre-given) geopolitical entity. Precisely because there are no "natural" political territories, the spatial zones successfully claimed by and/or allotted to any given state are always delineated through historically specific social practices that constitute, impose, and naturalize particular forms of knowledge – and, therefore, power – over space, scale, and territory (Agnew and Corbridge 1995; Agnew 1999; Coleman 2002; O Tuathail 1999). These practices operate "through the active simplification of the complex reality of places [and territories] in favour of controllable geopolitical abstractions" (Agnew and Corbridge 1995: 48–9). This is also reflected in changes in popular geographical assumptions about politics, political community, and political struggles. By including essays that explore these relatively neglected, "representational" practices, we hope to create a theoretical space for inquiry into the ways in which state space is represented and imagined, both in geopolitical struggles and in everyday life.

State space in the narrow sense

In its narrow sense state space refers to the spatialities of the state itself, regarded as an ensemble of juridico-political institutions and regulatory capacities grounded in the territorialization of political power. This involves, in the first instance, the coupling of authoritative, collectively binding political power to a specific territory. It is crucial to recognize that political power has frequently been exercised without resort to territorialization, for instance, among nomadic and other stateless peoples where the boundaries of political power are defined in terms of mobile subjects rather than fixed territories. Yet, even when political power has been effectively territorialized, it does not always assume the form of the modern sovereign state and its associated inter-state system. Earlier forms of territorialization include city-states, empires, the medieval state system, and absolutism (Braudel 1984; Dodgshon 1987, 1998). Thus, the modern territorial state must be viewed as a very late – and by no means final – development in the history of state formation.

In the modern inter-state system, territoriality operates not merely as a principle of internal geographical enclosure, but also as the foundational organizational principle of the entire system of geopolitical interaction on a global scale.

Accordingly, as the contributors to part I elaborate, it is the territorial organization (territorialization) of political power that appears to give a common form to all states within the inter-state system in the modern period. This territorialization process involves the systematic parcellizing of a potentially global political system into a series of mutually exclusive spaces controlled by separate and formally sovereign states. It thereby also establishes the material basis for the distinction between "domestic" politics (supposedly a realm of internal peace and the rule of law) and "foreign" relations (generally construed as a realm of anarchy, war, and violence), which has long underpinned mainstream approaches to international relations theory (Agnew and Corbridge 1995; Murphy 1996).

In the opening chapter, historical geographer Marcelo Escolar usefully highlights the crucial role of representational practices in the original territorialization of political power involved in the formation of the modern (inter-)state system during the long sixteenth century. Thus Escolar explores the radical reorganization of inherited medieval institutional landscapes, in which borders had served as relatively fluid zones of transition between overlapping, interpenetrating realms of political, religious, military, and other forms of authority. As Escolar's account clearly shows, the modern inter-state system was not constructed on a terrestrial tabula rasa but crystallized out of a complex, polymorphic medieval landscape that was itself inherited from earlier rounds of state building. As Escolar demonstrates, the degree of political centralization and state modernization crucially affected the nature of territorial demarcations and their associated representational practices in different zones of modern state building. Indeed, given the multiplicity of historical (and geographical) starting points for modern state formation during the early Renaissance period, it is hardly surprising that modern states continue to exhibit such divergent institutional and spatial forms, rather than converging around a generic model of the modern bureaucratic-democratic state.

Although the Treaty of Westphalia formally instituted the principle of state sovereignty, territorial borders have never been static features of state power. Rather, their forms and functions within the geopolitical system have been modified continually – sometimes quite dramatically – through political struggles on various spatial scales (Agnew and Corbridge 1995; Paasi 1996; Newman and Paasi 1998). Nonetheless, as historical sociologist and social theorist Michael Mann notes in chapter 2, it is precisely the state's centralized territorial form that underpins its unrivaled usefulness to diverse social forces – including both capital and labor – in promoting particular projects to restructure socioeconomic relations. Accordingly, as political geographer Peter Taylor notes in chapter 5, since the origins of the modern inter-state system during the long sixteenth century, the state's role as a territorial "power container" has expanded in several directions. These include: (1) war-making and military defense; (2) the containment and development of national economic wealth; (3) the promotion of nationalized politico cultural identities; (4) the institutionalization of democratic forms of political legitimation; and (5) the provision of various forms of social welfare. Thus, from the war machines of early modern Europe and the wealth containers of the mercantile era to the national developmental/imperialist states of the second industrial revolution and the national welfare states of the Fordist-Keynesian period, states have deployed a great variety of politicoregulatory strategies, and have attempted to use the principle of territoriality to "contain" very different types of socio economic activities within their borders. In short, even though the modern state has indeed "acted like a vortex sucking in social relations to mould them through its territoriality" (p. 102), the territorialization of politics was never accomplished "once and for all" but has remained a precarious, deeply contentious outcome of historically specific "state projects" (Jessop 1990). Thus territorial borders are best viewed as a medium and outcome of historically specific strategies and ceaselessly renewed attempts to shape the geographies of political-economic activities both within and between states (Newman and Paasi 1998).

As political geographers have long emphasized (e.g., Gottmann 1973; Taylor 1993), national states assume a variety of forms depending on their internal administrative hierarchies and inter-governmental arrangements. All modern national states, with the possible exception of small city-states, subdivide their territories into jurisdictional units and distribute administrative and/or political power among them according to certain legal-bureaucratic principles. In addition to the conventional distinction between unitary and federal states, there are further significant differences that shape the "spatial selectivity" (Jones 1997) of state forms. These are liable to change over time through measures to reduce or increase the number, scale, and scope of administrative and political units and/or to redesign and reallocate their tasks and responsibilities. Indeed, as several contributors to parts II and III of this book indicate, the present period is one in which the internal geographical differentiation of state space is being thoroughly reworked, as inherited forms, functions, and divisions of state space are called into question and redefined throughout western Europe, North America, and East Asia. For present purposes, the essential point is that these internal geographies of subnational administration and regulation represent fundamental elements of state space in its "narrow" sense.

Crucially, however, as our contributors demonstrate, territoriality represents only one dimension within the complex geographical architectures of modern state spatiality. For there are many other, equally important dimensions of state spatiality that may also be interpreted as products, arenas, objects, and stakes of ongoing sociopolitical struggles. Within the global politicogeographical system established by the (Westphalian) practices of state territoriality, states have mobilized a variety of historically specific strategies for parcellizing, regulating, monitoring, and representing social space. The analysis of such state spatial strategies leads us to the second dimension of state space mentioned above, namely, state space in its integral sense.

State space in the integral sense

The mobilization of state spatial strategies involves attempts to influence the geographies of socioeconomic activities such as industrial agglomeration, infrastructure investment, and demographic movements within a state's territory (Lefebvre 1978; Prescott 1987). On the one hand, as the Marxist theoretician Henri Lefebvre argues, "each state claims to produce a space wherein something is accomplished – a space, even, where something is brought to perfection: namely, a unified and hence homogeneous society" (1991: 281; cf. chapter 4, this volume). In their chapters, Lefebvre and Mann both detail the ways in which state institutions under modern capitalism tend to encage socioeconomic relations within an encompassing territorial grid. Likewise, in chapter 3, the Marxist state theorist Nicos Poulantzas suggests that state territoriality imposes a specifically capitalist "spatial power matrix" in which antagonistic class relations are (1) partitioned among distinct national frontiers and borders, and (2) homogenized within those borders according to the principle of national unification. For Poulantzas, this spatial power matrix has two main effects. First, it "nationalizes" the conditions for economic and social development, for class struggles and class alliances, and for other forms of social mobilization so that these processes and practices tend to operate within national rather than international and/or local horizons. Second, it establishes the basis for national (democratic) politics to define the general (public) interest and attempts to mobilize the 'people-nation' behind the national interest (whether to defend national security or to promote international competitiveness).

On the other hand, as other contributors to this volume emphasize, even in the midst of these tendencies toward the territorialization and homogenization of social relations within the framework of the national state, established grids of state spatial regulation are frequently unsettled, particularly under conditions of deep socioeconomic instability or systemic crisis (see also Harvey 1989b, 1982). When such crises erupt, entrenched patterns of state spatial regulation may be thoroughly reworked, in part as a means to reconfigure established geographies of capital accumulation and uneven spatial development (Smith 1984; Lefebvre 1977, 1978). In this sense, state spatial strategies must be viewed as historically specific practices through which state institutions attempt to adjust to the constantly changing geoeconomic and geopolitical conditions in which they operate: their modalities, targets, and effects evolve qualitatively during the history of capitalist development.

State space in the representational sense

In considering the representation of state space, our contributors address three key themes that pervade the more innovative recent literature, namely: (1) the power/knowledge relations involved in the construction of state territorial divisions, the parcellizing of territory as landed property, the demarcation of distinct political jurisdictions, and so forth; (2) the ways in which state spatial practices continually shape and reshape subjectivities and spatial horizons in everyday life; and (3) the ways in which social alliances are formed and mobilized on a territorial basis, leading to a variety of scale- and place-specific political strategies intended to defend and/or promote particular interests grounded within already established, emerging, or potential state spaces.

To varying degrees, the contributions of Escolar, Poulantzas, and Lefebvre (as well as the essays in parts II and III by Cameron and Palan, Sum, and Yuval-Davis) all discuss the essential role of power–knowledge relations in the construction, mapping, and continual restructuring of state space. The question of state hegemony, everyday life, and subjectivity is posed most prominently in part I by Lefebvre and Poulantzas, both of whom are deeply concerned to understand the manifold ways in which the modern state's power over territories and places becomes a taken-for-granted and mystified feature of everyday life under capitalism. For Lefebvre, the state's capacity to hide its own shaping effects upon social relations is absolutely essential to its operations of sociospatial regulation, control, and domination (see also Abrams 1988). Poulantzas in turn stresses the role of class struggle (especially between the bourgeoisie and the working class) in producing such naturalized, everyday epistemologies of state space, above all those associated with modern nationalism. Lefebvre is more interested in the politics of everyday resistance, the rise of new social movements, and the growth of new, potentially transformative uses of space.

The chapters in part I thus provide an initial set of conceptual tools and categories through which to decode the geographies of state space under modern capitalism and hence to denaturalize the geographical assumptions associated with traditional analyses of the national territorial state. They explore the contingent character of its historical constitution, the extraordinarily diverse political geographies associated with its historical evolution, the extensive cross-national variations in its spatial form, the often hidden structural and strategic biases associated with such variations, and the articulation of state space to contextually specific forms of spatial imaginary, discourse, and representation. The contributions thereby illuminate many key aspects of the three dimensions of state space alluded to above. Overall, they emphasize that states are not simply located "upon" or "within" a space. Rather, they are dynamically evolving spatial entities that continually mold and reshape the geographies of the very social relations they aspire to regulate, control, and/or restructure. This continual production and transformation of state space occurs not only through material-institutional practices of state spatial regulation but also through a range of representational and discursive strategies through which the terrain of sociopolitical struggle is mapped and remapped by actors who are directly involved in such struggles.

Remaking State Territoriality: Beyond the Westphalian Model?

The contributions to parts II and III turn from foundational theoretical issues to the more immediate question of how inherited geographies of state space are being reworked in a period of rapid geoeconomic and geopolitical change. These chapters also denaturalize established assumptions regarding state space in powerful ways. But they do so by analyzing the ways in which (1) state territoriality is being reforged as a principle of geographical enclosure; (2) the primacy of nationally scaled forms of state regulation is being destabilized in the face of newly emergent supranational and subnational forms of political-economic activity; and (3) new forms of political mobilization, conflict, and struggle are crystallizing that cross cut, bypass, or transcend inherited geographies of the national state.

Crucially, the contributions to parts II and III reject the narratives of state "decline," "decay," or "erosion" that pervade popular approaches to contemporary global change. While they diverge in their theoretical, empirical, and political starting points and in their interpretations of contemporary political-economic trends, they share a concern with two core issues: the transformation of inherited geographies of state space, and the ongoing production of new state spaces at various geographical scales and territorial sites around the world. The contributors to part II explore, in particular, various ways in which the inherited Westphalian system of state territoriality is being reorganized under contemporary capitalism (see also, among other authors, Anderson 1996; Kobrin 1998; Hettne 2000). Inter alia, the authors suggest that the primacy of the national territorial state is best interpreted as a parenthesis in the long history of state formation rather than as a necessary feature of political life. However, while the contributors to this part all question whether the Westphalian model of state territoriality still survives, they offer markedly contrasting visions of newly emergent geographies of state power, socioeconomic governance and political struggle.

Despite otherwise deeply rooted methodological and empirical differences, chapter 6 by international relations theorist Martin Shaw and chapter 7 by world systems theorist Giovanni Arrighi both contend quite explicitly that the Westphalian model of state territoriality is today being systematically dismantled. Shaw develops this argument primarily through a reinterpretation of the history of state forms in the West. On this basis he elaborates the daring claim that a new, internationalized western state form is currently emerging. Building upon and expanding Mann's fourfold characterization of the features of the modern territorial state (see chapter 2), Shaw argues specifically that state boundaries (especially in their military and geopolitical crystallizations) are being powerfully redrawn to produce a hemispheric, if not fully global, state (cf. Hardt and Negri 2000). Shaw does not regard this as an entirely novel arrangement. On the contrary, he argues that the dominant state form from the eighteenth to the mid-twentieth century was not the nation-state but a world or regional European empire centered on the western European heartlands of world capitalism. Nonetheless, Shaw suggests that the new western state is novel because it is dominated by a single core state rather than being structured through the coexistence of several European empires (late nineteenth century until World War II) or two postwar superpowers (World War II until the late 1980s). For Shaw, the Westphalian model overprivileges the national and the global scales and thereby neglects the continentally configured geopolitical "blocks" that, in his view, now constitute the most important units of state power. Despite criticisms (e.g., Panitch 2001), Shaw's seminal discussion of the "global western state conglomerate" illuminates the highly important role of supranational state alliances and institutions in what are increasingly multi-scalar and multi-centric political geographies.

Arrighi likewise critiques the Westphalian model by exploring the historical lineages of the Sinocentric state system and thereby reinterpreting the conventional history of state development in the capitalist world system (see also Arrighi 1994). In particular, he argues that both the capitalist world economy and the modern inter-state system contain pre-modern and modern characteristics. For Arrighi, the leading agencies in the formation and expansion of the capitalist world system have either been something less (city-states and quasi-states), something more (quasi-empires), or something different (business diasporas and other trans-territorial capitalist organizations) compared to the stereotypical nation-states that dominated the Westphalian geopolitical imagination. Nonetheless, as Arrighi suggests, at a decisive moment of its evolution, the Eurocentric capitalist world system did indeed become embodied in a worldwide system of nation-states that has continued to develop unevenly across time and space. Focusing on East Asia after 1945, Arrighi argues that many East Asian states were little more than "quasi-states" that functioned largely as "military protectorates" under US hegemony rather than as genuinely sovereign states. However, the linchpin of Arrighi's critique is his suggestion that the collapse of Communism, the deepening crisis of US global hegemony, and the incipient shift of capitalism's center of gravity (back) toward East Asia together have entailed a major threat to established global and national political geographies. Arrighi's work offers a sophisticated challenge to "neo-medievalist" claims that we are witnessing a return to pre-modern political geographies (see, e.g., Ruggie 1993; Kobrin 1998) and an insightful counterpoint to Shaw's suggestion that an integrated western or world-scale state is being forged. Yet Arrighi's chapter also converges with such analyses in claiming to discern a significant remaking of inherited formations of (national) state territoriality.

While Shaw and Arrighi focus on the global level from both geohistorical and contemporary viewpoints, the other contributors to part II examine the various reterritorializations and rescalings of state power that have ensued since the crisis of North Atlantic Fordism in the 1970s. For example, political sociologist and international political economist Bastiaan van Apeldoorn (chapter 8) addresses the development of European state space as a (geo)economic crystallization of state power and class domination following the dissolution of the Fordist-Keynesian class compromise during the early 1970s. He explores the significance of cultural and representational factors in state formation by drawing on the neo-Gramscian school of transnational historical materialism (on which see Gill 1993). One of the key contributions of his chapter is to distinguish between the institutional form and the socioeconomic content of European integration; the former involves what we have called state power in its narrow sense, the latter can be said to involve state power in its integral sense (p. 148). Van Apeldoorn also underscores the essential role of classes and rival class fractions – including both their material interests and their associated ideologies – in this remaking of political space. On this basis, in an elegant and concise case study, he traces the recent emergence of a new "comprehensive concept of control" (combining an accumulation strategy, state project, and hegemonic vision) for the European Union. Van Apeldoorn labels this state-mediated class strategy "embedded neoliberalism" and suggests that it has been promoted by the dominant "globalist" fraction of transnational capital. This implies that new state spaces are contingent, politically charged, and often highly unstable institutional creations rather than necessary and automatic responses to globally induced pressures or emergent governance problems. Nor are state spaces merely an arena in which political-economic struggles occur; they also constitute a key weapon in such struggles (see also chapter 3, this volume).

In their contribution to part II, international relations theorists Angus Cameron and Ronen Palan (chapter 9) highlight two additional emerging sites of economic and political restructuring that have in turn generated new representations and imaginations of economic life. These are the off-shore economy (the realm of international financial transactions and speculative investment activities) and the anti-economy (the realm of policies oriented toward excluded, marginalized, and decommodified populations and individuals). Although the off-shore economy is often described as if it were somehow extra-territorial and beyond the control of the national state (e.g., Castells 1996; O'Brien 1993; cf. Yeung 1998), Cameron and

Palan argue that its apparent "extra-territoriality" is actually a reified ideological reflection of new state projects and accumulation strategies. For Cameron and Palan, states are actively involved in constructing, reproducing, and exploiting the very distinction between "off-shore" and "on-shore" (private) economies. Indeed, they argue that national states are active "drivers" of the off-shore economy and the neo-liberal private economy rather than their helpless victims. As Cameron and Palan suggest, in redrawing territorial and institutional boundaries in these ways and thereby contributing to the development of a post-Westphalian geopolitical order, national states are deeply complicit in the establishment of putatively "deterritorialized" or "borderless" flows in the emerging, neo-liberal global economy.

If the new forms of statehood identified by Shaw, van Apeldoorn, and Cameron and Palan seem to be emerging primarily in a top-down manner, other authors have examined the emergence of new state and political spaces from the bottom up, through the initiatives of local and regional territorial coalitions and diverse, civil society-based social forces. Particularly noteworthy here is political scientist Joachim Blatter's chapter on cross-border regions in western Europe and North America (chapter 10; see also the chapters in part III by Keating, Keil, and Lipietz). Blatter argues that studies of border regions offer useful insights into contemporary processes of state spatial restructuring and the changing operations of borders, boundaries, and territories in global capitalism (see also Nevins 2002). Accordingly he develops a fourfold classification of the various political institutions associated with cross-border cooperation, namely, commissions, connections, coalitions, and consociations. He then shows how these institutions contribute in turn to the governance of four distinct border regions in Europe and North America. As Blatter argues, major differences in cross-border institution-building exist between the two continents. While the European path to debordering is described appropriately as a "multi-level system," Blatter suggests that the US–Mexican and US–Canadian cases are developing non-territorial political institutions on a bottom-up basis; consequently, in the latter context, the nation-state continues to serve as the key institutional agent of territorial governance. This analysis resonates closely with Escolar's emphasis on the divergent paths along which early modern processes of state territorialization unfolded. Blatter's insights also suggest that there is still ample scope for multiple and divergent post-Westphalian regulatory settlements and inter-scalar "fixes" to develop in different zones of the world economy.

Finally, in contrast to these top-down and bottom-up approaches, several novel accounts have emerged in recent years that emphasize the tangled, transversal properties of newly emergent state spaces. In contrast to the traditional, hierarchical conception of political space as a scaffolding of scales stretching vertically from the global and the national downward to the regional and the local, such approaches explore the proliferation of new, horizontally articulated, "rhizomatic" linkages among state (and non-state) institutions at diverse spatial scales. Chapter 11, by critical international political economist Ngai-Ling Sum, provides a particularly fascinating analysis of such "networked" and "rhizomatic" political spaces in contemporary East Asia. She coins the concept of "geo-governance" to analyze the strategic networks of trans-border actors (both public and private) involved in the self-reflexive coordination and stabilization of diverse trans-border modes of growth. These networks typically seek to promote territorial competitiveness by linking together economic activities at divergent scales (in particular, the global, the regional, and the local) and by shaping, disciplining, and controlling the time-space dimensions of production and exchange at each of these geographical scales. Sum develops this approach by examining four key "moments" of capitalist restructuring: finance, industry, commerce, and culture. In exploring the emergence of the "Greater China" region as a distinctive, networked geo-governance regime, Sum identifies another important escape route from the Westphalian territorial trap. This involves neither a simple reordering of entrenched scalar hierarchies nor a straightforward process of de- and re-territorialization through the reworking of the forms and functions of borders. Instead it involves processes of inter-scalar/inter-territorial rearticulation to establish new modes of interdependence, coordination, and governance across previously unconnected positions within inherited regimes of state territorial regulation.

The contributions included in part II of this volume raise a number of fundamental questions about emergent forms of state spatial organization. Taken together, these works suggest that, while national territorial states continue to play key roles in the regulation of global, national, regional, and local capitalisms, they are now no longer the exclusive locus of political authority in the contemporary world. In this sense, Ruggie's (1993) suggestion that the nexus between (national) territoriality and state sovereignty is today being "unbundled" is very germane. However, rather than viewing this unbundling process as the expression of a broader erosion of state power or as evidence that new "postmodern" political formations are being consolidated, most contributors to part II are more tentative in their interpretations. With the exception of Shaw, whose forecast of an emergent global-western state conglomerate represents a particularly bold argument regarding the future of state space, the other analyses in part II represent initial attempts to decode some basic contours of an emergent geopolitical reality that is still being forged through ongoing sociopolitical strategies, struggles, and conflicts at a range of scales and in diverse institutional sites around the world. Clearly, as these analyses indicate, the Westphalian model is being systematically destabilized, if not thoroughly dismantled, under contemporary conditions. But the question of what form(s) of state spatiality will emerge to address the regulatory deficits that have emerged in the wake of this major political-geographic rupture remains undecided. One of Antonio Gramsci's famous aphorisms therefore provides an appropriate epigraph to this section: "The crisis consists precisely in the fact that the old is dying and the new cannot be born" (1971: 276).

Reshaping Political Spaces: New Sites and Scales of Engagement

The contributions in part III attempt in various ways to connect the reterritorializations and rescalings of state power outlined in part II to the emergence of new forms of sociopolitical mobilization, contestation, and politico-cultural identity. They do so by linking many of the major themes surveyed in part II to the rise of new political spaces. This research agenda examines how new social forces are getting constituted as political actors and engaging in new forms of struggle to reconfigure inherited forms of state power or, more generally, to pursue new socioeconomic objectives.

This agenda is part of the growing interest in the "politics of scale" (Smith 1993) in which inherited scalar arrangements are rearticulated upward and downward to establish rehierarchized social, economic, and political geographies. These contributions thus concretize Swyngedouw's (1997: 140) provocative contention that scale is "the arena and moment, both discursively and materially, where sociospatial power relations are contested and compromises are negotiated and regulated." These chapters also show that, because scales do not exist in mutual isolation, but are always interconnected in a broader, often-changing inter-scalar ensemble (cf. Cox and Mair 1991; Lefebvre 1991; Brenner 2001), a serious and critical engagement with state space must always relate even the most dominant scale(s) to the broader inter-scalar processes through which political geographies are continually constituted and reconstituted. Against this background, part III explores different aspects of contemporary struggles to transform state space, to directly influence the exercise of state power on one or more scales, to escape or bypass the exercise of such power by opening up new political spaces, or to influence it through struggles that are conducted at a distance from the state and in the name of new politicocultural identities.

In chapter 12, for example, urban geographer Neil Smith suggests that geographical scale is best conceptualized as the always-contested and fragile spatial condensation of contradictory social forces as they seek to contain or enable particular forms of social interaction. He also emphasizes the role of cultural factors in ongoing rescaling processes in western Europe. In particular, Smith identifies two intertwined scalar trends in Europe that have major implications for the geographies of sociopolitical contestation. The first is the emergence of a post-national European space as capitalist enterprises seek to "jump scales" to the supranational level of the European Union in order to escape inherited national constraints on accumulation. However, in contrast to authors who believe that a new level of state power is currently being consolidated at a European scale (e.g., Majone 1997; Sbragia 2000), Smith emphasizes that European integration is a highly contested and politically charged political-economic project in which the key protagonists remain nation-states (cf. the chapters by Blatter, Lipietz, and Keating, this volume). The second and closely related trend emphasized by Smith is a resurgence of new types of regional movements, which likewise open up new scales for the articulation of sociopolitical claims, both by capital and by diverse subnational sociopolitical forces. For Smith, both of these developments underscore the deeply contested ways in which inherited scales of political-economic activity and sociocultural life are now being rearticulated in contemporary Europe. Even though state scalar structures are being massively transformed, Smith suggests that national states remain key institutional actors both in promoting rescaling processes and in managing inter-scalar relations within a multi-level institutional hierarchy.

Regulation theorist Alain Lipietz and political scientist Michael Keating also explore aspects of regionalization processes in their chapters. Lipietz (chapter 13) analyzes the dynamics of regional territorial alliance formation – or, in his neo-Hegelian terms, the transformation of regions "in themselves" into regions "for themselves" in contemporary capitalism. His chapter suggests that, following the crisis of North Atlantic Fordism in the early 1970s, the national scale of state territoriality is no longer the primary arena for political alliance formation and sociopolitical contestation. Instead, subnational scales such as regions and localities are becoming increasingly important sites for a variety of (neo-liberal and social democratic) regulatory experiments that attempt to rejuvenate capitalist growth. Emphasizing the complex and uneven character of political-economic development on various scales from the global to the local, Lipietz examines the conditions under which regionally based dominant classes can mobilize state institutions to promote territorial development within a subnational territorial economy such as a city or city-region. In this context he introduces the concept of "regional armature" to describe newly emergent regional power blocs that are anchored in specific regional state apparatuses and armored with relatively autonomous political capacities to pursue regional development projects – even in the face of opposition from the central state. On this basis, Lipietz emphasizes that the rise of such regional blocs requires the concerted mobilization of diverse sociopolitical forces oriented toward specific regional identities and political projects. Compared with other contributions in part III, Lipietz's key insights are (1) his emphasis on the extraordinary diversity of political-ideological projects (conservative, modernizing, and reactionary) that are crystallizing in and around contemporary regionalization movements; and (2) his recognition that, even as regional rescaling projects transform entrenched national hierarchies of state power, they are still conditioned in essential ways by the inherited institutional landscapes in which they emerge.

Keating (chapter 14) likewise explores some of the new forms of regional political mobilization that are currently emerging in western Europe. He notes that regional strategies in the era of North Atlantic Fordism were generally technocratic and sought to overcome the patterns of uneven development that had been produced by earlier projects of national modernization. Since the 1980s, however, regionalism has re-emerged largely through bottom-up social forces in a context of accelerated geoeconomic change. We suggest that there are two aspects to this development. First, in response to the pressures of globalization, new regional spaces are emerging from the search for economic prosperity based on agglomeration economies, institutional thickness, and embedded forms of social capital (cf. Storper 1997; Amin and Thrift 1995; Scott 1998). And, second, in response to the ongoing territorial rescaling of government, new spaces of regionalism are also emerging to (re)assert regional claims to democratic participation. These responses are evident in various countries and contexts where an identity politics based on separatist regional/ national movements has often been accompanied by the rise (or reinvention) of regional government and devolved territorial administration (Agnew 1995; Giordano 2000; MacLeod and Jones 2001). Reflecting these changes, Keating's chapter identifies six empirically grounded ideal types of regional movements and regionalist projects that are oriented toward the creation of new political spaces. For Keating, therefore, regionalist projects and movements are not simply top-down, technocratic creations but emerge on various scales and are premised on the unpredictable combination of various old and new political identities. And, as he indicates, any given instance of regionalism is likely to be based on a more-or-less conflictual, more-or-less negotiated mixture of different strategies and visions configured at a range of local, national, and even supranational scales. Keating's chapter thus develops a number of methodological strategies for the investigation of newly emergent spaces of regionalism and also introduces a number of analytical typologies that usefully characterize the broad institutional terrain within which divergent forms of regionalization are unfolding.

Whilst the contributions of Smith, Lipietz, and Keating are concerned primarily with the regional level, urbanist Roger Keil (chapter 15) explores several perspectives on local (state) agency in the age of the global city. In particular, he demonstrates various ways in which processes of globalization are currently transforming state power even as states in turn serve as a key institutional infrastructure in and through which globalization processes unfold. Keil acknowledges that the practical sovereignty of national states is being "hollowed out" and specific state capacities are tendentially disempowered through the assertion of (globalized) market powers and supranational governance institutions. But he also insists, along with other recent commentators (e.g., Weiss 1998; McMichael 1996; Yeung 1998), that national competition states have become major protagonists of globalization projects and that other state capacities are simultaneously being reasserted on many scales both above and below the national state. Nonetheless, Keil identifies some important blind-spots in the vast literature on globalization and state restructuring. These include the neglect of the local state's role in the making of globalization; the failure to examine the continuing and, indeed, reinvigorated regulatory power of the urban scale under globalized conditions; and the bracketing of the major role played by world cities as sites, stakes, and agents in the formation of post-national state forms. Under these conditions, for Keil, urban politics becomes an important forum in and through which competing scalar strategies are played out. It is also, Keil suggests, in the sphere of urban politics that radically democratic alternatives to contemporary neo-liberal forms of political and economic life may be developed (see also Keil 1998). His chapter thus usefully underscores the ways in which urban movements may generate sociopolitical consequences that transcend the urban scale to affect the institutional geographies of national and even global processes.

In chapter 16, anthropologists James Holston and Arjun Appadurai likewise explore the rearticulation of political space and social struggles in the urban context. Like Keil, they view the city as the arena for new modes of political action and for new forms of political identity. Under conditions of intensified globalization, they argue, cities have become strategic sites in which diverse transnational flows (of labor, commodities, information, and culture) are localized. In this context, the meaning of citizenship is being fundamentally reworked: the traditional liberal concept of national citizenship is decomposed and new forms of political subjectivity emerge that focus specifically on the conditions of everyday life within post-national cities. In contrast to Keil, however, Appadurai and Holston give more weight to the regressive side of contemporary denationalization processes. Noting the growing disjunction between the form and substance of national citizenship, they suggest that the two main responses to this crisis are equally unsatisfactory. Thus, whilst welfare retrenchment has encouraged social exclusion, xenophobia, and other politically induced forms of polarization, projects to broaden citizenship rights have frequently entailed their blunting into merely passive entitlements. On this basis, Holston and Appadurai highlight the dystopian elements of the modern city, especially its increasing division into new zones of intense social conflict and the intensification of everyday violence and generalized social insecurity. This is leading to the establishment of exclusive fortified enclaves, particularly in elite zones of the city, which undermine established forms of public space and, by implication, territorial democracy. In essence, then, the city is for Appadurai and Holston a strategic political space characterized both by new possibilities for popular-democratic mobilizations and by new, localized forms of domination, disempowerment, and exclusion. In this sense, their work usefully highlights the double-edged character of contemporary struggles to create new political spaces: while they may open up new chances for empowerment, resistance and struggle, they may also systematically delink decision making powers from popular-democratic control under the rubric of a new "glocal" authoritarianism (see also Swyngedouw 2000).

A number of closely related issues are raised in feminist political theorist Nira Yuval-Davis's chapter on the multi-scalar and multi-layered dynamics of contemporary identity politics in relation to citizenship and political democracy (chapter 17). She stresses the polymorphism of political boundaries and their changing relation to different forms of political imaginary. On this basis, she argues that citizenship practices are configured within politically constructed, and therefore malleable, physical and imagined territories. Because the boundaries of nations and states do not usually overlap with each other, and because the individual boundaries of each nation-state are often contested, Yuval-Davis suggests that people's membership in communities and polities is dynamic and multiple. Particularly under contemporary conditions, she claims, citizenship is becoming a multi-layered and relational construct rather than serving as the basis for singular, pre-given, or fixed political identities. Thus, just as Keil emphasizes the importance of urban civil society in the making of contemporary political spaces, Yuval-Davis stresses the role of bounded urban spaces as a daily theater for the performance of (struggles over) citizenship (cf. Jenson 1991). This performance of political identity involves the intersection and (re)articulation of ethnic, class, and gender differences. It also involves continuing struggles over the socioinstitutional boundaries delimiting the exercise of citizenship, such as that between the private and public, within particular territories. In this context, Yuval-Davis argues that women are especially important as symbols of collectivities, as symbolic border guards, and as bearers of "the private" domain in and across local, regional, national, and supranational boundaries. This emphasis on gender relations is a fundamentally important contribution to current discussions of state space – not merely for the contemporary period, when gender is openly recognized (if not always accepted) as a major component in the multiple political geographies of identity, but also for earlier periods, when patriarchy in various forms was arguably a key foundational element in the geographies of state formation.

The concluding contribution likewise develops a rather dystopian view of contemporary state spaces. Like Appadurai and Holston, anthropologist Carolyn Nordstrom also starts at the interface of the global and the local – this time in Africa, where many states have been devastated by decades of war, extreme poverty, and economic crisis. Drawing upon extensive ethnographic research in sub-Saharan African countries such as Angola and Mozambique, Nordstrom argues that the rise of internationalized, extra-legal "shadow networks" of informal exchange challenges academics to fundamentally rethink established theories of state sovereignty. She emphasizes that different flows of non-legal goods/services (including arms, gems, pornography, drugs, prostitution, and laundered money) do not move in distinct orbits but are closely interconnected within the same global trade networks. Crucially, in Nordstrom's analysis, non-formal production systems, quasi-legal "gray" markets, and illegal enterprises all play key roles in the constitution of global commodity flows; and state actors are in turn said to be essential to the financing, management, and reproduction of these shadow networks. At the interface between "licit" and "illicit" economic activities, Nordstrom argues, "networked" shadow states emerge that perform a variety of quasi-governmental functions in social and economic life. Thus Nordstrom emphasizes the degree to which, in many of the most war-torn countries of sub-Saharan Africa, non-state actors (including profiteers, bankers, and smugglers) frequently acquire state-like functions. Indeed, she argues that the people involved in international extra-state networks often forge trade agreements, foreign policy, and currency exchanges. This leads Nordstrom to conclude that, insofar as these interconnected webs of power generate mechanisms of accountability and provide a predictable basis on which people can attempt to plan their everyday lives, they have gained a significant degree of social, if not formal juridico-political, sovereignty. This opens entirely new ways of looking at state space. Like Blatter's analysis of cross-border regionalism in Europe and North America, Nordstrom's account of shadow networks underscores the extraordinarily diverse pathways of state spatial restructuring that are crystallizing in the current period throughout the world economy. Most crucially, Nordstrom's work also powerfully destabilizes traditional conceptions of sovereignty as the territorialized monopoly of formal state institutions.

In sum, the contributions to the third part of this anthology highlight five key issues. First, they emphasize the pivotal role of popular social struggles in generating, contesting, and overturning established inter-scalar orders – thereby reaffirming that spatial, territorial, and scalar relations are neither automatic nor naturally necessary features of statehood but rather deeply processual and practical outcomes of strategic initiatives undertaken by a wide range of social forces. Second, the contributions underscore the importance of studying different forms of state spatial organization, the opportunities they give to different social forces to pursue their interests through different spatial, territorial, and scalar strategies, and the significance of attempts to redefine these configurations of state space by jumping scales, rebordering territories, and/or reordering their functions. Third, these chapters highlight the degree to which ongoing struggles to transform state space emerge in the institutional interstices between public/private, state/civil society, and legal/illegal, leading in turn to new articulations among these dualities and a concomitant reworking of the socioinstitutional boundaries between state action and everyday life. Fourth, the contributions attempt to explore states and politics in their entirety – thereby taking full account of the implicit, the unspoken, the taboo and the dystopian aspects of state space as well as their more transparent, fetishized, and celebrated aspects. Finally, these chapters examine the impact of new configurations of space, territory, and scale upon the geographies of inclusion/exclusion, empowerment/disempowerment, and power/resistance.

Conclusion

The chapters in this volume have been chosen to illuminate the inherently processual character of state spatiality and to illustrate the explanatory and critical power of spatialized approaches to statehood. They treat processes of state spatial transformation as uneven, contested, incomplete, and unpredictable fissures within established geographies of state regulation rather than as totalizing ruptures or as unilinear transitions. In this spirit, they also highlight the extent to which the crisis of the national scale during the post-1970s period has not yet been resolved through the construction of a new primary scale on which social life as a whole can be organized and regulated. This should not surprise us, because, as several chapters emphasize, the existence of a single primary scale of political-economic organization represents the exception rather than the rule even under modern capitalism. This conclusion is reflected in the contributors' lively and provocative discussions of the legacies of premodern state forms within the Westphalian geopolitical order; its inherently multiscalar nature, despite the tendential nationalization of the inter-state system; the currently enhanced importance of new, or resurgent, scales ranging from the global to the local; the major role of new types of inter-scalar relay in shaping state spatialities; and the emergence of local and transversal social movements that challenge all forms of territoriality. More surprising, perhaps, is the extent to which all of the contributors also emphasize the continued, if significantly redefined, role of national state institutions in regulating and reproducing capitalism, managing inter-scalar relations, and mediating sociopolitical struggles across various geographical scales.

Drawing on these contributions, we can also identify some open questions and missing links in the study of new state spaces that merit more systematic inquiry. Among those adumbrated in this volume are:

1 *Theorization.* Much theoretical work is still needed on several key historical and/ or contemporary aspects of state space. These include territoriality, scalar divisions of regulation and spatial selectivity, and associated processes of state spatial restructuring, such as debordering, reterritorialization, and rescaling.

2 *Periodization.* While some chapters operate within the parameters of debates on the putative end of Westphalian territoriality and the decentering of nationally scaled forms of state regulation, others suggest more complex periodizations and spatializations of state restructuring that undermine simplistic, unilinear transition models. This points to the need to develop more nuanced approaches to the periodization of state spatial development and to operate with multiple temporal as well as spatial horizons.

3 *Case studies and comparisons.* Many of the concepts and arguments developed below are firmly grounded in individual case studies and/or in comparative analyses of state spatial restructing. While further case studies would help to differentiate interpretations of historical and contemporary state spaces in diverse contexts, territories, and scales, comparative studies would shed more light on the divergent pathways in and through which state space is reorganized and on their often markedly different outcomes in social, political, institutional, and geographical terms.

4 *Space, power, and the production of difference.* While many chapters emphasize class-based as well as territorially based social divisions, some also underscore the role of gender, race, and ethnicity in the production of state spatiality. This is attracting more and more attention, but there is still an urgent need to explore the dialectic between the gendered, racialized, and ethnicized character of state spaces and the state's own distinctive contributions to the gendering, racialization, and ethnicization of social life (but see Kofman 1995; Pettmann 1996; Soysal 2000).

5 *State space, critical theory, and the geographies of (in)justice.* Finally, much recent theorizing moves beyond mere "description" of spatial relations to uncover their complicity in the territorialization of diverse forms of political domination and everyday violence (Horkheimer 1972; Bourdieu 1998). By illuminating how unjust, exclusionary, and disempowering social structures are inscribed into spatial and institutional forms, critical approaches to state space also point toward the possibility of forging alternative political geographies based upon progressive, radically democratic priorities and practices. Exploring such possibilities – both in theory and in practice – is one of the most urgent intellectual and political tasks to emerge from recent work on the production of new state spaces. It is certainly a task to which we subscribe.

In sum, the theoretical creativity, analytical rigor, and intellectual curiosity displayed in the contributions to this volume suggest that we are indeed living in "interesting times" for the study of state space. And, clearly, as the aforementioned list of questions indicates, there is plenty of theoretical, methodological, empirical, and political work to do as our understanding of state space matures. We hope that this volume will promote the further dissemination of spatialized approaches to state theory and political studies, to the enrichment of ongoing debates on the future of statehood, and to the widening and deepening of our understanding of new state spaces.

BIBLIOGRAPHY

Abrams, P. (1988) "Notes on the difficulty of studying the state," *Journal of Historical Sociology*, 1 (1), 58–89.

Agnew, J. (1994) "The territorial trap: the geographical assumptions of international relations theory," *Review of International Political Economy*, 1, 53–80.

Agnew, J. (1995) "The rhetoric of regionalism: the Northern league in Italian politics, 1983–94," *Transactions of the Institute of British Geographers*, 20 (2), 156–72.

Agnew, J. (1999) "Mapping political power beyond state boundaries: territory, identity and movement in world politics," *Millennium*, 28 (3), 499–521.

Agnew, J. and Corbridge, S. (1995) *Mastering Space: Hegemony, Territory and International Political Economy*, London: Routledge.

Amin, A. and Thrift, N. (1995) "Institutional issues for the European regions: from markets and plans to powers of association," *Economy and Society*, 24 (1), 41–66.

Anderson, J. (1996) "The shifting stage of politics: new medieval and postmodern territorialities?," *Environment and Planning D: Society and Space*, 16 (4), 133–53.

Appadurai, A. (1996) *Modernity at Large: Cultural Dimensions of Globalization*, Minneapolis: University of Minnesota Press.

Arrighi, G. (1994) *The Long Twentieth Century*, London: Verso.

Bourdieu, P. (1998) *Acts of Resistance: Against the Tyranny of the Market*, New York: Free Press.

Braudel, F. (1984) *The Perspective of the World*, Berkeley: University of California Press.

Brenner, N. (1997) "Global, fragmented, hierarchical: Henri Lefebvre's geographies of globalization," *Public Culture*, 10 (1), 137–69.

Brenner, N. (1998) "Between fixity and motion: accumulation, territorial organization and the historical geography of spatial scales," *Environment and Planning D: Society and Space*, 16 (5), 459–81.

Brenner, N. (2001) "The limits to scale? Methodological reflections on scalar structuration," *Progress in Human Geography*, 15 (4), 525–48.

Castells, M. (1983) *The City and the Grassroots: A Cross-Cultural Theory of Urban Social Movement*, Berkeley: University of California Press.

Castells, M. (1996) *The Rise of the Network Society*, Oxford: Blackwell.

Coleman, M. (2002) "Thinking about the World Bank's 'accordion' geography of financial globalization," *Political Geography*, 21 (4), 495–524.

Collinge, C. (1996) *Spatial Articulation of the State: Reworking Social Relations and Social Regulation Theory*, Birmingham: Centre for Urban and Regional Studies.

Cox, K. R., ed. (1997) *Spaces of Globalization: Reasserting the Power of the Local*, New York: Guilford.

Cox, K. R. and Mair, A. (1991) "From localised social structures to localities as agents," *Environment and Planning A*, 23 (2), 197–214.

Dodgshon, R. A. (1987) *The European Past: Social Evolution and Spatial Order*, London: Macmillan.

Dodgshon, R. A. (1998) *Society in Time and Space: A Geographical Perspective on Change*, Cambridge: Cambridge University Press.

Giddens, A. (1985) *The Nation-State and Violence*, Cambridge: Polity.

Gill, S., ed. (1993) *Gramsci, Historical Materialism and International Relations*, Cambridge: Cambridge University Press.

Giordano, B. (2000) "Italian regionalism or 'Padanian' nationalism – the political context of the Lega Nord in Italian politics," *Political Geography*, 19 (4), 445–71.

Goodwin, M. and Painter, J. (1996) "Local governance, the crises of Fordism and the changing geographies of regulation," *Transactions of the Institute of British Geographers*, 21 (4), 635–48.

Gottmann, J. (1973) *The Significance of Territory*, Charlottesville, VA: University of Virginia Press.

Gramsci, A. (1971) *Selections from the Prison Notebooks*, London: Lawrence and Wishart.

Gregory, D. and Urry, J., eds (1985) *Social Relations and Spatial Structures*, Basingstoke: Macmillan.

Gupta, A. (1993) "The song of the nonaligned world: transnational identities and the reinscription of space in late capitalism," *Current Anthropology*, 7 (1), 63–79.

Hardt, M. and Negri, T. (2000) *Empire*, Cambridge, MA: Harvard University Press.

Harvey, D. (1982) *The Limits to Capital*, Oxford: Blackwell.

Harvey, D. (1989a) *The Condition of Postmodernity: An Enquiry into the Origins of Cultural Change*, Oxford: Blackwell.

Harvey, D. (1989b) *The Urban Experience*, Oxford: Blackwell.

Hettne, B., ed. (1995) *International Political Economy: Understanding Global Disorder*, London: Zed Books.

Hettne, B. (2000) "The fate of citizenship in post-Westphalia," *Citizenship Studies*, 4 (1), 35–46.

Horkheimer, M. (1972) *Critical Theory: Selected Essays*, New York: Herder and Herder.

Jenson, J. (1991) "All the world's a stage: ideas, spaces and times in Canadian political economy," *Studies in Political Economy*, 36 (Fall), 43–72.

Jessop, B. (1990) *State Theory: Putting Capitalist States in their Place*, Cambridge: Polity.

Jessop, B. (1998) "The rise of governance and the risks of failure: the case of economic development," *International Social Science Journal*, 155, 29–46.

Jessop, B. (1999) "The (il)logic of globalization," in K. Olds, P. Dicken, P. F. Kelly, L. Kong, and H. W.-C. Yeung, eds, *Globalization and the Asia Pacific: Contested Territories*, London: Routledge, 19–38.

Jessop, B. (2002) *The Future of the Capitalist State*, Cambridge: Polity.

Jessop, B. and Sum, N.-L. (2001) "Pre-disciplinary and post-disciplinary perspectives in political economy," *New Political Economy*, 6 (1), 89–101.

Jones, M. (1997) "Spatial selectivity of the state? The regulationist enigma and local struggles over economic governance," *Environment and Planning A*, 29 (5), 831–64.

Jones, M. (2001) "The rise of the regional state in economic governance: 'partnerships for prosperity' or new scales of state power?," *Environment and Planning A*, 33 (7), 1185–211.

Keating, M. (1998) *The New Regionalism in Western Europe: Territorial Restructuring and Political Change*, Chelmsford: Edward Elgar.

Keil, R. (1998) *Los Angeles: Globalization, Urbanization and Social Struggles*, Chichester: John Wiley.

Knox, P. and Taylor, P. J., eds (1995) *Global Cities in the World System*, Cambridge: Cambridge University Press.

Kobrin, S. J. (1998) "Back to the future: neomedievalism and the postmodern digital world economy," *Journal of International Affairs*, 51 (2), 361–86.

Kofman, E. (1995) "Citizenship for some but not others: spaces of citizenship in contemporary Europe," *Political Geography*, 14 (2), 121–35.

Kratochwil, F. (1986) "Of systems, boundaries, and territoriality: an inquiry into the formation of the state system," *World Politics*, 39 (1), 27–51.

Lefebvre, H. (1974) *La production de l'espace*, Paris: Anthropos.

Lefebvre, H. (1977) *De l'état: le mode de production étatique*. Volume 3. Paris: Union Générale d'Éditions.

Lefebvre, H. (1978) *De l'état: les contradictions de l'état moderne*. Volume 4. Paris: Union Générale d'Éditions.

Lefebvre, H. (1991) *The Production of Space*, Oxford: Blackwell (translation of Lefebvre 1974).

Lovering, J. (1999) "Theory led by policy: the inadequacies of the 'new regionalism' (illustrated from the case of Wales)," *International Journal of Urban and Regional Research*, 23 (3), 379–95.

Lukes, T. W. (1994) "Placing power/siting space: the politics of global and local in the New World Order," *Environment and Planning D: Society and Space*, 12 (4), 613–28.

MacLeod, G. (2001) "Beyond soft institutionalism: accumulation, regulation, and their geographical fixes," *Environment and Planning A*, 33 (7), 1145–67.

MacLeod, G. and Jones, M. (2001) "Renewing the geography of regions," *Environment and Planning D: Society and Space*, 19 (6), 669–95.

McMaster, R. and Sheppard, E., eds (2002) *Scale and Geographic Inquiry: Nature, Society, Method*, Oxford: Blackwell.

Macmillan, J. and Linklater, A., eds (1995) *Boundaries in Question: New Directions in International Relations*, London: Pinter.

Majone, G. (1997) "From the positive to the regulatory state: causes and consequences in the mode of governance," *Journal of Public Policy*, 17 (2), 139–67.

Mann, M. (1986) *The Sources of Social Power. Vol. I: A History of Power from the Beginning to AD 1760*. Cambridge: Cambridge University Press.

Mann, M. (1993) *The Sources of Social Power. Vol. II: The Rise of Classes and Nation-states, 1760–1914*, Cambridge: Cambridge University Press.

McMichael, P. (1996) *Development and Social Change: A Global Perspective*, Thousand Oaks, CA: Pine Forge Press.

Murphy, A. B. (1996) "The sovereign state system as political-territorial ideal: historical and contemporary considerations," in T. J. Bierstecker and C. Weber, eds, *State Sovereignty as Social Construct*, Cambridge: Cambridge University Press, 81–120.

Nevins, J. (2002) *Operational Gatekeeper: The Rise of the "Illegal Alien" and the Making of the U.S.–Mexico Boundary*, New York: Routledge.

Newman, D. and Paasi, A. (1998) "Fences and neighbours in the postmodern world: boundary narratives in political geography," *Progress in Human Geography*, 22 (2), 186–207.

O'Brien, R. J. (1993) *Global Financial Integration: The End of Geography*, London: Pinter.

Osiander, A. (2001) "Sovereignty, international relations, and the Westphalian myth," *International Organization*, 55 (2), 251–87.

O Tuathail, G. (1996) *Critical Geopolitics: The Politics of Writing Global Space*, Minneapolis: University of Minnesota Press.

O Tuathail, G. (1999) "De-territorialised threats and global dangers: geopolitics and risk society," in D. Newman, ed., *Boundaries, Territory and Postmodernity*, London: Cass, 17–31.

Paasi, A. (1996) *Territories, Boundaries and Consciousness: The Changing Geographies of the Finnish–Russian Border*, Chichester: John Wiley.

Panitch, L. (2001) "Theorising the 'global-Western State'," http://www.theglobalsite.ac.uk/review/107Panitch.htm

Peck, J. (2001) *Workfare States*, New York: Guilford.

Pettman, J. J. (1996) "Border crossings/shifting identities: minorities, gender and the state in international perspective," in M. Shapiro and H. Alker, eds, *Challenging Boundaries: Global Flows, Territorial Identities*, Minneapolis: University of Minnesota Press.

Prescott, J. R. V. (1987) *Political Frontiers and Boundaries*, London: Unwin and Hyman.

Radice, H. (1984) "The national economy: a Keynesian myth?," *Capital and Class*, 22, 111–40.

Ruggie, J. G. (1993) "Territoriality and beyond: problematizing modernity in international relations," *International Organization*, 47 (1), 139–74.

Sassen, S. (2001) *The Global City: New York, London, Tokyo*, Princeton, NJ: Princeton University Press, 2nd edn.

Sbragia, A. (2000) "The European Union as coxswain: governance by steering," in J. Pierre, ed., *Debating Governance*, Oxford: Oxford University Press, 219–40.

Scott, A. J. (1998) *Regions and the World Economy: The Coming Shape of Global Production, Competition, and Political Order*, Oxford: Oxford University Press.

Scott, A. J. and Storper, M. A., eds (1986) *Production, Work, Territory: The Geographical Anatomy of Industrial Capitalism*, London: Unwin Hyman.

Smith, N. (1984) *Uneven Development: Nature, Capital and the Production of Space*, Oxford: Blackwell.

Smith, N. (1993) "Homeless/global: scaling places," in J. Bird, B. Curtis, T. Putnam, and T. Tickner, eds, *Mapping the Futures*, London: Routledge, 87–119.

Soja, E. W. (1989) *Postmodern Geographies: The Reassertion of Space in Critical Social Theory*, London: Verso.

Soysal, Y. N. (2000) "Citizenship and identity: living in diasporas in postwar Europe," *Ethnic and Racial Studies*, 23 (1), 1–15.

Spruyt, H. (1994) *The Sovereign State and its Competitors: An Analysis of Systems Change*, Princeton, NJ: Princeton University Press.

Storper, M. A. (1997) *The Regional World: Territorial Development in a Global Economy*, New York: Guilford.

Swyngedouw, E. A. (1997) "Neither global nor local: 'glocalization' and the politics of scale," in K. R. Cox, ed., *Spaces of Globalization: Reasserting the Power of the Local*, New York: Guilford, 137–66.

Swyngedouw, E. A. (2000) "Authoritarian governance, power, and the politics of rescaling," *Environment and Planning D: Society and Space*, 18 (1), 63–76.

Taylor, P. J. (1993) *Political Geography: World-Economy, Nation-State, and Locality*, Harlow: Longman.

Taylor, P. J. (1995) "Beyond containers: internationality, interstateness, interterritoriality," *Progess in Human Geography*, 19 (1), 1–15.

Taylor, P. J. (1996) "Embedded statism and the social sciences: opening up to new spaces," *Environment and Planning A*, 28 (11), 1917–28.

Walker, R. B. J. (1993) *Inside/Outside: International Relations as Political Theory*, Cambridge: Cambridge University Press.

Wallerstein, I. (1988) "Inventions of timespace realities: towards an understanding of our historical systems," *Geography*, 73 (4), 289–97.

Weber, M. (1946) *Essays from Max Weber*, London: Routledge & Kegal Paul.

Weiss, L. (1998) *The Myth of the Powerless State: Governing the Economy in a Global Era*, Cambridge: Polity.

Wessels, W. (2000) *Die Öffnung des Staates: Modelle und Wirklichkeit grenzüberschreitender Verwaltungspraxis 1960–1995*, Opladen: Leske and Budrich.

Yeung, H. W.-C. (1998) "Capital, state and space: contesting the borderless worlds," *Transactions of the Institute of British Geographers*, 23 (2), 291–309.

Part I

Theoretical Foundations

I

Exploration, Cartography and the Modernization of State Power

Marcelo Escolar

Introduction

The absolute states which began to develop in Western Europe during the Late Middle Ages and which were consolidated during the Renaissance laid the political and institutional foundations of the different types of representative democratic states which evolved after the last quarter of the eighteenth century. On the whole, these states are distinguished by the fact that they exercised the power of political domination uniformly and on an exclusive basis throughout the territory. This led to the slow build-up of a monopoly of legitimate coercion, the concentration of tax-collecting and the bureaucratic centralization of public administration (Alliès, 1980, pp. 23–25).

Both for modern absolute states and contemporary representative democratic states the exercise of political sovereignty involves the people and property located within a given geographical area.

Although the existence of a territory is a part of both kinds of state, this does not mean that other types of territorial states do not also exist, not only in Western Europe but throughout the world. In fact, modern dynastic patrimonial states are not substantially different from other ancient or extra-European models. However, representative democratic states do differ from all the rest in one fundamental respect: they must recognize a people who delegate their sovereignty by means of a system of political representation, which, in turn, requires a clearly defined territory (Escolar, 1995, p. 5).

For this reason, the absolute states of Western Europe are the political and institutional forerunners of all contemporary states (Escolar, 1994, pp. 44–46), to the extent that the first representative democratic systems were set up in some of them or in their colonies, spreading, in the course of successive historical stages, to include almost all the states in existence today.

In this process, which lasted basically from the beginning of the fifteenth century until the present day, the modernization of the power of the state concentrated on developing methods and techniques aimed at making the bureaucratic and administrative apparatus function more efficiently, permitting more effective control of the territory and the population, but it also involved expending considerable energy developing methods of broadening and legitimizing the power of the state as well as gathering information regarding the different aspects of the social and natural reality both inside and outside the geographical boundaries of each individual state.

Consequently, the building up of state power in the absolute states of Western Europe entailed five basic aspects: the institutional consolidation of a centralized political and administrative apparatus; the organization of the bureaucracy and infrastructure within the territory ruled by the monarch; the projection and assessment of alternative strategies for the expansion of the state; the implementation of alternative offensive and defensive tactics launched from the territorial base; and the legitimization of the political rights of the people both within and beyond the borders of the state. Although these factors were formulated during the Renaissance and generally incorporated into the organization and style of state management during the seventeenth and eighteenth centuries, they were inherited by the democratic states which were to follow, reproduced in the absolute states of Western Europe and the Near East, and transported to the colonial empires, where they become a part of the states which emerged after the nineteenth century as a result of the various historical processes of decolonization.

Gradually, intellectual and practical undertakings developed simultaneously: on the one hand, collecting, classifying and drawing up an inventory of the information and documents dealing with the discovery and, on the other, analysing and processing, describing and depicting the results of exploration activity in the geographical areas which had been discovered or surveyed. In this context, the boundaries between the reality represented and the imaginings of the specialists involved had a direct impact on the depiction of these results by the intellectual authorities of each period (Harley, 1992, p. 234) and also on the empirical exactness of the data provided by the exploration, either directly when the specialist was also an explorer or observer, or indirectly when the data provided by the survey and field notes was processed by the specialist in his study.

Cartography was never a mirror image of the reality represented but a visual schema where the mapmaker or scholar involved aimed to reflect that reality using the means available at that time within the framework of the problems involved in the use made of the maps he produced and the parameters defining his particular approach to the world as 'geography' (Jacob, 1992, p. 240).

On this basis we can define a number of different periods where a connection exists between the prevailing worldview, the most important characteristics of the process of forging states and territories and the technical means for drawing maps using the information available.

The period between the sixteenth and eighteenth centuries, when the absolute states were evolving and being consolidated in Europe, may be subdivided into two eras which are significant from the point of view of exploration and mapmaking. The first of these is the Renaissance, when the geographical view of the world inherited from antiquity was gradually abandoned and the social and cultural impact of the discoveries and the process of centralization of state power was felt. The second is the Baroque and Neo-classical periods during the zenith of European Absolutism, when the metropolitan territories were surveyed and inspected, the colonies consolidated and the world was regarded as a stage for possible territorial expansion.

The nineteenth century, when the representative democratic states developed and were consolidated, is marked by the various political and administrative transformations which occurred in the central states as a direct result of the French and American revolutions (running parallel to the rapid development of capitalism in Western Europe and the United States). This led to the promotion of descriptive statistics and the development of monographic exhibitions associated with standardized methods of land surveying and cartographic representation. The aim of both of these disciplines was to define the differences which existed in the geography of the state lands and to classify the stocks of human and natural resources in the world beyond Europe.

Although this division into periods aims to distinguish processes which are significant in the relationship between cartography, exploration and the development of the power of the state before the scientific institutionalization of geographical knowledge towards the end of the nineteenth century, many of these developments are not restricted to one particular period but overlap so that, throughout the course of this work, we shall have to draw attention to the existence of certain anachronisms in one period and of other elements which foreshadow future periods. The history of cartographic representation and the spread of knowledge of *oekoumene* cannot be regarded linearly: we must be aware of continuity, steps backwards and hiatuses in the different stages of the territorialization of state power.

The Double Discovery and the Transformation of the Worldview during the Renaissance

Associating the worldviews prevalent in a given period with the political perspectives in relation to the increase of power and the bureaucratic and administrative structure of the state involves considering the alternative relationships between the images of state power and those of the real world, regarding them both as coherent natural and geographical entities.

The discovery at the beginning of the fifteenth century of ancient authorities which described the world in a way which differed from the Western Christian view served as a kind of epistemological doorway within the framework of which it was feasible to legitimize the opening up of new paths of inquiry and concrete possibilities for empirical research.

So, in the field of geography, the appearance of the texts and letters of Ptolemy, the Alexandrian astronomer and geographer who lived during the second century BC, contributed in large measure to the development of scientific knowledge during the Renaissance (Broc, 1980, pp. 34–35). Translated initially into Latin by Jacobus Angelus in 1409 and later retranslated into various vulgar tongues, these documents, along with cartographic documentation which was added during the following 200 years, constituted the basis of the geographical view held by the Western world until it was finally rejected in 1570, when Ortelius's *Theatrum Orbis Terrarum* was published and Mercator accorded merely historical value to Ptolemy's *La Geographia* in his atlas published in 1578. In the sense that they acted as stepping-stones (O'Sullivan, 1984, pp. 3–4), in our opinion these documents bear the intellectual responsibility for opening up the door during the whole of the fifteenth and the first half of the sixteenth centuries to exploration and the empirical discovery of the real shape of the world in an intellectual context constrained by respect for *auctoritas* and where knowledge was controlled by Judeo-Christian revelation.

As well as the Ptolemaic maps of the world and regional maps, with the technical innovation of organizing information based on the geographical co-ordinates of latitude and longitude, there were also portolan charts and hydrographic charts.[1] The latter, which had been developed initially during the fourteenth and fifteenth centuries in Italy and Catalonia for use in trade and the colonization of the Mediterranean, were subsequently used in the Portuguese schools of navigation and later by Spain in the fifteenth and sixteenth centuries as an aid in overseas exploration and expansion in the Atlantic, Indian and finally the Pacific Ocean basins.

In Portugal the early establishment of a centralized monarchy at the beginning of the fourteenth century and the existence of a clearly defined territory with stable borders which was effectively controlled during the fourteenth and fifteenth centuries created the right conditions for the development of a systematic policy of expansion associated with oceanic exploration based on technical knowledge linked to navigation and cartography (Boorstin, 1983, pp. 157–58). [. . .]

Against the background of the opening up of the known world as a result of Iberian expansion, the monarchs and political and administrative officials of the other absolute states of Europe began to fashion their own metropolitan geography, drafting projects of territorial expansion in geographical scenarios, both real and imaginary. Hence, a relationship was established between their institutional and political aspirations and the instruments of legitimization, control, expansion and surveying provided by the inherited worldviews and those which gradually emerged, at first in partial harmony with, and later diametrically opposed to, authorized knowledge.

Different types of academic cartographic knowledge, topographic and geodetic survey techniques and methods of representing the accumulated geographical and cadastral information were organized in line with the new requirements for the organization and consolidation of state power during the Renaissance (Alliès, 1980, p. 51).

Gradually, all the emerging absolute states required cartographic techniques in order to represent their own geography, both for the purpose of the social legitimization of their dominions and as a means of broadcasting the geographical profile of the country throughout the realm and in order to draw up an inventory of their natural, social and human resources and to set up jurisdictional institutions to facilitate government and state administration.

The pictorial maps which adorned palaces and official buildings as well as the maps of the world, globes and charts of the state territory which monarchs used to express their effective control fall into the first category. The identity of the state and its geographical profile required massive representations where, treading a fine line between pictorial representation and cartography proper, the component parts of the kingdom could be represented in a graphic manner (Jacob, 1992, p. 410).

Even in the Italian states, where the state territory as the object of public administration and the basis of sovereign power had attained the highest degree of institutionalization, this kind of cartographic representation of the state territory is only to be found after the middle of the sixteenth century.[2] Excellent examples of this type of map are the strategic-political wall maps painted by Enzio Danti between 1563 and 1575 in the *Palazzo Vecchio* in Florence and the maps painted by Antonio Danti between 1580 and 1583 found in the Vatican map room (Marino, 1987, p. 5).

In the remaining states of Western Europe this type of map production was limited to rudimentary drawings based on medieval or Ptolemaic maps of the world, where the profile of the state territory was purely decorative or propagandistic in nature, sometimes incorporating didactic, commemorative or spiritual functions or, at the most, only partially or unsystematically completed, based on the topographic surveys commissioned by the various sovereigns. [...]

The second category comprises different types of map showing very disparate levels of technical perfection. These were mainly used for setting up primitive land registers, defining administrative and government jurisdictions and preparing inventories of the state territory (Alliès, 1980, p. 53). With each new step forward in the institutional organization of the state, advances were made superseding the merely allegorical nature of such representations (Jacob, 1992, p. 355).

By the middle of the sixteenth century the political, institutional, technical and scientific conditions were finally ripe for maps to be used as planning instruments for the bureaucratic and administrative management and territorial control of state power in the states of Western Europe.

England in late Tudor times and France under the late Valois felt the impact of early overseas colonial expansion on trade and public administration. This had a direct impact on cartography which was then more likely to attract private or mixed funding which would guarantee not only the printing and graphical publication of the maps but also the necessary topographic surveys, documentary assessment and cartographic representation.

Although initially the English Crown was unable to offer true royal patronage in the conflict with the Spanish Empire (Barber, 1987a, pp. 58–59), unlike France where Catherine de Médicis guaranteed sustained support for expansionist adventures in America (Buisseret, 1987, p. 106), after 1580 or thereabouts the policy of both monarchs emulated that of the Iberian monarchs, entering into direct competition with the latter in the fields of overseas exploration and expansion.

Following the precedent of the land registration, water control and canal works in Venice, and to a lesser extent in Milan, Florence and the Papal States (Marino, 1987, pp. 6–11), mapmaking achieved official status in England and France.

On the basis of Saxton's great *Atlas* published in 1579, where British territory is described in (hundreds of) individual (cluster) units as opposed to the diocese traditionally used up till that time (Barber, 1987a, p. 65), Burghley, minister under Elizabeth I, and the main civil servants of the state bureaucracy, began to make systematic use of information on the density of the urban population, the location of large estates and communications to organize a taxation system and to calculate the resources of the kingdom (Barber, 1987b, pp. 75–81). This attitude was finally institutionalized with the 'Great Survey' ordered by James I in 1607, the aim of which was to produce a detailed survey of the Crown lands. Although this project did not prosper, the political, administrative and taxation requirements which led to the proposal resulted in the founding of the State Paper Office in

1610 (Barber, 1987b, p. 83). This was the first office for technical control of cartographic information on royal lands.

On the other side of the English Channel the main problems were similar, the aim basically being to regulate the feudal sway of the *Bando* by setting up a centralized jurisdictional system of justice and implementing planned economic and fiscal policies (Buisseret, 1987, p. 99). In 1560, Catherine de Médicis, the figure behind most of the political decisions taken by her various sons who occupied the French throne during the second half of the sixteenth century, commissioned Nicolas de Nicolaï, seigneur d'Arfeuille, to carry out a general cartographic survey of the provinces of the kingdom. Obviously, this commission was largely motivated by a desire to emulate Saxton's work in England. Even so, Nicolaï's atlas was never completed, and the parts which were remained in manuscript form (Buisseret, 1987, p. 106).

Apart from the various projects carried out until the time of the death of Catherine de Médicis in 1589, there was only one firm policy aimed at officializing scientific and technical activities of a cartographic nature after Sully's collaboration during the reign of Henry IV (1589–1610). It was Henry who promoted mapmaking with a view to planning the infrastructure of the kingdom and to help plan the distribution of the defensive forts and military garrisons throughout the territory (Buisseret, 1987, p. 112). We must wait until the time of Richelieu to find true political geography, the main manifestation of which occurred in 1624 when the Cardinal commissioned the engineer and cartographer, Nicolas Sanson, to draw up a map of France comprising 30 charts (Buisseret, 1987, p. 113). For the first time in Europe this large-scale map divided the cartographic representation according to subject-matter, thus breaking with the tradition of all-embracing images where the map, apart from being a technical tool, continued to be a symbolic representation of the geographical profile of state territory (Buisseret, 1987, p. 117).

In both the cases described above the desire of the monarchs to obtain detailed, localized information concerning the estates to be found within their territories clashed head-on with the regional power of the nobles who refused to provide the necessary data or to co-operate in the surveys of their private lands (Barber, 1987b, pp. 80–81; Buisseret, 1987, p. 106). Only the Spanish monarchy, perhaps owing to the strict centralizing policies implemented after the defeat of the *comuneros* in 1520–1522,[3] managed around 1577 to produce a complete map of the peninsula (part of an atlas which was started by Pedro Esquivel and later completed by Diego de Guevara at the request of Philip II). This may be regarded as the most accurate single map of this period both in geodetic terms and in terms of the amount of information included for its size and geographical coverage (Parker, 1987, pp. 130–31). After the defeat of the Spanish Armada and the onset of Spanish decadence, Spanish monarchs and their ministers only engaged the services of foreign specialists who, from that time onwards, were responsible for producing most of the administrative and political maps of the kingdom. However, as far as possible, the Iberian monarchs continued to retain the inventory and topographic survey of their colonial possessions for their own information (Parker, 1987, p. 145).

An interesting example which stands in contrast to the previous three is that of the Habsburg monarchy in Austria, for it provides the clearest illustration of the relationship which existed between the centralization of state power and the characteristics of the cartography promoted or financed directly by the state.

Unlike the other absolute states, Austria was organized on the basis of military and dynastic alliances between princes. This made the state structure very similar to the feudal grouping of subordinate dependencies. The monarchy could not central- ize mapmaking activities which, therefore, remained in the hands of the regional powers, managing only to promote maps of the territory necessary for a late construction of its self-image as the object of political domination. These maps aimed to express both the desire for autonomy and the desire to belong to the bloc (Vann, 1987, pp. 153–54). Consequently, in the maps produced in Austria during the latter years of the Renaissance the geographical limits were ideological rather than jurisdictional and were always linked to the concept of the principality and not the central state (Vann, 1987, pp. 158–59).

After the middle of the sixteenth century, discovery and cartography merged in a single project which was old before it was born: 'paradoxically, cosmography, which is being reformed as the great discoveries are being made, is developing at a time when the state of the world may render it obsolete' (Lestringant, 1993, p. 18). Renaissance cosmography tried to superimpose its images, increasingly standard- ized and ever less pictorial and more committed to the art of locating places faithfully, on the image of the world where the idea of the whole was didactically transmitted through the harmonious combination of the different dimensions of that reality which, as such, could be represented on maps which had no geograph- ical pretensions but which aimed merely to present the image of revealed truth (Lestringant, 1993, p. 35).

All the European monarchs of the sixteenth century employed 'cosmographs' who represented, read and described the world and the territories belonging to the state in graphic fashion: [...] This does not mean that the knowledge provided by oceanic exploration and the topographic survey of the districts of each European state was accumulated mainly in the works of these men. In fact, the spread and refinement of measurement, projection and map-drawing techniques were most evident in the works of Ortelius, Mercator and Gastaldi in the middle of the century, which were related to the work of cosmographers such as Sebastian Münster (Broc, 1980, pp. 75–84) and his followers (Broc, 1980, pp. 85–97). The main centres for the dissemination and technical development of printing were initially located in Northern Italy, later shifting to Southern Germany and the Rhineland and finally Flanders (Broc, 1980, pp. 121–32; Jacob, 1992, pp. 87–96).

The techniques developed to represent the spherical shape of the earth on a flat surface and the desire to produce an exhaustive geographical inventory sought epistemological guarantees and neutral yet practical methods of assessment. There- fore, they were regarded as instruments for the pragmatic implementation of state policy and administration and not as a symbolic decree of the extent of royal dominion. In this sense, the gradual separation of Renaissance cosmography from chorography and topography may be regarded as the basic contribution of the discoveries to the modernization of state power. This break signified a decisive change which led to the institutional drafting of territorial rules of administration and justice as well as the delimitation and systematic description of the Crown lands.

The surveying and instrumental representation of the territory of the state associated with administrative and scientific cartography in the seventeenth and

eighteenth centuries were made possible by the development of cartographic techniques during the Renaissance as a result of the 'double discovery', on the one hand,
and, on the other, the transformation of conspicuous state power into geographical
jurisdiction.

Survey, Inventory and Description: Cartographic Neutralization of State Territory in the Seventeenth and Eighteenth Centuries

During the first half of the seventeenth century, the main centre for designing,
drawing and printing maps moved to the new state of the United Provinces set up as
a result of the independence revolt of 1468–1569 in the northern area of Spanish
Flanders (the seven secessionist provinces headed by Holland and Zeeland). For
more than two centuries (the period between the Union of Utrecht in 1579 and the
Batava Republic in 1795) this new state, based on the autonomy of the bourgeoisie
and distinguished by a clearly liberal economic policy, enjoyed a decentralized
government, from the administrative point of view, and ample political, religious
and commercial freedom.

The first thirty years of existence of the United Provinces were marked by
continuous military confrontations with the Habsburgs. This did not hinder the
development of trade and intensive agricultural and industrial activity, with the
result that by the end of the sixteenth century the new state headed the states of
Europe. During a period of some seventy years, during which they held the leading
position in the economy of the capitalist world, the Dutch built up an overseas
empire which compounded and extended Portuguese possessions in the South
Atlantic and in the Indian Ocean, as well as consolidating their privileged trading
position with the Levant and Northern Europe. Although during this first period
England and France also promoted a more modest expansionist policy in both East
and West, they undoubtedly did so exploiting the space opened up by the Dutch
maritime companies and the 'naval shield' which these provided.

The economic liberalism, religious tolerance and administrative decentralization
which characterized the society and culture of the United Provinces meant that
pictorial and cartographic representations of the world, the state territory and its
geographical peculiarities attained a degree of popular familiarity, and that there
was some connection between the visual representation and the non-authoritarian
capacity to transform and control the landscape. In this they differed considerably
from the tight relationship between cartography, administration and territorial
management which was established in the main absolute states during modern
times.

In the Dutch state of the early half of the seventeenth century, it is difficult to
draw a precise dividing line between cartographic representation and descriptive
painting. Both activities demanded a common view of reality which did not draw a
clear distinction between the area of coded information (cartography) and the
figurative illustration of local and exotic scenes (Alpers, 1983, p. 84). In Holland
the most important thing was not the people but the land (Alpers, 1983, p. 88) and
the importance attributed to the land as a place constructed by society brought
together pictorial composition and the desire to depict the features of that landscape

(Rees, 1980, p. 62). Isomorphism of the pictorial-cartographic scene provided the most effective representational technique of approaching a visual description of the real experience, as though cartography distanced painting from the creation of imaginary landscapes. This peculiarity of style in no way detracted from the rigorous application of geometric, geodetic and topographic knowledge to cartography. Neither did it detract from the capacity for artistic communication and the aesthetic significance of pictorial works. On the contrary, it produced a realistic effect where art and science together sought to express the visualization of the world both near and far in the most complete manner possible in order to dominate and transform it.

Collective participation of the different strata of Dutch society in a framework of continuous economic growth and intellectual development meant that visual expression played a preponderant role in the transmission of experiences and knowledge systematically produced. In this respect, as has already been pointed out, the Dutch experience differed substantially from that of the other European states of the period.

On the other hand, the overseas enterprises and their impact on the nascent capitalism of the United Provinces meant that cartography was widely used, making descriptive, analytical and inventory descriptions of the world and the metropolitan regions available not only to the agents of state power but to the majority of the population (Alpers, 1983, p. 97). Highly developed techniques for the gathering of information and the visual representation of topographic and geodetic data together with a detailed and expressive pictorial technique for visualizing and interpreting reality meant that burghers, gentlemen and the people in general could approach reality and locate themselves within it.

From the great atlases of Mercator and Ortelius at the beginning of the century until Blaeu's atlases which appeared in 1636 and 1663, as well as the inventory of cities in Braun and Hogemberg's *Civitates Orbis Terrarum* between 1572 and 1617, cartography followed a course parallel and linked to the chorographic pictoric work of Goltzius, Koninck, Van Goyen and Ruisdael or the syncretic treatment of Breughel, where images of the landscape are placed in a boundless space in which the human species is one of the figurative elements. Cartography and painting finally merged in urban landscapes seen from an aerial viewpoint, such as Micker's 'View of Amsterdam' or Ruisdael's 'Panoramic View of Amsterdam, the Harbour and the Ij'.

In material terms, the modernization of Dutch state power took shape as the land mass itself came into being and, intellectually, with the socialization of the technical and aesthetic resources which allowed it to accommodate its geographical reality both scientifically and artistically and to represent it visually.

Decentralization of the state and liberalism transposed cartography to the realms of science and art without distinguishing clearly between them (Alpers, 1983, p. 78). 'Cartographic subversion', defined as the specialist's break with the utilitarian representations of political arithmetic promoted by the modern absolute states (Harley, 1988, p. 303), was not necessary, since state power was related to the political and social modernization programme promoted by civil society and not exclusively by the sovereignty of the monarch.

The situation was different in the other two powers of the period, France and England, where, in accordance with 'mercantilist' policy, the Renaissance cartographic scheme was gradually dismantled: geography was included in the scientific sphere of enlightened thought and cartographic knowledge in the technical sphere of the administration and state government.

Mercantilism, as applied in both these states, never was a clearly defined economic doctrine nor a monolithic economic development programme. Rather, the underlying concept is to be seen in the various institutional organizations which, during the seventeenth and eighteenth centuries, left their unmistakeable mark on the public treasury and government policy as tools for the accumulation of riches in the absolute states of Western Europe.

These institutional organizations sought to fashion a geographical arena in which to exercise a trade monopoly. It was therefore necessary to destroy the jurisdictional relationships of personal dependence and feudal vassalistic subordination characteristic of the medieval era. This breakdown was orchestrated in line with a variety of historical vicissitudes by a centralized political power which found expression in the bureaucratic apparatus of state.

However, two aspects must be stressed. The first is the pre-eminence of the process of unification of the geographical area under the control of the monarchy and the second the implementation of a series of administrative, judicial and economic rules with a view to standardizing the state territory and delimiting exclusive areas of responsibility subject to the central power (Alliès, 1980, pp. 29–37, 101–8).

During the Late Middle Ages, England was probably the state where political power was most centralized. From this initial situation emerged the reign of Henry VIII where power was concentrated to a high degree and the administration was centralized, although links were maintained with the highly consolidated power of the nobles of the commercial gentry and the yeomen. Within this institutional framework, a premature model of mercantilism took root under Cromwell during the first half of the sixteenth century. During the reign of Elizabeth and the Stuarts this early attempt was transformed into a kind of liberalism promoted and protected by the state which, by the middle of the seventeenth century, was competing with the Dutch state, finally ousting it in the last quarter of the century.

A relationship exists between this initial centralization of the English monarchy and the early development of rudimentary maps of the territory belonging to the feudal state. The most representative examples of this were the Gough Map of England produced in the thirteenth century and the first exhaustive cartographic inventory of the Crown lands carried out by Saxton in 1574.

Parallel to this tradition of allegorical and government uses of cartography, during the second half of the sixteenth century, England stood out on account of the proliferation of visual representations and descriptive accounts of its regions and of the world. These documents, drawn up from a patriotic and naturalistic standpoint (Cormarck, 1991) and consisting of different kinds of printed texts describing the discoveries, regional chorographic descriptions and treatises on astronomy, cosmography and navigation, appeared against an epistemological background created by the close link between science, magic and astrology which characterized the approach of authors such as John Dee, Cunningham, Blundeville and Recorde in the early days of the science of Bacon in that country (Livingstone, 1992, pp. 74–83). A foremost position must also be accorded to travel literature, the main exponents of which were Richard Hakluit and Walter Raleigh. These texts, whose aim was to preach a political message regarding British rights in North America, were the earliest forerunners of geographical works with patriotic aims based on an expansionist colonial philosophy (Comarck, 1994).

The moderate Protestant Reformation and the later Puritan reaction led to the development of new philosophies based on a view of the world which favoured both empirical knowledge of natural, cultural and social diversity (Livingstone, 1992, pp. 88–92) and a theological link with the doctrine of predestination. So, within the framework of the German Reformed Church, authors such as Keckermann and Varennius influenced the Briton Nathaniel Carpenter, for whom verbal and cartographic representation of empirically reconstructed geography was the expression of the harmony and perfection of the work of the Creator.

The rapid growth of a commercial bourgeoisie after the seventeenth century, the triumph of parliamentary power and, with it, the distribution of power among the different sectors of British society took constitutional form after the revolution of the 1640s. This situation made the English monarchy, whose power was effectively limited in any case, less prone to centralization. In this context, the cultivation of geography as a branch of knowledge independent of the needs of the state, in association with cartography as a scientific tool for describing the world, found fertile ground to develop. In many respects the situation was similar to Holland. However, the two approaches mentioned followed a parallel path as far as cartography for use by the public administration and as a tool for monarchical representation is concerned. In this respect they adapted to the dual powers which existed in the kingdom.

At this stage, during the second half of the seventeenth century and the whole of the eighteenth century, the development of geodetic and topographic knowledge together with cartographic techniques was easily linked to the establishment of cartography for fiscal, economic, judicial and administrative purposes without a need for the patronage or official control of the throne as had generally occurred and would continue to occur on the other side of the Channel.

In the case of France, on the other hand, the state which emerged after Richelieu and Mazzarino was markedly centralist, having evolved on the basis of direct coercion exercised during the first half of the seventeenth century on the various established territorial powers and on the formation of other new ones organized by the central power.

As a result of the gradual change undergone since the fourteenth century by the innumerable feudal and municipal prerogatives, the fiscal jurisdiction of the *intendants* and the hereditary judicial districts of the *officiers*, there was an overlap in the functions and responsibilities appropriated mainly by the bureaucracies of the monarchy and the legal profession and, to a lesser extent, by the local and regional powers. This gave the institutional and administrative map of France a polychromatic and even chaotic appearance which reflected to a large extent the difficulties being experienced by the dynastic power in the task of unifying the country around it and exercising effective control over its territories.

When this centralized state virtually devoid of legislative control was inherited by Louis XIV in 1661, it grew more radical in its more authoritarian aspects, such as the silencing of the *parlements* in 1663, the establishment of military garrisons in the town halls of the *bonnes villes*, reducing the courts to obedience and obliging the nobility, and in many cases the provincial governors, to reside at Versailles. For all these reasons the French state soon became the model of the European absolute state during the period which was to follow.

It was in France that mercantilism attained the status of a doctrine capable of promoting the reform of the institutional and normative patrimony of the monarchy. This was absolutely essential if the funds necessary for the autonomization of sovereign power and the institutional guarantee of the eminent territorial properties were to be secured (Escolar, 1994).

The emergence of unofficial geographical knowledge, as in England during the first half of the seventeenth century, was marginal, since it was linked to the circulation of knowledge which was not updated or of a highly general nature and to knowledge of a cartographic-descriptive nature. The main exponents of this type of information were the atlases of Le Clerc (a number of editions of which appeared between 1619 and 1632), Melchior Taverner's atlas (re-edited between 1634 and 1637), and those of Tassin, Nicolas Nicolaï and Guillaume Sanson, although the latter owe more to the state sponsorship of their authors. The 'love of maps', corroborated by the wide circulation of the atlases mentioned above as well as numerous regional descriptions, travel guides and itineraries (Revel, 1989, p. 151), stands in marked contrast to the 'Géographie du Roi' centred on the exaltation of the expansion of monarchic power, the naturalization of the territory and the drawing up of a systematic inventory of its natural and human resources.

The excessive reformist aims of French mercantilism, confronted with a society which had not yet found a satisfactory solution to the contradictions between a state which exercised political power implacably but which had not consolidated the social bases for administrative centralization, could scarcely do without the descriptive cartographic instruments appropriate for systematic management of the territory at different levels and which, therefore, served not only as generic tools for interpreting the geographical profile of the kingdom and its main localized attributes (Revel, 1989, p. 146) but mainly as an empirical basis for the calculation of strategies for political and administrative intervention (Revel, 1989, p. 152).

Although already following the ideas of Bacon, French science did not entirely share with contemporary English science the thrust of nascent capitalism carving out for itself an autonomous economic and political sphere within civil society. Science 'pour la Gloire du Roi' combined scientific geographical knowledge and official cartography (Broc, 1974, pp. 232–33). As a result of the appropriation by the state of scientific and technological knowledge linked to mapmaking, advances in geodetic measuring techniques, the physical conditions for recording topographic measurements and systems of graphic representation of the information obtained suffered the impact of the opportunity costs of projects which, in most cases, were strictly linked to the fashioning of the state territory and the centralized bureaucratic management of the state.

After 1670 England gradually took over from Holland as the leader of the world economy. During this period the two imperial powers in London and Paris vied with one another to win new overseas markets and extend their colonial possessions. This continued until England won the Seven Years War (1756–1763) which culminated in the British occupation of Quebec and French possessions in India and South-West Asia.

From the middle of the eighteenth century, knowledge and exploration of the new worlds was not limited to topographic surveys and an eclectic description of their natural and human resources – as had generally been the case during the Renaissance – but centred on inventorying, classifying and interpreting scientifically the data obtained as a result of discovery. This led to the involvement of empirical science in the exploration, economic exploitation and political appropriation of the various areas of the world. The journeys of Cook between 1768 and 1780, Bougainville in 1766 and Perouse between 1785 and 1788, as well as a vast number of similar smaller enterprises which, in the course of half a century, extended the limits of the known world by approximately 25 per cent, were supported economically both by the dominant powers of the period (England and France) and, to a lesser extent, by Russia, Scotland and Spain. The distinctive characteristic of these new exploratory enterprises was the link between imperialistic and scientific aims. This meant that mastery of nature and territorial dominion went hand in hand in eighteenth century colonial policy, converting the systems for recording information (verbal, statistical and graphic) into neutral tools for gathering, inventorying and representing information (Berthon and Robinson, 1991).

Between 1713 and 1716 the administration of *Ponts et Chaussées* was established in France and in 1747 the *Ecole des Ingénieurs des Ponts et Chaussées* was founded based on the work carried out during the reign of Henry IV by the military corps of *Ingénieurs du Roi* and *Maréchaux des Logis*, one of whose foremost exponents was Sebastien le Preste Vauban (1633–1707). From that time onwards, this institution was responsible for planning, drawing up blueprints, carrying out and supervising the construction of roads and canals, which was essential if movement throughout the kingdom was to be improved. This gave rise to a plethora of detailed topographic cartography directly related to the works being carried out. After the middle of the seventeenth century, surveys and works of statistical interpretation, such as those commissioned by Turgot in 1634 and 1664, as well as the first census were carried out as a result of the introduction of a poll tax in 1694, based on Vauban's proposal in the *Dîme Royale* (Revel, 1989, p. 125). Probably related to the information already collated, a descriptive genre of regional monographs with statistical back-up also flourished (Broc, 1974, p. 419). Both the 'regional' and the statistical aspects were ways of representing the geographical diversity of the kingdom qualitatively and quantitatively in order to provide descriptive tools of 'political arithmetic' to help the government and public administration plan their strategies (Revel, 1989, p. 125). This series of technical and intellectual activities could not have been supported without an aggressive policy of fiscal, customs, judicial and territorial regulation and standardization (Alliès, 1980, pp. 164–65) which, from the time of Henry IV, was undertaken by Sully, Richelieu, Mazzarino and later, in greater depth, by Colbert and the various ministers of the Bourbon sovereigns up to the time of Turgot.

In England, on the other hand, a more decentralized, less statist policy in the field of public works and territorial management gave rise to the concession of the Turnpike Roads, toll roads run by private trusts under the supervision of the county. Towards the middle of the seventeenth century social statistics began to develop vigorously, based on William Petty's essays on political arithmetic published between 1676 and 1787 as well as a series of official cartographic and local supervision projects such as those of General William Roy and the Duke of Richmond, which laid the foundations during the eighteenth century for the founding of the Ordnance Survey in 1791. In fact, throughout the seventeenth century English works of statistical description were more closely linked to works of a chorographic nature or more general natural history which might easily be included in the field of natural theology and geopietism (Livingstone, 1992, pp. 105–15).

On the whole, the overseas exploration and domestic surveys carried out by the absolute states of England and France promoted scientific and technical activity and, in turn, progress in these fields led to the acceleration of overseas expansion and the consolidation of the modern territorial states.

In both England and France, institutions for the promotion of science with state patronage were set up: in England the Royal Society and in France the *Académie des Sciences*, the *Jardin du Roi*, the *Observatoire Royal* and the *Académie des Inscriptions* (Broc, 1974, pp. 15–22; Livingstone, 1992, pp. 125–26).

The most important projects for surveying, systematizing and inventorying the data obtained as a result of overseas exploration and most of the land surveys of the State territory were promoted by these institutions.

The knowledge acquired by these institutions promoted the struggle for science produced for state purposes to be separated from scientific activity carried out purely in the pursuit of knowledge *per se*. This tension beween practical aims and intellectual interests was also evident in the methods of cartographic representation available at that time. Gradually a strictly neutral and abstract cartographic discipline emerged which, from the epistemological point of view, was related to the argument that knowledge of an area should be 'the result of scientific work not produced with political aims in mind' (Alliès, 1980, p. 59) and which, from the methodological point of view, was distinguished by the greatest possible theoretical and instrumental complexity in terms of the geodetic, topographic and cartographic techniques used (Harvey, 1980).

A good illustration of this state of affairs might be the laborious preparation of the map of France, which lasted almost 100 years. In 1663, Turgot, Louis XIV's Minister of Finance, commissioned the *Académie des Sciences* in Paris, with the help of the *Observatoire*, to draw up a large-scale map of the kingdom which was to be as precise and exhaustive as possible to be used to plan and manage his centralized development policy (Alliès, 1980, p. 58).

Once a methodological protocol for triangulation had been obtained in order to determine geometrically the positions of latitude and longitude, the work of calculating the astronomical co-ordinates of measured points throughout French territory began, being carried out successively by the Cassini dynasty until the Revolution. The first partial data produced scientifically gave rise in 1681 to a map showing the real shape of France which undermined the traditional map produced by the Royal Geographer, Nicolas de Sanson, in 1679. Only in 1745, seventy years after Colbert's request, did the *Description Géometrique de la France* appear, comprising eighteen charts. This was extended in 1755 with the *Carte Générale et Particulière de France* and finally completed with the publication in

1789 of the 180 sheets of the *Carte de Cassini* or *Carte de l'Académie*, where more than 3,000 triangulation points were marked on the terrain.

The main paradox of this enterprise, which was excessive for the period, was that the topographic and thematic information included in this first map of the state drawn from exact geodetic measurements was not equally precise and abundant (Revel, 1989, p. 154). This meant that the original aim of the map was completely undermined.

In Britain, on the other hand, the drafting of a map of the kingdom was mostly the result of the activities of William Roy, who undertook the task of drafting the first cartographic representations of the Highlands based on modern geodetic measuring techniques once the Scottish rebellion of 1745 had been put down. Later, with the support of the Royal Society, he prepared a complicated triangulation of England and Ireland based on 218 measuring stations. These works form the basis of the Ordnance Survey, an institution which undertook the task of preparing a map of Great Britain based on exact astronomical measurements and which enjoyed the scientific collaboration of the Cassinis. This was the first official institution in Europe which linked geodetic measurements and topographic surveying systematically and with some degree of continuity.

During the seventeenth century, Holland cleared the way for cartography and illustration, linking them to the fashioning and management of the territory from a perspective where science and art were brought together adapting to the decentralized nature and proliferation of the activities of inventory surveying and graphic representation of the metropolitan territory and the colonies. In seventeenth- and eighteenth-century France, the purposes served by cartography and the activities of drawing up inventories and producing statistical and monographic descriptions were to unify a state divided up into different pre-existing territorial units and standardize bureaucratic practices and administrative jurisdictional responsibilities. In the case of England, cartographic representation was used to organize methods of controlling and levying taxes agreed between the civil society and the dynastic state, but based on a unified territory and a much looser administrative structure.

By the end of the eighteenth century, then, the conditions were ripe for cartography to branch out as an independent discipline and for the political and institutional transformation of the territory as both the subject and the object of state sovereignty. The dichotomy which had existed between the representation of the world and the abstract representation of the geographical shape of the globe now disappeared.

Political and State Representation: Scientific Cartography and Territorial Naturalization during the Nineteenth Century

After the French and American Revolutions, the transfer of dynastic power to the state and the autonomous development of civil society invested the territory with a new symbolic, political and social significance. For this to occur, the Renaissance monarchist image of the land had to give way to the scientific representation of the map of the state during the Enlightenment and this process [...] formed the discipline of mapmaking as a survey, projection and representational tool, distancing it from other branches of knowledge of a geographical and statistical nature conceived as descriptive tools, systematized inventorying techniques and regional interpretations.

Eighteenth-century scientific cartography, firmly neutralized in its topographic and geodetic survey techniques, became the element socially legitimized between states for the fixing of state boundaries. Moreover, this true domestication of geographical material turned cartography into the institutionalized locus of sovereign power, making the state sphere independent of the ownership rights of the monarchy. Consequently, when Revolution demolished the ideological foundations of the Divine Rights of Kings as natural law and defined the society of the state as the consequence of a constitutional contract between the members of that society, the citizens became the depositaries of political sovereignty, and the territorial norm which delimited the state in geographical terms acquired a definitive abstract status. On the one hand, then, cartographic knowledge was officially recognized as a branch of instrumental knowledge and, on the other, the cognitive and social foundations were laid for the institutionalization of geography as a discipline which was to occur towards the end of the nineteenth century.

The forging of citizenship posed serious difficulties for the social and political theorists of the Revolution who had to justify the universal nature of the new order imposed by the French bourgeoisie without accepting, implicitly or in a directly doctrinaire fashion, the territorial inheritance of the *Ancien Régime* (Escolar, 1994).

A shift from a semi-patrimonial territory of domination to a territory of representation juridically defined by the people who delegated their sovereignty in the government of the state was required (Escolar, 1995). During this period of transition from coercive and ideological uses to political and social uses of the territory, the bureaucratic structure of the state underwent substantial changes as far as its institutional role was concerned. This was due to the fact that it was no longer exclusively a centralizing apparatus, the aim of which was to consolidate the monarchy, but had become a public arena – not without contradictions and internal struggles – where the government of the people could express itself through the administration and management of the natural and human resources of the territory subject to popular sovereignty (Alliès, 1980, pp. 182–83).

The destruction of the provincial system and the introduction of departmental administrative divisions in 1789 sought explicitly to dismantle the atavistic peculiarities upon which the French monarchy had been based (Revel, 1989, p. 129) and to incorporate the principles of equality and fraternity within the sphere of the geography of the state.

The period of twelve years after the Thermidor coup was characterized by the production of departmental information organized in a decentralized fashion. This was prompted by the circular issued to the departmental administrators by the first Minister of the Interior of the Directory, Bénézech, in 1795. This intense activity of surveying and interpreting descriptive and statistical data did not generate thematic local maps. Cartographic knowledge of the territory remained within the geodetic and topographic sphere linked to the construction of the map of France, an activity which was to follow the lines laid down by the Cassini dynasty since the time of Colbert (Revel, 1989, p. 154).

The main initiative was the compilation of general and detailed statistics of France carried out, but not completed, by Chaptal between 1801 and 1804. The mass of information which emerged as a result of this work organized on a departmental basis became the seed-bed for reinventing the provincial outlines within the new departmental format (Revel, 1989, p. 131).

With the advent of the Napoleonic Empire, the situation reverted to that of the previous monarchical period, and territorial statistics were once more a state secret. Two kinds of activity prospered during the Napoleonic period: on the one hand, statistical-cartographic surveys carried out by military engineers and, on the other hand, works describing places, countries and regions produced by civilians, who can be classed more or less as 'geographers', with an interest in the resources and potential of the territories conquered by the Empire.

The result of both these activities was that, for the first time, a grand system of geographical information was institutionalized (Godleweska, 1994). The cognitive and political importance of this lay in the idea of modernization as an expression of the ascendancy of rationalism in the technical control of society and government management and, in this regard, imperialism was linked to the idea of spreading progress legitimized in the right to conquest of civilization, and of French civilization in particular (Godleweska, 1994, p. 53).

The downfall of the Napoleonic Empire plunged France into a state of introspection with regard to its universalizing aims. The Restoration and then the July Monarchy restricted reflection regarding the territory, and hence society, to the level of the tools necessary for the selection of the various models of social and political organization of the state, since there was an urgent need to identify existing inequalities in order to plan possible changes (Chartier, 1980, p. 29). Duphin, who undertook this task during the decade of the 1820s, maintained the departmental divisions although strictly for descriptive purposes (Chartier, 1978). With Angeville and Guerry, during the decade of the 1830s, surveys gave way to inventories in line with the later interpretation of a single item which was French territory. Surveys became more abstract, since the natural geographical differences which constituted methodologically independent units were eliminated from the statistical design. In order to build a neutral space for statistical research, local units for the collection and addition of information were conceived as continuous areas in accordance with conventional zoning protocols (Chartier, 1980, pp. 29–30).

The scientific profile of the territory was already guaranteed by the maps drawn up on a solid geometric foundation. Using this as a starting-point, it was feasible to reconstruct the differences within the kingdom and plan the steps which had to be taken for an orderly transformation to occur. The idea of a geographical catalogue on a neutral and homogeneous space took root then. This would serve as the basis for the codification and control of social reality, since the exercise of 'effective power requires an unobstructed area in which to operate free from the constant distractions of the baroque design of contrasts' (Chartier, 1980, p. 30).

On the other side of the Atlantic, the thirteen British colonies emancipated in 1776 formed the first modern democratic state. The French Revolution set an important precedent, although there were notable differences in the respective processes of territorial formation and the political regimes which emerged in each case.

American democracy was first organized as a confederation in 1782 to become a federal state in 1795 after a wide-ranging parliamentary and political debate, whereas, from the outset, French democracy was monolithic, even taking into consideration Girondin's federal digressions during the last decade of the eighteenth century.

The construction of the territory of France had begun long before at the time of the first Capetian kings and was consolidated in the seventeenth and eighteenth centuries. During this same period other states had developed institutionally and territorially around it so that, when the Revolution occurred, French territory had already been defined by absolutism, and the frontiers could not be altered without impinging directly upon other neighbouring states.

None of this occurred in the United States, even if we accept that the thirteen colonies were surrounded by French and British colonial dependencies. In fact, the latter were far from being organized, effectively occupied territories like the European territories and, to a point, the American and Quebec territories were mere jurisdictions, more or less defined for the exercise of British or French imperial sovereignty. Throughout the nineteenth century the coastal strip occupied by the Union on the eastern seaboard of North America served as a launching-pad for expansion towards the more extensive unknown territories lying to the west (Goetzmann, 1986, pp. 76–79) within an imaginary continental territory which was rapidly established during the decades following the end of the War of Independence.

For this reason the progressive, civilizing discourse which had fanned the imperialist experience of the *Grande Nation* of France – with its belief in the superiority of its political institutions, culture and national science – was lacking in the ideological direction of the Union, where the discourse was directed towards civilizing the territory inherited jurisdictionally and the vast neighbouring territory as yet undiscovered, unexplored and unoccupied (Goetzmann, 1986, p. 115).

The idea of freedom forged in an individualistic, democratic society was steeped in images of virgin lands which could be transformed by the industrious efforts of American citizens who would tame the wilderness. The spectacular countryside foreshadowed the future of the nation.

From the very outset, patriotic imagination was connected to territorial expansion of the state. Both aspects were based on similar features: the idea of developing American science in order satisfactory to fulfil the manifest destiny of the nation – a discourse characteristic of the work of President Jefferson and the explorers Clark and Lewis between 1779 and 1830 (Livingstone, 1992, pp. 142–49) – and the theological-natural providentialism contained within the allegory of 'the geographical grandeur which foreshadowed the greatness of the state' found in the works of Guyot and Maury (Livingstone, 1992, pp. 149–55). No European state demonstrates such a close link as existed in the United States between exploration of non-metropolitian territories, the inventorying and description of the territory of the state, and the symbols for the self-identification of the nationality of that state.

The neutralization of the territory which had taken place during the process of state modernization was not limited merely to the scientific institutionalization achieved by cartographic knowledge, but aimed to reflect the real profile of the territory in the geodetic and topographic surveys which were carried out in Europe during the nineteenth century.

As in France, Britain undertook activities aimed at achieving a map of the state using astronomical triangulation. After 1791 the Royal Survey was charged with drawing these maps and with the general cartography of the kingdom using larger scales as the century progressed. In the other European states, similar bodies were also set up with the same aims.[4]

In the sixteenth century various topographic surveys had been carried out in order to produce national maps of different scales and varying degrees of precision with regard to the localized information used. In the Holy Empire, influenced by the German chorographic school, a wide-ranging inventory of Saxony was carried out between 1500 and 1600 on a scale of 1:26,000 and another of Bavaria between 1554 and 1563 (regarded as the best for that period) made up of 40 sheets on a scale of 1:50,000. In the following century, in 1652 Denmark produced a 36-sheet cadastral map as well as an annex containing descriptive cartographic details of a thematic and regional nature. In 1626 Sweden produced a more modest engraved six-sheet map, while Russia did not produce its first map of the European part of its Empire until 1720 and Austria carried out only partial surveys of a primitive nature between 1768 and 1790.

In general terms, a certain connection may be seen between the depth of the process of political centralization and state modernization in the various dynastic European powers and the progress made in the definition of their sovereign territories. [...]

The naturalization of the territory of the representative democratic states merits separate attention. Leaving to one side the vagaries of the officialization of cartographic representation and the institutionalization of surveying and territorial census tools in France after the Revolution, the United States stands out on account of the geometric radicalization of the practices of political-administrative division and the generalized production and use of cartographic information in the various parts of the state.

Early expansion towards the West, from the Appalachian Mountains to the Mississippi-Missouri basin, in the final decades of the eighteenth century and the first decade of the nineteenth century, provided the first proving ground for the practice of drawing linear borders which was consolidated during the second period of expansion towards the far West and the Pacific coast once the War of Secession had come to an end in the 1880s. In both cases, the territory was regarded geometrically, and state and country borders were drawn in accordance with the rectangular plots which were the norm throughout the territory of the United States.

In America there was not the same urgency as in Europe to produce cartographic representations which were geodetically precise and epistemologically legitimate in order to institutionalize and control the borders of the state, so, during the period between 1776 and 1818, most of such work was carried out sporadically, exploration going hand in hand with field surveys and the description and classification of the features of the landscape which was systematically surveyed. Some small-scale triangulation projects were carried out with a view to plotting the lines dividing the new states incorporated into the Union on the map.

Until the 1880s, geographic surveys were carried out by a variety of bodies which promoted and sponsored them sporadically. First the coastal survey carried out by the Treasury Department in 1807. This formed the basis of the stable budget granted by Congress in 1847 to keep coastal charts permanently updated using trigonometric triangulation techniques. Years later, in 1845, the United States Census Office was finally set up. This body carried out an ongoing job of producing and compiling federal statistical cartography. In 1813 the Topographer Engineers Corps was set up within the army. After 1863 this organization implemented an active policy of hydrological surveys, trigonometric triangulation and astronomical calculation of political boundaries. This office was eventually transferred to the War Department in 1879. Finally, also in 1879, the Geological Survey was set up, and one of its first tasks was territorial planning during the expansion towards the 'Far West'. It was finally charged with most of the cartographic work required by the War Department and the General Staff.

The wide variety of institutions involved in topographic surveys, geodetic measurement and cartographic representation in the United States shows the impact of a state structure directly linked to a government which represented the political will of the citizens and where the administration set up public bodies specifically charged with ensuring modernization and the material progress of the inhabitants of the state.

In the second half of the nineteenth century most of the central states, including the United States, had laid the foundations of their cartographic institutions. During this period the expansion of capitalism, until the crisis of 1880, wrought a profound transformation in the social structure of the developed countries, altering their consumer and production habits, labour relations and the relative importance of rural and urban society. Thus a climax was reached in the restructuring of the territory as well as in the administration responsible for controlling, managing and planning that territory.

But these same territories, organized socially and politically, which had already been methodically surveyed and represented, began to reproduce themselves as platforms of state with a virulence unknown since the Renaissance until a global colonial world, [coerced into] crudely [...] aping the West and covering almost the whole planet, was established.

Works classifying and interpreting descriptions of statistical series, monographs, travelogues, field reports, pictorial and cartographic representations and an endless variety of intellectual endeavours following certain standardized technical patterns achieved widespread legitimacy, which allowed them to attain independent institutional status.

In fact, exploration and representation became the two elements associated with discovery and the codification of the geographical diversity of the world on solid theoretical and experimental bases laid by positive science.

After the 1870s or thereabouts, mass education gradually began to use images of the metropolitan and overseas territories in order to form a collective identity among the citizens of the nation-states and the inhabitants of the colonial territories. Nations and empires were transformed into real mappable objects and, for the second time in 100 years (although on a larger scale), the administrative boundaries defined by Europe in the rest of the world solidified politically, until they functioned as instruments of ethnic discrimination between the numerous national entities which appeared in the course of the successive waves of decolonization which occurred during the twentieth century (Escolar, 1996).

Geographical societies – bodies for the promotion of geography and geographers – imbued with economic, political and scientific aims, constituted the privileged locus of the socialization of geographic knowledge and its practical use and intellectual circulation (Capel, 1981). On the other hand, the school systems gradually incorporated geography into the curriculum, transmitting the images, information and arguments to aid understanding of the natural character of the state territories and the non-arbitrary logic of colonial domination. Both these aims were based on the objective data on human and physical geography current at the end of the century (Escolar, 1996).

Conclusion

When the construction of the modern states began, knowledge of the territory was linked to the monarchy's capacity of ownership over its jurisdictional and eminent possessions. The emergence of an autonomous social sector which formed the state bureaucracy and the centralization of dynastic power from the fifteenth century onwards brought in their wake the search for ways of representing the territory which would enable the administration to foresee, calculate and exercise its functions and responsibilities.

Consequently, exploration was not merely a facet of the policy of conquest implemented during the Renaissance by the Western European states bent on overseas expansion but also a part of the task of surveying their territories in Europe.

Representing, describing and interpreting the world were not unrelated actions. The geographical reality of the planet was discovered and brought under control by breaking with the images inherited from antiquity and incorporating the images which the imagination and empirical surveys provided in vast numbers. Pictography, cartographic techniques and science formed a single intellectual field linked to the systematic preparation of domestic and overseas scenarios where the central power of the monarchy could plan and exercise effective territorial sovereignty.

However, the technology of cartographic representation could never achieve the Renaissance ideal of a complete picture, an image which included all the available information and which could be used for all purposes. For this reason, maps began to diverge from the true outline and the real subject-matter. During the seventeenth and eighteenth centuries, mapping meant controlling and having the capacity to move about on the ground.

Coercive centralization in the absolute states defined a world of necessary information which could not be left to the arbitrary nature of Renaissance cartographic pictography. From that time onwards, learning about the shape of the earth was a scientific process which neutralized the explicit ideological uses and figurative practices employed in cartography.

When the revolution came, the territory had already been formed and established by the absolute state. It had achieved a degree of political autonomy as an administrative and government jurisdiction, thus paving the way for an abstract, non-personalized idea of power and the idea of the state as an entity. Representation of the citizens became the mechanism for delegating the sovereign power of the citizens within a given territory. The national map, i.e. the neutral figure of the fatherland, then began to emerge as a tool for the formation of a national political identity among the members of that state.

When cartography and the state bureaucratic structure had become established as official institutions, the first scientific and the latter administrative in nature, surveying and exploration became ways of localizing thematic information. Consequently, from that time onwards, 'mapping' no longer meant inventing geography and producing a territory. From the latter decades of the nineteenth century onwards, neutralization of cartographic representation and naturalization of the geographic shape of the state allowed geography to take its place as an autonomous scientific discipline.

Translated from Spanish

NOTES

1   Charts which could be used to facilitate navigation following coastal sailing directions and geographical courses.
2   Of the 10,000 maps to be found in the Venice archives, only 1.5 per cent are dated around 1565 and of these only 1 per cent are pre-1560, whereas the Magistrature responsible for the control and management of the canals functioned for 300 years before maps were used for taking economic and judicial decisions (Marino, 1987, pp. 7 and 9).
3   Charles V put down the rebellion of the communities of Castile which rose up against the centralizing policy of the Emperor and in defence of the privileges of the Castilian boroughs.
4   The following data, referring to different examples in the European State and the United States, were taken from Harvey 1980.

REFERENCES

Alliès, P., 1980. *L'invention du territoire*. Grenoble: Presses Universitaires de Grenoble.
Alpers, S., 1983. 'L'oeil de l'histoire: l'effet cartographique dans la peinture hollandaise au 17ème siècle'. *Actes de la Recherche en Sciences Sociales* 49, pp. 71–101.
Barber, P. 1987a. 'England I: Pageantry, Defence and Government: Maps at Court to 1550'. In B. Buisseret (ed.), *Monarchs, Ministers and Maps: The Emergence of Cartography as a Tool of Government in Early Modern Europe*, Chicago and London: The University of Chicago Press.
Barber, P., 1987b. 'England II: Monarchs, Ministers and Maps, 1550–1625'. In B. Buisseret (ed.), *Monarchs, Ministers and Maps: The Emergence of Cartography as a Tool of Government in Early Modern Europe*, Chicago and London: The University of Chicago Press.
Berthon, S.; Robinson, A., 1991. *The Shape of the World. The Mapping and Discovery of the Heart*. London: George Philip.

Boorstin, D. J., 1983. *The Discoverers. A History of Man's Search to Know His World and Himself.* New York: Random House.

Broc, N., 1974. *La géographie des philosophes. Géographes et voyageurs français au XVIII siècle.* Paris: Ophrys/Associations des Publications près les Universités de Strasbourg.

Broc, N., 1980. *La Géographie de la renaissance.* Paris: C.T.H.S. (2nd edn, 1986).

Buisseret, D., 1987. 'Monarchs, Ministers and Maps in France before the Accession of Louis XIV'. In B. Buisseret (ed.), *Monarchs, Ministers and Maps: The Emergence of Cartography as a Tool of Government in Early Modern Europe*, Chicago and London: The University of Chicago Press.

Capel, H., 1981. 'Institutionalization of Geography and Strategies of Change'. In D. R. Stoddart (ed.), *Geography, Ideology and Social Concern*, Oxford: Blackwell.

Chartier, R., 1978. 'Les deux Frances: histoire d'une géographie'. *Cahiers d'Histoire* 4, pp. 393–415.

Chartier, R., 1980. 'Science sociale et découpage régional. Note sur deux débats, 1820–1920'. *Actes de la Recherches en Sciences Sociales* 35, pp. 27–36.

Cormarck, L. B., 1991. 'Good Fences Make Good Neighbours: Geography as Self-definition in Early Modern England'. *Isis* 82, pp. 639–61.

Cormarck, L. B., 1994. 'The Fashioning of an Empire: Geography and Empire in Elizabethan England'. In A. Godleweska and N. Smith (eds), *Geography and Empire*, Oxford: Blackwell.

Escolar, M., 1994. 'Elementos históricos para una teoría de la diferenciación e integración territorial. Geografía política del estado-Nación moderno'. In P. Chiolella, E. Laurelli, A. Rofman and L. Yanes (eds), *Integración Latinoamericana y Territorio*, Buenos Aires: Ediciones FfyL-UBA/CEUR.

Escolar, M., 1995. 'Territorios de representación y territorios representados'. Paper presented at the *V Reunião de antropologia do (merco) sul*, Tramandaí (Rs-Brazil).

Escolar, M., 1996. *Crítica do Discurso Geográfico.* São Paulo: Hucitec.

Godleweska, A., 1994. 'Napoleon's Geographers (1797–1815): Imperialist and Soldiers of Modernity'. In A. Godleweska and N. Smith (eds), *Geography and Empire*, Oxford and Cambridge, Mass.: Blackwell.

Goetzmann, W., 1986. *New Lands, New Men. America and the Second Great Age of Discovery.* New York: Viking.

Harley, J. B., 1988. 'Maps, Knowledge and Power'. In D. Cosgrove and S. Daniels (eds), *The Iconography of Landscape. Essays on the Symbolic Representations, Design and Use of the Past Environments*, Cambridge: Cambridge University Press.

Harley, J. B., 1992. 'Deconstructing the Map'. In T. J. Barnes and J. S. Duncan (eds), *Writing Worlds: Discourse, Text and Metaphor in the Representation of Landscape*, London and New York: Routledge.

Harvey, P. D. A., 1980. *The History of Topographical Maps: Symbols, Pictures and Surveys.* London: Thames & Hudson.

Jacob, C., 1992. *L'empire des cartes: approche théorique de la cartographie à travers l'histoire.* Paris: Albin Michel.

Lestringant, F., 1993. *L'atelier du cosmographe, ou l'image du monde à la Renaissance.* Paris: Albin Michel.

Livingstone, D., 1992. *The Geographical Tradition. Episodes in the History of a Contested Enterprise.* Oxford: Blackwell.

Marino, J., 1987. 'Administrative Mapping in the Italian States'. In B. Buisseret (ed.), *Monarchs, Ministers and Maps: The Emergence of Cartography as a Tool of Government in Early Modern Europe*, Chicago and London: The University of Chicago Press.

O'Sullivan, D., 1984. *The Age of Discovery 1400–1550.* London and New York: Longman.

Parker, G., 1987. 'Maps and Ministers: The Spanish Habsburgs'. In B. Buisseret (ed.), *Monarchs, Ministers and Maps: The Emergence of Cartography as a Tool of Government in Early Modern Europe*, Chicago and London: The University of Chicago Press.

Rees, R., 1980. 'Historical Links between Cartography and Art'. *Geographical Review* 70, pp. 57–72.

Revel, J., 1989. 'Connaissance du territoire, production du territoire: France XII–XIXe siècle'. In A. Burguière and J. Revel (eds), *Histoire de la France*, Vol. I. (ed. Revel), *L'espace français*, Paris: Seuil.

Vann, J., 1987. 'Mapping under the Austrian Habsburgs'. In B. Buisseret (ed.), *Monarch, Ministers and Maps: The Emergence of Cartography as a Tool of Government in Early Modern Europe*, Chicago and London, The University of Chicago Press.

2

The Autonomous Power of the State: Its Origins, Mechanisms and Results

Michael Mann

This essay tries to specify the origins, mechanisms and results of the autonomous power which the state possesses in relation to the major power groupings of 'civil society'. I will argue that the state is merely and essentially an arena, a *place*, and yet *this* is the very source of its autonomy. [After expanding on this definition, I will pursue its implications.] I discuss two essential parts of the definition, centrality and territoriality, in relation to two types of state power, termed here *despotic* and *infrastructural* power. I argue that state autonomy, of both despotic and infrastructural forms, flows principally from the state's unique ability to provide a *territorially centralized* form of organization.

Defining the State

The state is undeniably a messy concept. The main problem is that most definitions contain two different levels of analysis, the 'institutional' and the 'functional'. That is, the state can be defined in terms of what it looks like, institutionally, or what it does, its functions. Predominant is a mixed, but largely institutional, view put forward originally by Weber. In this the state contains four main elements, being:

1   A *differentiated* set of institutions and personnel embodying
2   *centrality* in the sense that political relations radiate outwards from a centre to cover
3   a *territorially demarcated area*, over which it exercises
4   a monopoly of *authoritative binding rule-making*, backed up by a monopoly of the means of physical violence.[1]

Apart from the last phrase which tends to equate the state with military force (see below), I will follow this definition. It is still something of a mixed bag [. . .] Nevertheless, my principal interest lies in those centralized institutions generally called 'states', and in the powers of the personnel who staff them, at the higher levels generally

The text of the above article has been previously printed in the *European Journal of Sociology*, XXV (1984), 185–213. Reprinted with permission.

termed the 'state elite'. The central question for us here, then, is what is the nature of the power possessed by states and state elites? In answering I shall contrast state elites with power groupings whose base lies outside the state, in 'civil society'. In line with the model of power underlying my work, I divide these into three: ideological, economic and military groups. So what, therefore, is the power of state elites as against the power of ideological movements, economic classes and military elites?

Two meanings of state power

What do we mean by 'the power of the state'? As soon as we begin to think about this commonplace phrase, we encounter two quite different senses in which states and their elites might be considered powerful. [...] The first sense concerns what we might term the *despotic power* of the state elite, the range of actions which the elite is empowered to undertake without routine, institutionalized negotiation with civil society groups. The historical variations in such powers have been so enormous that we can safely leave on one side the ticklish problem of how we precisely measure them. The despotic powers of many historical states have been virtually unlimited. The Chinese Emperor, as the Son of Heaven, 'owned' the whole of China and could do as he wished with any individual or group within his domain. The Roman Emperor, only a minor god, acquired powers which were also in principle unlimited outside of a restricted area of affairs nominally controlled by the Senate. Some monarchs of early modern Europe also claimed divinely derived, absolute powers (though they were not themselves divine). The contemporary Soviet state/party elite, as 'trustees' of the interests of the masses, also possess considerable despotic (though sometimes strictly unconstitutional) power. Great despotic power can be 'measured' most vividly in the ability of all these Red Queens to shout 'off with his head' and have their whim gratified without further ado – provided the person is at hand. Despotic power is also usually what is meant in the literature by 'autonomy of power'.

But there is a second sense in which people talk of 'the power of the state', especially in today's capitalist democracies. We might term this *infrastructural power*, the capacity of the state to actually penetrate civil society, and to implement logistically political decisions throughout the realm. This was comparatively weak in the historical societies just mentioned – once you were out of sight of the Red Queen, she had difficulty in getting at you. But it is powerfully developed in all industrial societies. When people in the West today complain of the growing power of the state, they cannot be referring sensibly to the despotic powers of the state elite itself, for if anything these are still declining. It is, after all, only 40 years since universal suffrage was fully established in several of the advanced capitalist states, and the basic political rights of groups such as ethnic minorities and women are still increasing. But the complaint is more justly levelled against the state's infrastructural encroachments. These powers are now immense. The state can assess and tax our income and wealth at source, without our consent or that of our neighbours or kin (which states before about 1850 were *never* able to do); it stores and can recall immediately a massive amount of information about all of us; it can enforce its will within the day almost anywhere in its domains; its influence on the overall economy is enormous; it even directly provides the subsistence of most of us (in state employment, in pensions, in family allowances, etc.). The state penetrates everyday life more than did any historical state. Its infrastructural power has increased enormously. If there were a Red Queen, we would all quail at her words – from Alaska to Florida, from the Shetlands to Cornwall there is no hiding place from the infrastructural reach of the modern state.

But who controls these states? Without prejudging a complex issue entirely, the answer in the capitalist democracies is less likely to be 'an autonomous state elite' than in most historic societies. In these countries most of the formal political leadership is elected and recallable. Whether one regards the democracy as genuine or not, few would contest that politicians are largely controlled by outside civil society groups (either by their financiers or by the electorate) as well as by the law. President Nixon or M. Chaban-Delmas may have paid no taxes; political leaders may surreptitiously amass wealth, infringe the civil liberties of their opponents, and hold on to power by slyly undemocratic means. But they do not brazenly expropriate or kill their enemies or dare to overturn legal traditions enshrining constitutional rule, private property or individual freedoms. On the rare occasions this happens, we refer to it as a *coup* or a revolution, an overturning of the norms. If we turn from elected politicians to permanent bureaucrats we still do not find them exercising significant autonomous power over civil society. [...] Their power to change the fundamental rules and overturn the distribution of power within civil society is feeble – without the backing of a formidable social movement.

So, in one sense states in the capitalist democracies are weak, in another they are strong. They are 'despotically weak' but 'infrastructurally strong'. Let us clearly distinguish these two types of state power. The first sense denotes power by the state elite itself *over* civil society. The second denotes the power of the state to penetrate and centrally coordinate the activities of civil society through its own infrastructure. The second type of power still allows the possibility that the state itself is a mere instrument of forces within civil society, i.e. that it has no despotic power at all. The two are analytically autonomous dimensions of power. In practice, of course, there may be a relationship between them. For example, the greater the state's infrastructural power, the greater the volume of binding rule-making, and therefore the greater the likelihood of despotic power over individuals and perhaps also over marginal, minority groups. All infrastructurally powerful states, including the capitalist democracies, are strong in relation to individuals and to the weaker groups in civil society, but the capitalist democratic states are feeble in relation to dominant groups – at least in comparison to most historical states.

From these two independent dimensions of state power we can derive the four ideal-types shown in table 2.1

The *feudal* state is the weakest, for it has both low despotic and low infrastructural power. The medieval European state approximated to this ideal-type, governing

Table 2.1 Two dimensions of state power

Despotic power	Infrastructural coordination	
	Low	High
Low	Feudal	Bureaucratic
High	Imperial	Authoritarian

largely indirectly, through infrastructure freely and contractually provided and controlled by the principal and independent magnates, clerics and towns. The *imperial* state possesses its own governing agents, but has only limited capacity to penetrate and coordinate civil society without the assistance of other power groups. It corresponds to the term patrimonial state used by writers like Weber (1968) and Bendix (1978). Ancient states like the Akkadian, Egyptian, Assyrian, Persian and Roman approximated to this type. I hesitated over the term *bureaucratic* state, because of its negative connotations. But a bureaucracy has a high organizational capacity, yet cannot set its own goals; and the bureaucratic state is controlled by others, civil society groups, but their decisions once taken are enforceable through the state's infrastructure. Contemporary capitalist democracies approximate to this type, as does the future state hoped for by most radicals and socialists. *Authoritarian* is intended to suggest a more institutionalized form of despotism, in which competing power groupings cannot evade the infrastructural reach of the state, nor are they structurally separate from the state (as they are in the bureaucratic type). All significant social power must go through the authoritative command structure of the state. Thus it is high on both dimensions, having high despotic power over civil society groups and being able to enforce this infrastructurally. In their different ways, Nazi Germany and the Soviet Union tend towards this case. But they probably traded off some loss of infrastructural penetration for high despotic powers (thus neither attained as high a level of social mobilization during the Second World War as the 'despotically weak' but participatory Great Britain did). Nor is this to deny that such states contain competing interest groups which may possess different bases in 'civil society'. Rather, in an authoritarian state power is transmitted through its directives and so such groups compete for direct control of the state. It is different in the capitalist democracies where the power of the capitalist class, for example, permeates the whole of society, and states generally accept the rules and rationality of the surrounding capitalist economy.

These are ideal-types. Yet my choice of real historical examples which roughly approximate to them reveals two major tendencies which are obvious enough yet worthy of explanation. First, there has occurred a long-term historical growth in the infrastructural power of the state, apparently given tremendous boosts by industrial societies, but also perceptible within both pre-industrial and industrial societies considered separately. Secondly, however, within each historical epoch have occurred wide variations in despotic powers. There has been *no* general development tendency in despotic powers – non-despotic states existed in late fourth millennium BC Mesopotamia (the 'primitive democracy' of the early city-states), in first millennium BC Phoenicia, Greece and Rome, in medieval republics and city-states, and in the modern world alike. The history of despotism has been one of oscillation, not development. Why such wide divergencies on one dimension, but a developmental trend on the other?

The development of state infrastructural power

The growth of the infrastructural power of the state is one in the logistics of political control. I will not here enumerate its main historical phases. Instead, I give examples of some logistical techniques which have aided effective state penetration of social life, each of which has had a long historical development.

1 A division of labour between the state's main activities which it coordinated centrally. A microcosm of this is to be found on the battlefields of history where a coordinated administrative division between infantry, cavalry and artillery, usually organized by the state, would normally defeat forces in which these activities were mixed up – at least in 'high intensity' warfare.
2 Literacy, enabling stabilized messages to be transmitted through the state's territories by its agents, and enabling legal responsibilities to be codified and stored. Giddens (1981) emphasizes this 'storage' aspect of state power.
3 Coinage, and weights and measures, allowing commodities to be exchanged under an ultimate guarantee of value by the state.
4 Rapidity of communication of messages and of transport of people and resources through improved roads, ships, telegraphy etc.

States able to use relatively highly developed forms of these techniques have possessed greater capacity for infrastructural penetration. This is pretty obvious. So is the fact that history has seen a secular process of infrastructural improvements.

Yet none of these techniques is specific to the state. They are part of general social development, part of the growth of human beings' increasing capacities for collective social mobilization of resources. Societies in general, not just their states, have advanced their powers. Thus none of these techniques necessarily changes the relationship between a state and its civil society; and none is necessarily pioneered by either the state or civil society.

Thus state power (in either sense) does not derive from techniques or means of power that are peculiar to itself. The varied techniques of power are of three main types: military, economic and ideological. They are characteristic of all social relationships. The state uses them all, adding no fourth means peculiar to itself. This has made reductionist theories of the state more plausible because the state seems dependent on resources also found more generally in civil society. If they are all wrong, it is not because the state manipulates means of power denied to other groups. The state is not autonomous in *this* sense. Indeed, the fact that the means used are essentially also the means used in all social relationships ensures that states rarely diverge far from their civil societies. [. . .]

Two conclusions emerge. First, in the whole history of the development of the infrastructure of power there is virtually no technique which belongs necessarily to the state, or conversely to civil society. Secondly, there is some kind of oscillation between the role of the two in social development. I hope to show later that it is not merely oscillation, but a dialectic.

The obvious question is: if infrastructural powers are a general feature of society, in what circumstances are they appropriated by the state? How does the state acquire in certain situations, but not others, despotic powers? What are the origins of the autonomous power of the state? My answer is in three stages, touching upon the *necessity* of the state, its *multiplicity of functions* and its *territorialized centrality*. The first two have often been identified in recent theory, the third is, I think, novel.

Origins of State Power

The necessity of the state

[. . .] Societies with states have had superior survival value to those without them. We have no examples of stateless societies long enduring past a primitive level of development, and many examples of state societies absorbing or eliminating stateless ones. Where stateless societies conquer ones with states, they either themselves develop a state or they induce social regress in the conquered society. There are good sociological reasons for this. Only three alternative bases for order exist, force, exchange and custom, and none of these are sufficient in the long run. At some point new exigencies arise for which custom is inadequate; at some point to bargain about everything in exchange relations is inefficient and disintegrating; while force alone, as Parsons emphasized, will soon 'deflate'. In the long run normally taken for granted, but enforceable, rules are necessary to bind together strangers or semi-strangers. It is not requisite that all these rules are set by a single monopolistic state. Indeed, though the feudal example is extreme, most states exist in a multi-state civilization which also provides certain normative rules of conduct. Nevertheless most societies seem to have required that some rules, particularly those relevant to the protection of life and property, be set monopolistically, and this has been the province of the state.

From this necessity, autonomous state power ultimately derives. The activities of the state personnel are necessary to society as a whole and/or to the various groups that benefit from the existing structure of rules which the state enforces. From this functionality derives the potentiality for exploitation, a lever for the achievement of private state interests. Whether the lever is used depends on other conditions, for – after all – we have not even established the existence of a permanent state cadre which might have identifiable interests. But necessity is the mother of state power.

The multiplicity of state functions

Despite the assertions of reductionists, most states have not in practice devoted themselves to the pursuit of a single function. 'Binding rule-making' is merely an umbrella term. The rules and functions have been extremely varied. As the two-dimensional models recognize, we may distinguish domestic and international, or economic, ideological and military functions. But there are many types of activity and each tends to be functional for differing 'constituencies' in society. I illustrate this with reference to what have been probably the four most persistent types of state activities.

1 The maintenance of internal order. This may benefit all, or all law-abiding subjects of the state. It may also protect the majority from arbitrary usurpations by socially and economically powerful groups, other than those allied to the state. But probably the main benefit is to protect existing property relations from the mass of the property-less. This function probably best serves a dominant economic class constituency.

2   Military defence/aggression, directed against foreign foes. 'War parties' are rarely coterminous with either the whole society or with one particular class within it. Defence may be genuinely collective; aggression usually has more specific interests behind it. Those interests may be quite widely shared by all 'younger sons' without inheritance rights or all those expansively minded; or they might comprise only a class fraction of an aristocracy, merchants or capitalists. In multi-state systems war usually involves alliances with other states, some of whom may share the same religion, ethnicity, or political philosophy as some domestic constituency. These are rarely reducible to economic class. Hence war and peace constituencies are usually somewhat idiosyncratic.

3   The maintenance of communications infrastructures: roads, rivers, message systems, coinages, weights and measures, marketing arrangements. Though few states have monopolized all of these, all states have provided some, because they have a territorial basis which is often most efficiently organized from a centre. The principal constituencies here are a 'general interest' and more particular trade-centred groups.

4   Economic redistribution: the authoritative distribution of scarce material resources between different ecological niches, age-groups, sexes, regions, classes etc. There is a strongly collective element in this function, more so than in the case of the others. Nevertheless, many of the redistributions involve rather particular groups, especially the economically inactive whose subsistence is thus protected by the state. And economic redistribution also has an international dimension, for the state normally regulates trade relations and currency exchanges across its boundaries, sometimes unilaterally, sometimes in alliance with other states. This also gives the state a particular constituency among merchants and other international agents – who, however, are rarely in agreement about desirable trade policy.

These four tasks are necessary, either to society as a whole or to interest groups within it. They are undertaken most efficiently by the personnel of a central state who become indispensable. And they bring the state into functional relations with diverse, sometimes cross-cutting groups between whom there is room to manoeuvre. The room can be exploited. Any state involved in a multiplicity of power relations can play off interest groups against each other. [. . .]

[There are many] examples of the state balancing between what are predominantly classes or class factions. But the balancing possibilities are much more numerous if the state is involved in a multiplicity of relations with groups which may on some issues be narrower than classes and on others wider. Because most states are pursuing multiple functions, they can perform multiple manoeuvres. The 'Bonapartist balancing act' is a skill acquired by most states. This manoeuvring space is the birthplace of state power.

And this is about as far as the insights contained within current two-dimensional theory can be expanded. It is progress, but not enough. It does not really capture the *distinctiveness* of the state as a social organization. After all, necessity plus multiplicity of function, and the balancing act, are also the power source and stock-in-trade of any ruthless committee chairperson. Is the state only a chair writ large? No, as we will now see.

The territorial centrality of the state

The definition of the state concentrates upon its institutional, territorial, centralized nature. This is the third, and most important, precondition of state power. As noted, the state does not possess a distinctive *means* of power independent of, and analogous to, economic, military and ideological power. The means used by states are only a combination of these, which are also the means of power used in all social relationships. However, the power of the state is irreducible in quite a different *sociospatial* and *organizational* sense. Only the state is inherently centralized over a delimited territory over which it has authoritative power. Unlike economic, ideological or military groups in civil society, the state elite's resources radiate authoritatively outwards from a centre but stop at defined territorial boundaries. The state is, indeed, a *place* – both a central place and a unified territorial reach. As the principal forms of state autonomous power will flow from this distinctive attribute of the state, it is important that I first prove that the state does so differ sociospatially and organizationally from the major power groupings of civil society.

Economic power groupings – classes, corporations, merchant houses, manors, plantations, the *oikos* etc. – normally exist in decentred, competitive or conflictual relations with one another. True, the internal arrangements of some of them (e.g. the modern corporation, or the household and manor of the great feudal lord) might be relatively centralized. But, first, they are oriented outwards to further opportunities for economic advantage which are not territorially confined nor subject to authoritative rules governing expansion (except by states). Economic power expansion is not authoritative, commanded – it is 'diffused', informally. Second, the scope of modern and some historic economic institutions is not territorial. They do not exercise general control of a specific territory, they control a specialized function and seek to extend it 'transnationally' wherever that function is demanded and exploitable. General Motors does not rule the territory around Detroit, it rules the assembly of automobiles and some aspects of the economic life-chances of its employees, stockholders and consumers. Third, in those cases where economic institutions have been authoritative, centralized and territorial (as in the feudal household/manor of historic nobilities) they have either been subject to a higher level of territorial, central control by the (imperial) state, or they have acquired political function (administering justice, raising military levies etc.) from a weak (feudal) state and so become themselves 'mini-states'. Thus states cannot be the simple instrument of classes, for they have a different territorial scope.

Analogous points can be made about ideological power movements like religions. Ideologies (unless state-led) normally spread even more diffusely than economic relations. They move diffusely and 'interstitially' inside state territories, spreading through communication networks among segments of a state's population (like classes, age-cohorts, genders, urban/rural inhabitants etc.); they often also move transnationally right through state boundaries. Ideologies may develop central, authoritative, Church-like institutions, but these are usually functionally, more than territorially, organized: they deal with the sacred rather than the secular, for example. There is a socio-spatial, as well as spiritual, 'transcendence' about ideological movements, which is really the opposite of the territorial bounds of the state.

It is true, however, that military power overlaps considerably with the state, especially in modern states who usually monopolize the means of organized violence. Nevertheless, it is helpful to treat the two as distinct sources of power. I have not the space here to justify this fully (see Mann, 1986, ch. 1). Let me instead make two simple points. First, not all warfare is most efficiently organized territorially centrally – guerrillas, military feudalism and warrior bands are all examples of relatively decentred military organizations effective at many historical periods. Second, the effective scope of military power does not cover a single, unitary territory. In fact, it has two rather different territorial radii of effective control.

Militaristic control of everyday behaviour requires such a high level of organized coercion, logistical back-up and surplus extraction that it is practical only within close communications to the armed forces in areas of high surplus availability. It does not spread evenly over entire state territories. It remains concentrated in pockets and along communications routes. It is relatively ineffective at penetrating peasant agriculture, for example.

The second radius enables, not everyday control, but the setting of broad limits of outward compliance over far greater areas. In this case, failure to comply with broad parameters such as the handing over of tribute, the performance of ritual acts of submission, occasional military support (or at least non-rebellion), could result in a punitive expedition, and so is avoided. This radius of military striking power has normally been far greater than that of state political control, as Owen Lattimore (1962) brilliantly argued. This is obviously so in the world today, given the capabilities of modern armaments. It is also true of the superpowers in a more subtle sense: they can impose 'friendly' regimes and de-stabilize the unfriendly through client military elites and their own covert paramilitary organizations, but they cannot get those regimes to conform closely to their political dictates. [...] The logistics of 'concentrated coercion' – that is, of military power – differ from those of the territorial centralized state. Thus we should distinguish the two as power organizations. The militarist theory of the state is false, and one reason is that the state's organization is not coterminous with military organization.

The organizational autonomy of the state is only partial – indeed, in many particular cases it may be rather small. General Motors and the capitalist class in general, or the Catholic Church, or the feudal lords and knights, or the US military, are or were quite capable of keeping watch on states they have propped up. Yet they could not do the states' jobs themselves unless they changed their own socio-spatial and organizational structure. A state autonomous power ensues from this difference. Even if a particular state is set up or intensified merely to institutionalize the relations between given social groups, this is done by concentrating resources and infrastructures in the hands of an institution that has different socio-spatial and organizational contours to those groups. Flexibility and speed of response entail concentration of decision-making and a tendency towards permanence of personnel. The decentred non-territorial interest groups that set up the state in the first place are thus less able to control it. Territorial centralization provides the state with a potentially independent basis of power mobilization being necessary to social development and uniquely in the possession of the state itself.

If we add together the necessity, multiplicity and territorial centrality of the state, we can in principle explain its autonomous power. By these means the state elite possesses an independence from civil society which, though not absolute, is no less absolute in principle than the power of any other major group. Its power cannot be reduced to their power either directly or 'ultimately' or 'in the last instance'. The state is not merely a locus of class struggle, an instrument of class rule, the factor of social cohesion, the expression of core values, the centre of social allocation processes, the institutionalization of military force (as in the various reductionist theories) – it is a different socio-spatial organization. As a consequence we can treat states as *actors*, in the person of state elites, with a will to power and we can engage in the kind of 'rational action' theory of state interests advocated by Levi (1981). [...]

Results: Infrastructural Power

Any state that acquires or exploits social utility will be provided with infrastructural supports. These enable it to regulate, normatively and by force, a *given* set of social and territorial relations, and to erect boundaries against the outside. New boundaries momentarily reached by previous social interactions are stabilized, regulated and heightened by the state's universalistic, monopolistic rules. In this sense the state gives territorial bounds to social relations whose dynamic lies outside of itself. The state *is* an arena, the condensation, the crystallization, the summation of social relations within its territories – a point often made by Poulantzas (1972). Yet, despite appearances, this does not support Poulantzas' reductionist view of the state, for this is an *active* role. The state may promote great social change by consolidating territoriality which would not have occurred without it. The importance of this role is in proportion to its infrastructural powers: the greater they are or become, the greater the territorializing of social life. Thus even if the state's every move toward despotism is successfully resisted by civil society groups, massive state-led infrastructural reorganization may result. Every dispute between the state elite and elements of civil society, and every dispute among the latter which is routinely regulated through the state's institutions, tends to focus the relations and the struggles of civil society on to the territorial plane of the state, consolidating social interaction over that terrain, creating territorialized mechanisms for repressing or compromising the struggle, and breaking both smaller local and also wider transnational social relationships.

Let me give an example [...]. From the thirteenth century onward, two principal social processes favoured a greater degree of territorial centralization in Europe. First, warfare gradually favoured army command structures capable of routine, complex coordination of specialized infantry, cavalry and artillery. Gradually, the looser feudal levy of knights, retainers and a few mercenaries became obsolete. In turn this presupposed a routine 'extraction – coercion cycle' to deliver men, monies and supplies to the forces (see the brilliant essay by Finer, 1975). Eventually, only territorially centred states were able to provide such resources and the Grand Duchies, the Prince–Bishops and the Leagues of Towns lost power to the emerging 'national' states. Second, European expansion, especially economic expansion taking an increasingly capitalistic form, required (a) increased military protection abroad, (b) more complex legal regulation of property and market transactions, and

(c) domestic property forms (like rights to common lands). Capitalistic property owners sought out territorial states for help in these matters. Thus European states gradually acquired far greater infrastructural powers: regular taxation, a monopoly over military mobilization, permanent bureaucratic administration, a monopoly of law-making and enforcement. In the long run, despite attempts at absolutism, states failed to acquire despotic powers through this because it also enhanced the infrastructural capacities of civil society groups, especially of capitalist property-holders. This was most marked in Western Europe and as the balance of geo-political power tilted Westwards – and especially to Britain – the despotically weak state proved the general model for the modern era. States governed with, and usually in the interests of, the capitalist class.

But the process and the alliance facilitated the rise of a quite different type of state power, infrastructural in nature. When capitalism emerged as dominant, it took the form of a series of territorial segments – many systems of production and exchange, each to a large (though not total) extent bounded by a state and its overseas sphere of influence. The nation-state system of our own era was not a product of capitalism (or, indeed, of feudalism) considered as pure modes of production. It is in that sense 'autonomous'. But it resulted from the way expansive, emergent, capitalist relations were given regulative boundaries by pre-existing states. [. . .] The need for territorial centralization led to the restructuring of first European, then world society. The balance of nuclear terror lies between the successor states of these puny Europeans.

In the international economic system today, nation-states appear as collective economic actors. [. . .] This does not necessarily mean that there is a common 'national interest', merely that on the international plane there are a series of collectively organized power actors, nation-states. There is no doubting the economic role of the nation-state: the existence of a domestic market segregated to a degree from the international market, the value of the state's currency, the level of its tariffs and import quotas, its support for its indigenous capital and labour, indeed, its whole political economy is permeated with the notion that 'civil society' is its territorial domain. The territoriality of the state has created social forces with a life of their own. [. . .]

In this essay I have argued that the state is essentially an arena, a place – just as reductionist theories have argued – and yet this is precisely the origin and mechanism of its autonomous powers. The state, unlike the principal power actors of civil society, is territorially bounded and centralized. Societies need some of their activities to be regulated over a centralized territory. So do dominant economic classes, Churches and other ideological power movements, and military elites. They, therefore, entrust power resources to state elites which they are incapable of fully recovering, precisely because their own socio-spatial basis of organization is not centralized and territorial. Such state power resources, and the autonomy to which they lead, may not amount to much. If, however, the state's use of the conferred resources generates further power resources – as was, indeed, intended by the civil society groups themselves – these will normally flow through the state's hands, and thus lead to a significant degree of power autonomy. Therefore, *autonomous state power is the product of the usefulness of enhanced territorial centralization to social life in general.* This has varied considerably through the history of societies, and so consequently has the power of states. [. . .]

I also emphasized a second result of state infrastructural powers. Where these have increased, so has the territoriality of social life itself. This has usually gone unnoticed within sociology because of the unchallenged status of sociology's masterconcept: 'society'. Most sociologists – indeed, most people anywhere who use this term – mean by 'society', the territory of a state. Thus 'American society', 'British society', 'Roman society' etc. The same is true of synonyms like 'social formation' and (to a lesser extent) 'social system'. Yet the relevance of state boundaries to what we mean by societies is always partial and has varied enormously. Medievalists do not generally characterize 'society' in their time-period as state-defined; much more likely is a broader, transnational designation like 'Christendom' or 'European society'. Yet this change between medieval and modern times is one of the most decisive aspects of the great modernizing transformations; just as the current relationship between nation-states and 'the world system' is crucial to our understanding of late twentieth-century society. How territorialized and centralized are societies? This is the most significant theoretical issue on which we find states exercising a massive force over social life, *not* the more traditional terrain of dispute, the despotic power of state elites over classes or other elites. States are central to our understanding of what a society is. Where states are strong, societies are relatively territorialized and centralized. That is the most general statement we can make about the autonomous power of the state.

NOTE

1   See, for example, the definitions of Eisenstadt (1969, p. 5); MacIver (1926, p. 22); Tilly (1975, p. 27); Weber (1968, p. 64).

REFERENCES

Bendix R. 1978: *Kings or People*. Berkeley, Ca: University of California Press.
Eisenstadt S. N. 1969: *The Political Systems of Empires*. New York: The Free Press.
Finer S. 1975: 'State and nation-building in Europe: the role of the military', in C. Tilly (ed.), *The Formation of National States in Western Europe*. Princeton, NJ: Princeton University Press, [pp. 84–163].
Giddens A. 1981: *A Contemporary Critique of Historical Materialism*. London: Macmillan.
Lattimore O. 1962: *Studies in Frontier History*. London: Oxford University Press.
Levi M. 1981: 'The predatory theory of rule', *Politics and Society*, 10, pp. 431–65.
MacIver R. M. 1926: *The Modern State*. Oxford: Clarendon Press.
Mann M. 1986: *The Sources of Social Power*, vol. 1. *A History of Power from the Beginning to 1760 AD*. Cambridge: Cambridge University Press.
Poulantzas N. 1972: [*Political Power and Social Classes*. London: New Left Books.]
Tilly C. 1975: *The Formation of National States in Western Europe*. Princeton, NJ: Princeton University Press.
Weber M. 1968: *Economy and Society*. New York: Bedminster Press.

3

The Nation

Nicos Poulantzas

The nation – a complex case if ever there was one – combines all the impasses of a traditional variant of Marxism. In fact, we have to recognize that there is no Marxist theory of the nation; and despite the passionate debates on the subject that have taken place within the workers movement, it would be far too evasive to say that Marxism has underestimated the reality of the nation.

1 From Marxist reflection about the nation and from the debate in the workers movement,[1] the following initial point would seem to emerge: the nation is not identical with the modern nation and the national State, such as they appeared with the rise of capitalism in the West. The term designates 'something else' – a specific unit of the overall production of social relations that existed long before capitalism. Insofar as it mapped out new frontiers, new sites and temporalities of social reproduction, the constitution of the nation may be said to coincide with the passage from classless (lineage) society to class society. [. . .]

2 The second, related point concerns the dissociation of *State* and *nation* within the very framework of capitalism. Above all as a result of discussions on the Austro-Marxist analyses of Otto Bauer, Karl Renner and others, it is gradually becoming clear that, even within the national State, the State cannot entirely encapsulate the nation. Indeed, as is shown by the case of the multinational Austro-Hungarian Empire, one and the same capitalist State can embrace several nations. Conversely, a nation which has not yet succeeded in forging its own State on the basis of capitalism is no less of a nation for that; and it has no less right than others to self-determination. This lies at the root of Lenin's original and radical principle according to which peoples and nations have the right to decide their own future. Unlike the Austro-Marxists, Lenin does not reduce the right of self-determination to mere 'cultural autonomy', but extends it to the right of nations to establish their own State. Although a nation does not need to have its own distinct State in order to exist and be recognized as such, it still by its very nature has the right to establish one. [. . .]

3 Our third point concerns the analysis of the modern nation. There is no difficulty in recognizing that, in capitalist social formations, the nation is both of a specific character and closely bound up with the State. Even if the nation does not exactly coincide with the capitalist State, the latter has the peculiarity of being a national State: for the first time, the national modality becomes relevant to the State's materiality. Indeed, the State here exhibits the *historical tendency* to

encompass a single, constant nation (in the modern sense of the term); and while it thus actually pursues the establishment of national unity, modern nations themselves exhibit the historical tendency to form their own States. The social formation, which is the nodal point of the expanded reproduction of social relations, tends to intersect the boundaries of the nation-State; and that uneven development which has marked capitalism since its beginnings tends to root itself in, and bring into interrelationship, the nation-States themselves.

I shall concern myself above all with this last series of points, which, as we know, are confirmed by the totality of contemporary economic, political and historical research. In explicating this tendency of State and nation to coincide, we shall be referred back to the specificity of the nation in the modern sense of the term. For it is precisely here that the failings of previous Marxist investigation are most evident.

First of all, we must consider arguments that seek to base these historical realities on certain economic foundations – of which the most frequently invoked is again the famous realm of the circulation of capital and commodity-exchange. According to such conceptions, economic unity, as the essential element of the modern nation, hinges upon unification of the so-called internal market. The generalization of commodity exchange, and the realization of exchange-value in the circulation of money, require the abolition of customs-duties and other fetters on commodity circulation and monetary union. The State itself works to constitute the modern nation in its economic dimension by homogenizing, under the aegis of commodity capital, the space of the circulation of commodities and capital. Indeed, this is supposed to be the essence of its activity in forging national unity. Here too are located, albeit in a more subtle manner, the roots of the relationship between the modern nation and State, as well as of the peculiarities of the national State. Thus, the State's specific materiality is held to derive from the fact that it establishes the exchangers of commodities and owners of capital as formally free and equal political individuals-subjects; and that it represents-crystallizes the unity of these individuals. The modern nation itself, at least in its economic dimension, is supposed to rest essentially upon the homogenization of the 'people-nation' as the space in which these competing individuals or commodity-traders constantly move. The corresponding class analysis is deduced from the argument that both the nation and the modern State were created by commodity capital in a process going back to the mercantile bourgeoisie of early capitalism.

The above is an only slightly schematized account of such conceptions, which form part of a dominant and extremely tenacious Marxist tradition. However, not only is the explanation very one-sided; it serves to block genuine analysis of the modern nation and carries with it a number of serious consequences.

(a)   The generalization of commodity-exchange cannot adequately account for the creation of the modern nation. While it brings out the need for unification of the so-called internal market and for breaking the fetters that impede the circulation of commodities and capital, *it does nothing to explain why such unification is located at the level of the nation.* By all means let us talk in terms of unification of the internal market. But what defines this notion of 'internal'? What makes possible the emergence of a specific space whose contours designate an inside and an outside? Why do these limits-frontiers follow this precise demarcation? Indeed, why and how are such limits assigned to a particular field, which becomes the site of the problem of unification? All these questions have to be faced: for homogenization of the internal market presupposes the prior enclosure of precisely that space which has still to be unified.

(b) More generally, this evasive reference to the co-ordinates of commodity-exchange expresses a profoundly empiricist and positivist conception of all the elements that are supposed to constitute the nation: common territory, common language, common historical and cultural tradition. I shall not enter here into the dispute – which has truly shaken the workers movement – over the exact nature of the elements which should be identified as constituting the nation. I am concerned above all to clarify the underlying conception on the basis of which a certain set of elements are usually put forward. In a certain sense, these elements of territory, language and tradition are often understood as transhistorical essences possessing an immutable nature. The emergence of the modern nation and its specific relationship to the State are then considered to be the result of a principle (generalization of commodity-exchange) whose effect is the addition-accumulation of these essences – accumulation which gives rise to an encompassing nation-State. Of course, such an explanation misses the essential problem already posed in connection with the internal market: namely, why and how do territory, historical tradition and language chart, by means of the State, the new configuration that is the modern nation? What makes it possible for these seemingly transhistorical elements to be articulated at the focal point of the modern nation? Why do these elements function in diverse ways as the frontier-signs of the modern nation?

Failure to pose these questions obviously leads to underestimation of the present-day weight of the nation. If territory, language and historical tradition retain the essence which they had when the nation's role was less important, and if the tendency of capitalism really is towards internationalization of markets and capital, then it would be easy to conclude, together with a number of contemporary writers, that the role of the nation is diminishing in the current phase of transition to capitalism [...]

As I have shown elsewhere,[2] the current internationalization of the market and of capital does nothing to reduce the peculiar weight of the nation. This is so because the elements that come into play in the constitution of the modern nation are of quite novel significance. Thus, territory and historico-cultural tradition – to take but two, apparently 'natural' elements – acquire a meaning under capitalism that is completely different from the one they assumed in the past. It is this difference which defines the problem of the market as that of the unity of the 'internal' market. Furthermore, it produces the uneven development of capitalism as an unevenness of historical moments affecting those differentiated, classified and distinct spaces that are called nations or national social formations. This difference therefore appears as a condition for capitalist development.

I shall argue that territory and tradition now have this quite novel meaning because they are inscribed in the still more fundamental changes of the underlying conceptual matrices of space and time. The fact that capitalist space and time are not at all the same as their counterparts in previous modes of production implies that considerable changes have taken place in the reality and meaning of territory and historicity. These changes both allow and entail the constitution of the modern nation: by mapping out a new organization of the language and a new relationship of the State to territory and historicity, they bring into being the modern nation and the nation State. [...]

In reality, however, transformations of the spatio-temporal matrices refer to the materiality of the social division of labour, of the structure of the State, and of the practices and techniques of capitalist economic, political and ideological power; they are the *real substratum* of mythical, religious, philosophical or 'experiential' representations of space-time. Just as these changes are not reducible to the representations which they occasion, so they cannot be identified with the scientific concepts of space and time which allow us to grasp them.

As the primary material framework of the institutions and practices of power, these spatio-temporal matrices should also be distinguished from Foucault's 'diagram', which, in its epistemological function, is closely related to the concept of structure employed by structuralism (the diagram immanent in each power situation). They differ from it in that their foundation lies in the relations of production and social division of labour. Of course, I am not speaking of some mechanical causality according to which pre-existing relations of production give rise at a subsequent stage to spatial and temporal matrices. Themselves implied by the relations of production and social division of labour, these matrices appear at the same time as their presupposition – in the sense that Marx gave to the term *logical priority* (*Voraussetzung*) as opposed to 'historical preconditions' (*historische Bedingungen*). Transformations of these matrices thus punctuate changes in the mode of production; and for this very reason, they are present in the material framework of the given State, structuring the modalities in which its power is exercised. The presence of the spatio-temporal matrices in the State does not then refer to a mere relationship of structural homology between State and relations of production. Indeed, the capitalist State has the peculiarity of reserving social space and time for itself: it intervenes in the erection of these matrices by tending to monopolize those procedures of space-time organization which are established through it as networks of domination and power. The modern nation appears as a product of the State, since its constitutive elements (economic unity, territory, tradition) are modified through the State's direct activity in the material organization of space and time. The modern nation further tends to coincide with the State, since it is actually incorporated by the State and acquires flesh and blood in the state apparatuses: it becomes the anchorage of state power in society and maps out its contours. The capitalist State is functional to the nation.

I The Spatial Matrix: Territory

In whichever way we approach the problem of space, we become aware that space matrices vary with the mode of production and that they are themselves presupposed by the forms of historico-social appropriation and consumption of space. However, in order to unravel the secret of these matrices, it is not enough to recapitulate the historical sequence of the forms of appropriation of social space. From the growth of towns through communications, transport and military apparatuses and strategy, to the emergence of borders, limits and territory, we are dealing with so many mechanisms of organizing social space. Now, the attempt to trace the history and transformations of these mechanisms always runs up against the same problem: the historical changes which they undergo are not variations on an intrinsic nature, for these mechanisms have no such nature. Discontinuity is here of decisive significance. Towns, frontiers and territory do not at all possess a single reality and meaning in both capitalism and pre-capitalist modes of production. And even if we manage to avoid the snare of that linear and empirical historiography which seeks to unfold the development of towns, frontiers and territory at a level of their own, we must still face the task of explaining discontinuities.

As we know, the most advanced research in this field currently tends to place these mechanisms of appropriation and consumption of social space in a direct relationship to the specific features of the various modes of production. However, the real problem lies elsewhere; the transformation of these mechanisms is woven into a more intricate web. We are not dealing with different modes of organization, appropriation and consumption of a 'space' that possesses an intrinsic nature, nor with different trajectories and structurings of one and the same space. The here decisive distinction between town and country varies quite profoundly according to the mode of production: not only because the historical co-ordinates modify the two terms of the relationship (the ancient, medieval or modern town and the ancient, feudal, communal or modern countryside) but, more fundamentally, because the relationship is itself inscribed in sites that vary according to the mode of production. If these mechanisms produce space, it is not because they differentially structure or divide up a single space in the process of socially consuming it, but because they concretize the primary, differential space matrices which are already present in their skeletal structure. The genealogy of the production of space is prior to the history of its appropriation.

Although the spatial matrices of ancient societies and feudal societies differ in important respects, they present a number of common features when we compare them, at our very general level of analysis, with the spatial matrix of capitalism. I shall not return here to the specificity of the pre-capitalist relations of production and social division of labour, in which the direct producer is not yet separated by relations of possession from his means of production, and in which the division of labour does not generate the dissociations peculiar to the capitalist mode of production. Nor shall I discuss the characteristic features of pre-capitalist political power and forms of State. However, these latter do involve a specific space that is *continuous, homogeneous, symmetrical, reversible and open*. The space of Western Antiquity is a space with a *centre*: the *polis* (which itself has a centre: the *agora*). But it has no frontiers in the modern sense of the term. It is concentric, but, having no real outside, it is also open. This centre (the *polis* and *agora*) is inscribed in a space whose essential characteristics are homogeneity and symmetry, not differentiation and hierarchy. Moreover, this geometric orientation is reproduced in the political organization of the city and the 'isonomy' relationship among its citizens.

These spatially diffuse points (the cities) are separated from one another not because they are closed to the outside, but because they are turned in on their own centre – not as links in a chain, but as dispersions in a single place.[3] 'Men', writes Gernet, 'order [this centre] at their will. The mathematical disposition of what could be any territory at all, the centre is arbitrary or even purely theoretical.' In this space (which is the one represented by Euclid and the Pythagoreans) people do not change their position, they simply move around. They always go to the same place, because each point in space is an exact repetition of the previous point; when they found colonies, it is only to form replicas of Athens or Rome. Since every trajectory is merely a return to the initial centre, no distance can ever be covered; and since the towns are 'open' to the countryside, there can be no question of a territory with limits that extend beyond, or fall short of, other segments. The Greeks and Romans do not extend outwards by drawing in their frontiers to include new pieces or portions of space – for what is at stake is not the assimilation of heterogeneous fragments. They simply spread out in a homogeneous field, which, while exhibiting certain delimitations, knows no enclosure in the modern sense of the term. Through every twist and turn, this topographical ordering coincides with the sites of exploitation and the forms of political command: space is homogeneous and undifferentiated because the space of the slave is the same as that of the master; and the points at which power is exercised are replicas of the sovereign's body. In fact, it is this body which unifies space and instals public man within private man: it is a body with no place and no frontiers. All roads lead to Rome in the sense that Rome is at every point of the sovereign's moving around: in the towns, in the countryside, in the fleet, and in the armies. To be sure, although this homogeneous site has no outside, it has confines which are its absolute reverse: namely, the barbarians. But these barbarians are precisely a non-site: not only are they not a segment, however distinct, of a single space, they are the definitive end of all possible space; they are not a division of space but a without-space, not a no-man's-land but a no-land.

Let us now pass on to the feudal system and the Middle Ages. As we said earlier, although the spatial matrices of Antiquity and feudalism exhibit noteworthy differences, they also have certain points in common. These become readily visible on condition that we avoid the simplistic couplet territorialization–deterritorialization which is now the height of fashion in the Deleuze–Guattari School.[4] For these authors, feudal personal bonds and the peasant's 'link' with the 'soil' give rise to the territorialization of space and of social relations, while the 'freeing' of the direct producer from these bonds results in the deterritorialization of space under capitalism. In reality, however, these terms cannot keep the same reference through the transformations of the mode of production, since their meaning varies with the spatial matrix: such is the case of the land, which no more possesses an intrinsic nature than do the other means and objects of production. Of course, the personalized economic-political ties of the feudal countryside and the rights and freedoms peculiar to the towns turn each of these sites in on itself: the walls of medieval towns (which were closed towns, according to Braudel) also marked the limits of freedoms, while feudal links in the countryside tied the producer to the soil. But these were contours inscribed in a spatial matrix which changed relatively little, in keeping with the relations of production and (simple) division of labour of the feudal system.

Here too, we are talking of a homogeneous, continuous, reversible and open space. In point of fact, people have never moved about as much as they did in the

Middle Ages: peasant migration, both individual and collective, was a major demographic phenomenon in medieval society. On the road were to be found knights, peasants travelling during the rotation period of crops and fields, merchants, clerics either undertaking a regular trip or running away from their monasteries, students, pilgrims of all kinds, crusaders – it was the great age of the wanderer. Both the towns and feudal demesnes or fiefs were open and turned out, through a number of epicentres, towards that umbilical centre, Jerusalem. As Marx pointed out, the relations of production were such that religion played the dominant role in feudal social formations; it was directly present in the forms of the exercise of power and it patterned space by setting the seal of Christianity upon it. But from the very beginning, this was the matrix of a continuous and homogeneous space. As in Antiquity, people do not change their position: between the fiefs, large villages and towns, on the one hand, and Jerusalem and its diverse earthly incarnations on the other, between the Fall and Salvation, there is no break, fissure or distance. Frontiers and such intermediary points of demarcation as walls, forests and deserts refer not to a distance that has to be crossed in order to pass from one segment to another (one town to another), but to crossroads of a single route. The pilgrim or crusader – which is what every traveller is after a fashion – does not actually go to the holy places and Jerusalem, because these are already inscribed in his body. (This is also the case with Islam.) The body-politic of each sovereign incarnates the unity of this space as the body of Christ-the-King, and space is marked out by the paths of the Lord. Delimitations are constantly intersecting and overlapping in a series of twists and turns; and subjects, while remaining on the spot, move about in accordance with the changes of the lords and sovereigns to whom they are personally tied. The pyramid of medieval political power has a shifting base like the beam of a movable beacon: all its movement occurs on a surface whose directions are reversible. This explains why the cartography of the Middle Ages is not fundamentally different from that of Antiquity. Here too, what takes the place of territory is a non-place, even though it is unlike that of Antiquity in that it is composed of Unbelievers or Infidels.

The contrast with capitalism is quite evident. But we cannot here recapitulate the historical constitution of capitalist social space. The problem still concerns relations between the strictly capitalist social matrix and the 'strictly capitalist' relations of production and social division of labour: it is a problem of the role of *territory* in the constitution of the modern nation.

The direct producer, the worker, is now totally separated from the means of labour – a situation which is at the root of the social division of labour in machine production and large-scale industry. The latter involves as its precondition an entirely different spatial matrix: *the serial, fractured, parcelled, cellular and irreversible* space which is peculiar to the Taylorist division of labour on the factory assembly line. Although this space also becomes homogeneous in the end, it does so only through a second-degree and problematic homogenization, which arises on the basis of its essential segmentations and gaps. Already at this level, the matrix space has a twofold dimension: it is composed of gaps, breaks, successive fracturings, closures and frontiers; but it has no end: the capitalist labour process tends towards world-wide application (expanded co-operation). It may be said that the separation of the direct producer from his means of labour and his liberation from personal bonds involve a process of deterritorialization. But the naturalist image peddled by this term is no more exact in this context than it is elsewhere. The whole process is inscribed in a fresh space, which precisely involves closures and successive segmentations. In this modern space, people change position *ad infinitum* by traversing separations in which each place is defined by its distance from others; they spread out in this space by assimilating and homogenizing new segments in the act of shifting their frontiers.

Now, it is not the shifting of frontiers that is important, but the appearance of *frontiers in the modern sense of the term*: that is to say, limits capable of being shifted along a serial and discontinuous loom which everywhere fixes *insides* and *outsides*. Within this very space are inscribed the movements and expanded reproduction of capital, the generalization of exchange, and monetary fluctuations. While these constantly stretch towards the outside, they have to cross frontiers of a serial and discontinuous space rooted in the social division of the labour processes. Implicit in the capitalist relations of production – economic ownership and possession of the means of production by capital – this space appears as the splitting of the labour process into capitalist units of production and reproduction. The uneven development of capitalism is, in its spatialized dimension, actually consubstantial with this discontinuous morphology; the expansion of capital consubstantial with this irreversibly oriented topology; and modern imperialism consubstantial with those spatial frontiers. *The first fruits of territory, considered as a constitutive element of the modern nation, are written into this capitalist spatial matrix.*

It must be made clear, however, that this national territory has nothing to do with the natural features of the land. It is rather of an essentially political character, in that the State tends to monopolize the procedures of the organization of space. The modern State materializes this spatial matrix in its various apparatuses (army, school, centralized bureaucracy, prison system), patterning in turn the subjects over whom it exercises power. The individualization of the body-politic – as an ensemble of identical monads separated from the State – rests on the state framework that is inscribed in the spatial matrix implied by the labour process. Modern individuals are the components of the modern nation-State: the people-nation of the capitalist State is the content of a space whose frontiers are the pertinent contours of the material bases of power. The segmented chain of such individualized sites traces the interior of national territory as a state patterning of the exercise of power. In fact, the national territory is but the political expression of an enclosure at the level of the State as a whole; and towns become those 'well-kept' and 'disciplined' towns to which Braudel refers. The direct producers are freed from the soil only to become trapped in a grid – one that includes not only the factory but also the modern family, the school, the army, the prison system, the city and the national territory. We may verify this by looking at the modalities through which the capitalist State exercises power. Thus, *concentration camps* are a peculiarly modern invention, because, among other reasons, both they and the national territory concretize the same spatial power matrix. Camps are the form of shutting up non-nationals (or, more precisely, 'anti-nationals') within the national territory. They internalize the frontiers of the national space at the heart of that space itself, thus making possible the modern notion of 'internal enemy'. The exact configuration and topography followed by this territory will, of course, depend on a whole series of historical factors (economic, political, linguistic and so on). But what matters here is the appearance of territory and frontiers in the modern sense of the terms. The territory becomes national and, by means of the State, constitutes an element of the modern nation.

In order to grasp this second proposition, we must take account of the fact that territory is only one element of the modern nation and of the capitalist State's relationship to historical tradition and language. For the moment, let us note that while this serial, discontinuous and segmented space-territory implies the existence of frontiers, it also poses the new problem of its own *homogenization* and *unification*. *Here too the State plays a role in forging national unity.* Frontiers and national territory do not exist prior to the unification of that which they structure: there is no original something-inside that has later to be unified. The capitalist State does not confine itself to perfecting national unity, but sets itself up in constructing this unity – that is, in forging the modern nation. The State marks out the frontiers of this serial space in the very process of unifying and homogenizing what these frontiers enclose. It is in this way that the territory becomes national, tending to merge with the nation-State. It is in this way too that the nation tends to encapsulate the State: it either embraces the existing State *or* sets itself up as the autonomous State of a modern nation by creating a State of its own. (*Jacobinism* and *separatism* are thus two aspects of the same phenomenon: the peculiar relationship between the modern nation and the State.) The national State realizes the unity of the individuals of the people-nation in the very movement by which it forges their individualization. It secures the political-public (nation-State) homogenization of the 'private' dissociations in the very movement by which it contributes to their establishment; law thus becomes the expression of national law and sovereignty. The State does not have to unify a pre-existing 'internal' market, but installs a unified national market by marking out the frontiers of what thereby becomes the inside of an outside. We can follow this process in the totality of state apparatuses (economic, military, educational, and so on) and thus find an initial, and no doubt partial, answer to a problem that would otherwise be insoluble. Pierre Vilar has given the best formulation of this problem: why are national social formations the principal roots and focal points of the uneven development of capitalism?[5]

Now, through that very movement by which it both marks out frontiers and unifies national space, the State also turns beyond those frontiers towards an irreversible, clearly demarcated space which yet has no end or final horizon. In other words, it seeks to expand markets, capital and territory. For to mark out frontiers involves the possibility of redrawing them: there is no way of advancing in this spatial matrix except along the road of homogenization, assimilation and unification – except through demarcation of an interior that is always capable of being extended *ad infinitum*. These frontiers therefore become established as frontiers of the national territory only from the moment when capital and commodities are in a position to break through them. It is not possible to move in this space without crossing frontiers: imperialism is consubstantial with the modern nation in the sense that it cannot be other than *inter*nationalization, or rather *trans*nationalization, of the processes of labour and capital. This spatial matrix is rooted in the labour process and social division of labour. As Marx said, capital is a relationship between capital and labour; and it is because it moves in the *inter*national spatial matrix of the labour and exploitation processes that capital can reproduce itself only through *trans*nationalization – however deterritorialized and a-national its various forms may appear to be.

Thus, the tendency of the modern State to expand *ad infinitum* – which is itself one with the process of establishing national unity – cannot but encapsulate a shift in frontiers involving assimilation and homogenization. Modern conquest has a meaning quite different from that of the past: it no longer denotes spreading through, and unity with, a continuous and homogeneous space, but rather expanding through and filling in breaches. In other words, the national State now homogenizes differences, crushes various nationalities 'within' the frontiers of the nation-State, and wears away the rugged features of the land that is included in the national territory. *Genocide* is also a modern invention bound up with the spatialization peculiar to nation-States – a form of extermination specific to the establishment or cleaning up of the national territory by means of homogenizing enclosure. Pre-capitalist expansion and conquest neither assimilated nor digested: the Greeks and the Romans, Islam and the Crusaders, Attila and Tamerlane all killed in order to clear a path in an open, continuous and already homogeneous space; that accounts for the undifferentiated massacres which marked the exercise of power in the great nomadic empires. Genocide becomes possible only when the national space is closed on *foreign* bodies within its very frontiers. Is this a symbolic image? Well, the first genocide of this century, that of the Armenians, accompanies precisely Kemal Ataturk's foundation of the Turkish nation-State, the establishment of a national territory on the ruins of the Ottoman Empire, and the *closure* of the Golden Horn. Genocide and concentration camps are inscribed in one and the same space.

Here too, we can see the roots of that peculiarly modern phenomenon, *totalitarianism*: separation and division in order to unify; parcelling out in order to structure; atomization in order to encompass; segmentation in order to totalize; closure in order to homogenize; and individualization in order to obliterate differences and otherness. The roots of totalitarianism are inscribed in the spatial matrix concretized by the modern nation-State – a matrix that is already present in its relations of production and in the capitalist social division of labour.

II   The Temporal Matrix and Historicity: Tradition

The second element which enters into the constitution of the modern nation is generally designated by the term 'common historical tradition'. I shall deal with this more rapidly. Historians have analysed in greater depth the transformations of the temporal matrix and of the notion of historicity. Here too, the principal question concerns the association between these transformations and changes in the relations of production and social division of labour. Tradition is not at all the same in pre-capitalist and capitalist societies: it has neither the same meaning nor the same function.

The temporal matrix of Antiquity evidently differs from that of medieval feudalism, but the two also have basic features in common. In both these societies, the means of production are still possessed by the direct producer and there is no capitalist division of labour; they crystallize modes of production (grounded on

slavery or serfdom) *which know only simple reproduction and not that expanded reproduction* peculiar to the capitalist mode. No doubt their temporal matrices are those
of *plural and singular times*. But each of these times is itself *continuous, homogeneous,
reversible and repetitive.* Whether agricultural, civil and political, military, aristo-
cratic, or clerical, these multiple times exhibit the same matrix characteristics.
Being essentially fluid, they have no universal measure: for they are not strictly
speaking *measurable*, given that measure can only encode gaps between segments.
Although specific sequences do show up in this homogeneous temporal *continuum*
and although privileged moments make their appearance – for we are not talking of
the linear descent of primitive societies – nevertheless, they are basically at the
mercy of 'chance' (Antiquity) or of the presence of eternity (medieval Christianity).
There is no succession or series: indeed there are no events. These are times of *the
present*, which itself gives to the *before* and the *after* their respective meanings. In the
societies of Antiquity, time is largely the circular time of eternal recurrence: the past
is always reproduced in the present, which is nothing but its echo; and the journey
back through time does not lead us away from the present, since the past is an
integral part of the Cosmos. To remember through *anamnesis* is to find again other
regions of being – the essence that is manifested by the here-and-now. In this
homogeneous, reversible and continuous time, the present is included in the
origins, chronology remaining a repetition of the genesis, if not actually a genealogical transfer. Rediscovering the origins is not the same as to recapitulate the
history of an accumulation (of experiences, knowledge, events) or of a progression
towards the present; it rather involves the attainment of original omniscience. It is
not that a future dimension is absent. But although the *telos* of the Pythagoreans
halts the spiral of freshly–begun cycles, it does so by looping the loop, by knitting
both ends together.

Things are not basically different in medieval feudalism. Over and above the
dependence of temporalities on the 'natural time' peculiar to essentially agrarian
societies (seasons, work in the fields, and so on), what matters is the temporal
matrix underlying the agricultural, artisan, military or clerical times that appear as
so many singular times. While each of these involves certain datings, the various
chronologies are not ordered throughout times that are divisible into equal segments; and nor do the various moments have a numerical frame of reference. These
chronologies refer instead to a continuous time which, placed under the aegis of
religion, appears as a time of eternity punctuated by second meanings, acts of piety,
and belfry-chimes inserted into the rhythm of the mass. Rooted in this temporal
matrix, a linear materiality of time does, of course, come forth as distinct from the
cyclical materiality of Antiquity: history now has a beginning and an end, located
between the Creation and the Last Judgement. But it is still a present time:
beginning and end, *before* and *after* are fully *co-present* in the constant essence of
the Divine. Whether it is a question of immutable truth or of progressively revealed
truth, and whether individual salvation is predetermined or not, all that is ever
involved is a repetition or bringing-up-to-date of the origins. Here where the
irreversibility of time is a mere illusion, to reach for the end is always to regain the
beginning.

These temporal matrices are present in the forms and techniques of pre-capitalist
political power as it is transferred from the body of the sovereign. This body-politic

does not make history, it bathes in a continuous and homogeneous historicity of which the subjects of power partake in the process of transferring that body. If the succession of sovereigns is conceived as a series of events, then, strictly speaking, there is no such thing; there is just the circulation by transference of an uninterrupted power, the re-concretization of the past: *translatio imperii*. This history-recollection is never anything but an unfolding of genealogies – those of divinities, heroes or dynasties; and this time, the representation of history takes place in the mode of the chronical. The past is not separated from the present by a gap, but spreads through it like an echo; while, in its turn, the present is but an unceasing herald of that future which will meet up with the beginnings. Here history is not made, it is commemorated.

This political history cannot have constitutive relations with territory in the modern sense of the term, because the territory-frontier does not yet exist. Moreover, pre-capitalist spatial matrices have the same foundation as the pre-capitalist temporal matrices: political historicity is transferred from the body of the sovereign, who is not himself sovereign of a territory-frontier. Indeed, there is neither historicity nor territory in its modern form: pre-capitalist territories have no historicity of their own, since political time is the time of the prince-body, who is capable of extension, contraction, and movement in a continuous and homogeneous space. In other words, the peculiar features of the spatial and temporal matrices of a mode of production, which are implied by the prevailing relations of production and social division of labour, determine the relations which these matrices sustain between each other. This fact is designated by a binomial term that is itself a problem rather than a solution: namely, 'space-time'.

The capitalist temporal matrix is entirely different, being the pre-condition of the new relations of production and consubstantial with the capitalist social division of labour. Machine production, large-scale industry and assembly-line labour entail a *segmented, serial, equally divided, cumulative and irreversible time that is oriented towards the product* and, thereby, towards expanded reproduction and capital accumulation: in short, a production process which has an orientation and a goal but no fixed limit. This time is measurable and susceptible to strict control by means of clocks, foremen's stop-watches, clocking-on machines and calendars. But on account of its segmentation and serialization, it raises the fresh problem of unification and universalization: how to master time by means of a single, homogeneous measure, which only reduces the multiple temporalities (workers' time and bourgeois time, the time of the economic, the social, and the political) by encoding the distances between them. However, each temporality expresses the characteristics of one and the same matrix: indeed (and this is what escapes many authors who stress the 'universalization' of capitalist time) this temporal matrix for the first time marks out the particular temporalities as *differential temporalities* – that is to say, as rhythmical and metrical variations of a serial, segmented, irreversible and cumulative time. The moments of this time follow one another in a series and are totalized in a result: the present now marks a transition from the before to the after. Modern historicity is thus of an evolutionary and progressive character; it refers to a time which is constituted to the very extent that it runs through itself, each moment producing the next in an irreversible sequence or series of events opening towards a future that is ever being recreated. [. . .]

The capitalist temporal matrix – that segmented, serial and divided time – is already implicit in the peculiar institutional structure of the State and its various apparatuses (army, school, bureaucracy, prison). The modern State also concretizes this matrix in the process of moulding the subjects over whom power is exercised, and in the techniques of exercising power themselves, especially the procedures whereby the people-nation is individualized. Now this segmented, serial and divided time raises the new problem of its *unification*: once again, the essential role will fall to the State. The modern State must ensure its mastery and control of time by setting down the norm and the standard of measurement, or, in other words, the frame of reference of the variations of particular temporalities. The State regulates what is fast or slow in relation to the standard, and structures the various discrepancies. The uneven development of capitalism fastens on to those stoppages that are the diverse state formations; the rhythm of uneven development peculiar to each formation (in the economic, the political and the ideological, and among all three) fastens on to the moments of the State. The State unifies the sectors of the capitalist formation in the further sense that it is the code of their irregular movements. The capitalist social formation or nation-State is also a process homogenized by the State.

We can now grasp the new meaning of historical tradition in the constitution of the modern nation; the relationship of this tradition to the State; and the fact that the nation tends to coincide with the modern State in the dual sense mentioned above: it merges with the existing State *or* sets itself up as an autonomous State and constitutes the modern nation by creating its own State. (Here too, Jacobinism and separatism are two aspects of a single reality: the peculiar relationship of the modern nation to the State.) 'Tradition' does not at all have the sense that it had in pre-capitalist societies, for *before* and *after* are here located in quite different matrices. The historical present is but a transition between the before and the after; the past is not co-present with the here-and-now, but refers to cumulative slices pointed towards what becomes a new meaning of the future. Tradition is no longer the commemoration of a past which includes the after: it is no longer the truth of that reversible historicity oriented towards the great beginning which is but a repetition and resumption of the origins. Tradition becomes that which speeds up or that which slows down, encapsulating a succession of moments which produce an irreversible history punctuated by the State. The modern State concentrates the unity of these historical moments and the direction of their sequence: it itself has no original legitimacy in the body of a sovereign, but is successively grounded on the people-nation, whose destiny it represents.

This State realizes a movement of individualization and unification; constitutes the people-nation in the further sense of representing its historical orientation; and assigns a goal to it, marking out what becomes a path. In this oriented historicity without a fixed limit, the State represents an eternity that it produces by self-generation. It organizes the forward course of the nation and thus tends to monopolize the national tradition by making it the moment of a becoming designated by itself, and by storing up the memory of the people-nation. In the capitalist era, a nation without a State of its own is in the course of losing its tradition and history; for the modern nation-State also involves eradication of the traditions, histories and memories of dominated nations involved in its process. This is how we should understand Engels' (undoubtedly ambiguous) remarks, according to which nations without a State of their own become, in the capitalist era, 'peoples without a history'.[6] The State establishes the modern nation by eliminating other national pasts and turning them into variations of its own history: modern imperialism, too, involves homogenization of temporal sequences and assimilation of histories by the nation–State. The modern demands for national autonomy and a national State are equivalent, within capitalist historicity, to demands for a national history.

To be sure, *the State is not the subject of real history*: for this is a process without a subject, the process of the class struggle. But we can now understand why the modern nation–States constitute the focal-points and basic moments of that real history, even though it is capable of extension at a world level; and why the history of the international proletariat is segmented and punctuated by the histories of national working classes. This situation depends not on ideological mechanisms but on the role of these nation-States in the material organization of capitalist historicity. Here too lie the roots of the peculiarly modern phenomenon of totalitarianism: the mastery and unification of time through establishing it as an instrument of power; the totalization of historicities through obliteration of their differences; the serialization and segmentation of the various moments so that they maybe oriented and stored up; the homogenization of the people-nation by forging or eliminating the national pasts. The premisses of modern totalitarianism exist in the temporal matrix which is inscribed in the modern State and which is already implied by capitalist relations of production and social division of labour.

This becomes still clearer if we bear in mind that the State establishes the peculiar relationship between *history* and *territory*, between the spatial and the temporal matrix. In fact, the modern nation makes possible the intersection of these matrices and thus serves as their point of junction; the capitalist State marks out the frontiers when it constitutes what is within (the people-nation) by homogenizing the before and the after of the content of this enclosure. National unity or the modern unity thereby becomes *historicity of a territory and territorialization of a history* – in short, a territorial national tradition concretized in the nation-States; the markings of a territory become indicators of history that are written into the State. The enclosures implicit in the constitution of the modern people-nation are only so awesome because they are also fragments of a history that is totalized and capitalized by the State. Genocide is the elimination of what become 'foreign bodies' of the national history and territory: it expels them beyond space and time. The great confinement only comes to pass because it is at the same time the fragmentation and the unification of a serial and segmented time: concentration camps are a modern invention in the additional sense that the frontier-gates close on 'anti-nationals' for whom time and national historicity are *in suspense*. In the modern era, demands for a national State are demands for a territory and history of one's own. The premisses of modern totalitarianism exist not only in the spatial and temporal matrices incarnated in the modern State, but also, or above all, in the relationship between the two that is concentrated by the State.

Lastly, the constitution of the modern nation should be located in the relationship between the modern State and *language*. Here we can merely point out that the construction of a national language by the modern State is reducible neither to the problem of its social and political usage, nor to the State's positing of linguistic norms and regulations, nor to the consequent destruction of dominated languages within the nation-States. The very structure of the national language is profoundly reorganized by the State: the relationship of language to the capitalist spatial and temporal matrices is restructured insofar as it is cast in the mould of a State which crystallizes intellectual labour in its specifically capitalist separation from manual labour. Thus, the role of a common language in constituting the modern nation does not refer to a process whereby the State takes over a language, causing it to suffer purely instrumental distortions; it denotes the very *re-creation* of language by the State. The linguistic imperialism peculiar to the officialese of a modern nation does not result merely from the forms of its employment; it is already present in its structuring.

III The Nation and Classes

As in the preceding cases, we now have to grasp the articulation of these analyses with an analysis of the nation in terms of class struggle.

Here too, there is no question of two distinct approaches dealing with substantively heterogeneous objects. The spatial and temporal matrices are presuppositions of the relations of production only because they are concretized in them as class struggle: they appear historically as the product of this struggle. In this aspect, however, they are not the product of a class acting as subject of history. They are the result of a process, since history itself is the process of the class struggle. The modern nation is not then the creation of the bourgeoisie, but the outcome of a *relationship* of forces between the 'modern' social classes – one in which the nation is a *stake* for the various classes.

At this point, there arises a second problem. The concrete configuration of a particular nation and a particular State, as well as the forms of their inter-relationship, depend on the historical peculiarities of the class-struggle process and of the class relationship of forces. They appear as so many variants of the modern nation and State – and thus of their spatial and temporal matrices – as long as we understand that in no case is there ever really a pre-existing essence differentiated only in its particular manifestations; and that there can be no question of an ideal type which is concretized in various ways. Just like the modern State and nation, these matrices exist only insofar as they are concretized in specific formations. If these formations and class-struggle processes have something in common (the same spatio-temporal matrix) it is because, until the point of rupture, they are situated on the terrain of a single mode of production, whose modifications are so many moments of its own expanded reproduction.

Thus, not only do these spatial and temporal matrices, like the modern nation, vary in *significance* according to the specific class struggles; they exist as so many variants in the differential class practices. There is a bourgeois spatiality and historicity, and there is a working-class spatiality and historicity. And yet they are variants of a single matrix, because the latter appears as the historical result of the class-struggle process and the relationship of forces, and because this process is truly a process of struggle in a *capitalist* society. To be sure, the relations of production and social division of labour make of the working class (in a commonly expressed formulation) the 'bearer' of positivity and of the historical future. Already under capitalism, its practices bear what appear as the 'seeds' of other social relations, other spatial and temporal matrices, another nation; and history always moves forward on the side of the working class. But I have in mind a different problem: the struggle of the working class does not unfold in an airtight chamber, but exists only as a term of the relationship between the working class and the bourgeoisie. The history of the working class is the history of its struggle against the bourgeoisie: to adopt the viewpoint of the working class is to adopt the viewpoint of its struggle against the bourgeoisie.

We are now in a position to explain, first of all, the constitutive relationship between each bourgeoisie and the nation. It is a relationship which follows, on the one hand, the rhythms and phases of the accumulation and expanded reproduction of capital, and on the other hand, the broad outline of changes in the policy of the bourgeoisie. The modern nation bears the stamp of the development of the bourgeoisie and of relations among its various fractions. This affects both the transition to capitalism within the process of primitive capital accumulation *and* the role of the merchant bourgeoisie in the formation of the nation; both the stage of competitive capitalism *and* the stage of imperialism (including its current phase of internationalization of capital). The transformations of capitalist relations of production leave their mark on transformations of the nation and of bourgeois nationalism. Now, even in the current phase characterized by internationalization of capital, the (no doubt altered) modern nation remains for the bourgeoisie the focal point of its own reproduction – reproduction which takes the precise form of internationalization or transnationalization of capital. This hard core of the modern nation is to be found in the unchanging kernel of the *capitalist* relations of production.

The bourgeoisie's relationship to the nation varies according to the fraction concerned (national bourgeoisie, internationalized bourgeoisie, domestic bourgeoisie); it is itself established by the mediation of the State. Now, *this State is not just any State*: it has a class nature and, *qua* bourgeois, it constitutes the bourgeoisie as the dominant class. But here again, there are not two States: a first, pre-class State, organizing the modern nation prior to the nation's relationship with the bourgeoisie; and a second, bourgeois-class State, superimposed on the first and committed to recovering the nation for the profit of the bourgeoisie. By grounding this State and the modern nation on the relations of production and social division of labour, we show that the State possesses a materiality of its own and, thus, a specific class nature. It is precisely a national State that is a bourgeois State – and not simply because the bourgeoisie makes use of it to turn the nation to its own advantage, but because the modern nation, the national State and the bourgeoisie are all constituted on, and have their mutual relations determined by, one and the same terrain. There can be no doubt that bourgeois policy vis-à-vis the nation is subject to the hazards of its particular interests: indeed, the history of the bourgeoisie is one of continual oscillation between identification with and betrayal of the nation. For the nation does not have the same meaning for the bourgeoisie as it does for the working-class and popular masses. Nevertheless, the modern nation is not something that the bourgeoisie can at will allow 'its' State to cast aside or re-establish. The modern nation is written into the State, and it is this national State which organizes the bourgeoisie as the dominant class.

The real problem, of course, concerns the relationship between the working class and the modern nation. This profound relationship has to a large extent been underestimated by Marxism, which has continually tended to examine it either by exclusively referring to the ideological domination of the bourgeoisie (as was the case above all of the Third International) or by referring to the participation of each working class in the national culture (Austro-Marxism). Now, the ideological impact of bourgeois nationalism on the working class is not itself in any doubt, but it is by no means the only aspect of the problem.

Although the existence and diverse practices of the working class already presage the historical supersession of the modern nation, they cannot under capitalism take shape except as workers' variants of that nation. The spatiality and historicity of each working class are a variant of its own nation, both because they are caught in the spatial and temporal matrices and because they form an integral part of that nation understood as a result of the relationship of forces between working class and bourgeoisie. Only insofar as there are national working classes can there be inter-nationalization of the working class and, hence, working-class internationalism: we are now beginning to grasp this proposition, which should be understood in a quite radical sense. Internationalism and internationalization of the working class and, hence, working-class internationalism: we are now beginning to grasp this propos-ition, which should be understood in a quite radical sense. Internationalism and internationalization of the working class do not refer to an original supra-national or a-national essence, subsequently assuming national forms or being simply concret-ized in national specificities. The capitalist labour process, which entails expanded cooperation (internationalization of the working class), presupposes national ma-teriality and defines the objective bases of such cooperation as working-class inter-nationalism. The present tendency of the labour process and social division of labour to extend throughout the world, as well as that of capital to be articulated in this movement, are never anything other than processes of internationalization or transnationalization. Only *a national transition to socialism* is possible: not in the sense of a universal model simply adapted to national particularities, but in the sense of a multiplicity of original roads to socialism, whose general principles, drawn from the theory and experience of the workers' movement, cannot be more than signs on the road.

We are now touching on fundamental, and therefore formidable, political prob-lems. These concern long-standing organizational forms of the workers' movement: namely, the working-class Internationals which, founded on a major underestima-tion of national reality, all led in practice to the reproduction of national oppression and domination at the very heart of the workers' movement. But they also concern the political position of the Third International and 'orthodox Marxism' concerning the national question: in the best of cases (Lenin), the right to national self-determination is still recognized, but as a right that should be supported only when it conforms to the interests of the 'international proletariat'. This is a pro-foundly instrumental conception of the nation, which, by neglecting national ma-teriality, has contributed to all the abuses with which we are familiar; it supposes the prior existence of a substantialized international proletariat and therefore raises the question: *who* will define its interests, *who* will best exhibit its essence and be able to speak in its name? (The common answer is: its vanguard section which has given reality to its essence – Revolution.) But the question cannot but lead to abuses, above all because the terms in which it is posed are false.

Furthermore, the State that plays a decisive role in organizing the modern nation is not itself an essence: neither the subject of history nor a mere instrument-object of the dominant class, it is, from the point of view of its class nature, the condensation of a class relationship of forces. The territory and history crystallized by the State ratify the dominance of the bourgeois variant of the spatio-temporal matrix over its working-class variant; the dominance of bourgeois over working-class historicity. But without being reabsorbed into the State, working-class history sets its seal on precisely the national aspect of the State. In its institutional structure, the State is also the result of the national process of class struggle – that is to say, both the struggle of the bourgeoisie against the working class, and the struggle of the working class against the bourgeoisie. Just like the national culture, history or language, the State is a strategic field ploughed from one end to the other by working-class and popular struggle and resistance; these are inscribed in the State, albeit in a deformed manner, and they always break into it through the wall of silence with which the State hems in the workers' memory. To set the national State as the prize and objective of workers' struggles involves the reappropriation by the working class of its own history. To be sure, this cannot be achieved without a transformation of the State; but it also points to a certain permanency of the State, in its national aspect, during the transition to socialism – permanency not just in the sense of a regrettable survival, but also in that of a positive necessity for the transition to socialism.

These remarks are far from exhausting the problem. Numerous questions remain, concerning: (a) the quite specific relationship to the nation maintained by the other social classes of a capitalist formation (the old and new petty bourgeoisie, the peasant classes) and by social categories such as the state bureaucracy; (b) the concrete political meaning of the nation for the working class and its struggle (according to the stage and phase of capitalism, as well as to the precise character of the conjuncture) and, in particular, the crucial role played during the current phase of imperialism by the struggle for national independence in the dominant countries, and by the national liberation struggle in the dominated countries; (c) national working-class ideology, both as a correct expression of internationalism and in terms of the impact of bourgeois nationalism on the working class: bourgeois nationalism could not have had such an enormous impact on the working class (leading it into the bloodbaths of national-imperialist wars), unless it rested on the materiality of the constitution and struggles of the working class, and unless it was linked to the genuinely working-class aspect of national ideology.

NOTES

1   [See, for example, G. Haupt, *La deuxième internationale 1899–1914: étude critique des sources*, Paris: Ecole des Hautes Etudes dans les Sciences Sociales (1964); M. Löwy, 'Marxists and the national question,' *New Left Review* (1976), 96, 81–100; M. Réberioux, *La République radicale? 1898–1914*, Paris: Editions de Seuil (1975); G. Haupt and M. Réberioux, *Le deuxième Internationale et l'Orient*, Paris: Editions Cujas (1967); M. Rodin-

son, 'Le marxisme et la nation,' *L'Homme et la Société* (1968), 7, 131–49; P. Vilar, *La Catalogne dans l'Espagne moderne. Recherches sur les fondements économiques des structures nationales*, 3 vols, Paris: Ecole des Hautes Etudes dans les Sciences Sociales (1962); and P. Vilar, 'On nations and nationalism', *Marxist Perspectives* (1979), 5, 8–29.]

2   [N. Poulantzas, *Classes in Contemporary Capitalism*, London: Verso (1975).]

3   M. Serres, 'Discours et parcours', in *Critique* April 1975.

4   [G. Deleuze and F. Guattari, *Anti-Oedipus: Capitalism and Schizophrenia*, New York: Viking Press (1977).]

5   In his contribution to the collective work, *Faire l'Histoire*, Vol. 1 (ed. J. Le Goff and P. Nora), [Paris: Gallimard,] 1974.

6   'Die Polendebatte in Frankfurt', in *Neue Rheinische Zeitung*, 3 September 1848. *Aus dem literarischen Nachlass von K. Marx, Fr. Engels und F. Lassalle* (ed. Franz Mehring) 1902, vol. III, p. 238.

4

Space and the State

Henri Lefebvre

During the course of its development, the state binds itself to space through a complex and changing relation that has passed through certain critical points. Born in and with a space, the state may also perish with it. The moments of this relation can be described as follows:

(1) The production of a space, *the national territory*, a physical space, mapped (*balisé*), modified, transformed by the networks, circuits, and flows that are established within it – roads, canals, railroads, commercial and financial circuits, motorways and air routes, etc. Thus this space is a material – natural – space in which the actions of human generations, of classes, and of political forces have left their mark, as producers of durable objects and realities (rather than only of isolated things and products, of tools and of goods destined for consumption). During the course of this process, the city and the country develop a new relationship in and through the mediation of a third term – the state that has the city as its center. Although the city and the country can no longer be separated, this does not mean that they have somehow been harmoniously superseded. They each survive as places assigned to the division of labor within a territory. Morphologically, this relationship (in the modern state) results in a shapeless mixture, in chaos, despite the administrative order and spatial logistics of the state.

(2) The production of a *social space* as such, an (artificial) edifice of hierarchically ordered institutions, of laws and conventions upheld by "values" that are communicated through the national language. This social architecture, this political monumentality, is the state itself, a pyramid that carries at its apex the political leader – a concrete abstraction, full of symbols, the source of an intense circulation of information and messages, "spiritual" exchanges, representations, ideology, knowledge bound up with power.

  "No institution without a space" (Lourau 1974: 141). The family, the school, the workplace, the church, and so on – each possesses an "appropriate" space. Appropriate for what? For a use specified within the social division of labor and supporting political domination. In these spaces, a system of "adapted" expectations and responses – rarely articulated as such because they seem obvious – acquire a quasi-natural self-evidence in everyday life and common sense.

Thus, each state *has* its space; the latter belongs first to nature, which the state opposes historically and politically through its entire powerful mass (*stature*). Moreover, each state *is* a social space, symbolized by the pyramid and the circle of circles (Hegel). In this social space, there is a minimum of *consensus*: just as a dog is commonly labeled a "dog," every French person knows what he is talking about when he refers to the town hall, the post office, the police station, the prefecture, the *département*, a member of the National Assembly (*député*), the grocery store, the bus and the train, train stations and bistros.

(3) In this latter sense, comprising a social (but not immediately political) consensus, the state occupies a *mental space* that includes the representations of the state that people construct – confused or clear, directly experienced (*veçues*) or conceptually elaborated (*élaborées*). This mental space must not be confused with physical or social space; nor can it be fully separated from the latter. For it is here that we may discern the space of representations and the representation of space.

As the product, the child, of a space, the so-called national territory, the state turns back toward its own historical conditions and antecedents, and transforms them. Subsequently, the state engenders social relations in space; it reaches still further as it unfurls; it produces a support, its own space, which is itself complex. This space regulates and organizes a disintegrating national space at the heart of a consolidating global space (*l'espace mondial*). The space produced by the state must be termed *political* due to its specific features and goals. The state provides the *relations* (that is, the social relations of production) with a calibrated spatial *support*; it clashes with the pre-existent economic space that it encounters – spontaneous poles of growth, historic towns, commercialized fragments of space that are sold in "lots." It tends to renew not only the social relations inherent in industrial production, but also the relations of domination inherent in the hierarchy of groups and places. In the chaos of relations among individuals, groups, class fractions, and classes, the state tends to impose a rationality, its own, which has space as its privileged instrument. The economy is thus recast in spatial terms – flows (of energy, raw materials, labor power, finished goods, trade patterns, etc.) and stocks (of gold and capital, investments, machines, technologies, stable clusters of various jobs, etc.). The state tends to control flows and stocks by ensuring their coordination. In the course of a threefold process (*growth* – i.e., expansion of the productive forces – *urbanization*, or the formation of massive units of production and consumption; and *spatialization*), a qualitative leap occurs: the emergence of the state mode of production (SMP) (*mode de production étatique*). The articulation between the SMP and space is thus crucial. It differs from that between previous modes of production (including capitalism) and their manner of occupying natural space (including modifying it through social practice). Something new appears in civil society and in political society, in production and in state institutions. This must be given a name and conceptualized. We suggest that this rationalization and socialization of society has assumed a specific form, which can be termed: politicization, statism.

It is difficult to explicate and prove the above series of arguments. To start with, although we have elaborated them in other works,[1] the reader cannot simply be referred to these texts, nor will it do for us merely to allude to them. We must thus "explicate" these arguments, summarizing their components and claims. Indeed we must even complete them and update them. For new inventions and discoveries are emerging every day in this domain, which lies at the very crossroads (*frontière*) of the political, the social, and the economic. Thus the works cited above have hardly exhausted the topic of the state.

But this is not the only problem: there is also the burden of the recent past. So-called "marxist" thought, which purports to base itself on Marx, has long neglected precisely what is today most directly in the spotlight – the city and the urban, space, the state itself. Hence, due to a still underdeveloped vocabulary, we meet further difficulties in constructing and articulating concepts. Knowledge (*connaissance*) of (social) space is now being established as a science, even though this is still in an early stage. This knowledge appears no less complex than the sciences of abstract space (geometry, topology, etc.) and physical space (from physics to cosmology). For example, the science of (social) space must include a *history of space*. Similarly, many volumes would be needed for a simple analytical study of *monumentality* and the relationship between the monument and the building. Oppression and domination, and thus power – but also splendor and meaning – are inherent in the very word "monument." This is another doubtless inexhaustible trilogy...[...]

An analysis of western countries reveals, first, the demands of capitalism and neo-capitalism, of developers and investment banks. It reveals, second, that state intervention does not just occur episodically or at specific points but incessantly, by means of diverse organizations and institutions devoted to the management and production of space. This state space (*espace étatique*) – which we analyze below – lacks the same chaotic features as the space generated by "private" interests. On the contrary, the aim is to make it appear homogeneous, the *same* throughout, organized according to a rationality of the identical and the repetitive that allows the state to introduce its presence, control, and surveillance in the most isolated corners (which thus cease to be "corners"). The relation between "private" interests and the activities of "public" powers sometimes involves a collusion, sometimes a collision. This creates the paradox of a space that is both homogeneous and broken (*l'espace homogène-brisé*). This paradox will be self-evident, if hard to express, to all those who pay any attention to their surroundings.

In the third place, "users" movements (their protests and struggles) have become a worldwide (*mondial*) phenomenon – as have protests related to work and the workplace, albeit in a different manner.

"Users" movements in France cannot be compared to those in Japan, Spain, Italy, or even the USA. In these countries, "users" and even consumers seem more conscious of their interests and their goal – namely, to appropriate, for the first time, a space whose use was neglected by those who produced it. How can we explain this weakness in France? It is undoubtedly due to the state, which represents both a constraint and a means of appeal, a form of pressure and, it seems, a form of arbitration. Not only is the state's impact (*la pression étatique*) stronger in France than elsewhere; it is also reinforced by the Jacobin currents of the left with their centralizing agenda. This agenda contributes to the weakening of movements that only a certain far-left (*gauchiste*) faction is willing to support regardless of other, hidden political motives. Japan is probably the country where these movements have become most powerful and have voiced the most ambitious objectives [...]

These movements are resurrecting the concept of "use" without reducing it merely to the consumption of space. They emphasize the relations between people (individuals, groups, classes) and space, with its different levels (*niveaux*): the neighborhood and the immediate, the urban and its mediations, the region and the nation, and, finally, the worldwide (*mondial*). These movements are experimenting with modes of action at diverse scales (*échelles*), always in light of the participants' experience and knowledge. Their current development suggests a possible convergence between struggles regarding work (the workplace) and those concerning all of space, that is to say, everyday life.

Is not the secret of the state, hidden because it is so obvious, to be found in space? The state and territory interact in such a way that they can be said to be mutually constitutive. This explains the deceptive activities and image of state officials (*hommes de l'État*). They seem to administer, to manage and to organize a natural space. In practice, however, they *substitute* another space for it, one that is first economic and social, and then political. They believe they are obeying something in their heads – a representation (of the country, etc.). In fact, they are establishing an order – their own.

To illuminate the junction between the state and space, it is necessary that we stop misrecognizing the spatial, and, correspondingly, that we come to recognize the importance of a theory of (social) space. From this perspective, "users" movements throughout the world are allied with a science of space that can no longer be seen as external to practice.

The understanding (*connaissance*) of social space is the theoretical aspect of a social process that has, as its practical aspect, the "users" movement. They are the inextricable aspects of the same reality and the same potentialities. This corresponds, to a certain extent, to the situation in which Marx found himself vis-à-vis the workers' movement and its protests over work (and the workplace). In that epoch, the "vulgar" economists (as Marx called them) were preoccupied with products, indexing and comparing objects, estimating their respective costs. In short, they busied themselves with *things*. Marx inverts this approach. Instead of considering *products*, he examines *production*, that is, the labor process and the relations of production as well as the mode of production. In doing so, he founds a theory. Likewise, today, many people are describing spaces, writing discourses about space. So our task is to invert this approach by founding a theory of the production of space. The state becomes more and more clearly the agent, even the guiding hand (*maître d'ouvrage*), of this production [...]

It is difficult to describe or define capitalistic space [...] How can a space be simultaneously homogeneous and fractured? Isn't this absurd, impossible? No. On the one hand, this space is homogeneous because within it, all is equivalent, exchangeable, interchangeable; because it is a space that is bought and sold, and exchange can only occur between units that are equivalent, interchangeable. On the other hand, this space is fractured because it is processed in the form of lots and parcels, and sold on this basis; it is thus fragmented. These aspects of capitalistic space are shaped both within the realm of the commodity, in which everything is equivalent, and within the realm of the state, in which everything is controlled. This capitalistic space is fractured because it is processed in the form of parcels that are sometimes minuscule – yet these parcels cannot be made so small that they can no longer be used for constructing buildings; the parcels are sold for as much as the laws or the rules of speculation permit. It is a *logical* space – even though the logical character of the homogeneous whole is contradicted by the fragmentation of the parts [...]

Each mode of production has had its space; but the characteristics of space cannot simply be reduced to the general characteristics of the mode of production. Medieval symbolism cannot be defined by the rents peasants surrendered to the lords of the manor, or by the relations between towns and the countryside. The reduction of aesthetic, social, and mental phenomena to the economic was a disastrous error that some "Marxists" still perpetuate.

The current mode of production is characterized by the space of state control (*contrôle étatique*), which is simultaneously a space of exchange. Through its control, the state tends to accentuate the homogeneous character of space, which is fractured by exchange. This space of state control can also be defined as being optical and visual. The human body has disappeared into a space that is equivalent to a series of images [...] In modern space, the body no longer has a presence; it is only *represented*, in a spatial environment reduced to its optical components. This space is also phallic; towers with their arrogance provide sufficient testament to this. Phallic, optical, visual, logical-logistical, homogeneous and fractured, global (*global*) and fragmented – these terms enable us to label and conceptualize the features that mark the space of the SMP.

The Bauhaus and Le Corbusier had idealized this space; at the same time, they actualized it. Their idealization followed from the visual and optical character of this space, from which it derives its specular and spectacular allure. An analysis of Le Corbusier's works shows that he envisioned this space in a manner that produced and reproduced the exultant image of a strong man, joyfully contemplating light, nature, green spaces, and the figures of other humans moving about in the glorious brightness of the sun. This space implies not only that everyday life is programmed and idealized through manipulated consumption but also that spatiality is hierarchized to distinguish noble spaces from vulgar ones, residential spaces from other spaces. It also implies a bureaucratic centrality, termed "civic" but occupied by the decision making powers. It is a space organized in such a way that, unless they revolt, "users" are reduced to passivity and silence. Their revolt can and must start from the presentation of counter-projects, of counter-spaces, leading to sometimes violent protests, and culminating in a radical revolt that calls into question the entirety of interchangeable, spectacular space, with its implication of everydayness, centrality, and spatial hierarchization.

These contradictions of space are added to and superimposed upon the entrenched contradictions of the capitalist mode of production. Knowledge (*connaissance*) which is directly invested in the production of space can process it in vast expanses (highway construction); but this space is fragmented, pulverized by private property. Thus appears a modern form of the contradiction noted by Marx between the productive forces and the relations of production and of property.

Private property (that is, social relations) prohibits knowledge from being deployed. It paralyzes the intentions and inventions of architects as well as urbanists; it annihilates their critical and creative capacities. The impact of the relations of production and of the social relations (of property) becomes more pronounced. The actions of property developers embody this impact.

The concept of a *hierarchical stratified morphology* (and its corollary – the "space of catastrophe" [*espace de catastrophe*]) stems from the research of R. Thom (1974).[2] It can be generalized and applied to social space. Synchronic analysis (of the present) does not prohibit a diachronic analysis (a history of space). On the contrary, the latter leads to the former. Morphological analysis presupposes genetic analysis.

One can speak of a stratified morphology whenever definite forms composed of discrete units are embedded within one another in a definite order. In linguistics, for example: the *phoneme* (a sound or syllable without meaning); the *word* (an articulation of connected phonemes into a signifying unit); the *clause* or sentence; the series of sentences and the unfolding of meanings. An analogous morphology exists in social space – from the "room" or hut to the house and the building; from the building to the group of houses, the village, and the neighborhood; from the neighborhood to the city, the region, the nation, and the state.

Table 4.1 presents some observable morphologies that have been formalized to reveal the hierarchical embedding of levels. Contrary to the abuse of this term within technocratic ideology, the articulation between the levels is not simply a "positive," unchanging fact. It also entails negative effects: ruptures, catastrophes.

When studying a hierarchized morphology, one has to define its "space of catastrophe," that is, the conditions under which the space might disintegrate. Theory shows that, from a genetic perspective, the conditions for stability and the conditions for a rupture are produced simultaneously [...]

These concepts enable us to delineate and define the junction (the articulation) between space and the modern state from the "outside." This articulation may also be captured from the "inside."

(1) The close cooperation between the state and the automobile industry in reshaping pre-existent spaces, including the historical city, is well known. While varying from country to country, certain effects are evident to some degree everywhere – highways, parking lots, but also factories, garages, hotels

Table 4.1

Linguistics	Physics	Biology	(Social) space
Phonemes	Particles	Molecules	Room (hut, shack)
Syllables (morphemes)	Molecules	Groups of molecules	Building (house)
Words	Bodies	Organelles	Neighborhood
Clauses	Planets	Cells	City
Sentences	Solar system	Organs	District (country)
Sequence of sentences	Galaxies	Individuals (of a species)	Nation (state)
		Ecological system	Continent
			Planet

and motels, gas stations, etc. In the large modern countries, some 20 percent of production and the working population are devoted to the automobile and its use. Everything is being sacrificed to this form of growth: the historical past, convenience, amusement, "culture." The historical city is rebuilt according to the demands of growth "impelled" by the automobile. Automobile and construction lobbies link up with the state technostructure (*technostructure éta-tique*). Working together, they eventually circumvent popular opposition to traffic, pollution, the withdrawal of public transport, etc. However, a "critical point" (critical state) is being reached more or less everywhere as the automobile's predominance is called into question and this questioning becomes political. Resistance is becoming more intense and its sources multiply, ranging from dispossessed, deskilled "landowners" to "users" of all classes. From this critical point on, a new conception of space is sought, with new functions and new forms that cannot be reduced simply to traffic circulation. "Quality of space" "qualitative space" – these concepts impose themselves gradually during a period of utopianism, dreams, nostalgia, efforts to go back in time or to live "as if things were different" (elite neo-anarchism).

(2)   When the state, in any given country, took control of energy production (electricity, oil), some people assumed it would be transferred to "private" companies at low prices, while others assumed that the state was taking responsibility for investments that the "private" sector could not manage. Few people perceived that the state was continuing to install a dominant space, extending the space demarcated by motorways, canals, and railroads. This would only be confirmed for certain later on through the state's creation of networks of highways and air traffic routes, and the production of nuclear energy (everywhere controlled by the state). With its technostructure controlling energy questions, the state gradually becomes the master of them, not only because it controls the units of production, but because it partitions space under the double surveillance of its technicians and the police. The production of energy is closely tied to that of political space, that is, state space.

(3)   The techniques permitting the management of space on a large scale, ownership relations and the needs defined by residency – these all circumscribe the conditions for the small-scale management of space. But only the state is capable of taking charge of the management of space "on a grand scale" – highways, air traffic routes – because only the state has at its disposal the appropriate resources, techniques, and "conceptual" capacity.

The sale and management of space in parcels, often very small (co-op apartments), has brought about a catastrophic situation of urban chaos. In several countries, the state attempts to impose an order upon this chaos through diverse institutions (in France, research bureaus such as OREAM, etc.). What kind of order? That of an homogeneous, logistical, optico-geometrical, quantitative space.

State initiatives in France and elsewhere are often described as "failures" because there seems to be a lack of harmony in their results. Such judgments, whether aesthetic or ethical, mask the real situation. For the measures taken

by the relevant institutions and administrations are not without effect. However, rather than resolving the contradictions of space, state action makes them
worse. The space produced in this process is not entirely new; instead, state
action engenders a specific product of the collision (*télescopage*) between the
public and the private. The state's rational and organizational capacity works
to the extent that flows are made to circulate rather than being lost in the chaos
of spaces abandoned to "private" and local interests. The apparent result is no
less chaotic. Wherever the state abolishes chaos, it establishes itself within
spaces made fascinating by their social emptiness: a highway interchange or an
airport runway, for example, both of which are places of transit and only of
transit. This is what clarifies the apparent absurdity of this space with its
double characteristic of being both homogeneous (the same) and fractured
(not by difference but by a rupture in homogeneity). This result arises from
the collision between two practices and two conceptions of space, one *logistical*
(global [*globale*], rational, homogeneous), the other *local* (based on private
interests and particular goals). In so-called capitalist countries, the contradiction can be intensified significantly between, on the one hand, the specific
goals of individual property developers, speculators, and investors (the agents
through which this space is produced) and, on the other hand, the general
(strategic) goals of the state, as represented in the state technostructure. In
these cases, the state prevails. Although the conflict does not always become so
intense, its effects are felt more or less everywhere. Hence the discomfort and
uneasiness we experience when confronted with these spaces in which one sees
at work, simultaneously, operations at specific points in time and space that
correspond to particular interests, as well as a rationalizing, generic (*globale*)
thought which is completely indifferent to its "users" (that is, to the "living
bodies" as opposed to the "functions").

(4) The rational and scientific space produced and administered by the state
     encounters not only the commodified space which is marketed and sold in
     parcels. It also encounters spontaneous, almost blind growth poles which
     generally date back to the previous epoch (archeo-capitalism, paleo-technol-
     ogy, etc.). These growth poles include, first, the large corporations that de-
     veloped near natural sources of energy (coal), raw materials (ore), and
     supplies of labor (masses of workers previously trained through traditional
     craft or farm work); second, they include the large cities which used to
     function as accelerators of growth. The collision between these spontaneous
     modalities of growth which predate the flows of the modern economy, on the
     one hand, and state space, on the other hand, does not occur without causing
     damage. State rationality prevails. Only the state can control the flows and
     harmonize them with the fixed elements of the economy (stocks) because the
     state integrates them into the dominant space it produces. The huge invest-
     ments that accompany the disintegration of the spontaneous growth poles and
     the many resultant displacements (of equipment, of energy, of the labor force,
     and of raw materials) can only be properly accomplished with the agreement
     and support of political power. No one denies this. What is often less well
     understood, however, is the consolidation – at a national and even at a

supranational scale – of this new space, superimposed upon the previous spaces, and thoroughly reordering them. One need only consider, for example, the relocation of French heavy industry from Lorraine to Dunkerque and Fos-sur-Mer. One could also mention the colossal installations by Italsider in Tarente, the automobile factories in Sagonte, Spain, etc.

(5)   The modern state is confronted with open spaces, or rather, spaces that have burst open on all sides: from apartments to buildings to the national territory by way of institutions (the school, the neighborhood, the city, the region). As historical products of previous epochs, carrying within themselves the various remnants of those periods (analogical, symbolic, etc.), these spaces are devastated, disintegrated, and ripped apart; at the same time, they overflow their borders. This is just one part of the catastrophic picture being sketched here. Apartments and buildings form open links with (*s'ouvrent sur*) collective services (*les équipements*), neighborhoods with the city and the urban. The nation itself no longer has any borders – not for capital or technology, for workers and the workforce, for expertise, or for commodities. Flows traverse borders with the impetuosity of rivers.

If regulating flows, coordinating the blind forces of growth and imposing its law onto the chaos of "private" and "local" interests is the primary function of stato-political space (*l'espace étatico-politique*), it has another function which is opposed to this but which is no less important for being so. This is its role in holding together spaces that have been ripped apart and in maintaining their multiple functions. The dominant space is characterized by the following two elements: it imposes itself upon those who threaten to pulverize the conditions for social life; and it forbids the transgressions that tend to produce a different space (whatever that might be). These two functions are correlated and yet conflictual. How can both atomization (pulverization) and transgression (supersession [*dépassement*]) be prevented?

The state tends, once again, to establish chains of equivalence, in this case of interchangeable surfaces and masses. It pushes this tendency to the point of identifying the dominated spaces within the homogeneity of the dominant space. At the same time, it controls certain effects that tend to dissolve the extant space and thus to constitute a new space defined in a different way – namely, by the differences between places and between the activities linked to these places. State action is thus not limited to the management of the social and "private" life of millions of people (the "citizens," the political "subjects") by institutional and administrative means. It proceeds in a more indirect but no less effective way by making use of this privileged instrument – space.

The capitalist mode of production (CMP) is defined by the relations of production, but not by them alone. The concept of "relations of production" is *necessary, but not sufficient*. The CMP is constituted neither by an interaction of "subjects" (individual or collective, including classes) nor as a "system" endowed with an internal coherence. This latter interpretation, despite its bold claims, implicitly glorifies what it pretends to critique.

The CMP can be defined, first of all, by a chain of concepts, from exchange value to the organic composition of capital, emphasizing the production of surplus value and the accumulation of capital with its associated theoretical problems. In contrast to the analysis of production in general, the analysis of the production of surplus value involves considering how surplus value is *realized* (trade patterns) and how it is *allocated* (investment patterns). The production of surplus value occurs within companies – that is, workplaces. The realization and allocation of surplus value occurs in cities, a fact which by no means exhausts the concept of the *urban*.

This is not all. The CMP is also defined by the production of social and political relations, including the state and state power (*l'étatique*). It is defined, finally, by the production of a spatial *support* (a foundation for the relations of production and for their renewal or reproduction). This spatial support is not particularly mysterious. It is shaped out of pre-existing space – the (geophysical) "nation-space," historical spaces. In this sense it is also shaped by definite agents – developers, bankers, urbanists, architects, landowners, political authorities (local or national), and sometimes "users."

As this vast process unfolds, something new appears. The CMP is transformed. The *socialization* of the productive forces, of production, of society, of the product, is accomplished, as foreseen by Marx. The space thus engendered is "social" in the sense that it is not a thing among things, but the system (*l'ensemble*) of links, connections, networks, and circuits. Nevertheless "socialization" and "nationalization" took the form – unforeseen by Marx – of statification, of political space (or better: of logico-political space).

Let us continue, condensing and summarizing these arguments. As it develops, the CMP produces its space, and thus a *social product*. Once a certain level (of the growth of the productive forces) is reached, it utilizes pre-existent spaces, but it does not stop there. First, it *integrates* older spaces (nature, the countryside, historical cities) while destroying them; then it invests knowledge (*savoir*) more and more deeply in the management space (the soil, the subterranean and its resources, air space). The CMP produces its own space; in so doing, it is transformed and this is the advent of the SMP. During the course of this process, space enters simultaneously into:

1   *the productive forces* (for example, from an empirical and descriptive point of view, into what economists term "agglomeration economies");
2   *the relations of production and of property* (since space can be sold and bought; and since it includes all flows, circuits and networks, etc.);
3   *ideology* and the instruments of political power (since space becomes the basis for rationality, the technostructure, and state control);
4   *the production of surplus value* (investments in urbanization, in air space, in the tourism industry with its exploitation of mountains and the sea, i.e., of the empty spaces beyond industrial production, etc.); *the realization of surplus value* (the organization of urban consumption and everyday life, of the "bureaucratic society of controlled consumption"); *the allocation of surplus value* (ground rents and underground rents, banks specializing in real estate, speculation, etc.).

The moment at which space becomes predominant, that is, when a dominant (political) space is constituted, is also the moment when production no longer spontaneously and blindly guarantees the reproduction of social relations. Although necessary, reproduction inside the corporation (investments and amortizations) and beyond (reproduction of the labor force in and by the working-class family) is no longer sufficient. The primary role of the modern state is to prevent the collapse of the edifice which extends from the labor force to the political caste – to maintain a hierarchized system of places, functions, and institutions. The process of reproduction does not become functionally autonomous; it is actualized in a space, political space, the condition for generalized reproduction. The latter entails:

1 biological (demographic) reproduction;
2 the reproduction of the labor force (families grouped in "housing projects" or in working-class neighborhoods, suburban fringes (*banlieues*), etc.;
3 the reproduction of the means of production (equipment, technology, resources);
4 the reproduction of the relations of production (which the company is no longer able to ensure or guarantee) and the relations of domination.

From a certain point on, as capital investment expands, the task of ensuring the conditions for the reproduction of the relations of domination is left to the state. Strategically, the modern state organizes space in order to:

1 break up oppositions by redistributing groups of people, including opposing groups, into ghettos;
2 hierarchize places on the basis of power relations; and
3 control the entire system (*l'ensemble*).

The space which thereby ensures this generalized reproduction has the following familiar characteristics:

1 It is *homogeneous*. It is the same throughout, implying the interchangeability of places and even of moments (time), organizing the set of places for everyday life (*l'ensemble des lieux de la quotidienneté*) (work – family and private life – planned leisure). This requires a powerful centralization, and thus a center–periphery relation. Exchangeability and interchangeability take on the appearance of the identical and of the repetitive.
2 It is *fractured* (*brisé*). A homogeneous, optico-geometrical, quantifiable and quantified, and thus abstract space can only become concrete by being embodied in a practical use, in building activities that unfold in and through "parcels." The contradiction is exacerbated between the *functionality* which state control is supposed to ensure, and the *absurdity* of the results, which is more or less perceptible, if not obvious, everywhere.
3 It is *hierarchized*. Inequalities are a necessary outcome of the exchange of spaces, since use does not disappear, but reappears in the scheduling of time. Places are arranged unequally in relation to the centers, which are themselves unequal – from commercial centers to administrative centers. State action exacerbates this situation: spaces form extreme hierarchies, from the centers of domination to the peripheries that are impoverished but still all the more strongly controlled. Hence the paradoxical aspect of the space that is constituted in this way. It is difficult to locate (social) *classes* within it; however, *segregation* continues. Habi-

tats are closely entangled yet nonetheless the "residential" spaces of the elite, the bourgeoisie, and the middle classes are distinguished perfectly from those reserved for blue-collar and service workers (small houses or tenements in sprawling cities [*les villes éclatés*] and in working-class suburbs).

Social space then assumes the form of a *collection of ghettos*: for the elite, for the bourgeoisie, for the intellectuals, for foreign workers, etc. These ghettos are not simply juxtaposed; they are hierarchized in a way that represents spatially the economic and social hierarchy, dominant sectors and subordinate sectors.

The state coordinates. It prevents "properly" capitalistic space – that is, space broken into fragments (*en miettes*) – from breaking society itself apart. But the state can do no more than substitute the homogeneity of the identical-repetitive for this situation of pulverization. The state makes use of logic but cannot impose either an abstract coherence or a spatial cohesion upon the diverse moments of the process leading from the production of surplus value to its realization. While bound within and by the dominant space, this process remains fragmented: commercial capital, finance capital, industrial capital, and real estate capital fall under the control of groups whose interests often diverge and sometimes clash. The state prevents speculation from paralyzing the general functioning of civil society and the economy. It organizes, it plans directly or indirectly, on occasion even closing some spaces, or controlling some flows by means of computers. But the space that is thus created, which is meant to be both political and regulatory, proves to be both bureaucratizing and bureaucratized, that is, administered by "bureaus." It thus complements the primary form of the repetitive by a secondary form, whose repetitiveness originates in exchangeability-interchangeability. Last but not least, this space – which is made repressive by the mere fact that it is hierarchized – imposes *the reproduction of the relations of domination* (which in turn completes the reproduction of the relations of production).

The regulatory character of political space (and state space) can therefore be analyzed in three dimensions:

- *the ideological* – the technocratic representation of the social;
- *the practical* – instrumental, a means of action;
- *the tactical-strategic* – consisting principally in the subordination of a territory's resources to political ends.

The ideology is that of a coherence-cohesion, of a neutral and thus all the more effective logic, of a homogeneity that is optico-geometric, and thus both quantifying and quantified. This ideology also entails the representation of a certain transparency – of a space in which the elements of society would be made transparent and would coexist peacefully. But shouldn't certainties be questioned? The Cartesian spirit will rule as long as this proposition is not admitted as a certainty (counter-certainty). Among all certainties, aren't those concerning space the most suspect?

The rationality of this space is stripped off like a veil when one realizes that, in reality, it "regulates" and perpetuates the relations of domination. It accomplishes this by subordinating simple reproduction (of the labor force) to the more complex reproduction of the relations of production, and by subordinating the latter to the relations of domination, incorporated into space. These modalities of reproduction include and imply one another, constituting in turn a hierarchical morphology that guarantees their intelligibility but also threatens them: for there can be no such morphology without a rupture (catastrophe). This is how the relation of the dominant to the dominated can be explained. This relation must be reduced neither to the empirical nor to mere representation. A space that is dominated may itself be dominant over another space. We know that the spatial hierarchy presents itself as an entwining or imbrication of dominant–dominated spaces. This relation of inclusion/exclusion has a logical (logistical) character.

Here one may add that the following elements include and imply one another morphologically – *everydayness* (time programmed in and by space); *spatiality* (center–periphery relations); and the *repetitive* (the identical is reproduced under conditions in which natural differences and particularities are abolished). The social hierarchy thus presents itself, more evidently today than ever, as a *spatial hierarchy*.

We thus arrive at an expanded conception of the *mode of production*. Capitalism is defined not on the basis of production in general, but by the production of surplus value, by the accumulation of capital (Luxemburg 1963), as well as by the reproduction of determinate social relations. Starting from a certain critical point, the latter result is gradually accomplished through and in space, as well as through the identification-repetition of gestures, of actions, of everydayness, of the inscribed-prescribed. Fragments of spaces and of social activities are coordinated, but not without conflicts. Space: how practical (*Quelle aubaine, l'espace*)! It may be sold and bought. It expands the realm of the commodity. At the same time, it permits the social forces that would otherwise resist established political power to be controlled. And so the state mode of production is inaugurated.

All sorts of obstacles and conflictual situations resist this comprehensive process. The repetitive must made to appear new; the identical must be made to appear dynamic. Hence the incredible mixture of the neo, the retro, and the archaic in modern life. The repetitive fits ill with the realm of the lived, for its dependence upon logic and identity implies the abolition of lived experience (*du vécu*). Thus ensues sickness, boredom, rejection: the massive disgust that follows the establishment of the SMP. At this critical point, violence enters onto the scene. Hence the strange (alienating-alienated) climate of the modern world: on the one hand, a repetitive and identitarian rationality; on the other hand, violence, whether as a means to affirm lived experience and use, or as a means to extend them. Violence smolders everywhere as this rational world is reduced to the principle of interchangeability. Violence and the tranquillity of 'regulatory' space strangely intermingle. Can't we today consider social space to be the very incarnation of violence, whether virtual or actual? This in turn calls for a global project (*un projet global*), that of another society in another space.

But let us not skip ahead. In what sense is contemporary space a "space of catastrophe"? The point of Thom's arguments (1974) is to show how and why the *logical* character of morphological embedding (*des implications morphologiques*) generates ruptures rather than stability (contrary to the technocratic thesis). In other words, logic and violence belong together.

The agents of the state (*gens de l'État*) conceive and construct *dominant* spaces ruling over *dominated* spaces (for example, through the planning of air space, airlines, airports, runways, etc.). They subject space to a logistics, believing thereby that they can either suppress conflicts and contradictions, or at least understand them in order to combat them. Against this, however, the intrinsic connection between logic and violence suggests that these agents in fact revive conflicts and aggravate contradictions.

A worldwide integration (*mondialisation*) of production and production cycles is now occurring. Doesn't the word "internationalization" (*internationalisation*) limit the scope of the phenomena that are contingent upon the growth of the productive forces? The accumulation of investments and productive capital is occurring on a world scale. The so-called supranational corporations reflect this growth, while the relations of production (and of property) remain fastened to the national scale. A globalization of labor flows, of technology, of expertise, is also taking place. The so-called developed countries, the "centers," purchase massive quantities of labor power (generally low-skilled) in the peripheries. Moreover, capital and investments have begun to seek on site (*sur place*) the labor power which they set into movement. The relation between capital and the labor force has thus changed scale. This implies a *globalization of capital markets* (and thus of surplus value transfers) in which the so-called "socialist" countries are also included, for they too are sites of investments but also of accumulation (of the means of production), technology markets, enormous reserves of labor power, etc.

A globalization and diversification of the class struggle ensues which penetrates physical, social, and mental space, creating new cleavages. The production of a planetary space likewise ensues, whose frontiers oscillate between visibility and invisibility, and in which national states have until now maintained their functions – control and hierarchization (of dominant-dominated spaces), regulation. Even the space of the corporation can and must today be reconsidered in the light of global perspectives. An article in the journal *Place* (no. 6, 1977) states: "Due to its general character, the strategic importance of wages has already been sufficiently demonstrated, but there are other broadly significant factors that would require a comparable analysis. Space is one such factor." The employers, the article continues, have not neglected the impact of space as a variable, either inside or outside the factory. This is made clear, for example, by the organizational charts that delineate "the distribution of jobs and positions within a spatial apparatus," including the functions of surveillance, which are the pivot of smooth operations. Yet, the typical or traditional space inspired by Taylorism – with its double perspective of enclosure (narrowed for the machine and the worker; but widened for purposes of surveillance) – is no longer sufficient. It disintegrates. According to official texts, the relationship between the worker and the machine will be superseded (*dépasser*) by a complex system that is organized by three relations: worker–production process; process–building; building–environment. (This nonetheless leaves aside the relations among the workers themselves.)

The disintegration of a space which juxtaposes locations and the possible establishment of a space that articulates and hierarchizes them – the contours of these developments are clear enough. This reveals a new field of protest within the factory; but it also begins to transcend the division between work and non-work (that is to say, between everyday life and the environment, and thus between housing, collective services, and landscape). A new right emerges – *the right to space* (in and beyond the workplace), *the right to control investment insofar as it manages and operationalizes space.*

The new mode of production (let us label it "socialist" once again) must produce its own space, which can no longer be a capitalist space. Any transformation of the world that remains caught in the pre-existent morphology will do no more than reproduce the relations of domination in a more or less disguised form. Capitalist space is in the process of disintegrating; will it be reconstituted in the name of socialism? A new space must be created which builds upon the tendencies that are already perceptible in the capitalist mode of production. In the context of capitalist space, what does this destructive space – the "space of catastrophe" – look like, and how should we describe it? It is a space of differences or a *differential space*, which represents for capitalism an antagonistic and ruinous tendency.

The fact that a new space, which is formed on one or another level of the stratified morphology, devastates this or that inherited space – this event-emergence can no longer come as a surprise to us [...]

The history of space would emphasize destruction – be it on the scale of architecture and the house (the building), on the scale of the urban, or on that of a country. Such a history would extricate the meaning of these destructions – not as the will of a particular agent, but as the substitution of one space by another, including the destruction of antecedent spaces by subsequent spaces (catastrophe).

The same history of space would emphasize reappropriations (modifications of the purpose and meaning of buildings) through which the destruction of what exists is avoided.

Such destructions and reappropriations are accomplished around *critical points*, during a *critical situation* of a society or a state, when such a situation obtains (transition).

In order to define the link between the SMP and space, in order to demonstrate that logico-political space is a "space of catastrophe," we must also recall that the formation of this space is accompanied by convulsions, crises, and wars – which a fallacious analysis attributes to purely economic or political factors, thus eliminating the spatial dimension. Yet the transformation of space cannot be conceived as an accidental result of such convulsions. Nor can this transformation be represented as the effect of conscious reasoning, as the intended goal of crises and wars. The convulsions of the modern world were provoked by the displacements of settlements (colonization) and resources (raw materials) across space. This resulted, following each large war, in a redistribution of space, including its resources, and in changes in how space was settled (the transition from early forms of colonialism to contemporary neo-colonialism). These changes could be foreseen from the onset of crises and tragic events; however, they were neither expected nor planned as such.

These considerations concerning space as a field of (non-abstract) possibilities permit a conception of *virtual causality* that does not lead into teleological assumptions about "final causes" or into mystical-metaphysical visions of a "causality of absence" (that is to say, of the future) or of a "metonymic" or "structural causality" (see Althusser 1965: 165–6). The political conception of space makes possible an understanding of how history and its by-products enter into the globalization process (*s'ouvrent sur le mondial en marche*) and are thus transformed.

This same process through which historicity is transformed into "something else" – globality (*mondialité*) – may explain why war and peace are not "declared" clearly, if at all. Conventional history and historicity presuppose a distinction between these *two states of affairs* that tend to become identical within the modern state. The new modality for settling space seems today to have entailed the most extreme strategic consequences: occupation of the oceans, unbridled threats to planetary space as a whole, and even beyond this. One might contend that the space of property – which reaches from underground to the earth's surface and beyond – in itself represents a "space of catastrophe": it unsettles, atomizes, and pulverizes pre-existing space, tearing it into pieces. But the space of property cannot be established without its corollary: state space (*l'espace étatique*), which corrects and supports it. What is it exactly that has *disintegrated*? All specialized spaces that have been subsumed within an institution, and which are thus enclosed, functionalized. The *uses* of space persist nonetheless: spaces for sports, the body, children, transportation, education, sleep, etc. Pulverized space tends to be reconstituted in spaces that are *differentiated according to use* (time, the scheduling of time, cycles of time). Armed with its instrument of logistical space, the state inserts itself between pulverized spaces and spaces that have been reconstructed differentially. The state's pressure prevents both a chaotic pulverization and the formation of a new space produced through a new mode of production. It prevents disintegrated spaces from being reshaped according to a Reason that has been rendered more flexible and open (dialecticized) through the relation of time (cycles and rhythms) to space. The catastrophe consists in the fact that state space hinders the transformation that would lead to the production of a differential space. State space subordinates both chaos and difference to its implacable logistics. It does not eliminate the chaos, but manages it. On the other hand, it does capture differences at the moment of their emergence and abolishes them. It rules an empty order animated only by that which it negates, defined by chaos and dissolution on the one side, the differential and the concrete on the other. The logic of this space coincides with the state's strategy, and thus with the objectives and the stakes of power. We know too well that this logic is empty only in appearance; it serves as the pivot and the axis for the political forces which seek to maintain the equilibrium between the levels of the morphology (the infra- and the supranational) and which contravene the rupture of that equilibrium. But the logic of state space *is* already this rupture, since it interrupts the movement.

At this level of state logic (*la logique étatique*), the risk implied in the trilogy of representation–participation–institution comes into play. The real and concrete movements, those of the "users," their protests and struggles, fall into the trap set for them by the state (especially when it possesses the full power of centralization). The study of urban movements shows this. To the triad or trilogy mentioned above corresponds the triple trap of *substitution* (of authority for grassroots action), *transfer* (of responsibility from the activists to the "leaders"), and *displacement* (of the objectives and the stakes of social protests to the goals set by the "bosses" who are attached to the established order [...]). Only control by the base and *territorial* self-management (*autogestion*) – exerting pressure against the summits of state power and leading a concrete struggle for concrete objectives – can oppose an actualized democracy to administrative rationality, that is, can subdue state logic through a spatialized dialectic (concretized in space without neglecting time – on the contrary, integrating space with time and time with space).

Here, and in this framework, one may return to Marx's *Critique of the Gotha Program* and Lenin's *State and Revolution*. On the way to its depoliticization, the declining state should first take charge of space in order to repair the damage inflicted during the current period: the ruins, the chaos, the waste, the pollution (which eventually causes the death of the seas, the Mediterranean for example, and even the Atlantic Ocean!). This work (*oeuvre*) cannot be accomplished without conceiving a new *texture* of space. The declining state will be dissolved not so much into "society" in an abstract sense as into a reorganized social space. At this stage, the state would be able to maintain certain functions, including that of representation. The control (*maîtrise*) of flows, the harmony between flows internal and external to a territory, will require that they be oriented *against* the global firms and, by implication, will also require a general management (*une gestion globale*) of a statist type during a certain period. This can only lead toward the *end* (goal and conclusion) by means of the activity of the base: spatial (territorial) self-management (*autogestion*), direct democracy and democratic control, affirmation of the differences produced in and through that struggle.

NOTES

This essay is an abridged translation of "L'espace et l'état," originally published as chapter 5 of Henri Lefebvre's *De l'Etat IV. Les contradictions de l'état moderne. La dialectique et/de l'état*, Union Générale d'Editions: Paris, 1978, 259–324. Translated by Alexandra Kowalski-Hodges, Neil Brenner, Aaron Passell, and Bob Jessop. Efforts have been made to trace the current copyright holder. If any copyright entitlements have been inadvertertly overlooked, Blackwell will be pleased to make the appropriate accreditation at the first opportunity.

1   See, in particular, Lefebvre (1991/1973, 1996/1968). See also Lefebvre, *La révolution urbaine* (1970), where the word "revolution" designates a multi-faceted, global transformation and not simply a violent political operation.

2   *Translators' note:* Thom's work is discussed at greater length elsewhere in the text of *De l'Etat*.

REFERENCES

Althusser, Louis (1965) *Lire le capital*. Vol. II. Paris: Maspéro.

Lefebvre, Henri (1970) *La révolution urbaine*. Paris: Gallimard.

Lefebvre, Henri (1991/1973) *The Production of Space*. Trans. D. Nicholson-Smith. Cambridge, MA: Blackwell.

Lefebvre, Henri (1996/1968) *The Right to the City*. Trans. E. Kofman and E. Lebas in H. Lefebvre, *Writings on Cities*. Cambridge, MA: Blackwell.

Lourau, René (1974) *L'analyseur Lip*. Paris: Union Générale d'Editions.

Luxemburg, Rosa (1963) *The Accumulation of Capital*. London: Routledge.

Thom, René (1974) *Modèles mathémathiques de la morphogénèse: recueil de textes sur la theorie des catastrophes et ses applications*. Paris: Union Générale d'Editions.

5

The State as Container: Territoriality in the Modern World-System

Peter J. Taylor

Territoriality is a form of behaviour that uses a bounded space, a territory, as the instrument for securing a particular outcome. By controlling access to a territory through boundary restrictions, the content of a territory can be manipulated and its character designed. This strategy seems to be ubiquitous across individuals and groups in their constructions of social organization (Sack, 1983). For example, at the individual level the designation of a room as 'my study' keeps this territory out of bounds to certain individuals and their inappropriate behaviours (children). In cities, gangs lay claim to neighbourhoods to banish rivals from 'our turf'. And, of course, states lay claim to spheres of influence where they force special territorial privileges, for instance when the Caribbean is designated 'America's backyard'. These uses of territoriality are important within their particular contexts but they pale in significance when compared to the territoriality that underpins the interstate system. Across the whole of our modern world, territory is directly linked to sovereignty to mould politics into a fundamentally state-centric social process (Gottmann, 1973; Johnston, 1991), so much so that conflicts not involving the state are often seen as outside politics as generally conceived (Taylor, 1992). I will argue here that the state's 'capture' of politics, and much else besides, in the modern world is premissed upon territoriality.

The power of the modern state is based to a large degree upon the fusing of the idea of state with that of nation to produce the nation-state. The latter term is often abbreviated simply to 'nation', as in the use of the name United Nations to describe the world organization of states. State as nation or nation-state has accrued the power to persuade millions of young men willingly 'to lay down their lives for their country' in the twentieth century. This awesome power has been made possible by a fundamental territorial link that exists between state and nation. All social institutions exist concretely in some section of space but state and nation are both peculiar in having a special relation with a specific place. A given state does not just exist in space, it has sovereign power in a particular territory. Similarly, a nation is not an arbitrary spatial given, it has meaning only for a particular place, its homeland. It is this basic community of state and nation as both being constituted through place that has enabled them to be linked together as nation-state (Taylor, 1993a: 225–28). The domination of political practice in the world by territoriality is a consequence of this territorial link between sovereign territory and national homeland.

Anthony Giddens (1985) has famously described the state as a 'power container'. Since the ability to contain social relations is a prime function of territoriality (Sack, 1983; Johnston, 1991), this particular metaphor is used to order the arguments below. The article presents two theses. In the first, termed 'filling the container', the cumulative accretion of power by expansion of the function of states is charted. The thesis is that the state has acted like a vortex sucking in social relations to mould them through its territoriality. In this way states have graduated from warring states through to welfare states as we consecutively witness the construction of power, wealth, cultural and social containers. The outcome has been the seemingly all-powerful nation-state of the twentieth century. This historical interpretation then provides a necessary background for assessing the contemporary efficacy of this territoriality and its future relevance in an era of increasing globalization. In the second argument, termed 'a leaking container?', the contemporary status of the accreted state functions is described in the light of the currently popular 'end of the state' thesis. It is argued that, despite some leaks, the state as container still has plenty of life left in it: territoriality is too good a strategy to despatch to history but what is contained and why is, and always has been, changeable. But this territoriality is not eternal. In a short speculative conclusion, the ultimate conflict between states as containers and the global ecosystem is interpreted as leading to a future end of the state.

I   Filling the Container

When we look at the twentieth-century state in the core of the modern world-system we are immediately impressed by the sheer magnitude of functions it has acquired. I will argue here, however, that they can be reduced to just four basic tasks: states wage war, they manage the economy, they give national identity, and they provide social services. As strategies of territoriality these amount to containment of power, wealth, culture and society.

I   Power containers: warring states to defensive states

The mainstream of medieval European politics was not territorial in nature. Within feudalism, personal loyalties formed a social hierarchy of political relations with no recourse to sovereignties. At the top of the hierarchy were the papacy and the holy Roman empire but neither was powerful enough to impose its political authority across Europe. The effective defeat of the empire by the papacy in the twelfth century produced a power vacuum in which two forms of territoriality developed. In Italy a city-states system evolved a competitive territorial politics which gradually reduced the number of players through elimination by war. In the rest of Europe outside the empire, what Strayer (1970) calls 'law states' developed at a scale between city-state and empire. These medium-sized polities constructed central-ized administrations based upon law courts and exchequer. But such internal functions were not complemented by external organs of state since there was as yet no interstate system in place (Strayer, 1970). This began to change in the 'long' sixteenth century. The year 1494 is usually seen as the key date, with the invasion of Italy by France, one of the most centralized of the law states. This precipitated Spanish intervention and culminated in two consequences: first, Italian city-states were reduced from being major players on the European political scene; secondly, the competitive Italian states system was in some sense imported into the rest of Europe but at a larger geographical scale. Law states were transformed from internal centralizers into members of an interstate system requiring an external arm to the state.

During the sixteenth century the complex political mosaic legacy of medieval Europe was gradually transformed into a more contiguous pattern of territories (Luard, 1986): for instance, treaty agreements between England, France and Spain in 1559 were aimed at producing more cohesive state territories. Dynastic patch-works of land were not defensible in the gunpowder age when fortresses had to give way to large state territories as the basis for success in war. At the treaty of Westphalia in 1648 an interstate system was recognized which confirmed the success of medium-sized states by eliminating rival power foci both above and below. Basically, state centralization was accepted through the principle of noninterference in each other's internal affairs, thus formally eliminating all rival power centres in their territories. At the same time the last vestiges of papal and empire political supremacy were re-moved. The end result was the modern sovereign state as power container, formally all powerful within its territory.

This outcome has been called a 'liberty of states' (Gross, 1959: 27). The Westpha-lia treaty brought to an end the disorder of the thirty years war but replaced it by a competitive political order in which states were free to extend their territory in an endless series of border wars. Although this political arrangement was a far cry from its medieval European antecedents, it was not that unusual outside Europe. According to Mann (1986), political forms of power have always been innately territorial in nature so that the creation of such power containers is bringing Europe into a common political order after its feudal aberration. Systems of states in other parts of the world have usually created 'eras of warring states' which Europe seemed to be embarking on after 1648. As the centralizing states became absolute states, their *raison d'état* became warfare for the enhanced glory of the warrior king. The usual result of such incessant warring outside Europe had been the conversion of the competitive states system into an empire either by the successes of one of the warring states or by an outside polity taking advantage of weaknesses produced by the warfare. Europe's post-1648 era of warring states did not produce such an outcome. Why?

There are two basic political reasons for this European exceptionalism. First, a mechanism of control was introduced into the system which prevented one state taking over the rest. This was the notion of balance of power whereby in any military contest, outsiders would come to the aid of the losing side instead of following their immediate interests by joining the winning side and sharing the spoils. Although balances of power have had a long history in terms of local regional arrangements, it seems that this application at the level of the interstate system is new (Luard, 1992). Although not always perfectly applied, the balance-of-power mechanism did achieve the goal of its proponents in preserving political competition. In this it was helped by a second mechanism which has come to supplant balance of power as political stabilizer in our century. This is the invention of the defensive state which uses war only to deter or defeat threats to its territory. All states which join the United Nations formally renounce the use of war to expand their territory. Hence since 1945, the military arms of all states have had to change their labels – from ministries of war or war departments to ministries of defence or defence departments. This is the reason why international boundaries have never been as stable as in the second half of the twentieth century (Coplin, 1964).

In some senses the power container as war machine has been controlled in the modern interstate system from the seventeenth century. But this was always much more than a political outcome. States were becoming more than simple power containers.

2   Wealth containers: mercantile state to development state

We get a very strong hint about the bases of the changes to the state in the seventeenth century by looking at which particular European state was at the forefront of the two political innovations just described. The Dutch are usually attributed as being the inventors and leading promoters of system-wide balance of power (Luard, 1992: 5). They also viewed themselves as a pacific state with no claims on other's territory (Taylor, 1993b). In the thirty years war their fight with Spain was completely different from the devastation across the Rhine in Germany. Theirs was a war of defence along their borders leaving a peaceful haven behind their military lines. And therein lies one of the secrets of Holland's incredible economic success, for the mid-seventeenth century is this country's 'golden age'.

The 'long' sixteenth century, as well as generating the interstate system that we have described, also saw the creation of a nascent capitalist world-economy. The Low Countries were strategically located between the Baltic, the Atlantic, the Rhine and the Mediterranean to become a leading economic growth pole of these new developments. But they were originally part of the Hapsburg realm so that their initial economic contribution was to further the power of the greatest dynasty in Europe. As such they could have been instrumental in converting the evolving interstate system into an empire. Instead, the northern Netherlands rebelled to create their own state in the most commercialized zone of Europe. Without the hindrance of a monarch the new republic operated with an alternative *raison d'état* to warfare (Boogman, 1978). Instead of viewing accretion of new territory as an enhancement of political glory, it could be viewed through economic cost-benefit lenses. From this perspective, despite the bounty and spoils, war could be seen as destructive of economic prosperity. Hence their pacific state and defensive war. Instead their *raison d'état* was that of the merchant: to pursue policies to aid trade and production with the ultimate goal of promoting capital accumulation. The state was to become a wealth container, not to fight wars better but to beget more wealth.

The success of the Dutch in this policy was astounding. While the rest of Europe experienced the 'crisis of the seventeenth century', The Netherlands had their golden age. As the great exception of the times, it was inevitable that other states would emulate them. And so economic policy became a crucial component of the business of states as containers of wealth. The generic name for this is mercantilism which consisted of state *economic* warfare in order to accumulate wealth, often quite literally through the prevention of the export of bullion. Such policies were based upon economic theories that assumed a finite quantity of wealth and each state's purpose was to get as large a share as possible for itself. Mercantile states were wealth containers *par excellence.*

It is important to note here that these new economic functions did not replace the older political ones; they were grafted on to produce a more complex and sophisticated state. The outcome varied among states. Cromwell's England was the mercantilist challenge to the Dutch which most resembled their economic focus. In France, on the other hand, Colbert employed mercantilist policies to provide resources for war to enhance the glory of his king, Louis XIV. No matter: the key point is the grafting of the notion of an economy coterminous with the state and which the state had to manage. Although the theories of mercantilism were subsequently discredited by the new political economy of the eighteenth and nineteenth centuries, the very term confirms the mercantile practice of state responsibility for its economy – the idea of economy originally only referred to household activities, but by adding the adjective 'political' its meaning was moved up to the level of the state.

As state exchequers moved from being taxation agencies and military procurers to becoming economic facilitators we can begin to see a recognizably modern state. By the end of the nineteenth century, close relations between government, industry and banks were generally accepted in what was to be called state monopoly capitalism. The renewed bout of state economic competition at this time is sometimes known as the 'new mercantilism'. More recently, in the period after the second world war, economic growth has become the key criterion for assessing state success from whatever part of the world. *Per capita* GNP league tables have become common fare and every state is a development state whose prime function as a wealth container is to promote economic growth within its territories. Nobody today would doubt the importance of the original Dutch *raison d'état.*

3   Cultural containers: imagined communities to nation-states

The political economy that arose to criticize mercantilism fundamentally disputed the idea that the world-economy operated as a zero-sum game. Adam Smith and other political economists were all concerned with economic improvement, with devising policies that would not only profit a single state but the system as a whole as well. Progress came to be viewed not just as possible but as being the norm. This idea of progress lies at the heart of the enlightenment reassessment of the nature of the world-system which was taking place throughout Europe in the eighteenth century. Basically this movement was the result of a cultural time-lag when the intellectual construction of the world was catching up with the reality of a capital-expanding world-system that had emerged two centuries earlier. This intellectual coming to terms with incessant change had the effect of discrediting not just mercantilism but the whole traditional edifice of society. A new secular rationalism emerged to advise state managers but this did little to cushion massive upheavals in society as a whole resulting from continual capital restructuring.

When the new rationality focused on the sovereignty basis of states, the 'people' were discovered as the true source of legitimation, replacing the sovereign and his discredited religious claims to authority. In the American revolution the people were interpreted as consisting of the commercial classes but with the French revolution the full fundamental implications of the change in sovereignty was revealed (Billington, 1980). The people became the nation, all citizens of the state. Furthermore, as a nation the people were deemed to share crucial cultural attributes so that their citizenship was not an arbitrary matter of location. The nation was, in Benedict Anderson's (1983) famous phrase, an imagined community. It became a collective group with a common destiny. In this way national identity replaced religious identity as the basis for incorporating individuals into the political arena. In addition, the community was indissolubly linked to the land in which it developed. This completely changed the nature of territory, especially the integrity of its borders. From being parcels of land transferable between states as the outcome of wars, all territory, including borderlands, became inviolate. We can see this changing meaning of territory in the 1793 French constitution which debarred the state from ever making peace with a foreign power that occupied any part of French territory (Billington, 1980: 66). In short it became the state's duty to defend the national homeland.

The national homeland became a cultural container. And herein lies the secret of how nationalism helped ordinary men and women cope with the social upheavals they experienced. It is no accident that the rise of nationalism coincided with great nineteenth-century capitalist restructurings known as urbanization and industrialization (Nairn, 1981). The land was being made sacred just as vast numbers of the people were being forced to leave it and move to towns and cities. National culture gave people a continued identity with their land. As its landscape became imbued with historical significance the community of people who had once lived there, sharing the same language, were given a glorious, if sometimes tragic, shared past which pointed the way to their future common destiny.

In the first half of the nineteenth century, nationalism continued in the French tradition as a revolutionary movement at war with multinational dynastic states. This was transformed in the second half of the century with the emergence of 'official' nationalisms (Anderson, 1983). The state discovered the efficacy of the new cultural container and nurtured it. Basically state managers found the idea of nation very conducive to mobilizing its citizens behind the state: from the sponsoring of national 'high culture' to feeding the people their national history in the schools and the much more sinister nationalizing programmes (policies such as russification, germanification, anglification, etc.), states hitched their destinies to nationalism. Those that didn't disappeared in 1919.

In the twentieth century the nation-state has become ubiquitous. All states, whatever their cultural make-up, are assumed to be nation-states and carry out internal policies accordingly. The world consists of nearly 200 cultural containers (the numbers having recently risen) within which national ideals are being reproduced in schooling, the mass media and all manner of other social institutions.

4 Social containers: democracy to welfare states

Whatever use is made of it, the idea of the people as a nation is a profoundly democratic concept. If we are all part of the same community, surely we should all have the same rights and obligations? This was explicit in the original French revolutionary nationalism where manhood suffrage and military conscription were soon implemented. When nationalism became widely adopted in Europe as official state doctrine a century later, the implications for the political process were soon to be found on each state agenda. Suffrage reform proceeded at different rates in different countries but no state avoided a widening of its political citizenry (Rokkan, 1970).

This had a profound effect on the state and its operations. Political parties that had been parliamentary clubs had to reform and become vote-getting organizations out there in the country. Mobilizing voters required policies targeted at the newly enfranchised citizens. In addition new parties – socialist, peasant, church – were taking advantage of the widened suffrage to compete with established parties using completely new programmes. What this did was to bring the concerns of ordinary people on to the state agenda. As right- and left-wing political élites competed for government, a new set of functions was added to the state's repertoire. Whether the social imperialism of the right, the new liberalism of the centre or the socialism of the left, all contributed to the emergence of a welfare state. Although taking different forms in different countries, its essence was to treat the people of a state as a society, a cohesive social grouping that constituted a moral and practical social system. That is to say, the state had a moral obligation to look after its people (provide a social safety net) and a practical task of making sure the society functioned properly (prevent a breakdown of social order). In this way the idea of society became coterminous with the sum of persons living within a state's territory (French society, British society, American society, etc.): states had become the social containers of our world.

The nation-state of the twentieth century has been the end result of these processes. It has become the great container of activities, first capturing politics, then economics, followed by cultural identity and finally the idea of society itself. This fusing of polity, economy, nation and society has produced the most powerful of all institutions in our times, so powerful in fact that for much of modern discourse it masquerades as a natural phenomenon rather than the historical creation it is. Brown (1981: ix) has captured this situation superbly:

> It is sometimes said that the last thing a fish would discover is water. As a basic feature of its environment it is taken for granted. So it appears to be with twentieth century men and women and the nation-state. But we not only take the nation-state as a fixed element of our circumstances; we think – or rather we assume without reflection – that its existence settles other questions.

This is the immanent power the nation-state has wielded throughout most of the twentieth century. But it is no longer an unquestioned part of our political world. As we come to the end of this century, more and more commentators are reporting that the containers are leaking their hard-won contents.

II   A Leaking Container?

Is the territorial state that has accumulated military defence, economic development, national salvation and social welfare functions over nearly half a millennium
really coming to the end of its dominance? Certainly the great weight of history
sketched in the last section must make us wary of assertions that the end of the state
is nigh. What is happening is much more subtle than an early demise of the state,
not least because of the large amount of vested interest in the continuing existence
of states. Quite simply, the efficacy of territoriality is too apparent and the container
is too full for the demise of the state not to be a long-term affair.

   Having set out this initial caveat, however, we must recognize that in the second
half of the twentieth century there has been a large literature on the difficulties states
are having in coming to terms with contemporary social change. In Rosenau's
(1989) memorable description, the state has become 'a withering colossus'. For
Deutsch (1981) there is simply 'a crisis of the state' which Brown (1973) describes
as 'a world without borders'. This widespread uncertainty about the power of states
is certainly a new phenomenon in our modern world. But what makes this literature
so remarkable is the fact that the difficulties revealed cover such a wide range of
disparate social activities. At times it seems that everything the state does is under
threat. Something is happening and the purpose of this section is to evaluate the
evidence brought forward and to interpret it in the light of our previous description
of the rise of the nation-state in all its power. We treat each of the four containers in
their historical order dealing with both the leaks that weaken the states and the fixes
that attempt to check any diminution of power.

1   Whither the warring states?

John Herz (1976) was one of the earliest writers to re-evaluate the state in the world
after the second world war and find it wanting. In 1957 he argued that the coming of
the atomic age with its intercontinental missiles meant that the state could no longer
carry out its most basic function, the defence of its people and territory. The new scale
of warfare meant that no territory could be large enough to protect its people from
annihilation. Hence Herz proclaimed 'the end of the territorial state'. But since this
statement the number of states in the world has more than quadrupled. Clearly given
the avoidance of nuclear war, the territorial state idea has diffused across the whole
world since the 1950s to make this identification of its demise premature to say the
least. The very nature of nuclear weapons seems to have been a factor in their nonuse
despite frequent threats. At the moment we can say the state as power container has
survived the atomic age.

   We can go further and say that the contemporary states are more secure and stable
than at any time in the history of the modern world-system. By this I mean that
the international régime since 1945 has effectively protected states by guaranteeing
their international existence. Hence despite the many political upheavals since 1945,
the physical boundaries on the political map have changed little. Neighbours respect
neighbours; in Europe all the signatories of the 1975 Helsinki agreement make no

claims on others' territories – a previously unheard of situation for Europe. But this situation operates in practice across the world. In Africa, for instance, the complete breakdown of government in several countries has not led to the neighbours taking advantage of the political vacuum to grab some territory for themselves. Nobody is carving up Somalia or Liberia in the way, say, Poland has been partitioned in the past. Even the breakdown of the USSR and Yugoslav federations has not led to outside claims on territory; generally old provincial boundaries have been converted into new state boundaries. The major exception to this respect for sovereign borders was Iraq's incorporation of Kuwait, a situation quickly reversed. Defence of the territorial integrity of states has, it would seem, never been simpler in complete contradiction to Herz's contention of the loss of the defence function.

John Gaddis (1987) has termed the period after the second world war 'the Long Peace', but this must seem a sick joke to the vast majority of the world's population living in the physical insecurity of the third world. The peace is a highly militarized one throughout the world. Arms sales have never been higher than in our times and, even after the end of the cold war, we are finding it difficult to produce a worthwhile 'peace dividend'. In most countries the state is very much a power container but it is citizens rather than external foes who feel its effects. Internal coercion is the rule but without the legitimacy of the early modern European absolute monarchs. Anybody who thinks the state is no longer a power container, and a ruthless one at that, should look to the third world. But even in the richer countries the defence function seems to be particularly inviolate to change. In moves towards European unity, for instance, it is the integration of the defence decision-making that will be the most difficult to achieve. States are certainly very reluctant to give up their monopoly of legitimate force however or wherever it is applied.

Conclusion: even without a world of warring states, politically the state remains the major power container in the world.

2   The national economy in the era of globalization

The erosion of the power of states is most documented and discussed in the sphere of economics. It is the wealth container that is springing most leaks. Expectations of politicians as leaders of development states are having to be scaled down rapidly by both the politicians themselves and their publics. Many commentators now doubt the continued existence of national economies leaving, in effect, nothing to manage in the state. All of this is the result of a rapid globalization of economic activities that has made territorial economic containment obsolete.

The interstate system has always operated within a world-economy and from the era of mercantilism onwards states pursued policies of capturing economic activities in their territory, as we have argued above. The globalization thesis argues that the balance between political and economic forces has fundamentally changed to the latter's great advantage. Starting with the rise of US multinational corporations in the decades following the second world war, the world-economy has become more and more integrated under the control of larger and larger economic units. The key date for these changes is 1971 with the demise of Bretton Woods currency controls. With the aid of new computer and telecommunication technologies, a global money market has been constructed that dwarfs all national markets (Thrift, 1989). In all sectors of the economy, global strategy is now the watchword as one country is played off against another. The importance of globalization can be appreciated by noting that both political superpowers have been brought down to size by a leaking of their wealth, albeit at rather different rates.

It has been pointed out that the economic actors in this globalization all have countries of origin which is important both for how they operate and for providing the ultimate security of their capital. But it would be disingenuous not to recognize that economic processes have been developing beyond the control of states to an increasing extent in recent years (Taylor, 1994b). The main response of states has not been to put pressure on their leading corporations to invest 'at home' – a new, new mercantilism – but to form economic blocks. By changing geographical scale, politicians hope to be in a better position *vis-à-vis* global capital and regain some lost economic control. There is nothing new in economic groupings of states for mutual benefit but it does seem that contemporary efforts are more ambitious than previous ones. Of course unless the politicians manage to combine Europe, North America and Japan they will never recover their previous overlordship of economic affairs.

Conclusion: the old wealth containers are no longer operative but politicians have not given up on territoriality. New economic blocs represent another attempt at creating wealth containers but at a scale that may stem at least some of the leaks.

3   The nation-state in an era of fragmentation

Globalization is not the only contemporary process sweeping our world; in seeming contradiction, fragmentation is a force to be reckoned with (Agnew, 1987). While the integrity of states has been under threat from economic processes above it has simultaneously suffered attacks from below. This has come as much more of a surprise than globalization which had long been predicted. Until about two decades ago studies of the state assumed that regional challenges to state centralization were merely of historic interest (e.g., Rokkan, 1970). The welfare state was seen as the final stage in centralization with its state-wide services homogenizing opportunities throughout the country: there was no longer any reason for local protest. But just as the welfare state was becoming consolidated throughout Europe, separatist movements sprang up across many countries. Even the oldest states found their centralization to be culturally incomplete as Scots, Bretons, Basques, among many others, began their struggles for independence. In eastern Europe such cultural resurgence was controlled until the demise of communism took away the centralizing state and allowed national separations; even Czechoslovakia has become two states. In western Europe such national aspirations have been largely contained by allowing a regional tier of government, but the story has by no means ended.

Just as with combining to form economic blocs, dividing into more homogeneous cultural units remains a territorial strategy although in this case at a smaller scale. The idea of a world of nation-states has always been a myth in practice, with virtually all states having cultural mixes of peoples including important minorities. Dividing up existing states along cultural lines may therefore actually strengthen the interstate system as its new members come closer to the national ideal.

Conclusion: These new states can be much more successful cultural containers than the old states being dismantled.

Our three conclusions have confirmed the continuing use of territoriality but at different scales – the state as power container tends to preserve existing boundaries; the state as wealth container tends towards larger territories; and the state as cultural container tends towards smaller territories. Interim conclusion: there is a triple layering of territoriality emerging (Taylor, 1994a). This may be politically astute but it is difficult to imagine how a triple-layered 'society' can be constructed.

4   Social confusion in a triple territoriality

The state as a social container is being battered from the right and left of the political spectrum. The erosion of the welfare state in the last decade by market-oriented conservative governments throughout the world has cast doubt on the meaning of the 'social' in a national society. The attack on social expenditures has many interpretations ranging from being part of expected public expenditure cuts in an economic recession to being a new round of social engineering to convert a 'dependence society' to an 'enterprise society'. But does enterprise need a society? British Prime Minister Margaret Thatcher thought not, with her oft-quoted remark that there is no such thing as society, just individuals and their families. This is a most remarkable statement from such a 'nationalist politician', implying as it does no territoriality! Given this politician's record I think we can treat this statement as an aberration but one that does reveal the ultimate implications of 'new right' politics.

The meaning of society is equally problematic when viewed from 'new left' politics. Commonly viewed as the acme of left-wing political achievement, the welfare state has been so poorly defended that the very word welfare is now widely accepted as a derogatory term. The state, and hence the society that it encompasses, is viewed with suspicion in many radical circles. The result has been that new left politics tend not to be organized through traditional political parties because they are seen as naive instruments of the state. Instead we have a wide spectrum of social movements that are very careful about their association with states (Walker, 1988). In fact their ubiquitous slogan explicitly excludes the state: 'Think global, act local'. But where does this leave the society behind the excluded state?

Despite the politics of the 1980s, the state and its society are not so easily dismissed. There are signs that what we may term a 'new centre politics' is emerging. Clinton Cabinet member Robert Reich (1991) has pointed out that to be successful, ultimately any government has to support its territorial economy (and the people who produce, consume and vote there) not its off-shore economy from which only the few benefit. Similarly the global agendas of radical organizations like Greenpeace are facing increasing competition from concerns focused on the 'home society'. Swanning around the world highlighting threats to the earth can be easily countered by a rigorous campaign for a particular piece of the earth, 'our territory'. This is what nation-states can do so well. Hence we can expect the new centre politics to be an alliance of state élites and the people in an explicit recognition of the social container versus the anti-territoriality of new right off-shore economy and new left globalism. Despite the many leakages reported above, states should not be written out of world politics just yet.

III Beyond Mark Twain

Our conclusion is remarkably like Mark Twain's famous response, on reading his obituary, that reports of his death were premature. But Mark Twain was mortal and we can be positive that he is indeed dead now. Similarly states are not eternal, whatever their national apologists may claim. Historical constructions can become historical deconstructions; that is the spirit of the 'demise of the state' literature and I have no intention of disputing this. In this conclusion, therefore, having countered premature dismissals of contemporary territoriality, I speculate on the future futility of territoriality since I think the state as container is ultimately doomed.

The threat to the state comes not from the cause of globalization, an economic one world, but the consequence, the destruction of the environmental one world. It is not only the fact that pollution is no respecter of boundaries: the whole structure of the world-system is predicated on economic expansion which is ultimately unsustainable. And the states are directly implicated as 'growth machines' – it is unimaginable that a politician could win control of a state on a no-growth policy. The people expect more, that is the essence of progress. But progress cannot be for ever if the earth is too small for ever-expanding capitalism (Taylor, 1993c).

I have no idea how future generations of politicians will solve this conundrum, if indeed they do, except to say that containers will be part of the problem since states are not ecosystems. Territoriality was finally accepted as the primary political strategy after the anarchic implications of a negative-sum game – the anti-territoriality of the central European thirty years war – became widely appreciated. In a neat reversal, as we approach another negative-sum game – testing the fragility of the earth's ecology – anti-territoriality will have to be part of the solution with territoriality the problem.

REFERENCES

Agnew, J. A. 1987: *Place and politics*. London: Allen and Unwin.

Anderson, B. 1983: *Imagined communities*. London: Verso.

Billington, J. A. 1980: *Fire in the minds of men*. London: Temple Smith.

Boogman, J. C. 1978: The *raison d'état* politician, Johan de Witt. *The Low Country's History Yearbook 1978*, 55–78.

Brown, L. R. 1973: *World without borders*. New York: Vintage.

Brown, P. G. 1981: Introduction. In Brown, P. G. and Shue, H., editors, *Boundaries*. Totoawa, NJ: Rowman & Littlefield.

Coplin, W. D. 1964: International law and assumptions about the state system. *World Politics* 17, 615–35.

Deutsch, K. W. 1981: The crisis of the state. *Government and Opposition* 16, 331–43.

Gaddis, J. 1987: *The long peace*. New York: Oxford University Press.

Giddens, A. 1985: *The nation-state and violence*. Cambridge: Polity Press.

Gottmann, J. 1973: *The significance of territory*. Charlottesville, VA: University of Virginia Press.

Gross, L. 1959: The peace of Westphalia, 1648–1948. *The American Journal of International Law* 53, 1–29.

Herz, J. H. 1976: *The nation-state and the crisis of world politics*. New York: McKay.

Johnston, R. J. 1991: *A question of place*. Oxford: Basil Blackwell.

Luard, E. 1986: *War in international society*. London: Tauris.

—— 1992: *The balance of power*. London: Macmillan.

Mann, M. 1986: *Sources of social power, volume 1*. Cambridge: Cambridge University Press.

Nairn, T. 1981: *The break-up of Britain*. London: New Left.

Reich, R. B. 1991: *The work of nations*. New York: Knopf.

Rokkan, S. 1970: *Citizens, elections, parties*. New York: McKay.

Rosenau, J. N. 1989: The state in an era of cascading politics. In Caporaso, J. A., editor, *The elusive state*. Beverly Hills, CA: Sage.

Sack, R. D. 1983: Human territoriality: a theory. *Annals, Association of American Geographers* 73, 55–74.

Strayer, J. R. 1970: *On the medieval origins of the modern state*. Princeton, NJ: Princeton University Press.

Taylor, P. J. 1992: Political geography in world-systems analysis. *Review* 14, 387–402.

—— 1993a: *Political geography: world-economy, nation-state and locality*. London: Longman.

—— 1993b: Ten years that shook the world: the United Provinces as first hegemonic state. *Sociological Perspectives* 37, 25–46.

—— 1993c: The last of the hegemons: British impasse, American impasse, world impasse. *Southeastern Geographer* 33, 1–22.

—— 1994a: States in world-systems analysis: massaging a creative tension. In Palan, R. and Gills, B., editors, *Transcending the state-global divide: a neostructuralist agenda in international relations*. Boulder, CO: Reinner.

—— 1994b: World cities and territorial states: the rise and fall of their mutuality. In Knox, P. and Taylor, P. J., editors, *World cities in a world-system*. Cambridge and New York: Cambridge University Press.

Thrift, N. 1989: The geography of international economic disorder. In Johnston, R. J. and Taylor, P. J., editors, *World in crisis*. Oxford: Basil Blackwell.

Walker, R. B. J. 1988: *One world, many worlds*. Boulder, CO: Reinner.

Part II

Remaking State Territorialities

6

The State of Globalization: Towards a Theory of State Transformation

Martin Shaw

This article is about the theory of the state in conditions of globalization. It is based on the idea that globalization is much more than the market liberalization of the last quarter of the twentieth century and the associated changes, important though this new phase is. Globalization, it is assumed here, is not simply or mainly either an economic or a recent historical phenomenon, indeed not a single process at all. It can be defined as a complex set of distinct but related processes – economic, cultural, social and also political and military – through which social relations have developed towards a global scale and with global reach, over a long historic period. Globalization has been developing for some centuries, in the sense that what Mann calls the 'multi-power actor civilization' of the west,[1] originating in Europe, has come to dominate more or less the entire world. Globalization in this sense includes the development of regional and transnational as well as explicitly global forms.

Even the current phase of globalization, which has been understood as dominated by economic processes, has many roots in complex political, military and ideological transformations. The collapse of communism and the end of the Cold War have not only symbolized and dramatized the socioeconomic and cultural changes which are taking place: they require a definitive place in any explanation of the current phase of globalization. This article challenges the conventional view that recent trends in globalization have been led by economic, social and cultural processes, and offers a distinctively politicist and militarist historical explanation.

If we approach globalization from this point of view, our view of its significance for understanding the state will be transformed. This article argues that it is wholly erroneous to counterpose globalization to the state, as many increasingly sterile debates in the social sciences have done. Globalization does not undermine the state but includes the transformation of state forms. It is both predicated on and produces such transformations. The reason for the false counterposition of the state and globalization is that the debates rest on inadequate theorizations of the state, and it is these which the article seeks to address. This article is therefore in two parts: first, I seek to *identify* the contemporary state; then I ask how it can be *understood* in terms of state theory.

I   What is the State of Globalization?

So much literature assumes that it knows what the contemporary state is: the nation-state, in a system of nation-states. In reality, just as states have not always been nation-states, so their transformations in recent times have produced state forms which go far beyond the nation-state as classically understood. So the key error in globalization debates, which this article seeks to correct, has been the identification of the modern state with the nation-state.

In contradiction to a large body of literature which assumes this identity, it can be shown quite easily that even at the highest point of the classic nation-state, in the first half of the twentieth century, the state was typically far from approaching a pure nation-state form. The dominant form of the state from the eighteenth to the mid-twentieth century was the European empire – i.e. a world or regional empire centred on various forms of local state in the European heartlands of world capitalism – rather than the nation-state in any simple sense.

From the earliest phases of globalization – the fifteenth century onwards – the growth of European influence involved the global projection of European military and political as well as economic and cultural power. Typical early imperial states such as Spain and Portugal were not nation-states in any modern sense. It is true that later phases of globalization, especially in the late nineteenth and early twentieth centuries, accentuated the national character of European imperial states. Let us take, however, the example of the the British empire, the greatest in the later period: this was a highly complex state which utterly belies any simple notion of the nation-state as either a national or a political unity. The imperial British state rested on an integration of nations within the British isles (notably the English and Scots, although the Irish, both Protestant and Catholic, and Welsh also had important roles) into the 'British' state-nation which was forged after the Union of 1707. But it also included a multiplicity of proto-nations, both settler-colonial and colonized, which partook of 'British' nationality in different degrees. The imperial state was also a highly complex structure, in which a great range of local institutions developed with large but very variable autonomy.

Only with the demise of the imperial European state, over the course of the twentieth century, has the 'nation-state' become a more or less universal political form, spreading first to the rest of Europe, then to what became known as the 'Third World', and finally to the remains of the Soviet Union. Accounts of this process often fail to grasp, however, that as the national state form has become more universal, it has also been shorn of the key characteristics of autonomous state power.

In perhaps the classic definition of the modern state, Max Weber specified that: 'A compulsory political organization with continuous operations will be called a "state" insofar as its administrative staff successfully upholds the claim to the monopoly of the legitimate use of physical force in the enforcement of its order.'[2] Following him, Anthony Giddens defines the modern nation-state as a 'bordered power container'.[3] The borders of states are not merely administrative divisions but potentially, at least, lines along which violence might erupt. States are typically autonomous centres of political-military power whose conflicts can erupt in violence.

If we accept this as a characterization of the state, the dominant imperial nation-state of the nineteenth and early twentieth centuries – which was also the classic militarist state – achieves a good fit. However, most contemporary 'nation-states' (in the period since 1945 in which the number of 'nation-states' has multi-plied dramatically) can hardly be considered states in this sense. Very many states are small, weak, with problematic national coherence, and above all minimal capacities to mobilize violence and only limited autonomy in any sense. At the other extreme, many even of the strongest nation-states have lost or given up the capacity to mobilize violence independently of their allies. Borders between these states – within the North Atlantic alliance, the European Union and more broadly and loosely the western bloc of states – are no longer borders of violence.

The paradox is therefore that now that the nation-state form has been universal-ized, most 'nation-states' are no longer autonomous states in the classic sense. The most recent phase of globalization, in the second half of the twentieth century, has certainly involved a decline in the autonomy of the nation-state, as simplistic theories of globalization imply. But this autonomy has been undermined chiefly by the outcomes of nation-states' own projections of military power, rather than by economic or even cultural and social globalization.

The beginning of the end for the nation-state was in reality the Second World War. The victory of the 'superpowers' – a new world power, the United States, and a regional power, the Soviet Union – led to the demise not only of the European empires, but of the nation-state itself. Even the greatest imperial nation-states, Britain and France, survived or were restored as shadows of their former conditions, courtesy of the new world power, with real loss of military-political autonomy. Defeated states such as Germany and Japan were reconstructed by the victors. Lesser western states effectively gave up all military-political autonomy, pooling their sovereignty in the new institutions of the western bloc. Certainly, some processes of economic globalization in recent decades have made the economic management capacity of 'nation-states' more problematic, but the 'nation-state' was already no longer really a nation-state.

It was war, therefore, not globalization in its most recent economic-liberalization phase, which overcame the classic nation-state. But if the nation-state has been surpassed, what has been the dominant state form of the last fifty years? We might define it as the state bloc, of which both the western and Soviet blocs could be considered examples. In the Soviet case, however, the subordinate 'nation-states' were little more than 'satellites'. The enforced nature of the bloc – at both the inter-state and societal levels – meant that its internal cohesion was so weak that it could hardly be considered a stable example of a new state form. The bloc began to fracture as soon as it was established in the late 1940s: violence between communist states loomed as early as the 1949 split between Stalin and Tito's Yugoslavia, and violence within them erupted in eastern Germany within weeks of Stalin's death in 1953. By the late 1950s, there was a split between the two greatest communist powers, the Soviet Union and China, whose borders bristled with military hardware and intermittent tension. Later these tensions erupted into open warfare between China and its client Cambodia, on the one hand, and the Soviet client, Vietnam, on the other. From the 1956 revolutions in Hungary and Poland through the 'Prague

Spring' of 1968 to the Polish Solidarity movement of the 1980s, a history of revolt constantly threatened the bloc's stability.

The western bloc, on the other hand, has developed and grown more closely integrated over the last half-century. Despite undoubted economic rivalries and political tensions between national elites, and deep social conflicts, these have not taken the form of serious violence. The coherence and stability of the western state bloc have been problematic, internally in the relations of its component states and in their relations with society, and externally in their relations with other centres of state power. But its coherence has been developed and its stability managed, overall with considerable success.

The western state, as I propose to call it, has developed into a massive, institutionally complex and messy agglomeration of state power centred on North America, western Europe, Japan and Australasia, but whose writ has extended even during the Cold War to Latin America, parts of the Middle East, parts of Asia and much of Africa, and has had in many senses genuinely global reach. The western state can be defined as a single state conglomerate because borders of violence have been largely abolished within, and have shifted to the edges of, this bloc. During the Cold War, there was a highly dangerous, militarized border with the Soviet bloc, and outside the blocs there were borders with old-style nation-states, while insurgents opened up new borders of violence within nation-states.

It was tempting for some critics to describe the western state as an American world empire, and so it may have appeared in the 1950s and 1960s when American power was at its peak. But American hegemony, in its relative decline, has been replaced not by a hegemonic vacuum but by the hegemony of the west as a whole. As America acts out its political-military leadership of the western bloc, it becomes increasingly clear that – despite the protests of nationalists in the USA – its state is embedded in a global western raft of institutions. The relative importance both of other national centres of power, and of multinational and global institutions themselves, has grown over the last half-century, and with them the interdependence and legitimacy of the whole conglomerate.

With the end of the Cold War, further shifts in the borders of violence have dramatically altered the role of the western state along with other state forms. The borders between the west and the newly emergent states of the former Soviet bloc have become highly permeable. On a world scale, the pacified area has been greatly extended, although new borders of violence have developed within former so-called nation-states (many of these such as the Soviet Union and Yugoslavia were actually multinational states; others such as many post-colonial states in Africa had very little genuinely national character). Former administrative structures have become organizing centres of violent conflict, while chaotic new borders have been made across villages and towns, separating former neighbours.

In this context, the global role of the western state has undergone further important transformations. First, with the collapse of the Soviet bloc and state, the western state is the only global centre, and has been able to utilize legitimate global institutions, notably the United Nations, to underwrite its own global projection of power. Second, the primary military-political role of the western state has changed from rivalry with a similar if weaker world centre to management of the new fracturing of states and societies, in order to limit the damage to the state system and also – often under pressure from media and civil society – the damage which new wars and new borders do to society.

There is therefore a new phase in the globalization of western state power. Paradoxically this is developing despite the absence of a clear political will by western leaders to develop their state institutions into clear mechanisms of global leadership and management. Certainly, western leaders have developed a growing rhetoric of global responsibility, but there is a great reluctance to commit real resources or thought to the development of global institutions or to forms of global social change which might offer greater stability. Global state intervention develops, however, despite any conscious drive towards it by world leaders, as a result of pressures generated by a wide variety of forces.

These are the conditions which have permitted the larger part of global space, fractured by competing world empires, nation-states and blocs during the earlier phases of globalization, to become an increasingly integrated political space. The unification of this space has been a gradual process over several decades of institutionalizing common forms and standards and developing international institutions. It is not difficult to see, however, that the military-political unification of the greater part of the world – the dominant western centre of world capitalism together with much of its so-called 'Third World' periphery – has had huge significance for the processes of economic and cultural globalization. The western state which developed through the Second World War and the Cold War was the political-military framework within which globalization (in the sense of recent economic liberalization) developed.

The year 1945 – considered as both the end of the Second World War and the beginning of the Cold War – was therefore the single most important turning point in the history of globalization. The owl of Minerva flies at dusk, and it is only at the end of the Cold War that we can appreciate the significance of the historical transformations which it involved. The manifest danger of nuclear annihilation and formal parity of armaments masked the latent development of a western-dominated global order. The importance of 1945 in leading to a profound reorganization of global military-political and hence socioeconomic and cultural space is only fully recognizable today.

After 1989, it is becoming possible to see the western state as a global form of state power. The resulting political-military changes have involved very important processes of globalization in their own right and have facilitated the extension of the wider range of globalization processes. Although the Iron Curtain was already highly permeable, its removal ended the political-military bifurcation of global space and opened the east far more fully to incorporation in processes of globalization of all kinds.

2 Theorizing the Emergent Global State

How do we understand the emerging global state forms centred on the western state conglomerate? So far, theory has tended to see the global context of state power in one of two limiting ways, both of which tacitly assume the old identity of state as nation-state. On the one hand, global forms of state power are subsumed under the 'international', which itself assumes the national as the fundamental unit of analysis.

The study of international organizations and regimes, for example, sees these as extensions of the nation-state.

On the other hand, there are new, generally more radical, discourses which move beyond the international to global politics, but assume that globalization diminishes the state element of 'governance'. A literature on 'governance without government',[4] in a 'post-statist world order',[5] focuses on how regulation takes place through international organizations and civil society as well as through nation-states. While this literature correctly sees that governance now involves more than the nation-state, it mistakenly implies that this should lead us to replace a 'state' perspective with the perspective of governance. To conclude from the relative decline or bypassing of the nation-state that the state as such has become less important is to miss the central contexts of globalization discussed in the first half of this article.

I argued above that we need to understand the globally dominant contemporary form of the state as the western state conglomerate, which is developing increasing global reach and legitimacy in the post-Cold War world. Provocatively perhaps, I would take this further and argue that we should understand this state form as an emergent *global state*. This state is fragmentary, undoubtedly, and possibly unstable. It constitutes, however, a more or less coherent raft of state institutions which possess, to some degree, global reach and legitimacy, and which function as a state in regulating economy, society and politics on a global scale.

A large body of literature now recognizes globalization in economic, social and cultural senses, and with it 'global society'.[6] Why then is it so unthinkable to look at the globalization of political and military power, and with it the global state? The concept is unfamiliar, certainly, but much of its difficulty is to do with the culture of the social sciences which is saturated with a concept of state as centralized nation-state. In this context, a global state can only be understood in terms of a 'world government' which obviously does not and is not likely to exist. I use the term in a rather different way, and in the remainder of this article I provide an elaboration and justification.

One reason for our difficulty in recognizing global state developments is that they are manifested in complex, rapidly changing and often highly contrasting forms. Different theoretical approaches tend to latch on to different sides of these developments. For marxists and 'Third World' theorists, for example, the Gulf War represented a manifestation of 'imperialism', centred on strategic control of oil. In contrast, western military action to protect Kurdish refugees, following the war, represented for many International Relations analysts a new form of 'humanitarian intervention'.

These and other paradigms compete to offer simple characterizations of global state power. In reality, however, global state power crystallizes as both 'imperialist' and 'humanitarian', and indeed in other forms. Mann's argument that states involve 'polymorphous crystallization', and that different crystallizations dominate different institutions, is particularly important here.[7] He gives as an example the American state, crystallizing

as conservative-patriarchal one week when restricting abortion rights, as capitalist the next when regulating the savings and loans banking scandal, as a superpower the next when sending troops abroad for other than national economic interests. These varied crystallizations are rarely in harmony or in dialectical opposition to one another; usually they just differ. They mobilize differing, if overlapping and intersecting, power networks.[8]

We need to extend this analysis in understanding the emergent global state. In the Iraqi wars of 1991, Western and global state power crystallized as both 'imperialist' and 'humanitarian', as well as in other forms, at quickly succeeding stages of the crisis.[9] Within this kind of global crisis, the American state crystallizes sometimes as a nation-state, at other times as centre of the western state, at others still as the centre of global state power. Without understanding this diversity, we will lapse into one-sidedness or downright confusion and fail to grasp global political change.

In order to understand the global state which crystallizes in these diverse forms, we must first define the state. In particular, the continuing significance of military-political power as the primary criterion for the existence of 'a state' needs to be explained. Most discussion of states in the social sciences has implied a slippage from a military-centred definition towards a juridical or economic management-based definition. It is because of this slippage that many have concluded that the state is weakened by globalization. I am assuming that the classic military-political definition is still relevant: that military relations still define the relations between distinct states and hence the parameters of global relations of power.

To understand what is a state – and conversely, when a state is not a state – I return to Weber's definition quoted above, which centres on the monopoly of legitimate violence in a given territory. Before 1945, state leaders (and others) often acted as if Weber's definition was true and they did in fact hold a monopoly of legitimate violence. In a world of nation-states, the demarcation of one state from another was the potential for violence between them. Our discussion has raised the issue of what then happens to states, and to our understanding of state, when this potential has been removed, as it has since 1945 between western states – and more problematically since 1989 between western states and Russia.

The most important change is that the control of violence is ceasing to be divided vertically between different nation-states and empires. Instead, it is being divided horizontally between different levels of power, each of which claims some legitimacy and thus fragments the nature of 'state'. On the one hand there is the internationalization of legitimate force. On the other there are the processes of 'privatization' (or 'reprivatization') of force, which have been increasingly discussed in the 1990s, in which individuals, social groups and non-state actors are more widely using force and claiming legitimacy for their usage. At the same time, some nation-states, at least, retain some of their classic control of violence.

This situation calls for a revision of Weber's definition. Fortunately Mann, in his study of nineteenth-century states, has already provided a looser version. For him,

1   The state is a differentiated set of institutions and personnel
2   embodying centrality, in the sense that political relations radiate to and from a centre, to cover a
3   territorially demarcated area over which it exercises

4   some degree of authoritative, binding rule making, backed up by some organized political force.[10]

As Mann points out, this is an institutional rather than a functional definition and crucially for our purposes it abandons the idea of a monopoly of legitimate force. A state involves, Mann suggests, merely 'some degree of authoritative rule making' and 'some organized political force'.

This definition is particularly suited to the complex, overlapping forms of state power which exist in the late twentieth century in conditions of globalization. Taking Mann's criteria in turn, I argue that the emergent global state can be considered a state, and that an additional fifth criterion needs to be added if we are to make sense of the situation of overlapping levels of state power.

States, according to Mann's first point, involve 'a differentiated set of institutions and personnel': differentiated, he means, in relation to society. The important word here is actually 'set'. Mann makes it clear that states are not necessarily homogenized and closely integrated institutions, but they consist of more or less discrete and often disjointed apparatuses. 'Under the microscope, states "Balkanize"', he argues, quoting Abrams's neat formulation that 'The state is the unified symbol of an actual disunity.'[11] Mann avers that 'Like cock-up-foul-up theorists I believe that states are messier and less systematic and unitary than each single theory suggests.'[12] The idea that states are institutional 'messes' rather than the homogenous structures of ideal type is of central importance to my understanding of the global state.

Just as the emergent global society is highly distinctive in 'including' a large number of national societies, the global state is unusual in 'including' a large number of nation-states. Nevertheless, this is not an entirely unprecedented situation. Multinational states do not always take the relatively neat centralized forms of the UK or (in a different sense) the former Soviet Union. Mann himself analyses the highly complex (and from an ideal-typical point of view, idiosyncratic) forms of the Austro-Hungarian empire. The western-centred global state is, however, an aggregation of institutions of an unprecedented kind and on an unprecedented scale. If we examine it in action, for example in Bosnia-Herzegovina, we see an amazing plethora of global, western and national state institutions – political, military and welfare – complemented by an equally dazzling and complex array of civil society organizations. As this example underlines, the global state is truly the biggest 'institutional mess' of all.

The second question is in what sense the global state meets Mann's second criterion of 'embodying centrality, in the sense that political relations radiate to and from a centre'. To put the issue another way, when is an institutional mess so messy that it cannot be seen as a single set of institutions at all? In what sense do the UN, NATO and various other international organizations, together with the USA and the various western nation-states, constitute a single set of institutions?

Clearly there is no straightforward constitutional order in the global state, but there is an order and it does have elements of a constitution. The centre – Washington rather than New York – seems clear, and the fact that political relations radiate to and from it has now been confirmed in all serious global crises of the post-

1989 period, from Kuwait to Dayton. The continuing centrality of the USA to war management worldwide, and to all the major attempts at 'peace settlements' from the Middle East and Yugoslavia to South Africa and even Northern Ireland, underlines this point.

There are two apparent anomalies in this situation which lead probably to much of the theoretical confusion. First, the centre of the western and emergent global state is constituted primarily by the centre of a nation-state, the USA. Second, political relations radiate to and from this centre through diverse sets of institutions. There is the UN itself, which confers global legitimacy on the US state (and in which that state does have a constitutional role as a permanent member of the Security Council, and a de facto role which goes beyond that). There is NATO, which is increasingly confirmed as the effective organization of western military power on a global as well as a regional scale. There are the numerous western-led world economic organizations, from the exclusive G7 to the wider OECD and the increasingly global WTO. And last but not least, there are the bilateral relations of the American state with virtually all other nation-states.

All these networks overlap, however, and the critical point is that the role of the US administration in each of them is determined not only by its 'national' interests but by the exigencies of global leadership. Of course, other nation-states, especially the UK and France but in different ways Germany and Japan and also Russia and China, as well as regional organizations, notably the EU, also have very important roles in the developing global state. The internal structure of the global state is uncertain and evolving. The roles of the various states and power networks are all contested, problematic and changing, and in the Russian and Chinese cases espe-cially unstable. Nevertheless their development is governed not just by the interplay of national interests but by the demands of world political and economic manage-ment.

Mann's third criterion, that a state possesses a 'territorially demarcated area' over which it exercises some degree of authoritative, binding rule making, backed up by some organized political force, is obviously also problematic, but does not in my view negate the concept of a global state. The territorially demarcated area of the interlocking global power networks is, in principle, the world. The fact that other state organizations claim lesser territorial jurisdictions, regional in the case of the EU, national in the case of nation-states, subnational in the case of local state authorities, does not contradict this. The idea of overlapping territorial jurisdictions is not new but it has a particular contemporary salience. There is a systematic sharing of sovereignty which is relativizing the previously unique sovereignty of the nation-state.

This leaves us with Mann's fourth point, the existence of 'some degree of authoritative, binding rule making', backed up by 'some organized political force'. Authoritative global rule making actually takes several different forms. There are the institutional arrangements which bind states together in the various inter-state organizations, so that they regulate the internal structure of the global state and the roles of nation-states within it. There is the body of international law which binds individuals and institutions in civil society as well as state institutions. There are the wide range of international conventions and agreements which regulate global economy and society. Rule making is undoubtedly patchy and in some areas incoherent, but it is proceeding apace. Mann's 'some degree' seems particularly apposite.

Rule making in the global state clearly has the backing of 'some organized political force': the armed forces of the USA, UK, France, in some circumstances Russia, and many other states, have been deployed in the names of NATO and the UN. Increasingly, too, international law is acquiring a machinery of courts, tribunals and police, even if it remains heavily dependent on nation-states, and has selective application and limited real enforcement capacity.

The global state appears to meet Mann's definition of a state. However, although this definition clearly permits a conceptualization of overlapping levels of state power, it says nothing specifically about the situation of overlapping and the ways in which different 'states' in this sense will articulate. We need therefore to add a new criterion: that a state (particular) must be

5   to a significant degree *inclusive* and *constitutive* of other forms or levels of state power (i.e. of state power in general in a particular time and space).

This criterion is essential. Clearly nation-states, in the present period, are still generally inclusive and constitutive of subnational forms, although perhaps less so than in the recent past (in the European Union, for example, regions are starting to be constituted by EU as well as national state power). To a considerable extent, too, nation-states also constitute regional and global forms of state, as well as (by definition) the international. In contrast, local and regional state forms within nation-states are generally only weakly inclusive or constitutive.

The inclusiveness and constitutiveness of the various transnational forms of state is not easy to determine. Clearly the global state institutions of the UN system have been, in principle, inclusive of the entire range of nation-states, even if in practice important states have been excluded or have excluded themselves from all or parts of the system. To date, however, the UN system has been only weakly constitutive of its component nation-states. The western state, on the other hand, became highly constitutive of its component nation-states during the Cold War, and largely remains so. The European state (European Union) has gradually strengthened both its inclusiveness and its constitutiveness of member nation-states – although this is very much a matter of contention – but its articulation with the transatlantic western state is problematic.

Once we examine this criterion, the global state is evidently a problematic level of state power. In many ways its western core remains stronger than the global form itself. It is evident, however, that the western state is operating globally, in response to global imperatives and the need for global legitimation. The western state has begun to be constituted within broader global rather than narrowly western parameters. The global level rather than the narrowly western is *becoming* constitutive, too, of the component nation-states. Still, it seems best to define the global state, even more than global society or culture, as an emergent, still contingent and problematic reality.

The fact that the western state acts as a global state is due to the manifold pressures and contradictions of global governance. These include not merely threats to western interests (as with Kuwaiti oil or the danger of a wider Balkan war), but also the imperatives of globally legitimate principles, the claims of insurgent and victimized groups (such as the Kurds and Bosnians), the contradictions of global media coverage and the demands of an emergent global civil society. The fact that the west has largely continued to cohere, despite the end of the Cold War, and has assumed global roles despite the manifest reluctance of the main western states to pursue a global leadership role, testifies to the structural significance of these trends in global society.

At rare moments, such as the Gulf mobilization, the Somalian and Haitian interventions and the Dayton settlement, western governments appear to have chosen leadership. The scarcity of these moments, compared to the occasions on which they have seemed to want to turn their backs, suggests, however, that in the end they have had leadership thrust upon them. In the end it is the logic of the new global political-military situation, including the articulation of domestic politics with global issues, which has compelled the west and especially the USA to act as the centre of an emergent global state.

These pressures function to hold together, more or less, a western-centred global state, just as the pressures of world war and Cold War formed the context of earlier stages in the development of a coherent western state. The fact that these pressures are more diffuse does not necessarily mean that they are ineffectual, although it does raise a question mark over the process. While global crises push the process of global state formation forward and make it visible, they also bare its weak coherence and contradictions, including the internal conflicts of the western core. Although the western state proved itself relatively stable during the Cold War, it may be that the challenges involved in its new global role may ultimately threaten that stability. It is therefore theoretically possible that the global state could simply fragment, and the world could revert in the medium term at least to an anarchy of national and regional state institutions fundamentally at odds with the globalization of economy, society and culture. Such a development is, however, unlikely, but to acknowledge its possibility underlines the uncertainty and incoherence of the current forms of global state. It may also imply the need for constructive thinking about their development.

So far on balance the trends discussed above have worked to maintain the general cohesion of the western-global state. Despite important temporary disagreements, it appears that the common interests of the component national and regional forms of state within the west favour its long-term stability. The major contradictions of the western-centred global state are its relatively weak effectiveness in controlling violence and its relatively poor legitimacy with state elites and societies in the non-western world. The nexus of the western state with the UN as a legitimating institution is manifestly fragile. In the long term, it will only survive if it manages to achieve greater effectiveness and legitimacy, which will require substantial social change as well as institution building.

There are, moreover, important issues in the articulation of the global state with the regional and national states which it partly includes and constitutes. These relationships are plural and variable. A full analysis of the contemporary state needs to examine these forms alongside the globalized western state power.

To explicate the nature of contemporary 'nation-states' and their relations with global state power, it is necessary to grasp the huge variation which exists in the 'states' described by this term. Robert Cooper has proposed a three-fold categorization of contemporary 'nation-states' as 'postmodern', 'modern' and 'pre-modern'.[13] While the terminology carries questionable theoretical overtones, it catches a division of states which is useful for this analysis.

First, within the west, 'nation-states' are no longer classic nation-states. They are 'postmodern' in the sense that they are very fully articulated with transnational western and global power networks. Of course, states vary enormously in the extent to which they mimic the characteristics of traditional nation-states. The USA and post-imperial Britain and France each retain a clear capacity for significant independent military action in some circumstances – although even in the American case, dependence on the wider framework of western and global power networks has increased. At the other extreme, the Canadian, Benelux and Scandinavin states have largely surrendered their capacity for independent initiative to NATO and the UN. Western states are also variably embedded in more or less dominant positions in the wide range of global economic institutions. These institutions powerfully reinforce the political-military integration of western states.

Within the west, it is important to note the special significance of the European state. This is a unique state form as well as a key component of the western state in general. It too meets all but one of Mann's criteria, in some cases better than the western-global state as a whole. The key qualification is that the forms of force available to the EU are very limited and its capacity for mobilizing military power, or even political power to deal with military issues, is still very weak. The European situation is the extreme case of the general feature of modern state organization which we have discussed. For the foreseeable future, there are likely to exist in Europe several distinctive levels of state organization, at the national, European, western (transatlantic) and global levels (not to mention sub-national regional state forms).[14]

Beyond the western state lies a never-never land of minor states, like the central and eastern Europeans, smaller East Asian and many Latin American and African states, which also have weak autonomous power. Although some states – especially those which have only recently claimed independence – pride themselves on their 'nation-state' status, these are also not really nation-states in the classic sense. They shelter under western power: although they are currently more weakly integrated into it than western states, they have no serious strategic options apart from closer relationships with the western-centred global state. In the European context, this reality is reflected in the aspirations of the smaller central and eastern states to join the EU, NATO, etc.

The relations of western and these allied 'nation-states' to regional, western and global state forms are increasingly institutionalized. Mann dubs the period after 1945 'the age of institutionalized nation-states', partly because states were based on institutionalized compromises between classes, but also – more relevant to our purposes – because relations between states were highly institutionalized.[15] The role of each nation-state corresponds to a complex set of understandings and systems of regulation within the west as a whole.

The second major group of states consists of major independent centres of state power, which correspond best to the classic model of the 'modern' nation-states. Beyond the west and its periphery lie the great non-western states including India and Brazil as well as Russia and China, and lesser powers such as Iraq, Iran and

Serbia. These states mostly acknowledge the reality of western global dominance by partial incorporation into western-led global institutions and by avoiding potential military confrontations with the west. On the other hand, many of them mobilize substantial military power which they may well use in confrontations with each other and with minor states or insurgent movements, and which may then bring them into conflict with the western-UN centre. The most critical long-term issues for the western and emergent global state are their relations with the states in this group. The latter's fuller incorporation into global state institutions would largely neutralize any danger of serious inter-state war.

The third category consists of territories where the state does not even reach the level of a stable nation-state, let alone full participation in global institutions. Here the conditions for stable state forms of any kind are weak. Instead, state power is fragmentary, often based crudely on violence with threadbare legitimacy. In some cases state power has degenerated into warlordism and gangsterism. This has been an increasingly common pattern in parts of Africa and the former Soviet Union (not to mention Yugoslavia). Cooper labels this case 'pre-modern' although this high-lights the problem of his terminology. Although 'ancient' ethnic or tribal hatreds may be mobilized, the technologies of communication and armament used in mobilizing are often state-of-the-art, and diaspora-based global power networks are exploited. During the 1990s, managing the violent disintegration of states in this group has been a major challenge generating pressures for continuing global state development.

This account of the articulation of different categories of 'nation-state' with global state developments shows the continuing interdependence and mutual con-stitutiveness of these two major forms. This is the problem which the state theory of the twenty-first century will need to address, and which globalization theory will need to understand if it is to escape from the sterile counterposition of state and globalization.

NOTES

1 Michael Mann, *The Sources of Social Power*, Vol. I (Cambridge: Cambridge University Press, 1986).
2 Quoted in ibid., p. 55.
3 Anthony Giddens, *The Nation-State and Violence* (Cambridge: Polity, 1985).
4 James N. Rosenau and Otto Czempiel, *Governance without Government: Order and Change in World Politics* (Cambridge: Cambridge University Press, 1992).
5 Richard N. Falk, 'State of siege: will globalisation win out?', *International Affairs* 73 (1) (January 1997): 125.
6 See Martin Shaw, *Global Society and International Relations* (Cambridge: Polity, 1994).
7 See Mann, *The Sources of Social Power*, Vol. II, pp. 75–88. Mann identifies six 'higher-level' crystallizations in his analysis of nineteenth-century western states, as capitalist, ideological-moral, militarist, patriarchal and at points on continua of representativeness and nationality. This categorization needs expansion to deal with the greater complex-ities of late twentieth-century state crystallizations.
8 ibid., p. 736.

9 I have analysed this phenomenon in *Civil Society and Media in Global Crises* (London: Pinter, 1996).

10 Mann, *The Sources of Social Power*, Vol. II, p. 55.

11 ibid., p. 53.

12 ibid., p. 88.

13 Robert Cooper, *The Post-Modern State and the World Order* (London: Demos, 1996).

14 The argument about a nation-state versus a federal concept of European integration is therefore misnamed on both sides, since neither mere linkages of nation-states nor a classic federation is on offer, but rather this interdependent plurality of forms of state power.

15 Michael Mann, 'As the twentieth century ages', *New Left Review* 214 (November-December 1995): 116.

7

The Rise of East Asia and the Withering Away of the Interstate System

Giovanni Arrighi

History continually messes up the neat conceptual frameworks and the more or less elegant theoretical speculations with which we endeavor to understand the past and forecast the future of our world. In recent years, two events stand out as eminently subversive of the intellectual landscape: the sudden demise of the USSR as one of the two main loci of world power and the gradual rise of East Asia to epicenter of world-scale processes of capital accumulation. Although each event has received much scholarly attention, it is their joint occurrence that has the most significant conceptual and theoretical implications.

I

World-systems studies are as likely to be revolutionized by this joint occurrence as any other field of historical inquiry. Thus, André Gunder Frank has claimed that these two events provide a new perspective on the origins and development of the world economic system. For, although both Braudel and Wallerstein have argued that the latest world system emerged in Western Europe by at least 1450, then spread outward from Europe to encompass the rest of the world (Frank 1994: 259), Frank now proposes that the formation of a world economic system encompassing Eurasia and parts of Africa antedates 1450 by several millennia. Within this ancient world economic system, Europe in the modern era did not "incorporate" Asia. Rather, after 1500 it used American silver to buy its way into an Asian-dominated trading system. Even then, "Europe's incursions into Asia . . . succeeded only after about three centuries, when Ottoman, Moghul, and Qing rule was weakened for other reasons. In the global economy, these and other economies competed with each other until Europe won" (Frank 1994: 273, 275).

Frank does not spell out the dynamic of this "victory." He nonetheless insists on two things. First, at the origins of the victory there is "no dramatic, or even gradual, change to a capitalist economy, and certainly none beginning in Europe in the sixteenth century" (1994: 275). And second, the victory now seems to have been very short-lived. Indeed, it seems that Asia will again play a leading role in the world economy (Gills and Frank 1994: 6–7).

Starting from altogether different premises, a group of Japanese historians, most notably, Takeshi Hamashita and Heita Kawakatsu, have also recently advanced a reinterpretation of "modernization" in East Asia. Unlike Frank, Hamashita and Kawakatsu focus on East Asian rather than world history. But like Frank, they deny that the expanding European world economy ever "incorporated" what they call the Sinocentric tribute-trade system of East Asia.

For Hamashita, the several sea zones that stretch from Northeast to Southeast Asia have constituted for at least a millennium an integrated ensemble of regions, countries, and cities held together by a tribute-trade system centered on China. The regions, countries, and cities located along the perimeter of each sea zone "are close enough to influence one another, but are too far apart to assimilate or be assimilated."

The Sinocentric tribute-trade system provided them with a political-economic framework of mutual integration that was loose enough to endow its peripheral components with considerable autonomy vis-à-vis the Chinese center (Hamashita 1997: 117–20). Within this system, tribute missions performed an "imperial title-awarding" function that was both hierarchical and competitive. Thus, Korea, Japan, the Ryukyus, Vietnam, and Laos, among others, all sent tribute missions to China. But the Ryukyus and Korea sent missions also to Japan; and Vietnam required tribute missions from Laos. Japan and Vietnam, therefore, were both peripheral members of the Sinocentric system and competitors with China in the exercise of the imperial title-awarding function (Hamashita 1994: 92).

The system of tribute missions was intertwined and grew in symbiosis with extensive trading networks. In fact, the relationship between trade and tribute was so close that "it is quite legitimate to view tribute exchange as a commercial transaction."

> Even the Chinese court...acted as a party to business transactions. The mode of payment was often Chinese currency, whether paper money or silver. Seen from an economic perspective, tribute was managed as an exchange between seller and buyer, with the "price" of commodities fixed. Indeed, "price" standards were determined, albeit loosely, by market prices in Peking. Given the nature of this transaction, it can be shown that the foundation of the whole complex tribute-trade formation was determined by the price structure of China and that the tribute-trade zone formed an integrated "silver zone" in which silver was used as the medium of trade settlement. The key to the functioning of the tribute trade as a system was the huge [foreign] "demand" for [Chinese] commodities...and the difference between prices inside and outside China. (Hamashita 1994: 96–7)

European expansion in Asia did not end the Sinocentric tribute-trade system. It simply influenced its inner dynamics, most notably, by strengthening the preexisting disposition of peripheral countries to seek better terms for their exchanges with the center or even to replace China as the system's center. But the formation of national identities among these countries long preceded the European impact and was based on their own understanding of Sinocentrism (Hamashita 1994: 94; 1997: 118, 121, 125). Thus, through its seclusion policy in the Edo period (1603–1867) "Japan was trying to become a mini-China both ideologically and materially." And Japanese industrialization after the Meiji Restoration "was not so much a process of catching up with the West, but more a result of centuries-long competition within Asia" (Kawakatsu 1994: 6–7; also 1986).

Although Hamashita and Kawakatsu tell us little about the Sinocentric tribute-trade system after 1945, their analyses are nonetheless presented as having major implications for intra-regional relations and for political and economic relations between the region and the rest of the world. (see, for example, Hamashita 1997: 116–17). For Hamashita these implications can plausibly be summed up in two propositions.

First, the present political, economic, and cultural configuration of East Asia is a legacy of the tribute-trade system that regulated relations among the various political jurisdictions of the region for centuries before its incorporation into the modern interstate system. This incorporation is very recent and cannot be expected to have displaced, let alone erased, shared understandings of interstate relations that have deep roots in the geography and history of the region. These shared understandings will continue to influence the way in which interstate relations operate in East Asia and between East Asian and non-East Asian states.

Second, the legacy of the Sinocentric tribute-trade system is likely to weigh even more heavily on relations among business enterprises in the region than on relations among governments. For tribute was inseparable from a regional trading system which, over time, became increasingly autonomous from the actual dispatch of tribute missions. The main expression of this autonomy was the growth of large interstitial business communities, most notably an Overseas Chinese business diaspora, that connected the local economies of the region to one another in complementarity and, increasingly, in competition with tribute missions (Hamashita 1994: 97–103; 1997: 123, 127–8). When the Sinocentric tribute system began to wither away under the combined impact of endogenous nationalism and exogenous incorporation in the Eurocentric interstate system, these interstitial business communities did not vanish. On the contrary, they continued to constitute an "invisible" but powerful connector of the East Asian regional economy.

This conceptualization of East Asian history contains an implicit critique of established world-systems theories that present both analogies and differences with Frank's critique. The two critiques are analogous in emphasizing the premodern ancestry of the contemporary world system and the superficiality of Western hegemony in Asia in general, and in East Asia in particular. Since modernity and Western hegemony have been associated in Braudel's and Wallerstein's conceptualizations of world history with the rise and expansion of a Eurocentric *capitalist* world system, this emphasis is tantamount to rejecting capitalism as a useful notion for analysing world historical social change. Frank rejects the notion explicitly, as we have seen; but Hamashita does so implicitly by ignoring capitalism in his account of the Sinocentric world system and of its transformation under Western influence.

The two critiques also diverge in one important respect. Frank's critique underscores the basic continuity *in time* of a single global world system before and after the European discovery and conquest of the Americas (Frank 1994: 273; see also Gills and Frank 1993). Hamashita's implicit critique, in contrast, underscores the basic discontinuity *in space* of regional world systems that retain their geo-historical identity even after they are incorporated in a single global world system. In short, the main thrust of Frank's critique is to erase modern (and capitalist) history from the map of the contemporary global economy, while the main thrust of Hamashita's critique is to put regional geopolitics at the center of contemporary world history.

This paper argues that, taken jointly or separately, these critiques go both too far and not far enough. They go too far, because their legitimate preoccupation with the premodern ancestry of the modern world system tends to negate the undeniable specificity of the modern era, as defined by the extraordinary expansionary thrust of the Eurocentric system both absolutely and relative to the Sinocentric system. Wallerstein's theory of the rise in Europe of an inherently expansionary *capitalist* system is meant to highlight and explain this phenomenon and, as such, it cannot be dismissed unless we produce an alternative and more plausible explanation. Neither Frank nor Hamashita provide this. Thus their critiques of established world-systems theories do not go far enough, and so they cannot see the challenge that the collapse of the USSR and the rise of East Asia pose to our understanding of capitalism as world historical social system. The rest of this paper sketches the East Asian dimension of this challenge and then proposes a reconceptualization of historical capitalism that accommodates Frank's and Hamashita's legitimate pre-occupation with the premodern ancestry of the contemporary world system.

II

The rise of East Asia and the present crisis of the system of nation-states are closely related phenomena. Yet this close relationship has gone largely unnoticed, with each phenomenon being explored more or less independently. Ever since Kindleberger (1969) declared the nation-state to be "just about through as an economic unit," the crisis of the system of nation-states has been associated with, and traced to, the emergence of a system of deracinated and potentially footloose transnational corporations. In recent years, other facets of the disempowerment of nation-states have been introduced. Thus, Drucker (1993: 141–56) traces the disempowerment to the combined impact of three forces: the "transnationalism" of multilateral treaties and suprastatal organizations, including transnational corporations; the "regionalism" of economic blocs like the European Union and the North American Free Trade Agreement (NAFTA); and the "tribalism" of increasing emphasis on diversity and identity. Either way, the symptoms and the causes of the ongoing crisis of the system of nation-states are sought and found in all regions of the world without any special attention to East Asia. Accounts of economic expansion in East Asia, for their part, make almost no reference to the disempowerment of nation-states as a significant aspect of the phenomenon (for a partial exception, see Bernard and Ravenhill 1995). Worse still, the neo-liberal fantasy of a greater respect for, and reliance on, self-regulating markets on the part of economically successful East Asian governments has channeled debates on the wrong track. In dismantling authoritatively and effectively this fantasy, Johnson (1987, 1988), Amsden (1989), and Wade (1990), among others, have conveyed the impression that the crisis of nation-states, if at all real, does not concern East Asia, where states are well and strong.

Leaving aside the question of whether the states of East Asia are well and strong – some are, others are not – let us first note how peculiar East Asian states appear when compared with the ideal type of nation-state. Three peculiarities stand out above all others: the "quasi-state" nature of the economically most successful states of the region; the importance of informal business networks in connecting the economies of these quasi-states to one another and to the rest of the region; and the extreme imbalance of the distribution of military, financial, and demographic resources among the states operating in the region.

The expression "quasi-states" designates states that have been granted juridical statehood, and have thereby become members of the interstate system, but lack the capabilities needed to carry out the governmental functions associated historically with statehood (Jackson 1990: 21). Jackson introduced the expression to refer to the less successful among the Third World states following the post-Second World War wave of decolonization. Nevertheless, to varying degrees and in different ways the five most successful capitalist states of East Asia – Japan and the so-called Four Tigers – all qualify as quasi-states.

For the internal and external aspects of national sovereignty are essentially theories about the legitimacy of nationally-scaled political authority vis-à-vis super-ordinate and local polities. Yet key facts of the history of the modern world system violate the theory of nation-states as the pinnacle of legitimate authority and nowhere and at no time more conspicuously than today in the case of East Asia as an emerging center of world capitalism. Among the region's most successful capit-alist states, only the largest, Japan, is a nation-state in the full sense of the term. Regionally and globally, however, even Japan is still a US military protectorate. In this sense it can be seen, just like the Federal Republic of Germany, as a "semi-sovereign state" (Katzenstein 1987). South Korea and Taiwan, the two states of intermediate size, are also US military protectorates and neither is a full nation-state – with Korea divided in two and Taiwan having a tense relationship with Mainland China. Finally, semi-sovereign Hong Kong and Singapore are city-states, exercising in the East Asian region functions not altogether different from those performed by Genoa and Venice in early-modern Europe. Thus Singapore's commercial-industrial entrepôt functions make it resemble Venice, while Hong Kong's comme-rical-financial entrepôt functions make it resemble Genoa (Arrighi 1994: 78).

This peculiar configuration of East Asian capitalist states is matched by an equally peculiar configuration of the region's business organizations. Up to very recently, East Asia (Northeast Asia in particular) has been a secondary source and destination of foreign direct investment in comparison not just with North America and Western Europe, but also with Latin America, Southern and Central Africa, North Africa, and the Middle East. As a result, the vertical integration of economic activities across political jurisdictions typical of US corporate capitalism never became as important in East Asia as it did in most regions of the non-Communist world.

Although in the 1970s and, above all, in the 1980s foreign direct investment within East Asia and between East Asia and the rest of the world grew rapidly (Petri 1993: 39–42), the crossborder organization of business enterprise in the region relied heavily on informal networks among juridically independent units rather than vertical integration within a single multi-unit enterprise. In the 1970s and early 1980s, the leading agencies in the formation of regional business networks of this kind were Japanese trading and manufacturing companies, which transplanted across the region their domestic multilayered subcontracting system (Arrighi, Ikeda and Irwan 1993). From the mid-1980s onwards, however, the leading role of Japanese companies in the formation of regional business networks was supplemented, and in key areas surpassed, by the activities of the Overseas Chinese business diaspora (Arrighi 1996; Irwan 1995). These two agencies, in the words of a senior economist for Deutsche Bank Capital Markets in Tokyo, "don't really mix, but complement each other well. The Overseas Chinese are the oil – the lubricant that makes deals possible – and the Japanese are the vinegar – the technology, capital, and management that really packs a punch" (quoted in Kraar 1993: 40).

Po-keung Hui (1995) has documented the derivation of the Chinese capitalist diaspora that is emerging as a leading agency of processes of capital accumulation in East Asia from the business communities that grew in the interstices of the Sinocentric tribute-trade system before and after the European impact. His analysis supports Hamashita's contention of the continuing relevance of the Sinocentric tribute-trade system for an understanding of the present and future dynamic of the East Asian region. But it also invites a comparison with similarly structured business agencies that played a critical role in the formation and initial expansion of the Eurocentric capitalist world economy.

I am referring specifically to the Genoese capitalist diaspora which, in association with the territorialist rulers of Portugal and Spain, promoted and organized the transoceanic expansion of the European world economy in the late fifteenth and early sixteenth centuries (Arrighi 1994: ch. 2). For now, let us simply underscore two striking similarities between the sixteenth-century Genoese and the late-twentieth-century Chinese capitalist diasporas. First, like the networks of commercial and financial intermediation controlled by the sixteenth-century Genoese diaspora, the business networks controlled by the Chinese diaspora occupy places (Hong Kong, Taiwan, Singapore, as well as the most important commerical centers of Southeast Asian countries and Mainland China) but are not defined by the places they occupy. What defines the networks is the space-of-flows (the commercial and financial transactions) that connect the places where individual members or subgroups of the diaspora conduct their business (cf. Arrighi 1994: 82–4).

Second, like the business networks of the sixteenth-century Genoese diaspora, the business networks of the Overseas Chinese are an interstitial formation that thrives on the limits and contradictions of very large territorial organizations – organizations whose networks of power are so extensive as to resemble premodern world empires rather than nation-states.

This brings us to the third peculiarity of the political economy of the East Asian region: the extreme imbalance of the distribution of power resources among political jurisdictions. This extreme imbalance is the obverse of the other two peculiarities. Broadly speaking, the "semi-sovereignty" of the most successful capitalist states of the region is the obverse of their incorporation into US power networks. And the growing importance of the Overseas Chinese in promoting the economic expansion and integration of the region is one aspect of the reincorporation of Mainland China in regional and world markets.

The extreme imbalance of military power in the region is primarily a legacy of Japan's defeat in the Second World War and of the US policy of "containment" during the Cold War era. The unilateral military occupation of Japan by the USA in

1945 and the division of the region five years later into two antagonistic blocs created, in Cumings' words, a US "vertical regime solidified through bilateral defense treaties (with Japan, South Korea, Taiwan and the Philippines) and conducted by a State Department that towered over the foreign ministries of these four countries" (1997: 155). Thus, despite minor perforations in the military curtain between capitalist and communist states, the dominant tendency was a unilateral American regime heavily biased towards military communication (ibid.).

From the start this "unilateral American regime" combined features that made it resemble the pre-modern Sinocentric tribute-trade system as well as the early-modern Genoese-Iberian regime of rule and accumulation. The main resemblance with the Sinocentric system was the interpenetration of tribute and trade relations between an imperial center whose domestic economy was of incomparably greater size than that of its vassal states. Thus we might say that the Pax Americana in East Asia transformed the periphery of the former Sinocentric tribute-trade system into the periphery of a US-centric tribute-trade system.

The US-centric East Asian regime, however, fostered a functional specialization between the imperial and the vassal states that had no parallel in the old Sinocentric regime. Rather, it reminds us of the sixteenth-century Genoese-Iberian quasi-imperial regime. The main feature of the latter regime was a relationship of political exchange between an (Iberian) territorialist organization – which specialized in the provision of protection and in the pursuit of power – and a (Genoese) capitalist organization, which specialized in trade and pursuit of profit. A similar relationship can be clearly recognized in US–Japanese relations throughout the Cold War era. For "semi-sovereignty" enabled Japanese capital to externalize protection costs and to specialize in the pursuit of profit as successfully as Genoese capital had done four centuries earlier (Arrighi 1994: 120, 338).

Freed from the burden of defense spending, Japanese governments have funneled all their resources and energies into an economic expansionism that has brought affluence to Japan and taken its business to the farthest reaches of the globe. War has been an issue only in that the people and the conservative government have resisted involvement in foreign wars like Korea and Vietnam. Making what concessions were necessary under the Security Treaty with the Americans, the government has sought only involvement that would bring economic profit to Japanese enterprise (Schurmann 1974: 143).

For all its similarities with pre- and early-modern modes of rule and accumulation, the post-Second World War US-centric East Asian regime differs radically from its predecessors in at least one respect: the incomparably greater size, dispersion, and technological sophistication of the US military-industrial apparatus (Krasner 1988: 21). Neither Imperial China nor Imperial Spain ever enjoyed such extensive and potentially destructive military muscle. And yet, it was precisely in the military sphere that the US-centric East Asian regime began to crack. For the Vietnam War destroyed what the Korean War had created. It initiated a reversal of the economic fortunes of the USA and Japan that, over time, made US world power dependent on Japanese finances. More importantly, it forced the USA to readmit Mainland China to normal commercial and diplomatic intercourse with the rest of East Asia (cf. Arrighi 1996).

This outcome transformed without eliminating the previous imbalance of the distribution of power resources in the region. The rise of Japan to industrial and financial powerhouse of global significance transformed the previous relationship of Japanese political and economic vassalage vis-à-vis the USA into a relationship of mutual vassalage. Japan continued to depend on the USA for military protection; but the USA came to depend ever more critically on Japanese finance and industry for the reproduction of its protection-producing apparatus. That is to say, power resources became more evenly distributed between the USA and Japan but the structural differentiation between the two states that was at the basis of their relationship of political exchange, if anything, increased further.

At the same time, the reincorporation of Mainland China in the regional and global market economies brought back into play a state whose demographic size, abundance of labor resources, and growth potential surpassed by a good margin that of all other states operating in the region, the USA included. This giant "container" of labor power would once again become the powerful attractor of means of payments it had been in premodern and early-modern times. To be sure, the PRC [People's Republic of China] has been reincorporated in regional and global markets at the lowest levels of the value-added hierarchy of the capitalist world economy. And in spite of the extraordinary expansion of its domestic production and foreign trade over the last fifteen years, its GNP per capita at world market prices has remained among the lowest in the world (Lu 1995). Nevertheless, this failure of relative GNP per capita at world market prices to rise has further increased the attractiveness of the PRC's huge reserves of labor for foreign capital and entrepreneurship, as reflected in the explosive growth of capital flows to China since the late 1980s (Arrighi 1996).

If the main attraction of the PRC for foreign capital has been its huge and highly competitive reserves of labor, the "matchmaker" that has facilitated the encounter of foreign capital and Chinese labor is the Overseas Chinese capitalist diaspora.

Drawn by China's capable pool of low-cost labor and its growing potential as a market that contains one-fifth of the world's population, foreign investors continue to pour money into the PRC. Some 80 percent of that capital comes from the Overseas Chinese, refugees from poverty, disorder, and communism, who in one of the era's more piquant ironies are now Beijing's favorite financiers and models for modernization (Kraar 1993: 40).

But the most piquant irony of the situation is how premodern "postmodernity" looks in what has become the most dynamic region of the capitalist world system. According to most accounts, one of the main features of postmodernity is the waning of the usefulness and power of nation-states. They are declared either "too large" or "too small" to operate effectively and this is said to lead to the transfer of authority upwards and downwards from the national level. If so, the gifts of history and geography seem to have provided East Asia with a solution by endowing it with a variety of territorial and non-territorial organizations that are either something less, or something more, or something different than nation-states. There are city-states, and quasi-states; quasi-empires, and "nations" that are not states, like the Overseas Chinese; and above all, there is a structural differentiation among the most powerful organizations in the region that has left the USA in control of most of the guns, Japan and the Overseas Chinese in control of most of the money, and the PRC in control of most of the labor. In this "messy" but capitalistically most successful political economic formation there are plenty of nation-states. But they are either peripheral components of the regional formation – as Malaysia, Thailand, Indonesia, Vietnam, Laos, Cambodia, and the Philippines to different extents and in different ways all are – or they do not fit the image of the nation-state with which we have been trying to understand the origins and present dynamics of the modern world.

III

The peculiar political economic configuration of contemporary East Asia poses two main challenges to established world-systems theories. First, might some or all of its peculiarities actually be more ordinary features of historical capitalism than hitherto acknowledged? And second, if so, what kind of theoretical construct would best enable us to grasp the logic and implications of the rise of East Asia and the concomitant demise of nation-states as key actors in world politics? I concentrate here on the first challenge, considering the second briefly in my conclusions.

The peculiarities of the political economy of East Asia have already underscored how difficult it is to disentangle modern from premodern, and Eastern from Western, forms of organization in the East Asian "melting pot." But it is also evident that the political economic configuration of the entire history of the Eurocentric capitalist world system is as "messy" as, nay, "messier" than, the present configuration of East Asian capitalism. In particular, the notion that nation-states have been the key agencies of the process of formation and expansion of the Eurocentric capitalist system obscures as much as it clarifies.

City-states, diaspora capitalist classes, quasi-states, and quasi-empires have all played as critical a role as nation-states. In the original formation of the system, city-states led the way. As Mattingly (1988), Cox (1959), Lane (1966; 1979), Braudel (1984), and McNeill (1984) have emphasized in different but complementary ways, the late-medieval system of city-states centered on Venice, Florence, Genoa, and Milan anticipated by two centuries or more many of the key features of the European system of nation-states that was instituted by the Peace of Westphalia of 1648. In fact, according to Mattingly (1988: 178), the Peace of Westphalia was modeled after the Peace of Lodi of 1454 that institutionalized the balance of power among the Italian city-states.

The 200-year period that separates 1648 from 1454 corresponds almost exactly to Braudel's and Wallerstein's "long" sixteenth century. At the beginning of the period, capitalism as mode of rule and accumulation was still embedded primarily in the Italian system of city-states and, as such, it remained an interstitial formation of the European world economy. At the end of the period, it had become embedded in a European-wide system of nation-states and, as such, it had become the dominant mode of rule and accumulation of the entire European world economy. The obverse side of this transformation of the inner structure of the European world economy was an extraordinary expansion of its outer boundaries through the conquest of the Americas, major incursions in the Indian Ocean world economy, and the establishment of direct contacts with the Sinocentric tribute-trade system (Arrighi 1994: 32–47).

In terms of the present political economic configuration of East Asia, the most interesting aspect of this transformation-cum-expansion is that its agencies were either something less, or something more, or something different than nation-states. To be sure, nation-states were the main beneficiaries of the process. But they were not its promoters and organizers. Initially, its main agency was the above-mentioned Genoese-Iberian complex brought and held together by a mutually beneficial relationship of political exchange between the Genoese capitalist diaspora and the territorialist rulers of what very quickly became Imperial Spain. As the European world economy was reorganized and expanded under Genoese-Iberian leadership, various forms of proto-nationalism emerged in its midst in opposition to the imperial pretensions of the territorialist rulers of Spain and to the centralizing tendencies of the Genoese capitalist diaspora in European high finance. Even then, however, the leading loci and agencies of this countervailing power were not the more accomplished nation-states, like France, England and Sweden. Rather, it was the quasi-state of Holland – a semi-sovereign organization still struggling for juridical statehood and having more features in common with the declining city-states than with the rising nation-states (Arrighi 1994: 109–58, 177–95).

After the Peace of Westphalia, nation-states did become the main agencies of change in the Eurocentric world system. Nevertheless, the nation-state that was most active and successful in promoting the outward expansion of the system, Britain, relied heavily on forms of governmental and business organization that had been pioneered by city-states, business diasporas, quasi-empires, and quasi-states. This pre- and early-modern heritage became particularly evident in the nineteenth century, when Britain briefly, but almost literally, ruled the entire world through a combination of techniques of power derived equally from Venice and Holland on the one side, and from Genoa and Imperial Spain on the other (Arrighi 1994: 57–8, 167–71, 195–213).

Britain's half-territorialist, half-capitalist world empire eventually collapsed under the weight of its own contradictions. Yet, by the time of its collapse, the world had been transformed out of recognition and the ground prepared for the subsequent universal expansion and simultaneous supersession of the European system of nation-states. The "industrialization" of war, transport, and communication led to an unprecedented breakdown of temporal and spatial barriers both within and between the previously discrete regions of the global economy. In its turn, this "time-space compression" revolutionized the conditions under which states formed and related to one another.

On the one hand, state-making and national-economy-making could now be pursued effectively on a much greater scale than before. As a result, the typical nation-state of the European core came to be perceived as being "too small" to be able to compete militarily and commercially with the continent-sized national economies that were forming in the Russian Empire on its eastern flank and in the USA on its western flank. Germany's obsession with *Lebensraum* – paralleled in the Sinocentric system by Japan's obsession with *tairiku* – was but an aspect of this perception, which soon became a self-fulfilling prophesy by exacerbating the conflicts that led to two World Wars. Even before the Second World War was over, notes Kennedy (1987: 357), "The bipolar world, forecast so often in the nineteenth and early twentieth centuries, had at last arrived; the international order, in DePorte's words, now moved 'from one system to another.' Only the USA and the USSR counted ... and of the two, the American 'superpower' was vastly superior."

On the other hand, the low-volume, low-density web of exchanges that had linked loosely the world economies and world empires of Afroeurasia to one another since premodern times, and, in modern times, to the Americas and then Australasia, now grew in volume and density at a speed without historical precedent. As a result, the global economy came to be perceived as so highly interdependent as to make national economic independence anachronistic.

As Wade (1996) notes, much recent talk about globalization and the irrelevance of nation-states simply recycles arguments that were fashionable a hundred years ago. There are nonetheless two important differences between the realities, if not the perceptions, of the obsolescence of nation-states today and in the late nineteenth and early twentieth centuries.

First of all, a century ago the reality, and to a large extent the perception, of the crisis of nation-states concerned the states of the old European core relative to the continent-sized states that were forming on the outer perimeter of the Eurocentric system, the USA in particular. The irresistible rise of US power and wealth, and of Soviet power, though not wealth, in the course of the two World Wars and their aftermath confirmed the validity of the widely held expectation that the nation-states of the old European core were bound to live in the shadow of their two flanking giants, unless they could themselves attain continental dimension. The reality, and to a lesser extent the perception, of the present crisis of nation-states, in contrast, is that the giant states themselves are in trouble. The sudden collapse of the USSR has both clarified and obscured this new dimension of the crisis. It has clearly shown how vulnerable even the largest, most self-sufficient, and second-greatest military power had become to the forces of global economic integration. But it has obscured the true nature of the crisis by provoking a general amnesia of the USSR and, with ups and downs, has outlasted the end of the Cold War.

The second difference between the crisis of the nation-state today and a hundred years ago is that the strategies and structures of US hegemony in the Cold War era have deepened and widened the crisis by transforming small and medium-sized states into quasi-states, and by creating the conditions for a new time-space compression that has undermined the power of even the larger states. To be sure, under US hegemony the nation-state form of political organization became universal. But as the form of national sovereignty expanded, its substance contracted like never before (Arrighi 1994: 66–9).

In part, this was the direct outcome of the institutionalization of the idea of world government and of the actual exercise of world-governmental functions by the USA. The institutionalization of the idea of world government materialized through the creation of the United Nations and Bretton Woods organizations, which imposed restrictions of various kinds on the sovereignty of most of their member nation-states. But the greatest restrictions were imposed by the series of US-centric regional military alliances and by the US-centric world monetary system through which the USA at the height of its power actually governed the world. In part, however, the evaporation of the substance of national sovereignty was the indirect result of the new forms of regional and world economic integration that grew under the carapace of US military and financial power. Unlike the nineteenth-century world economic integration instituted by and centered on Britain, the system of regional and world economic integration instituted by and centered on the USA in the Cold War era did not rest on the unilateral free trade of the hegemonic power and on the extraction of tribute from an overseas territorial empire. Rather, it rested on a process of bilateral and multilateral trade liberalization closely monitored and administered by the USA, acting in concert with its most important political allies, and on a global transplant of the vertically integrated organizational structures of US corporations (Arrighi 1994: 69–72).

Administered trade liberalization and the global transplant of US corporations were meant to serve a double purpose: to maintain and expand US world power, and to reorganize interstate relations so as to "contain" not just the forces of Communist revolution, but also the forces of nationalism that had torn apart and eventually destroyed the nineteenth-century British system of world economic integration. In pursuit of these two objectives, the overseas transplant of US corporations had priority over trade liberalization. Thus, as Gilpin (1975: 108) has underscored with reference to US policy in Europe, the fundamental motivation of US support for Western European economic unification was to consolidate US and Western power vis-à-vis the USSR. In this pursuit, the US government was willing to tolerate some discrimination against the import of US goods in the newly created Common Market. But it was not willing to tolerate discrimination against the transplant of US corporations inside that market.

In Gilpin's view, the relationship of these corporations to US world power was not unlike that of joint-stock chartered companies to British power in the seventeenth and eighteenth centuries. This is true up to a point. The global transplant of US corporations did maintain and expand the world power of the USA by establishing claims on the incomes, and controls over the resources, of foreign countries. The importance of these US claims and controls should not be underestimated. In the last resort, they constituted the single most important difference between the world power of the USA and that of the USSR and, by implication, the single most important reason why the decline of US world power, unlike that of the USSR, has proceeded gradually rather than catastrophically (for an early statement of this difference, see Arrighi 1982: 95–7).

Nevertheless, the relationship between the transnational expansion of US corporations and the maintenance and expansion of the power of the US state has been just as much one of contradiction as of complementarity. For one thing, the claims on foreign incomes established by the subsidiaries of US corporations did not translate into a proportionate increase in the incomes of US residents and in the revenues of the US government. On the contrary, precisely when the fiscal crisis of the US "warfare-welfare state" became acute under the impact of the Vietnam War, a growing proportion of the incomes and liquidity of US corporations, instead of being repatriated, flew to offshore money markets. In the words of Eugene Birnbaum of Chase Manhattan Bank, the result was "the amassing of an immense volume of liquid funds and markets – the world of Eurodollar finance – outside the regulatory authority of *any* country or agency" (quoted in Frieden 1987: 85; emphasis in the original).

Interestingly enough, the organization of this world of Eurodollar finance – like the organizations of the sixteenth-century Genoese business diaspora and of the

Chinese business diaspora from premodern to our own times – occupies places but is not defined by the places it occupies. The so-called Eurodollar or Eurocurrency market "has no headquarters or buildings of its own. . . . Physically it consists merely of a network of telephones and telex machines around the world, telephones which may be used for purposes other than Eurodollar deals" (Harrod 1969: 319). This space-of-flows falls under no state jurisdiction. And although the US state may still have some privileged access to its services and resources, the main tendency of the last twenty-five years has been for all nation-states, including the US, to become the servant rather than the master of extraterritorial high finance.

Equally important, the transnational expansion of US corporations has called forth competitive responses in old and new centers of capital accumulation that have weakened, and eventually reversed, US claims on foreign incomes and resources. As Chandler (1990: 615–16) has pointed out, by the time Servan-Schreiber called upon his fellow Europeans to stand up to the "American Challenge" a growing number of European enterprises were beginning to meet the challenge and even beginning to challenge US corporations in the American market itself as well as outside the USA. In the 1970s, the accumulated value of non-US (mostly Western European) foreign direct investment grew one-and-a-half times faster than that of US foreign direct investment. By 1980, it was estimated that there were over 10,000 transnational corporations of all national origins, and by the early 1990s three times as many (Arrighi 1994: 73, 304).

Moreover, during the 1980s, it was the turn of East Asian capital to outcompete both US and Western European capital through the formation of a new kind of transnational business organization – an organization that was deeply rooted in the region's gifts of history and geography, and that combined the advantages of vertical integration with the flexibility of informal business networks. But no matter which particular fraction of capital won, the outcome of each round of the competitive struggle was a further increase in the volume and density of the web of exchanges that linked people and territory across political jurisdictions both regionally and globally.

IV

It now appears that the rise of East Asia and its "messy" political economic configuration is a special case of the even "messier" political economic configuration of the capitalist world system throughout its history. In both configurations, the leading agencies of the formation and expansion of the capitalist world system appear to have been organizations that are either something less (city-states and quasi-states) or something more (quasi-empires) or something different (business diasporas and other transterritorial capitalist organizations) than nation-states. At a decisive moment of its evolution, the Eurocentric capitalist world system did become embodied in a system of nation-states. But its further expansion continued to depend on the formation in its midst of organizations that resembled their pre- and early-modern predecessors.

Moreover, as the Eurocentric capitalist system came to encompass the entire globe, nation-states gradually lost their centrality as the main loci of world power.

World power came instead to be concentrated in structurally differentiated governmental and non-governmental organizations that reproduce on a much larger scale and in incomparably more complex forms many of the traits of pre- and early-modern modes of rule and accumulation.

This "messy" historical formation does not quite fit the concept of "capitalist world economy" that has become dominant in world-system studies. To capture the rise and present demise of the system of nation-states, that concept needs revising in a way that complements Chase-Dunn's and Hall's revision of the concept of "world empire." Wallerstein had claimed that what makes the modern world system unique is that it is the only world economy (competing polities within a single economic system) that did not transform into a world empire (a single polity encompassing an entire economic system). Conversely, Chase-Dunn and Hall suggest that the celebrated interstate system of the capitalist world economy is not as novel as is sometimes claimed. Accordingly they propose to replace the concept of "world empire" with that of "core-wide empire" to recognize that premodern state-based world systems oscillated between core-wide empires and interstate systems (Chase-Dunn and Hall 1993).

The reconceptualization proposed here, in contrast, concerns the very idea of "capitalist world economy." Just as Chase-Dunn and Hall have found more "modern" features in premodern world systems than Wallerstein's dichotomy "world empire" versus "world economy" allows for, so too are there more "premodern" features in the modern world system than allowed for by that same dichotomy. The reason why the celebrated interstate system of the capitalist world economy is not as novel as Wallerstein claimed is not just that several of its features were already present in premodern world systems. It is also that several features of premodern core-wide empires have played a critical role in the formation, expansion, and present supersession of the modern interstate system.

As the studies of early-modern Western Europe and of late-modern East Asia both suggest, we need a concept of "capitalist world economy" that defines capitalism as an interstitial formation of both premodern and modern times. Capitalism as mode of rule and accumulation did become dominant, first in Europe and then globally. But it never completely lost its interstitial character, which is as evident in today's emerging center of world capitalism (East Asia) as in its original sixteenth-century center (Western Europe). In between, there lies the era of the modern interstate system. But as long as we remain infatuated with the typical "containers" of power of this era, we shall be as ill-equipped to predict the future of our world as we are to understand its origins and evolution.

NOTE

This chapter is a shortened version of an article first published in the *Journal of World Systems Research*, II, 15, 1996.

REFERENCES

Amsden, Alice (1989). *Asia's Next Giant: South Korea and Late Industrialization.* Oxford: Oxford University Press.

Arrighi, Giovanni (1982). "A Crisis of Hegemony." In S. Amin, G. Arrighi, A. G. Frank and I. Wallerstein, *Dynamics of Global Crisis,* 55–108. New York: Monthly Review Press.

Arrighi, Giovanni (1994). *The Long Twentieth Century. Money, Power and the Origins of Our Times.* London: Verso.

Arrighi, Giovanni (1996). "The Rise of East Asia. World-Systemic and Regional Aspects." *International Journal of Sociology and Social Policy,* 16, 7/8, 6–44.

Arrighi, Giovanni, Satoshi Ikeda and Alex Irwan (1993). "The Rise of East Asia: One Miracle or Many?" In R. A. Palat, ed., *Pacific-Asia and the Future of the World-System,* 41–65. Westport, CT: Greenwood Press.

Bernard, Mitchell and John Ravenhill (1995). "Beyond Product Cycles and Flying Geese: Regionalization, Hierarchy, and the Industrialization of East Asia." *World Politics,* 47, 2, 171–209.

Braudel, Fernand (1984). *The Perspective of the World.* New York: Harper and Row.

Chandler, Alfred (1990). *Scale and Scope. The Dynamics of Industrial Capitalism.* Cambridge, MA: The Belknap Press.

Chase-Dunn, Christopher and Thomas D. Hall (1993). "Comparing World-Systems: Concepts and Working Hypotheses." *Social Forces,* 71, 4, 851–86.

Cox, Oliver (1959). *Foundations of Capitalism.* New York: Philosophical Library.

Cumings, Bruce (1997). "Japan and Northeast Asia into the Twenty-first Century." In P. Katzenstein and T. Shiraishi, eds, *Network Power: Japan and Asia,* 136–68. Ithaca, NY: Cornell University Press.

Drucker, Peter F. (1993). *Post-capitalist Society.* New York: Harper and Row.

Frank, Andre Gunder (1994). "The World Economic System in Asia Before European Hegemony." *The Historian,* 56, 2, 259–76.

Frieden, Jeffrey A. (1987). *Banking on the World. The Politics of American International Finance.* New York: Harper and Row.

Gills, Barry and André G. Frank (1993). *The World System: Five Hundred Years or Five Thousand?.* London: Routledge.

Gills, Barry and André G. Frank (1994). "The Modern World System under Asian Hegemony. The Silver Standard World Economy 1450–1750." Unpublished paper.

Gilpin, Robert (1975). *U. S. Power and the Multinational Corporation.* New York: Basic Books.

Hamashita, Takeshi (1994). "The Tribute Trade System and Modern Asia." In A. J. H. Latham and H. Kawakatsu, eds, *Japanese Industrialization and the Asian Economy,* 91–107. London: Routledge.

Hamashita, Takeshi (1997). "The Intra-Regional System in East Asia in Modern Times." In P. Katzenstein and T. Shiraishi, eds, *Network Power: Japan and Asia,* 113–35. Ithaca, NY: Cornell University Press.

Harrod, Roy (1969). *Money.* London: Macmillan.

Hui, Po-keung (1995). "Overseas Chinese Business Networks: East Asian Economic Development in Historical Perspective." Ph.D. diss., Department of Sociology, State University of New York at Binghamton.

Irwan, Alex (1995). "Business Networks and the Regional Economy of East and Southeast Asia in the Late Twentieth Century." Ph.D. diss., Department of Sociology, State University of New York at Binghamton.

Jackson, Robert (1990). *Quasi-States: Sovereignty, International Relations and the Third World.* Cambridge: Cambridge University Press.

Johnson, Chalmers (1987). "Political Institutions and Economic Performance: The Government–Business Relationship in Japan, South Korea, and Taiwan." In F. C. Deyo, ed., *The Political Economy of the New Asian Industrialization*, 136–64. Ithaca, NY: Cornell University Press.

Johnson, Chalmers (1988). "The Japanese Political Economy: A Crisis in Theory." *Ethics and International Affairs*, 2, 79–97.

Katzenstein, Peter (1987). *Policy and Politics in West Germany: The Growth of a Semisovereign State*. Philadelphia, PA: Temple University Press.

Kawakatsu, Heita (1986). "International Competitiveness in Cotton Goods in the Late Nineteenth Century: Britain versus India and East Asia." In W. Fischer, R. M. McInnis and J. Schneider, eds, *The Emergence of a World Economy, 1500–1914*, 619–43. Wiesbaden: Franz Steiner Verlag.

Kawakatsu, Heita (1994). "Historical Background." In A. J. H. Latham and H. Kawakatsu, eds., *Japanese Industrialization and the Asian Economy*, 4–8. London: Routledge.

Kennedy, Paul (1987). *The Rise and Fall of the Great Powers: Economic Change and Military Conflict from 1500 to 2000*. New York: Random House.

Kindleberger, Charles (1969). *American Business Abroad*. New Haven, CT: Yale University Press.

Kraar, Louis (1993). "The New Power in Asia." *Fortune*, October 31, 38–44.

Krasner, Stephen (1988). "A Trade Strategy for the United States." *Ethics and International Affairs*, 2, 17–35.

Lane, Frederic (1966). *Venice and History*. Baltimore: The Johns Hopkins University Press.

Lane, Frederic (1979). *Profits from Power. Readings in Protection Rent and Violence-Controlling Enterprises*. Albany, NY: State University of New York Press.

Lu, Aiguo (1995). "China's Reintegration in the World Economy: A Preliminary Assessment." UNU/WIDER, Helsinki.

Mattingly, Garrett (1988). *Renaissance Diplomacy*. New York: Dover.

McNeill, William (1984). *The Pursuit of Power: Technology, Armed Force, and Society since A. D. 1000*. Chicago: University of Chicago Press.

Petri, Peter A. (1993) "The East Asian Trading Bloc: An Analytical History." In J. A. Frankel and M. Kahler, eds, *Regionalism and Rivalry. Japan and the United States in Pacific Asia*, 21–52. Chicago: University of Chicago Press.

Schurmann, Frang (1974). *The Logic of World Power: An Inquiry into the Origins, Currents and Contradictions of World Politics*. New York: Pantheon.

Wade, Robert (1990). *Governing the Market. Economic Theory and the Role of Government in East Asian Industrialization*. Princeton: Princeton University Press.

Wade, Robert (1996). "Globalization and its Limits: Reports of the Death of the National Economy are Greatly Exaggerated." In S. Berger and R. Dore, eds, *Convergence or Diversity? National Models of Production and Distribution in a Global Economy*, 60–88. Ithaca, NY: Cornell University Press.

8

The Struggle over European Order: Transnational Class Agency in the Making of "Embedded Neo-Liberalism"[1]

Bastiaan van Apeldoorn

Introduction

This chapter presents an analysis of *transnational* social forces in the making of what is interpreted as a new European socio-economic order emerging out of the relaunching of the European integration process of the 1980s and 1990s. This transnational struggle over European order is seen as taking place within the context of a changing global political economy in which the social relations of capitalist production are increasingly constituted beyond the nation-state.[. . .] it is only by putting the process of European integration within a global context that one can fully capture present dynamics and see how that process has been bound up with a *transnational* restructuring of European state–society relations. This has, in turn, involved a transformation of the historical bloc underpinning the European project. In this perspective, European change is seen as linked to global change through the mediating agency of transnational social forces, understood as collective actors whose identities, interests and strategies take shape within a changing global structural context, and who struggle over the direction and content of the European integration process.

In this chapter, I thus conceive of the European integration process as a struggle between transnational social forces. This struggle may express itself ideologically, or on what Gramsci called the 'universal plane' of hegemony (Gramsci, 1971: 182), in the form of rival 'projects' contending for the construction of European order. On the one hand, these projects serve as rallying points around which disparate actors may coalesce into broad transnational coalitions. On the other hand, they are also consciously articulated and propagated by certain elite groups at the apex of (fractions of) transnational social forces. I argue that in this respect a particularly critical role is played by the agency of an emergent transnational capitalist class.

The chapter is structured as follows. The first section briefly elaborates the theoretical framework that informs my analysis, thus defining my position within the broad array of neo-Gramscian perspectives [. . .]. The second section then identifies three contending projects – identified as neo-liberalism, neo-mercantilism and 'supranational social democracy' – in the struggle over European integration as that process was relaunched in the mid-1980s. These are then linked to different transnational social forces, and especially to rival 'fractions' of an emergent European transnational capitalist class. The third section analyses the struggle between these rival projects up to the Treaty of Maastricht, emphasising in particular the struggle within Europe's transnational capitalist elite. In the final section I argue that, as the ideological orientation of this class (fraction) has, into the 1990s, definitively shifted away from its earlier neo-mercantilist tendencies and towards neo-liberalism, one witnesses the rise of a new comprehensive concept for European socio-economic governance. This is denoted as 'embedded neo-liberalism', which is neo-liberal at its core and reflects the outlook of the most globalised sections of European capital, while at the same time seeking to accommodate the orientations of other social forces.

'Gramscian Transnationalism' as an Approach to European Integration

European order has both a particular institutional *form*, and a particular socio-economic *content*.[2] Established approaches to European integration, particularly those bound up with the still dominant perspectives of intergovernmentalism (Moravcsik, 1991, 1998) and supranationalism/neo-functionalism (Haas, 1958; Sandholtz and Zysman, 1989; Sandholtz and Stone Sweet, 1998), have always focused rather exclusively on the institutional form of the integration process. In contrast, the primary concern here is with the socio-economic content of, or the social purpose underpinning, the European project. Understanding the social purpose underlying the emergent European order requires, I argue, an analysis of its social underpinnings, which remain hidden from established perspectives inasmuch as these narrowly define power in terms of political authority of either states or supranational/international public bodies (cf. Ruggie, 1982). In order to overcome this narrow focus, one should add a concept of *social* power, in both its material *and* ideological dimensions, derived not from political authorities, or from the state in a narrow sense, but from the social forces that underpin state power. As a result, any analysis of the *problématique* surrounding the social purpose of European integration necessarily demands an alternative approach to the study of European order. A neo-Gramscian perspective within the field of International Political Economy (IPE) can, in my view, provide fertile ground for such an alternative. This approach to European integration, which one might refer to as 'Gramscian transnationalism', integrates the following three elements: a focus on social forces; an emphasis on the role of ideas; and, finally, a radical abandonment of state-centrism in favour of a transnationalist view of (global) politics.[3] Let me briefly discuss each of them.

   The first element, then, calls for a focus on social forces within the process of European integration and views these as engendered by the capitalist production process. I thus proceed from a historical materialist understanding of 'the social' in which the social relations of production are seen as critical for an understanding of social power in capitalist societies.[4] Such a perspective also ought to consciously reclaim the centrality of the concept of class in the study of political economy. The point of departure of any class analysis should, however, be that the class domination by which capitalist societies are characterised cannot be understood from a structuralist perspective. Instead, the reproduction of the structural power of capital – and of the capitalist class – has to be explained in terms of collective human agency within concrete social power struggles.

Although it is the relation between capital and labour that engenders the basic class division in capitalist society, the class approach adopted here does not take classes as unified social actors. In particular, following the pioneering work of Kees van der Pijl and others (van der Pijl, 1984, 1998; Overbeek, 1993), I conceptualise the process of *capitalist* class formation as one in which the different concrete groups within the capitalist class crystallise into rival class *fractions*. The elites of such fractions might aspire to represent the capitalist class as a whole, articulating a 'general capitalist interest' from their own fractional perspective. Two primary structural axes along which class fractions are concretely formed may be identified: first, that of industrial (productive) versus financial (money) capital, and, second, that of domestic (or national) versus transnational capital, which becomes particularly relevant for analysing divisions *within* industrial capital (see also [Bieler and Norton, 2001] on this point). Within the latter, one can further differentiate with respect to the degree of globalisation: that is, whether the transnational activities of an enterprise take place on a truly global scale or are rather more confined to a particular macro-region (e.g., Western Europe).

A neo-Gramscian perspective also emphasises the ideological dimension of the struggles between social (class) forces (and indeed of the process of class formation). Entering what Gramsci called 'the most purely political phase' (Gramsci, 1971: 181), the struggle between social forces becomes a struggle between competing ideologies aspiring to hegemony. The second element of our approach is the critical role accorded to the power of ideas and ideological practices in the construction of European order and in defining its social purpose. This approach thus transcends the narrow rationalism of established approaches to European integration. The link between ideas and particular social forces is critical, however, inasmuch as ideas are produced by human agency in the context of social power relations, and are as such bound up with the strategic action of social actors.

The third element is the transnational dimension. Whereas intergovernmentalist accounts of European integration ignore the transnational level altogether, supranationalist (neo-functionalist) approaches do explicitly acknowledge the role of transnational actors. However, they tend to see that role as subservient to the alleged functional logic of the integration process and/or to the supranational leadership of the European Commission, thus denying the autonomy of these actors. The point of departure for the present analysis is that the social forces underpinning European order are not necessarily internal to the European Union (EU), or to its member states, but are rather located within a global political economy in which capitalist production and finance are undergoing a sustained transnationalisation and globalisation. This is reflected *inter alia* in the increasing dominance of transnational corporations (TNCs) as actors in the world economy (see, e.g., United Nations Conference on Trade and Development, or UNCTAD, 1997), and in the concomitant growing structural power of transnational capital (Gill and Law, 1993). These structural transformations thus engender *transnational* social forces, and indeed a process of *transnational class formation* (van der Pijl, 1998). It is from this perspective that in the sections below I will examine what can be seen as the transnational dynamics of European integration in the 1980s and 1990s.

Transnational Struggle over European Order: Contending Projects and Rival Class Fractions

In Western Europe, throughout the 1970s and early 1980s, there was a period of 'Euro-pessimism' as both the integration process and the post-war Fordist growth engine came to a rather sudden grinding halt. In what soon came to be the conventional view, the world economic crisis was regarded to have affected Europe in ways that traditional (Keynesian) policies could not answer as well as revealing structural weaknesses within the European economy which made it lag behind the competing blocs of Japan and the USA. It was within this context that the European integration process was relaunched as social and political forces – in particular sections of European big business – organised themselves at a European level, re-activating the political process. Here, different visions, different projects, came to compete with one another, each of which must be seen as linked to specific transnational social and political forces, and as constituting contending responses on the part of these forces to the crisis of European capitalism within the context of global capitalist restructuring.

The neo-liberal project

In the context of European integration, the rising power of neo-liberal ideology became first of all manifest in the 'Euro-sclerosis' discourse according to which the stagflation of the European economy was the result of 'institutional rigidities'. These, it was claimed, were engendered by 'excessive' government intervention, 'too powerful' trade unions and an 'overburdened' welfare state, among other things, that all hindered the efficient allocation of resources through the market mechanism, thus impeding necessary adjustments to the changing global environment.

In the neo-liberal conception of European integration, then, the process should be restricted to negative integration, resulting in more market and less state at all levels of governance. The benefits of the Internal Market project were thus seen as principally deriving from the freer market it would create, emphasising its deregulatory effects and expected efficiency gains. In the neo-liberal view, European integration should subordinate Europe's socio-economic and industrial space to what are seen as the beneficial forces of globalisation: Europe as an advanced free trade zone within a free trading world.

It was, however, only at the end of the 1980s and the beginning of the 1990s that neo-liberal adjustment really started to become a reality in continental Europe, moving beyond right-wing rhetoric. Indeed, as this analysis intends to show, neo-liberalism was not the only ideological force playing a role in Europe's relaunch.

The neo-mercantilist project

The world economic crisis also gave rise to a different discourse on Europe's alleged decline and how to reverse it. Whereas the neo-liberal ideology was primarily propagated by social forces bound up with global financial capital and industrial TNCs with a truly global reach, most of continental Europe was still dominated by firms that, although maybe no longer domestic, had yet to develop into 'global players'. The crisis of international Fordism, in the context of a deepening transnationalisation of production, provoked a global restructuring race – with the rise of Japan further intensifying global competition – that had profound impacts upon European industry (Van Tulder and Junne, 1988). These former national champions and 'would-be European champions' therefore perceived the forces of globalisation more as a threat to their market shares and competitive position than as an opportunity to force a structural transformation of Europe's 'sclerotic' socio-economic system. Within this perspective, the loss of international competitiveness was blamed less on labour market rigidity, trade union power or the welfare state, and more on the fragmentation of the European market, the (resulting) insufficient economies of scale and the perceived technology gap *vis-à-vis* the USA and Japan.

It was thus these forces that came to promote the creation of a European home market as the centre-piece of their strategy for a relaunching of Europe. As Grahl and Teague note, in the neo-mercantilist interpretation of the Internal Market project, 'national rivalries and the fragmentation of Community market, have ... deprived European companies of a key element in competitive success, which the 1992 programme will correct' (Grahl and Teague, 1990: 172). A strong European home market was expected to serve as both a stepping-stone to conquer the world market as well as a protective shield against outside competition. The neo-mercantilist project thus constituted a defensive regionalisation strategy oriented towards the creation of a strong regional economy, not only through the completion of the Internal Market, but also through an industrial policy aimed at the promotion of 'European champions', if necessary protected by European tariff walls (Pearce and Sutton, 1986).

The social democratic project

The social democratic project for Europe's socio-economic order developed within the context of the initial success of the Internal Market programme as pro-European social democrats came to see European federalism as the answer to the dilemmas of the European left in the era of globalisation. As a concrete political strategy, this project was first and foremost formulated and pursued by Jacques Delors and his entourage during Delors's presidency of the European Commission (for a detailed account of the 'Delorist' strategy see Ross, 1995). For Delors, as for other social democrats, a united Europe offered an opportunity to protect the 'European model of society', and its traditions of the mixed economy and high levels of social protection, against the potentially destructive forces of globalisation and neo-liberalism (on this see, e.g., Delors, 1992; Grant, 1994: 86–7; Ross, 1995: 15, and *passim*). Delors had accepted the creation of a competitive home market (and the market liberalisation that went with it) as both an economic and political *sine qua non* for a successful relaunching of the European integration process but, at the same time, he warned the neo-liberals that 'the Community is not and will not be, a free trade zone. It is up to us to make a *European organised space*' (Delors in Krause, 1991). As George Ross notes, it was 'for this reason [that] the backbone of Delors's strategy was to promote state-building programs on the back of market-building successes' (Ross, 1995: 109).

Transnational class formation within the European arena

As indicated, all three projects – including the social-democratic one – developed within a transnational setting. It is particularly the process of transnational class formation, as engendered by the transnationalisation of global capitalism, that is the key to understanding such a setting. Processes of class formation must always be located within concrete historical and institutional contexts. One can argue that the EU provides one such context: a political arena in which an emergent transnational capitalist class – consisting of the top managers and owners of Europe's largest TNCs – takes the European region as its primary frame of reference and organises itself to influence the (socio-economic) governance of that region. The organised power of this transnational capitalist class within the European arena contrasts starkly with that of European labour, which remains fragmented and weak (see, e.g., Streeck and Schmitter, 1991), and certainly does not constitute a transnational class as such.

A basic divide that has structured this European process of transnational class formation as it evolved in the 1980s has been the division within European capital between that part already integrated into global production networks, operating on the world market and having a concomitant 'globalist' outlook, and that part which was still much more exclusively oriented towards, and dependent upon, the European 'home market', thus adopting a more European 'regionalist' perspective. This has engendered the tendential formation of two rival fractions within Europe's emerging transnational capitalist elite. These are here denoted, first, as a 'globalist' fraction, deriving from the most mobile and most globalised parts of transnational capital, i.e., global financial institutions and other (industrial) 'global players'; and second, as a 'Europeanist' fraction consisting of those who control large industrial enterprises which, although operating on a transnational scale, nevertheless primarily serve the European market, competing against the often cheaper imports from outside Europe (in particular East Asia).[5] As demonstrated below, the perspective of the former fraction has tended towards neo-liberalism, whereas the latter came to promote the neo-mercantilist project. It is maintained here that in the 1980s the opposition between neo-liberalism and neo-mercantilism was the central axis around which the ideological struggles within the emerging transnational European capitalist class revolved. The outcome of this struggle, in interaction with the so-called social democratic project, has been critical in shaping the emergent European socioeconomic order.

This struggle will be analysed by examining the case of the European Round Table of Industrialists (ERT), one of the leading bodies within the organisational network of the European capitalist class, and at the same time a prime organisation through which that transnational capitalist class has formed. Founded in 1983 by a group of 17 major European industrialists, the ERT today consists of around 45 chief executive officers (CEOs) and chairmen leading Europe's biggest and most transnational industrial corporations. The membership of the ERT is personal (rather than corporate) but the fact that its members together control a large part of European transnational capital – a majority of the members' companies are Fortune 500 firms[6] and about half are amongst the 100 biggest TNCs in the world (UNCTAD, 1997) – of course contributes to explaining the large political influence that this group of people can command.[7] Generally recognised as 'the single most powerful business group in Europe' (Gardner, 1991: 47–8), the ERT is in particular credited with bringing the completion of the Internal Market back on to the European agenda. It thus represents one of the driving forces behind Europe's relaunching (see especially van Apeldoorn, 2000; Cowles, 1994, 1995; Holman, 1992).

The ERT can be viewed as an elite organisation of Europe's emergent transnational capitalist class in which – transcending the more conventional forms of corporate lobbying in the EU – the interests of that class (fraction) are organised, shaped and synthesised into a comprehensive strategy. Yet, while effectively representing the perceived material interests of European big business, the ERT ideologically transcends those interests as well by appealing to a wider set of interests and identities (for a more elaborate account, see van Apeldoorn, 2000). In contradistinction to the Union of Industrial and Employers' Confederations of Europe (UNICE, the EU's official employers' organisation which represents a more 'corporatist' class interest, defending the vested interests of the European employers' class), the ERT, as a private club of transnational capitalists, seeks to elevate its class strategy towards a higher, more universal level: that is, to the 'universal plane' of hegemony. The role of the ERT must thus be seen as operating primarily at the level of ideas and ideology formation. It is at this level that the ERT has been an important actor in the struggle over the socio-economic content of the relaunched European integration process.

Transnational Struggle over European Order: From Europe 1992 to Maastricht

The rivalry between the neo-liberal and the neo-mercantilist concepts of a relaunching of European integration was also manifest within the ranks of the ERT, in turn reflecting what constituted the central axis of intra-capitalist struggle in the Europe of the 1980s. After an early walk-out of three 'globalist' members (the British CEOs of Unilever, Shell, and ICI), the ERT became dominated by representatives of the Europeanist fraction. Thus its strategic orientation in the 1980s tended towards what one could call a protective regionalism, at the heart of which was the promotion of a big European home market, in which Europe's regional TNCs could grow to resist and challenge the rising global competition. Premised, albeit ambivalently, on a neo-mercantilist project for European order, this strategy included the advocacy of a European industrial policy – centred around European technology programmes and infrastructure projects – focused on the nurturing of European champions as well as a limited form of protectionism at the European level. The Internal Market was thus seen by a majority of the early ERT members in neo-mercantilist terms as the creation of a big home market that would enable European industry to reach 'the scale necessary to resist pressure from non-European competitors' (ERT, 1983).

The ERT's campaign for a European home market has indeed significantly contributed to, and was probably critical for, the successful relaunching of the integration process through Europe 1992. Yet the Internal Market that was created on the basis of the Commission's White Paper did not turn out to be the kind of home market that many of the early ERT members (of the Europeanist fraction) had envisaged in several respects: namely, a relatively protected home market in which Euro-champions could prosper in order to confront global competition. The latter turned out to be an illusion as most initiatives for a European industrial policy failed, in the end, to take off. The more straightforwardly protectionist measures met resistance from (neo-)liberal governments (e.g., Germany, the UK, and the Netherlands) which reflected in part the dominance of the globalist fraction of European capital in those countries. Although sectors of European industry – cars and electronics – lobbied hard for protectionist measures and had their demands partially met, these limited protectionist policies (such as anti-dumping duties and import quotas) were gradually ended and external trade liberalisation in the EU has progressed steadily ever since (Hanson, 1998). Therefore, as the internal barriers came down, no external barriers were erected and the Internal Market provided as much opportunity for US and Japanese as for European firms (Wyatt-Walter, 1998). Hence, the regionalisation of the European economy, in the sense of the further integration of its national economic systems, went hand in hand with a further globalisation of the European region.

In the transnational struggle over Europe's relaunching, neo-liberal social forces, strengthened by the on-going and deepening globalisation process, were gaining the upper hand over those that had favoured a neo-mercantilist interpretation of the Internal Market programme. This struggle had also been fought out within the ranks of Europe's transnational capitalist class in which the Europeanist fraction was slowly losing its dominant position and, moreover, gradually abandoning its own earlier neo-mercantilist perspective. This neo-liberal shift on the part of Europe's capitalist elite was also reflected in the changing strategic orientation of the ERT at the end of the 1980s and into the 1990s, when its membership witnessed a significant change in the balance of power between the globalist and Europeanist 'fractions'. From 1988 onwards, one can witness a change in the composition of ERT's membership that made the globalists the dominant group within the ERT. Not only did many globalist companies, such as Shell, Unilever, ICI, BP, La Roche, BT and Bayer, (re-)join the ERT, but older ERT companies, formerly producing primarily for the European market and competing against non-European imports, became more global themselves (see van Apeldoorn, 1999: ch. 6). This globalisation of European industry took place within the context of intensifying global competition, as well as the political failure of the neo-mercantilist project, in the light of which neo-liberalism gained appeal as an alternative strategy.

These structural changes enabled (but did not determine) a transcendence of the earlier opposition between Europeanists and globalists. The shift in the ideological and strategic orientation of the ERT – and of Europe's transnational bourgeoisie more widely – did not, however, come about without internal struggles. Indeed, in the final analysis it was through these struggles that this shift was achieved. The expansion of membership that had swelled the ranks of the neo-liberal globalists initially brought about a renewed opposition between the two camps, in which conflicts about trade policy occupied once more a central place. According to one representative of ERT's globalist fraction at that time, the (then) chairman of Unilever, Floris Maljers, the 'struggle between liberals and protectionists' became a constant feature of the internal policy debates at the end of the 1980s and beginning of the 1990s.[8] Rather than leading to a break-up of the ERT, this internal strife was in fact a (probably necessary) phase that preceded the emergence of a new consensus. In 1991 – when the ERT in the context of the Maastricht negotiations published its report, *Reshaping Europe* (ERT, 1991) – this new consensus still had the form of a rather unstable compromise between the two competing perspectives of protective regionalism and neo-liberal globalism; yet this compromise was later to develop into a new synthesis reflecting the dominance of the neo-liberal perspective (see below).

With regard to the Maastricht Treaty, which set the EU on course for Economic and Monetary Union (EMU), the ERT did not play the same initiating role as it did with regard to the Internal Market programme. When one analyses the (socio-economic) *content* of Maastricht, however, one encounters several of the ideas that the ERT, or at least part of the ERT membership, had been pushing for years, in particular ideas related to monetary union as a necessary complement to the Internal Market,[9] as well as an enhanced European role in infrastructure and research and technology (for further details, see van Apeldoorn, 2000).

The socio-economic content of Maastricht can in fact be interpreted as reflecting the transnational configuration of social and political forces within the European political economy at the beginning of the 1990s. The ERT here represented important sections of the ruling elite within that configuration and as such was one important forum from which that elite could shape the debates that at the ideological level conditioned the political bargaining process. However, trans-national social-democratic forces, which under the leadership of Delors temporarily gained momentum around the end of the 1980s, also played a significant role in this respect. Next to the social chapter, EMU in fact became an equally important centre-piece of the social democratic project. It was seen as serving the double function of regaining some democratic control over the global financial markets (Holland, 1995: 12), as well as paving the way to a (federal) political union that could then further advance the cause of 'organising European space'. The social democratic interpretation of Maastricht has, however, largely failed to materialise. The social chapter has not gone much beyond mere symbolic politics (even if such symbols do matter), thanks in large part to the lobbying efforts of big business (Rhodes, 1992; Streeck 1995a). Political union has for all intents and purposes been indefinitely postponed, and the Treaty of Amsterdam of 1997 notably failed to deliver on this score. Also, the hope that EMU might restore democratic control over policy making continues to be contradicted by the reality of a monetarist consensus among the European elite. This is expressed, in addition to the stability pact, by the ability of monetarist elites to rebut the challenge posed by a powerful figure such as the former German finance minister, Oskar Lafontaine (on EMU, see [Gill, 2001]; on the challenge by Lafontaine, see [van der Pijl, 2001]).

Maastricht was not a triumph for Thatcherite neo-liberalism, or for the social-democratic vision, or even, for that matter, for the neo-mercantilist strategy. In fact, it contained elements of all three rival projects, even though it was biased in favour of the neo-liberal project due to the neo-liberal orthodoxy underpinning EMU. At the same time, however, chapters on 'Trans-European [infrastructure] Networks' and 'Research and Technological Development' did provide a basis for some form of European industrial policy or *Ordnungspolitik*, clearly more in tune with the German model of Rhineland capitalism (Albert, 1993) rather than the (UK) neo-liberal model. These policies did not amount to a neo-mercantilist strategy, but they did speak to the interests of that part of European industry that – in its dependence on a strong European home base – had propagated a more mercantilist conception of the European project in the past. Finally, the albeit rather weak 'social chapter' nevertheless succeeded in incorporating European social democracy and the trade unions into the 'New Europe' (for the reasons behind, in particular, export-oriented unions' support of the Internal Market and EMU, see [Bieling, 2001; Bieler and Torjesen, 2001]).

The Emergent New European Order: 'Embedded Neo-Liberalism'

The Maastricht compromise reflects the gradual rise of what can be termed an 'embedded neo-liberal' synthesis that also points to the social purpose underpinning the emergent European order. Embedded neo-liberalism is neo-liberal inasmuch as it emphasises the primacy of global market forces and the freedom of transnational capital. Yet, as a result of such processes, markets become increasingly *disconnected* from their post-war national social institutions. Embedded neo-liberalism is thus 'embedded' to the extent that it recognises the limits to *laissez-faire*, and thus to the disembedding process, and accepts that certain compromises need to be made; hence at least a limited form of 'embeddedness' is preserved.[10] This means that within most European countries the dismantling of the welfare state has so far been limited, and that established corporatist institutions have not been abolished but rather – as in the case of the celebrated Dutch model – maintained and strengthened to implement neo-liberal labour market reform while maintaining social consensus (cf. Rhodes, 1997; see also [Bieling, 2001]). Such a reformulation of the original neo-liberal project, which had been developed in the Anglo-Saxon heartland, was necessary within the (continental) European context for a number of reasons. For instance, the neo-liberal offensive had to overcome the resistance of the institutionalised traditions of corporatist class relations, the social and industrial protection offered by an often interventionist state, and other elements of 'embeddedness' in a context within which rival social democratic and neo-mercantilist projects had developed.

On the one hand, then, one may interpret embedded neo-liberalism as the outcome of the transnational struggle between the three contending projects of neo-liberalism, neo-mercantilism and supranational social democracy. This was a struggle in which the neo-liberal project became dominant but still had to accommodate the concerns of both the former neo-mercantilists and of the social democrats that promoted a social dimension to the new European market. The neo-liberal project incorporated these rival concerns in such a way that they were ultimately subordinated to the interests of globalising capital (on the neglect of social democratic concerns in this compromise, see also [Bieling, 2001]). On the other hand, though, embedded neo-liberalism can also be interpreted as the emerging hegemonic project of Europe's transnational capitalist class. It is this class that has become dominated by the leadership of a globalist fraction both in terms of financial firms and global industrial TNCs.

It is in particular within global *industrial* capital that one can observe the dialectical conflict – captured so brilliantly in Polanyi's classic analysis (Polanyi, 1957) – between, on the one hand, the drive of capital for market liberalisation and, on the other hand, a recognition of the need for social protection. Pure *laissez-faire* policies would only harm the interests of this capital fraction as it still needs the state to educate the workforce, to provide infrastructure, to pursue macroeconomic policies that favour growth and investment, or to maintain social and political stability; in short, to sustain both economic and political hegemony.[11] At the same time that globalising capital seeks to detach itself from the constraints imposed by (national) institutions, it is also 'aware' that it cannot in fact become fully 'footloose' in this sense, and continues to need supporting institutions itself.

In sum, embedded neo-liberalism is here interpreted as a potentially hegemonic project unifying Europe's transnational capitalist class and expressing its collective interests, while at the same time appealing to a wider set of interests and identities. As such it is also reflected in the discourse and strategy of the ERT as it continued to play an important role in the evolving regime of European socio-economic governance into the 1990s.

Transnational class strategy and European governance in the 1990s

The post-Maastricht period witnessed the further consolidation of ERT's neo-liberal shift, reflecting a general re-orientation of the European transnational bourgeoisie, of which now both the (former) globalist and Europeanist fractions were united within the ERT's ranks. Whereas, in the early 1980s, the response to the world economic crisis (and the concomitant global restructuring race) was still defensive, and indeed protectionist, the deep recession of the early 1990s (which also saw the temporary return of 'Euro-pessimism') met with a rather unambiguous call for further neo-liberal restructuring. This means deregulation, labour market flexibility, 'downsizing' the public sector and an unequivocal commitment to global free trade (see ERT, 1993a, 1993b, 1994).

With regard to ERT's strengthened free trade orientation, the crucial battle was probably that over the conclusion of the Uruguay Round of the General Agreement on Tariffs and Trade (GATT) talks (in December 1993). This was because free traders within the ERT established a position of leadership and persuaded the French members to take a stance against the wavering position of their own government.[12] In retrospect, the Uruguay Round and the subsequent founding of the World Trade Organisation (WTO) signalled the 'final' defeat of the Euro-protectionists, both within the ERT and the European corporate elite more widely.[13] The post-Maastricht period also witnessed a strengthening of the consensus in favour of monetary union. This was not only because the crises of the European Monetary System (EMS) of 1992 and 1993 showed that only a single currency could provide European business with sufficient stability, but also because the convergence criteria were increasingly showing their 'salutary' disciplinary effects.[14]

Yet, just as ERT's original 'Europeanist' orientation was never unequivocally neo-mercantilist (although some members came close to this ideal type), the ideological outlook of ERT capitalists in the 1990s is not one of orthodox neo-liberalism either. Indeed, it rather reflects the potentially hegemonic synthesis of embedded neo-liberalism. Within ERT's own discourse, the limits of its neo-liberalism become most apparent with regard to the field of industrial policy broadly conceived. Within a pure neo-liberal model, the only legitimate industrial policy is the policing of the free market by competition policy. Whereas such a perspective may suit the interests of transnational financial capital, industrial capital, even its most transnationally mobile fraction, needs the state to go beyond this passive role, in an attempt to actively seek and secure the 'conditions for competitiveness' (ERT, 1993a). Hence, rather than the British neo-liberal model, it was the liberal German alternative of an active *Ordnungspolitik* that became the preferred concept around which all fractions could rally.[15]

The embeddedness of ERT's neo-liberalism also transpires from its attitude towards European social policies, and in particular from those that came out of the so-called social chapter of Maastricht. Although the ERT at the time waged war on the social chapter, it was also recognised by (at least part of) the ERT that, given the balance of social and political forces at that time, its inclusion (albeit as an 'appendix') was inevitable. Hence acceptance of the social chapter was possible given the extent to which it had been watered down. Most ERT members remain keenly aware of the need for social consensus by rejecting the neo-liberal (confrontational) mode of labour relations (characteristic of, say, British industrial relations), and emphasising that some degree of basic social harmony is indispensable for European industry to prosper (see ERT, 1993b: 9). Although transnational capital will of course remain categorically opposed to any form of European collective bargaining, it has not refused to participate in the 'neo-voluntarist' (Streeck, 1995b) European Social Dialogue. This was another initiative that was started under Delors and represented a form of 'social partnership' that fits well within the embedded neo-liberal model.

Still, the 'embeddedness' of ERT's neo-liberalism remains thin in this respect and seems to be primarily geared towards the creation of the 'conditions for competitiveness', and thus to serve the interests of transnational and globalising capital, rather than to protect subordinate social groups and classes. Indeed, the ERT bluntly states that the burden of 'adjustment' will have to be carried by labour. In the ERT's own words, 'a very large amount of the effort to adjust European labour markets will rely on labour' (ERT, 1993b: 16). The ERT is well aware that this 'adjustment' – which is offered as the only way to restore growth and employment –

implies a fundamental restructuring of state–society relations and that this in turn calls for the construction of a new hegemonic project capable of producing consent across social classes (and class fractions):

> Enabling Europe to return to high employment growth requires more than replacing policy instruments, it calls for a change of our economic and social structures. But governments are only able to change structures when there is a *new social consensus*, i.e. the convergence on principles and, ultimately, agreement on the goals for that change among the social partners, governments, the opinion leaders and ultimately, the population ... We need a consensus on the European level that *only a healthy, efficient and competitive private sector is able to provide sufficient jobs, and that markets should be left to allocate labour efficiently.* (ERT, 1993b: 9; original emphasis)

In creating this new consensus, a key role is played by the concept of *competitiveness*. Appealing equally to neo-liberals, neo-mercantilists and social-democrats, this concept enables the articulation of a predominantly neo-liberal ideology with elements of the alternative ideological discourses of the social democratic and neo-mercantilist projects in such a way that their opposition is neutralised. Hence the construction of hegemony.

Competitiveness, like globalisation, has become a key word in European socio-economic discourse. From the Delors White Paper on 'Growth, Competitiveness and Employment' (European Commission, 1994) onwards, it has become the unofficial key policy objective of the EU. In 1995 – following an initiative by the ERT – a Competitiveness Advisory Group (CAG) was set up by the Commission, which since then has been 'keeping competitiveness in the forefront of the policy debates' (ERT, 1993a: 27). Crucially, as transpires from both ERT and Commission publications, the meaning of the concept of competitiveness has now, first of all, come to be bound up with the (albeit embedded) neo-liberal project. This constitutes a break with the past in which the concept had tended to be defined more in neo-mercantilist terms, as in the case of the ERT, or in more social-democratic terms (i.e., mixed with Keynesian and other 'progressive' elements), as in the case of the (Delors) Commission.

As an operationalisation of this new competitiveness ideology, the ERT has, in tandem with the CAG, started to promote the concept of 'benchmarking' *vis-à-vis* the Commission and the member states. Bench-marking means not only 'measuring the performance' of individual firms, or sectors, but also that of nations against the other 'best competitors' in the world (ERT, 1994: 4). In its report, *Benchmarking for Policy-Makers*, the ERT is very explicit about how policy-makers should 'measure' competitiveness. The country or (macro-)region that is most competitive is the country that is most successful in attracting mobile capital: 'Governments must recognise today that every economic and social system in the world is competing with all the others to attract the footloose businesses' (ERT, 1996: 15).

Competitiveness and benchmarking have also become the key concepts within the public (socio-economic) policy discourse of the EU. Analysing the policy documents of the Commission one can also see how these concepts are mobilised to promote a programme of neo-liberal restructuring, aimed at removing, in the words of the Director-General for Industry, the still remaining 'rigidities and distortions ... that prevent Europe from fully exploiting its potential' (European

Commission, 1997b: 5). Invoking the inevitability of globalisation, and 'hence' the need for adaptation, the Commission defines benchmarking as a tool for improving competitiveness and 'for promoting the convergence towards best practice' (European Commission, 1996: 16). This involves the global 'comparison of societal behaviour, commercial practice, market structure and public institutions' (European Commission, 1997a: 3). The 'High Level Group on Benchmarking' – chaired by a board member of Investor, the investment company controlling the global Wallenberg empire – reinforces this stance. As it makes clear in its first report, the object of all these 'comparisons' is to promote rapid 'structural reforms' that will allow Europe to adapt to the exigencies of globalisation: 'this involves further liberalisation, privatisation, . . . more flexible labour laws, lower government subsidies, etc.' (High Level Group on Benchmarking, 1999: 13). Inasmuch as this neo-liberal restructuring programme will be successfully implemented, the contradictions of embedded neo-liberalism will of course become more acute.

Conclusion

This chapter has analysed transnational social forces in the making of what has been interpreted as an 'embedded neo-liberal' European order. Embedded neo-liberalism was interpreted as the outcome of the transnational struggle between the three rival projects of neo-liberalism, neo-mercantilism and social democracy. The 'embedded' component of embedded neo-liberalism addresses the concerns of both the former neo-mercantilists as well as those of the European labour movement and social-democratic political forces. But this incorporation is done in such a way that these concerns are, in the end, subordinated to the overriding objective of neo-liberal competitiveness. As Gramsci has put it (1971: 182), 'the development and expansion of the particular group are conceived of, and presented, as being the motor force of a universal expansion, of a development of all the "national" energies'. Indeed, the 'universal expansion' of neo-liberal competitiveness increasingly seems to be formulated as the primary goal of European socio-economic governance whilst intertwined with the development of ' "national" energies'. This is apparent, first of all, in the competitiveness discourse that is now underpinning the Commission's strategy with regard to industrial policy and macroeconomic management. Second, it transpires from the relative failure of the social dimension. Third, it follows from the way the EU has fully committed itself to global free trade. Finally, it is apparent from the neo-liberal character of the EMU, at the heart of the current integration project.

The European socio-economic order that is being constructed thus subordinates the European region to the exigencies of the global economy and global competition, and hence to the interests of global transnational capital. Under the banner of 'competitiveness', the EU pursues the, by now, familiar neo-liberal policies of budget austerity, deregulation ('freeing' the market), and 'flexibilisation' of the labour market. These are pursued even whilst also seeking to preserve the social consensus model that is still prevalent in most European countries. The limited elements of 'embeddedness' that one may discern in, for instance, the discourse of the ERT, as well as within that of the Commission and within similar elite discourses (such as that of the 'Third Way'), thus seem to be primarily oriented towards the interests of globalising transnational capital. The question remains, then, to what extent the social purpose of the emergent European order may yet be constructed on a different normative basis from that contained in the idea that the ultimate 'benchmark' for the 'performance' of a society is its ability to accumulate wealth in private hands.

NOTES

1 This chapter draws in part on an earlier and longer version, see van Apeldoorn (1998).
2 Here I borrow the words of John Ruggie (1982) in his critique of the international regimes literature. Form and content are of course interrelated, but in this chapter I will focus on the latter.
3 For a much more extensive development of this approach, see van Apeldoorn (1999: ch. 1). Also see [Bieler, 2001] for a more elaborate discussion of the limitations of conventional integration theories and how a neo-Gramscian perspective might provide an alternative. The neo-Gramscian perspectives developed, for example, by Overbeek (1993) or van der Pijl (1998) most closely inspire my own approach to European integration.
4 A historical materialist perspective on global politics is defined by Robert Cox as 'examin[ing] the connections between power in production, power in the state, and power in international relations' (Cox, 1981: 135). To be sure, it is not suggested here that 'the social' is exhausted by 'social relations of production'. However, in my view, the latter are primary in the production and distribution of wealth and thus central to both the constitution of forms of social power and the question of socio-economic content that concerns me in this chapter.
5 This division of European capital has been partly inspired by a similar one developed by Holman (1992).
6 *Fortune*'s 1998 Global 500; see http://cgi.pathfinder.com/fortune/global500. For a list of current ERT members (as well as other up-to-date information on the ERT), see the ERT website: http://www.ert.be.
7 Commenting upon this, former EU Commissioner (for competition), Peter Sutherland, stated that because membership 'is at head of company level, and only the biggest companies in each country of the European Union are members of it ... by definition each member of the ERT has access at the highest level to government' (telephone interview, 27 January 1998).
8 Interview with Floris Maljers, by Otto Holman and author, Rotterdam, 3 September 1993.
9 Although the ERT in its 1991 report did call for a single currency and a 'clear and unambiguous timetable to achieve this goal' (ERT, 1991: 46), it largely left the lobbying for monetary union to a big business forum especially set up for that purpose (in 1987), the Association for Monetary Union in Europe (AMUE).
10 'Embeddedness', then, does not denote a re-embedding in the sense of Polanyi's (1957) 'double movement' (in which 'society and politics' re-assert their control over the market). It must rather be seen as anticipating and preventing (we speak mainly about effects here, and only in a very limited sense about intentions) such a societal backlash.
11 Of course, this applies to capital in general as well, but, ideally speaking, productive capital is closer to the moment of the accumulation process with which these functional

needs are bound up than financial capital. Abstractly, productive capital is more concerned with the principle of social protection than financial capital, and national capital
is more so than transnationally-mobile 'global' capital (cf. van der Pijl 1984, 1998).

12 Interview (by Otto Holman and author) with former ERT Vice-Chairman Floris Mal-
    jers, Rotterdam, 3 September 1993.
13 At least this was the perception of former ERT Vice-Chairman, David Simon (interview,
    London, 12 September 1996).
14 Interview with former ERT Vice Chairman, André Leysen, Antwerp, 21 May 1996.
15 Interviews.

REFERENCES

Albert, M. 1993: *Capitalism vs. Capitalism*, London: Whurr Books.
van Apeldoorn, B. 1998: 'Transnationalism and the Restructuring of Europe's Socio-
    Economic Order', *International Journal of Political Economy*, 28 (1), 12–53.
van Apeldoorn, B. 1999: 'Transnational class agency and the Struggle over European Order',
    Unpublished Ph.D. thesis, European University Institute.
van Apeldoorn, B. 2000: 'Transnational Class Agency and European Governance: The Case
    of the European Round Table of Industrialists', *New Political Economy*, 5 (2), 157–81.
Bieler, A. and Morton, A. D. 2001: 'Introduction: Neo-Gramscian Perspectives in Inter-
    national Political Economy and the Relevance to European Integration', in A. Bieler and
    A. D. Morton, eds, *Social Forces in the Making of the New Europe: The Restructuring of
    European Social Relations in the Global Political Economy*, Basingstoke: Palgrave, 3–24.
Bieler, A. and Torjesen, S. 2001: 'Strength through Unity? A Comparative Analysis of Splits in
    the Austrian, Norwegian and Swedish Labour Movements over EU Membership', in
    A. Bieler and A. D. Morton, eds, *Social Forces in the Making of the New Europe: The Restructur-
    ing of European Social Relations in the Global Political Economy*, Basingstoke: Palgrave, 115–36.
Bieling, H.-J. 2001: 'European Constitutionalism and Industrial Relations', in A. Bieler and
    A. D. Morton, eds, *Social Forces in the Making of New Europe: The Restructuring of European
    Social Relations in the Global Political Economy*, Basingstoke: Palgrave, 93–114.
Cowles, M. G. 1994: 'The Politics of Big Business in the European Community: Setting the
    Agenda for the New Europe', Unpublished Ph.D. thesis, The American University.
Cowles, M. G. 1995: 'Setting the Agenda for a New Europe: The ERT and EC 1992',
    Journal of Common Market Studies, 33 (4), 501–26.
Cox, R. W. 1981: 'Social Forces, States and World Order: Beyond International Relations
    Theory', *Millennium*, 102 (2), 126–55.
Delors, J. 1992: *Our Europe*, London: Verso.
European Commission 1994: *Growth, Competitiveness, Employment: The Challenges and Ways
    Forward into the 21st Century. White Paper*, Luxemburg: Office for Official Publications of
    the European Communities.
European Commission 1996: *Benchmarking the Competitiveness of European Industry*, Brussels:
    Com (96) 436 Final, 9 October.
European Commission 1997a: *Benchmarking: Implementation of an Instrument Available to
    Economic Actors and Public Authorities*, Brussels: Com (97) 153 (2), 16 April.
European Commission 1997b: *The Competitiveness of European Industry*, Luxemburg: Office
    for Official Publications of the European Communities.
European Round Table of Industrialists 1983: 'Foundation for the Future of European
    Industry' (Memorandum to EC Commissioner Davignon) (Mimeo).

European Round Table of Industrialists 1991: *Reshaping Europe: A Report from the European Round Table of Industrialists*, Brussels: European Round Table of Industrialists.

European Round Table of Industrialists 1993a: *Beating the Crisis: A Charter for Europe's Industrial Future*, Brussels: European Round Table of Industrialists.

European Round Table of Industrialists 1993b: *European Labour Markets: An Update on Perspectives and Requirements for Job Generation in the Second Half of the 1990s*, Brussels: European Round Table of Industrialists.

European Round Table of Industrialists 1994: *European Competitiveness: The Way to Growth and Jobs*, Brussels: European Round Table of Industrialists.

European Round Table of Industrialists 1996: *Benchmarking for Policy-Makers: The Way to Competitiveness*, Brussels: European Round Table of Industrialists.

Gardner, J. N. 1991: *Effective Lobbying in the European Community*, Deventer: Kluwer.

[Gill, S. 2001: 'Constitutionalising Capital: EMU and Disciplinary Neo-Liberalism', in A. Bieler and A. D. Morton, eds, *Social Forces in the Making of New Europe: The Restructuring of European Social Relations in the Global Political Economy*, Basingstoke: Palgrave, 47–69.]

Gill, S. and Law, D. 1993: *The Global Political Economy: Perspectives, Problems and Policies*, Brighton: Wheatsheaf.

Grahl, J. and Teague, P. 1990: *The Big Market: The Future of the European Community*, London: Lawrence & Wishart.

Gramsci, A. 1971: *Selections from the Prison Notebooks*, London: Lawrence & Wishart.

Grant, C. 1994: *Delors: Inside the House that Jacques Built*, London: Nicholas Brearley.

Haas, E. B. 1958: *The Uniting of Europe: Political, Social, and Economic Forces 1950–1957*, Stanford, CA: Stanford University Press.

Hanson, B. 1998: 'What Happened to Fortress Europe? External Trade Policy Liberalisation in the European Union', *International Organisation*, 52 (1), 55–85.

High Level Group on Benchmarking 1999: 'First Report by the High Level Group on Benchmarking Paper', 2, European Commission, Directorate General III.

Holland, S. 1995: 'Squaring the Circle', *European Labour Forum* (summer), 15, 12–23.

Holman, O. 1992: 'Transnational Class Strategy and the New Europe', *International Journal of Political Economy*, 22 (1), 3–22.

Krause, A. 1991: *Inside the New Europe*, New York: HarperCollins.

Moravcsik, A. 1991: 'Negotiating the Single European Act', in R. O. Keohane and S. Hoffman, eds, *The New European Community: Decision-Making and Institutional Change*, Boulder, CO: Westview Press.

Moravcsik, A. 1998: *The Choice for Europe: Social Purpose and State Power from Messina to Maastricht*, Ithaca, NY: Cornell University Press.

Overbeek, H. (ed.) 1993: *Restructuring Hegemony in the Global Political Economy: The Rise of Transnational Liberalism in the 1980s*, London: Routledge.

Pearce, J. and Sutton, J. 1986: *Protection and Industrial Policy in Europe*, London: Routledge.

van der Pijl, K. 1984: *The Making of the Atlantic Ruling Class*, London: Verso.

van der Pijl, K. 1998: 'America over Europe: Atlantic Unity and Rivalry from Gorbachov to Kosovo', paper prepared for the 24th Annual British International Studies Association Conference, 20–2 December (UMIST/Manchester).

[van der Pijl, K. 2001: 'What Happened to the European Option for Eastern Europe?', in A. Bieler and A. D. Morton, eds, *Social Forces in the Making of New Europe: The Restructuring of European Social Relations in the Global Political Economy*, Basingstoke: Palgrave, 185–204.]

Polanyi, K. 1957: *The Great Transformation: The Political and Economic Origins of Our Time*, Boston, MA: Beacon.

Rhodes, M. 1992: 'The Future of the "Social Dimension": Labour Market Regulation in Post-1992 Europe', *Journal of Common Market Studies*, 30 (1), 23–51.

Rhodes, M. 1997: 'Globalisation, Labour Markets and Welfare States: A Future of Competitive Corporatism?', *EUI Working Papers, Robert Schumann Centre*, 97 (36).

Ross, G. 1995: *Jacques Delors and European Integration*, Cambridge: Polity Press.

Ruggie, J. 1982: 'Territoriality and Beyond: Problematising Modernity in International Relations', *International Organisation*, 36 (2), 379–416.

Sandholtz, W. and Stone Sweet, A. (eds) 1998: *European Integration and Supranational Governance*, Oxford: Oxford University Press.

Sandholtz, W. and Zysman, J. 1989: '1992: Recasting the European Bargain', *World Politics*, 17 (1), 95–128.

Streeck, W. 1995a: 'From Market-Making to State Building? Reflections on the Political Economy of European Social Policy', in S. Leibfried and P. Pierson, eds, *European Social Policy: Between Fragmentation and Integration*, Washington, DC: Brookings Institution, 389–431.

Streeck, W. 1995b: 'Neo-Voluntarism: A New European Social Policy Regime?', *European Law Journal*, 1 (1), 31–59.

Streeck, W. and Schmitter, P. C. 1991: 'From National Corporatism to Transnational Pluralism: Organized Interests in the Single European Market', *Politics and Society*, 19 (2), 133–64.

Van Tulder, R. and Junne, G. 1988: *European Multinationals in Core Technologies*, New York: Wiley.

UNCTAD 1997: *World Investment Report 1997: Transnational Corporations, Market Structure and Competition Policy*, Geneva: United Nations.

Wyatt-Walter, A. 1998: 'Globalisation, Corporate Identity and European Technology Policy', in W. D. Coleman and G. R. D. Underhill, eds, *Regionalism and Global Economic Integration: Europe, Asia and the Americas*, London: Routledge.

9

The Imagined Economy: Mapping Transformations in the Contemporary State

Angus Cameron and Ronen Palan

Ever since the publication of Michel Foucault's *Les Mots et les Choses* and Thomas Kuhn's *Structure of Scientific Revolutions*, the idea of large scale, systemic, and 'epistemic' transformation has become a central tenet of late twentieth century thought.[1] Claims for such diverse processes as globalisation, postmodernism, the 'information revolution', and so on, all carry the central message that rapid transformations in the structures of social life are intricately bound up with our knowledge about those changes.

Geographers, sociologists, and political economists of various hues and traditions have been active in describing and mapping out the consequences of these transformations.[2] They have sparked interest not only in the changing spatial and temporal dimensions of institutions and places, but equally in the more subtle and interesting changes to perceptions and functions of the multiplicity of overlapping borders that are used to define them. Kate Kirby, for instance, has demonstrated that boundaries between physical and social spaces are as much discursive dichotomies as they are coordinates plotted on the ground.[3] Similarly, Anthony Wilden's communication theory presents the mapping out of boundaries as 'punctuations', giving a necessary rhythm and form to social interactions that are both constituted and constitutive.[4]

A key idea throughout this line of research is that the materiality of boundaries is derived as much from their function as delineating 'systems of signs' as from their concrete demarcation of physical spaces. So in the case of the 'imagined community' of Benedict Anderson, it is the historical production of the particular category of community imagined, the 'nation', rather than the fact of its imagination, that is of primary interest.[5] All forms of community are ultimately 'imagined' since whatever the proximity of their members physically and biologically, their comprehension of each other, and of their individual and collective relationship to the environment, is of necessity inscribed in and mediated through myths, practices, metaphors, dialects, and language.[6] Boundaries are viewed therefore as material expressions of the logical necessities of systems of signs. For example, the rapid shift in European history from the amorphous zones of 'frontiers' to the stricter form of delineation of the 'boundary' is perceived to have been an effect with both epistemic and societal causes.[7]

Social geography has been particularly alive to these concepts, with the consequence that what Nigel Thrift calls 'rhetorical constructs' are considered legitimate subjects of analysis as shapers of practices and institutions and as constitutive elements in dynamic social processes.[8] Rhetoric is no longer simply viewed as an ideological mask for materialist interests but is the expressed codification of *discourses*, of 'practically oriented orders bent to the task of constructing more or less durable social networks'.[9] Thrift accepts Foucault's argument that reflections upon developments 'out there' cannot be reduced to either the *eros* of the pursuit of knowledge for its own sake and/or a form of domination and subjugation (ideology). Knowledge is generated by the practical needs of coping, adapting, commanding, and steering developments. Seen in this light, changing patterns of discourses are subjects of importance in themselves.

The advent of the discourse (or, as Roger Keil argues persuasively, *discourses*[10]) of globalisation, has lent a particular practical relevance to the remapping of social, political, and economic space. In what are viewed as 'ideological discourses', globalisation is widely perceived, and is increasingly being *deployed*, as 'a universal causal agent'.[11] There is a growing and apparently unshakeable consensus amongst political and business elites (not to mention many academic social scientists) that the state and business corporations must *adapt* to 'globalisation' and the 'borderless world'.[12]

However, the very notion of adaptation suggests that reflexivity lies at the heart of globalisation. Anthony Giddens, for example, presents us with an image of globalisation characterised by 'reflexive modernisation' that has not only transcended established traditions of social organisation, but which produces a world in which traditions can no longer be created.[13] For Giddens, the post-traditional and radically reflexive society is one where 'social bonds have effectively to be *made*, rather than inherited from the past'.[14] Giddens' global society is one of 'indefinite space' which is increasingly disembedded and therefore offers the possibility, however remote, of a political pluralism and cosmopolitanism in the future.[15] These ideas also inform David Held and Daniele Archibugi's (and others) conception of a 'cosmopolitan democracy', which seeks to re-imagine the nature and content of political community in response to the emerging global system.[16] The version of globalisation presented by Giddens and Held is attuned to the constructed nature of globalisation and the new spaces that its various processes have opened up for and of political action. Such an approach is grounded in the proposition that it is the *materiality* of globalisation, its empirical processes and institutions, that creates spaces of opportunity and constraint for reflexive development in the future.

This paper is also concerned with the nature of political and economic spatialisation in relation to globalisation, but differs in the way it conceives of social space. For Giddens and Held, spaces of political action are opened up by *processes* of globalisation, but the complexities surrounding the development and deployment of *discourses* of globalisation are not investigated. We are interested in both the embedded spatialisation of the discourse of globalisation and the evolving cognitive spatialisation that flows from it.

As many observers have noticed, the 'global' system to which corporate and political leaders and academics appeal with such regularity is a curious reality since it is always *absent*. It is removed from us in *space*, since it exists beyond and across the world of states and corporations, heedless of political and economic boundaries. It is also removed in *time*, since globalisation means, above all else, an inexorable process towards the future *telos* of 'globality'. Notwithstanding the ambiguities and contradictions inherent in this absent promise, however, its widespread acceptance is having the effect of generating an institutional structure for the 'global', mediated through policies and techniques of *necessary adaptation*. Drawing on similar perceptions of the 'realities' of globality, governments of all shades legitimise reductions in welfare spending and the privatisation of essential services, and corporate managers justify the 'downsizing' of their workforces. In the face of an ubiquitous and inexorable process of economic globalisation, governments and businesses see themselves as being compelled to reject and replace traditional patterns of social, political, and economic relations. It is a consequence of the widespread acceptance of these adaptive imperatives that discourses of globalisation have so rapidly become embedded in and reproduced by concrete institutions and practices.[17]

Critiques of 'ideological' discourses of globalisation have developed to show that the way it is most commonly presented fails to grasp its complex, dynamic nature.[18] Particular attention is drawn to the ways in which social and economic structures of the state are being reconstructed to accommodate and even create the global.[19] Far from being a transgression away from the state, the argument goes, much of what is understood to occupy the new, external space of the global is located (physically, conceptually, and juridically) within the state.[20] Processes of globalisation may indeed alter structures of the conventional state but they are also, as sociohistorical discourses, responsible for the reflexive establishment of those conventions in the first place. Globalisation, in other words, is a phenomenon in the life of the state system.

In this paper we would like to draw attention to another important development in relation to the evolving discourse of globalisation. Whilst social structures have indeed changed, they have not simply dissolved, as some critics of the 'discourse of globalisation' appear to believe, into a homogenous, reflexive soup. Contrary to the assumptions of some observers, 'they' – the decision-makers, mainstream political scientists, and economists – employ a much more complex and multifaceted concept of globalisation than the crude and simplistic definition often attributed to them. Though such people may well speak of the 'borderless world' or 'global village' and allude to the 'reality' of an undifferentiated global market, this imagery is more complex than it first appears since, paradoxically, it is predicated on a series of assumptions about the nature and function of *the state*. It appears to us that much of the meaning of orthodox globalism can be explained through the discursive fragmentation and reconstitution of the nation-state and, most importantly, the national economy.

We argue here that orthodox conceptions of contemporary state and the global system are comprised of three immanent and mutually constitutive socioeconomic spatialities. We have designated these the *offshore* economy, the *private* economy and the *anti*-economy: three overlapping elements that simultaneously delineate the content of the 'global' and generate a spatial and temporal hierarchy for the state in relation to it. Each is marked by different normative characteristics, types and levels of institution, dynamic historical processes, degrees of territorial embeddedness, and levels of access to reflexivity as an instrumental resource.

The first section of this article explores the processes by which the meanings of, and relationships between, institutions of state and economy have developed over time through discursive and reflexive practices. The second section then examines the ways in which the introduction of the 'new' space of the global economy has altered the spatial and conceptual terrain of the state by generating a tripartite structure of national political and social economies. This structure, we argue, creates a complex and dynamic spatialisation for the state whereby it both contains and is contained by the 'global'. It also, we suggest, produces a normative spatial hierarchy which differentiates between those able to participate in and benefit from the globalisation of the state, and those most often left out of the orthodox debate (particularly in International Relations),[21] the 'socially excluded'. The piece concludes by exploring the reasons why the conceptual and institutional environment of the state should have developed in this way.

The Reflexivity of the State

The most common presentation of globalisation in the late 1980s, as a linear movement from the state to the global, contained a hidden message: if the world is shifting from a particularistic system of nation-states and national economies to a more homogenous and, ultimately, politically integrated space, then this new space, while larger, still performs functions that were attributed to states. Globalisation, in other words, represents a challenge to the state, but not to politics or economics! The current transformation both of political and economic spaces and processes, and of the individual and institutional relationships through which they are mediated, suggests to us that something more fundamental is taking place.

Such an interpretation implies that something is 'gained' by those presiding over the disaggregation of the state and national economy under globalisation. It also suggests, of course, that something is being 'lost' with the disruption of coherent territorial domains. What, then, was embedded in the previous conception of the 'national' territory that can explain what has been lost and what has been gained?

Influenced by Foucault and Jacques Derrida, Nicos Poulantzas developed a theory of the relationship between space and political subjectivity in his later work.[22] The national territory, he argues, 'has nothing to do with the natural features of the land. It is, rather, of an essentially political character'.[23] So that 'in fact, the national territory is but the political expression of an enclosure at the level of the state as a whole'.[24] Poulantzas is, however, still ambiguous. Does he speak of the material features of the land or of the imaginary constitution of the nation-state as a collective entity with particular responsibilities? It seems that his point of reference is by and large the latter; his study is an anthropological investigation of the modern myths of the nation-state, myths that generate an intuitive, 'self-evident' understanding which represents individuals as 'citizens' of the nation-state. If, as Poulantzas sought to demonstrate, the nation-state consisted of mutually supporting discourses, we can see how in terms of a particular historical rationality it 'makes sense' and, indeed, is viewed as 'just' for the individual to inhabit a particular social and political formation. By corollary, this socio-political formation is in turn understood to be representative of that individual's aspirations.

Such relationships are also investigated from a genealogical perspective as constituting 'logical spaces'.[25] From this perspective, constructions of social, political,
and economic space form part of a logical whole which contains notions of reality
and truth as much as they serve to inform and constitute them. Categories such as
the 'individual', the 'territory', the 'national economy' and so on interrelate within
and across discourses to create sets of relations which provide basic, pre-cognitive
frameworks for the affirmation or denial of the real and the true. The meaning of an
alleged change in the concept of the spatiality of the nation-state can be interpreted,
therefore, only within an interpretation of the meaning of the nation-state itself.
What discursive baggage does the concept of the nation-state carry? What kinds of
practices does the concept legitimise?

Zygmunt Bauman maintains that the modern nation-state accompanied the rise
of calculative rationality.[26] The specific category of the nation-state is founded on
the notion of society as an organised and mechanical organisation of people:

> It was the breakdown of self-enclosed communities and the ensuing appearance of the
> 'masterless men' – vagabonds, vagrants, shifting populations nowhere at home ... that
> rendered the issue of social control, and of the reproduction of social order, problem-
> atic. The heretofore invisible, 'natural' flow of things had been brought abruptly into
> relief as a 'mechanism' – something to be designed, administered and monitored,
> something not functioning, or not functioning properly, unless attended to and oper-
> ated skilfully.[27]

This need to self-consciously design and monitor 'society' reveals above all that it
has always been a fundamentally reflexive form of social organisation. It may be
argued that from its earliest formal manifestations, the state has been constantly
(re-)created in pursuit of changing needs and conceptions of the nation; the material reality of the 'nation', of course, was represented in the state, hence these are
mutually referential concepts.[28]

The parliament of the *Fronde* movement in France in 1766, for example, represents one of the first explicit attempts to formally encapsulate the idea of the nation
state in its modern form, i.e., as a reflexively constituted political community
representing a unitary, territorially delineated 'people'. The *Fronde* parliament was
an institutional response to a process by which what was referred to at the time as
the 'social body' was taking on a more coherent and formal structure as a 'national
society'. The *Fronde* maintained a separation between the 'nation' and the body of
the king, but argued for an intermediary body that would be representative of this
formalised conception of 'the nation' in matters of state.[29] To the nationalist
theorist, then, the 'nation' is the origin and cornerstone of all subsequent forms of
political constitution.

There were certain logical imperatives embedded in the concept of the nation
which were soon to pervade political discourse. They served as 'intuitive' truths. As
an immanent and discrete collectivity, the nation-state represents, as Bauman notes,
a self-organising historical entity sharing in the formation and execution of collective goals.[30] The matter of collective goals simultaneously poses questions of ethics,
i.e., which of these goals are honourable, and questions of technique: how a
community is to go about self-organising itself to achieve such goals.

The representation of closure, of an homogenised 'national economy', for instance, was central to the idea of the subordination of market forces to the goals of the state. It may be debated at length whether there was indeed ever a 'nation' which corresponded to the ideal of closure (in our view, there was not), however the imperative of the logic of the nation legitimised a particular political economy centred around belief in the closure of the state. In other words, a political economy which aims at advancing 'national' goals of wealth and power creation can be advanced only on the basis of a belief in the reality of the nation. Belief in the nation is in turn supported by the concrete evidence offered by the pursuit of national goals. The idea that the state was the political arm of the nation or community was then translated into the practice that the state had responsibility for encouraging the welfare and cohesion of its population through redistributive taxation, universal education, social and physical security, health care, and so on. The state, as the collective arm of the nation, also had the right and duty to control and subordinate market forces for the benefit of the nation.

This identification of the 'nation' as constitutive of the social body generates a series of logical propositions which the state must then enact. The nation is predicated upon the presupposition that members of the 'nation' share in some epic spiritual journey as a single 'community of fate'.[31] The agglomeration of people residing within a given political boundary and/or sharing linguistic or other attributes were viewed as having a common destiny. In this context patriotic feelings were translated into nationalist ideologies which simultaneously prescribed the meaning of the collectivity and to the role of individual within it.

Consequently, nationalist theory is strongly prescriptive in that it suggests that the 'spiritual unity' of the nation must be translated into both a responsibility on the part of each individual towards the whole and, in turn, a responsibility on the part of the nation towards the individual. The lofty goals of the nation necessitated that the individual, legally and morally constituted as a 'member', subordinate him or herself to the common good.[32] Each member of the nation is charged with responsibility towards maintaining the physical and spiritual continuity of the 'father/motherland' and with providing future generations with the right conditions to continue the journey. Throughout its history, therefore, the nation has performed a central constitutive role with regard to the state, informing and legitimising new forms of social organisations and new forms of surveillance.

This is equally true with regard to specific formation of the national economy. The strongly territorial idea of the nation-state was from the outset closely bound up with the extension of regulatory control over the assets and transactions of the national population and the emergent institutions of the private and public sectors. At the same time, the state border as an economic boundary serves to separate and *create* the 'domestic' and the 'international' economies as discrete spaces. A bounded political economy was, for example, a prerequisite for the regulation of all forms of inter-*national* trade, a concept that has no meaning except in a world economy divided by national borders. The conception is of an international economy with the emphasis on the reflexively mediated goals of mutually recognised state sovereignty.

Notwithstanding its contradictions, the assumed spatial correlation between economy and society contains an assumption of subordination that remains commonplace throughout the social sciences. Among sociologists it is represented most clearly in the work of the structural functionalists. Talcott Parsons, for instance, viewed the economy and politics as two functional sub-systems of the 'social system'.[33] Similarly David Easton, followed the marginalists in defining the political system as an alternative mode of 'resource allocation' to the economy.[34] These ideas were then echoed in the first wave of development theory, namely modernisation, which is predicated on the necessity of the creation of 'proper' (economical, political, and moral) conditions for the economic success of the nation state in a world economy.[35]

But in advocating a particular political system, modernisation theorists and liberal economists, together with the rest of the literature predicated on the concept of a 'national economy', were already acknowledging the centrality of *political choice*. The notion of the national 'system' – which is in practice the discrete 'political' and 'economic' systems of the state working in combination as the 'national economy' – implied not only a discrete separation from an external environment (the world market), but also a self-organising and self-producing capacity on the part of the nation-state, what Humberto Maturana and Fransisco Varela call *autopoiesis*.[36] National economic policy is, after all, a matter of choice; a choice which is, ostensibly at least, open to 'the nation'. The nation may choose to adopt open borders and free trade policy, or it may choose instead varying degree of protectionist policies. Economists as a whole argued in favour of the former and against the latter, but the issue of choice, and hence the ideological debate surrounding national choices, was central to the political debate. Therefore, during the golden years of the national economy concept – the period between roughly 1940 and 1980 – we saw impassioned debates as to which national economic policy to be taken. It was a period characterised throughout the world by a battle between 'isolationists' and 'universalists', between advocates of protectionist, nationalist, and socialist policies and advocates of free trade and open borders. Under this ideological guise, governments of all political persuasions and all degrees of democracy presented their constituencies with a stark choice between 'going it alone' or submerging the national economy in an increasingly transnationalised economy.

These sorts of political debates were predicated on a single central assumption, namely that the state is the sole and proper intermediary between the demands of the international market and the demands of its citizens for social and economic equality and other social goals. It is our contention that the erosion of the second part of the equation, of the concept of a national economy, and its replacement by a discourse not of an homogenised but a *tripartite* state, undermines the first part of the equation. The ideology that places the emphasis on the state as supporting, sustaining, and introducing international goals to the 'domestic' context works within a changing perception of the nature of the national political economy. As Stephen Gill argues in his 'new constitutionalism', the rule of the market and transnational capital is actively being legitimised through a reconceptualisation and consequent remapping of the 'national economy'.[37]

The new map of the national economy that emerges is not, of course, a conventional two dimensional cartography. Rather it is a graphic representation of an evolving hermeneutic of the national economy in relation to the two 'new' spaces, those of globality and exclusion. These new spaces are manifest both discursively –

they are described and explained and, above all, *predicted* – and institutionally: they are both in the process of 'becoming' through the establishment of institutions and policies designed to 'cope with' these very institutions.

The Hermeneutics of the Contemporary 'National Economy'

In the tripartite scheme introduced below we attempt to map together the elements of an emerging imaginary configuration of the contemporary state. The dynamics driving this reconfiguration of national economic and social hierarchies are the related discourses of globalisation and exclusion. The offshore, private, and anti-economies presented here are constituted within and constitutive of the economic jurisdiction of the contemporary state. They are not intended as fixed or wholly separate spatial categories, but rather combine to form an overlapping hierarchy of normative economic domains which are located within and across states to varying degrees, are subject to varying degrees of political and legal influence, and are constituted through differing institutional structures. Whilst these 'spaces' are not intended to conform to a conventional territorial geography, they are not wholly separate from it. Their relationship to the conventional spatiality of the state is best envisaged as becoming less place bound, and therefore increasingly 'placeless' with increasing globality. The relative degree of access to and mobility between these three domains by individuals and firms has significant consequences for their respective degrees of access to the fruits of the global economy. Each element of this scheme has both a discursive and a concrete institutional form already, though they are understood to be in a process of active evolution. Significantly, they imply a form of spatial hierarchy illustrated in figure 9.1.

The offshore economy

Proponents of the globalisation thesis tend to emphasise open markets, swift and accelerating rates of capital mobility, the formation of global commodity chains, the 'borderless world', and so on. The image created is that of a new economic space spanning the globe, a 'space of flows',[38] transcending and penetrating all national boundaries without let or hindrance.[39] These images are normally presented by their enthusiasts as facts, as if a genuine global market is in existence or alternatively shows clear signs of coming into existence. Not surprisingly, this has in turn given rise to a host of critical literature pointing out the many empirical weaknesses of such representations.[40]

Both sets of literature are misleading but not entirely wrong. The institutions and practices that have come to be known collectively as 'globalisation' are evidently not universalised throughout the entire world economy. They do, however, refer to a very specific development in the past three decades: the emergence of the offshore economy.[41] The term offshore economy is a reference to the emergence of a 'third space' consisting of highly integrated capital markets, such as the Euromarkets, export processing zones (EPZs) – which although physically located within the territories of states, have very different legal and fiscal conditions – and tax havens,

PRIVATE SECTOR		PUBLIC SECTOR	THIRD SECTOR/ SOCIAL ECONOMY
OFFSHORE	PRIVATE		ANTI-
Institutions: World/Global economy Global markets Global firms Merchant banks Global cities Media corps. 'Global' organisations (WTO, etc.) TNCs	*Institutions:* National economy National state bodies Local state bodies Domestic firms Borders Domestic market Retail banking		*Institutions:* Local/Peripheral economy Community Family Household Welfare state
Processes: Globalisation Technicisation Securitisation	*Processes:* Privatisation Liberalisation Deregulation Enabling Modernisation Globalisation		*Processes:* Dependency Stagnation Decline Exclusion Marginalisation Obsolescence
Normative characteristics: Economic Dynamic Site of competition Impersonal Apolitical Economic Future-oriented Developing Expanding World market Technological 'Real'	*Normative characteristics:* Political Dynamic Competitive Flexible Globalising Privatising Enabling (business) Modernising Open to trade Market led Employed Onshore		*Normative characteristics:* Static Uncompetitive Inflexible Pre-global Residual Dependent (aid or welfare) Un- or De-skilled Outmoded Third World Unemployed Underclass
'MAINSTREAM' ECONOMY ('SOCIAL INCLUSION')			'WELFARE' AND/OR 'INFORMAL' ECONOMY ('SOCIAL EXCLUSION')
		← Potential change in status only available through: *Flexibilisation, Retraining, Reskilling, Insertion, Integration, Development, Formalisation, Modernisation.*	

Figure 9.1 The spatio-temporal hierarchy of the contemporary national economy

those places that carry the more traditional and exotic image of offshore.[42] Specifically, the rapid development of the realm of offshore has consisted of four processes.

One is the broadening of the Euromarket into a series of interconnected 'stateless' financial markets which together currently intermediate an estimated 80 per cent of all international banking transactions. Euromarkets operate beyond the regulatory control of states, indeed this is precisely why they were established in the first instance. The Euromarket was developed as a means of freeing up the flow of international capital during the post-war reconstruction, by providing mechanisms by which the US dollar could be traded by banks outside of the jurisdiction of the United States. Such transactions were not subject to the constraints of national taxation, reserve requirements, reporting, or capital controls. The apparent anarchy of offshore, therefore, belies its origins in conscious policy decisions taken by, amongst others, the Bank of England in the 1950s.[43]

A second process involves the concomitant rise in the number of tax havens (68 according to the latest authoritative accounts) which has been matched by a significant rise in both the density of transactions that they handle and the quantity of capital they contain.[44] It is estimated that about half of the global stock of money either resides in or passes through tax havens.[45] Tax havens offer several services to their clients including shipping registration, discrete and secure banking services, and, of increasing importance, corporate citizenship, all of which are specifically designed to circumvent regulatory restrictions in other jurisdictions. Tax havens essentially sell sovereign citizenship to wealthy individuals or more usually to firms wishing to minimise or even eliminate their exposure to regulations in their home (i.e., physically-located) territory.

A third is a dramatic rise in the number of export processing zones and free trade zones, from two in the early 1960s to an estimated 845 today, providing employment directly to 27 million workers world-wide.[46] EPZs, special economic zones, free trade zones, and the like represent the extension of the domain of offshore to manufacturing and trade by creating spaces which although located within the boundaries of the state, benefit from greatly reduced taxation, import duties, and more general regulations. Approximately one quarter of the world's manufacturing takes place in EPZs and free trade zones, the majority being assembly plants for components made elsewhere all of whose products are then re-exported.

Finally, the development of offshore has extended of the principle of 'flagging out' developed in the shipping industry to other spheres of activity such as aircraft leasing, telecommunications and Internet casinos, Internet pornography, and eventually Internet shopping. Flagging out involves the formal registration of an activity or institution physically located in one place in the legal jurisdiction of another. In the case of shipping, therefore, flagging out means, quite literally, flying the flag of the jurisdiction in which the boat is registered rather than that of the home country of the ship's owners and/or operators. States such as Panama, Sierra Leone, Singapore and Hong Kong have successfully 'sold' their relatively light safety and taxation regimes to foreign shipping owners for many years.[47]

As part of all four of these processes, and for a great variety of reasons, states have created juridical enclaves of two main types. First, there are physical enclaves such as the EPZs where a specific bounded area of state territory is deemed to lie outside of normal jurisdiction. Second, there are 'fictional' enclaves: forms of demarcations based on a legal separation of domestic and offshore law within which that state wholly or in part withholds its 'normal' regulatory and fiscal functions from particular types of organisation.

Due to its the sheer size (i.e., the volume of capital that passes through or is contained within it) and its degree of integration, the offshore economy creates a virtual regulatory space within which its 'citizens' are able to escape, by and large, the controls imposed by national regulatory frameworks, leading to a growing scale and velocity of particular types of market integration. Above all, offshore is claimed to represent a radical disjuncture between economic activity and physical space since fundamental to the idea of offshore is that it is 'placeless'.[48] It is this aspect of offshore that has led to its close association with globalisation, but which also has been least understood. Far from constituting an economic domain that is wholly beyond the states-system and even destructive of it, for the time being at least, offshore remains firmly rooted within states and their national economies.

Offshore undoubtedly represents the creation of a regulatory environment that both contradicts and undermines the very idea of a 'national' economy and a coherent national space.[49] However, contrary to the image the name 'offshore' tends to conjure up, it exists almost wholly within the physical and juridical boundaries of states and is sanctioned and encouraged by national governments. Offshore is not a homogenous phenomenon and nor is it wholly disengaged from the national economy. Rather, offshore develops new (and not so new) sets of regulatory boundaries that, whilst different from the conventionally understood territorial boundaries of the state, are no more or less real. These boundaries create spaces of differential regulation within and across states that add to the functionality of the border as much as they contradict it.

Offshore has certainly allowed those with access to its institutions and processes a range of economic spaces within which they are able to circumvent the exigencies of territoriality. But offshore does not represent a terminal dislocation of the national economy, its fragmentation prior to absorption by the global. The power of Euro-markets to circumvent national economic regulations does not, as many assume, mean that they are the antithesis of the national economy. Euromarkets still deal in 'national' currencies and other forms of securitised instruments and, whilst there is little doubt that their dynamics have altered the nature of money and its relationship to the state, this does not remove the function of the national economic space. The sovereign space of the state retains a very powerful mediating function in delivering the variety of regulatory spaces that is so important for the lubrication of capital flows. Offshore may include 'economies of signs and space' but they are still economies embedded in the concept of national sovereignty over economic activity, however much they may be disengaged from the territory.[50]

The private economy

While it is important to recognise the significance of the offshore economy and the tremendous scope for its extension, it is equally important to recognise that the integrated and open 'global' market of the globalist thesis takes place only within specifically designated realms of transaction. The economy as a whole has not gone down the road of offshore. The predominant framework of economic activities is that of a national *private* economy.

The national private economy is a normatively created regulatory space in which the state retains the function of law-maker and law-enforcer, a role which has if anything been strengthened by the rise of the offshore economy. That said, the state must affect deep changes within its territorial boundaries in response to 'globalisation' by increasingly attempting to accommodate the needs of the offshore economy to attract and protect investment. Unlike the offshore economy, the national private economy's globalising tendencies manifest themselves not directly as a new spatial terrain, but indirectly, through the notion of competitiveness. The private economy is increasingly linked globally as a competitive node within one overwhelming market-place.[51]

The national private economy has already found expression in a number of different concepts. The 'competition' state and the 'enabling' state both present images of the interaction between state and economy whereby the state is curiously both reinvigorated and withdrawn.[52] The conventional image of the enabling state is one that is essentially withdrawn from the economy. The state no longer replaces entrepreneurship through public ownership but enables, and *should* enable, it through a combination of privatisation, 'pre-competitive' measures, and structural adaptation. In this way the imagery and practices of the corporatist and/or Fordist state have been replaced by a much more fragmentary and fluid conception of the national economic space which, although still bounded and regulated, is beyond the capacity of the state to control. This is both a deliberate policy fostered by national governments anxious to resolve balance of payments and fiscal problems and a product of the massive expansion of the financial and securities sector.

The competition state – a concept which, as Paul Krugman has argued, is non-sensical – has a specific prescriptive resonance.[53] States are in effect becoming active drivers of entrenching neo-liberal forms of economic regulation.[54] The 'hollowing-out' of the state entailed in these processes of privatisation and globalisation/localisation is, however, much overstated. The presentation of the role of the state as progressively 'deregulating' economic space obscures the extent of *re-regulation* that is taking place.[55] (In many ways even that is an overstatement since the core function of the state with respect to the economy has not in fact changed all that much.) Rather than be constrained by an external force of globalisation across the board as the cruder versions of that theory tend to claim, the state has created conditions whereby it must make a normative differentiation between different aspects of its 'national' economy with respect to the global. The state has not retreated but has reconfigured the way it applies its regulations so that they are no longer 'national' in the sense of being universally and evenly applied throughout the territory of the state.

National economic policies and institutions are increasingly being geared towards promoting internal competition between different industrial regions for investment. Competition is engendered by a combination of spatial and fiscal policies including: regional development agencies, 'pre-competitive' infrastructural improvements, tax holidays, and all manner of financial 'sweeteners'. As a consequence, transnational capital is seen to negotiate directly with regional and local authorities over the terms and conditions of their investment, including labour conditions, levels of service provision and infrastructure, as much if not more than they do with national governments. It is as though local and regional economies have ceased to be embedded in a national economic space, but now compete directly with other similar places in other states in a global space.

As such the involvement of the state with its territorial economy has not diminished but its emphasis has changed. The private national economy is concerned to attune national economic policy to the realities of the 'global' economy and, even more vaguely, to the exigencies of the process of globalisation. The apparent powerlessness of the state in the face of the process of globalisation has been the cause of much controversy in both the academic and policy literature because of the perceived threat posed by globalisation to the sovereignty autonomy of the state. However, it is worth recalling that the well-established concept of the 'world economy' (or, as Fernand Braudel argues, world *economies*[56]) has long provided an all-encompassing economic space, which, although less clearly articulated in institutional terms than the global economy, has nonetheless had important constitutive and determinative effects for states. Specifically the alternative neutral space of the world economy creates a dual role for the national economic boundary. Although normally only considered as a territorial delimitation between one state and another (or others), the national economic boundary at the same time serves as a border between the territorial space of the state and the virtual space of the 'world economy'. The concept of the world economy, like its global successor, occupies a space that is variously above and between national economies and functions as a neutral space, providing a benchmark for prices arrived at through the aggregation of national economic statistics. All traded commodities are accorded a world market price against which national (or regional in the case of the EU, NAFTA, MERCO-SUR, etc.) prices are gauged.

Whilst the concept of the global economy greatly extends the idea of an all-encompassing 'world space', not least by legitimating the conferring of considerable legislative power to institutions such as the World Trade Organisation (WTO) that have an explicitly global remit, this is not as great a change as is sometimes claimed. There has undoubtedly been some loss of power and 'sovereignty' to such global institutions but it should be noted that membership also confers a considerable degree of legitimacy back on to states. Membership of the WTO, for example, is only open to a 'state or separate customs territory possessing *full autonomy* in the conduct of its external commercial relations'.[57] No state has, or ever has had such 'full autonomy'. However, by signing up to the WTO, a state government establishes a claim to a mutually recognised form of relative autonomy. There is no small irony in that fact that this 'autonomy' is articulated through and guaranteed by an organisation to which a member state must also agree to 'ensure the conformity of its laws, regulations and administrative procedures'.[58] However, the major change here is less a fundamental transformation of the operation of the world economy than the drawing of ever larger numbers of states into a system that was already constituted on a semi-informal basis by and between the core economies of the industrialised world.[59] The result has not been the weakening of national boundaries but their reconstitution.

Though these changes are of considerable significance, the discourse of the global economy has had its most profound effect in the domestic affairs of states and in particular in the nature of their relationship to their domestic populations. At the same time as the *eros* of the global has opened up the dynamic spaces of offshore and the private economy to which the state has had little perceived choice but to conform, so it has also necessitated a differentiation between those able to participate in the new order and those less fortunate and less 'competitive'.[60] In the process of transforming the spatial content of the 'imaginary economy' away from the territorial space of the state, discourses of globalisation have reinscribed the articulation of 'inclusion' and 'exclusion'. In place of a delineation between the inside and outside of 'society' that was understood to be coextensive with the physical boundaries of the state, the emerging hierarchy of the state draws a new internal boundary between those able to participate in the global economy, and those who cannot.

The anti-economy

By privileging and institutionalising particular norms of socio-economic behaviour and participation, the orthodox discourse of globalisation necessarily opens up the third of our conceptual spaces: the *anti*-economy. The anti-economy is that portion of economic activity that is often left out of the global-versus-national debate, except when it is wheeled out as evidence in support of one side or the other. The national economy has bifurcated into a performing, competitive portion, and a non-performing, uncompetitive 'anti'-economy that consists of various sections of hitherto national economies that are now presented as the 'left out' and 'left over'.

The anti-economy is so designated here not because it is in any way 'uneconomic', but because, for reasons that economists and policy-makers find difficult to explain, the new competitive economy seems to be unable to sustain employment at levels above 90 per cent of the potential work force. Various governments have tried to rig the figures and present a more optimistic account of the true capacity of the economy to absorb workers, but recently a broad consensus has arisen that the goal of 'full-employment' is incompatible with the notion of the national private economy.[61] Those occupying the anti-economy are the poor, the disemployed, the uncompetitive, and the 'inflexible'. Their status is perhaps best expressed by the currently fashionable concept of 'social exclusion'.[62] The task of the state with regard to such groups is either to 'reintegrate' them into the private economy as though they had somehow departed from it, or confine them within 'local' enclaves so that they do not threaten the vibrant national private economy.

Social exclusion is, like globalisation, a vague and ambiguous term. It is used to refer to chronic, multiple deprivation through discrimination, displacement, unemployment, disability, ill-health, and so on. These problems conspire to isolate individuals and communities physically, socially, and economically from the basic and/or 'normal' standards expected by the rest of society.

Whilst the concept of exclusion convincingly describes the lived experience of many people, it is a term with different meanings. In recent years the concept of exclusion has been adopted by both increasing numbers of national governments and international agencies. As it has become increasingly internationalised, and therefore removed from its essentially descriptive roots, social exclusion has become a *normative category* which is defined ultimately in relation to the 'global' economy. As such, the meaning and function of the term has changed dramatically. What began as a very powerful description of the cumulative effects of poverty and discrimination within the context of a globalising political economy, has itself become a form of discrimination or, as Ruth Levitas puts it, a 'New Durkheimian Hegemony'.[63] Social exclusion as a normative category is an important element in a proscriptive re-mapping and re-inscribing of the social world and, in particular, in redefining the function of the state with regard to both its 'citizenry' and the global system. Although other causes for exclusion are commonly acknowledged, unemployment or 'exclusion from the labour market' is now routinely paraded as the 'principal' form of social exclusion worldwide to which the automatic solution is assumed to be employment or reinsertion into the labour market.[64]

The idea of 'exclusion', whilst not always explicit, is a necessary aspect of any definition of 'society'.[65] Every society involves an exercise in normative delimitation, the creation of an 'in' and an 'out' based on complex combinations of institutions, traditions, languages, iconographies, identities, religions, ethnicities, territories, laws, and so on. For that reason, the pairing of 'social' and 'exclusion' seems a little paradoxical, even tautological, at first glance. In fact the rather curious nature of this pairing suits its function very well since social exclusion seeks to identify a phenomenon that is itself paradoxical. Social exclusion denotes a space of exclusion *within* a society, a normative separation that places certain individuals and communities into a discrete space that is simultaneously in the state but beyond the society or, as Scott Lash puts, it in reference to the associated concept of the underclass, into a 'class not in but of civil society'.[66] Social exclusion is a product of socio-spatial discourses which, as Thrift warns, 'unless they [bounded spaces of 'exclusion'] are used with great care [. . .] can . . . come dangerously close to reifying power by allotting it to its own abstract spaces'.[67]

The value of concepts used to describe the substantive effects of inequality and disadvantage lie in their ability to capture local social, cultural, and institutional complexities and dynamics. The essence of the concept of exclusion as it is currently used to define policy is the opposite: it replaces complexity with a single, blanket category of exclusion defined according to a preordained and prescriptive 'solution'. That solution, based on the ideology of the competitive world economy, stems not from the substantive problems of individuals and communities but from the orthodox discourse of globalisation.

The importance of social exclusion in respect of the prevailing orthodoxy is that it adds another, missing dimension to the state/global nexus. The result is a complex social space in which the state is simultaneously performing two very different roles. It is at the same time obliged to conform itself to the exigencies of the global economy, which it is instrumental in defining and in which it is increasingly integrated, and it must also address the socio-economic needs and the 'cohesion' of its population. As we have seen, that population is divided between the 'included' who participate in the global economy through paid work, and the excluded who do not. As the related categories of inclusion and exclusion are intended to imply, however, these are also (possibly primarily) *normative* categories defined according to their proximity to the ideals of the global economy. Put bluntly, the more global you are, the more included you are.[68]

Social exclusion implies a radical disjuncture in the conventional equation of the state and society. The two are no longer coextensive since the state itself administers an internal 'border' between the included (those in employment), and the excluded. In spite of its role in creating this distinction, the task of resolving the problem of social exclusion is still the *responsibility* of the state. Social exclusion may have been caused by the vagaries of the global economy but responsibility for it still ends at the border; there is no responsibility on the part of one state for the economically excluded of another. As the Czech gypsies who landed at Dover in 1997 and the Moroccan emigrants who brave the crossing to Spain have discovered, one state's socially excluded person, is another state's 'economic migrant'.[69]

Conclusion

Why then, has the spatial content of the imaginary, 'national' economy evolved in this way? On one level it is routinely argued that the creation of a normative economic hierarchy is no more than a consequence of changes in the structure of the world economy over which national governments have little or no control.[70] Perhaps. We would like to point out, however, an important consequence, whether intended or not, of this tripartite construction of a 'global state': the global system is no longer portrayed as simply 'the state writ large'.

The argument here is that globalisation relies crucially on the reconstitution of the concepts of the state and the national economy and that they are part and parcel of the same dynamic structure of the social world as the 'global'. The state and the national economy are reconstituted in two ways. First, they are accorded a concrete historical reality as the point of origin from which globalisation departs, a reality that has only been fully codified because of the need to define a 'state of nature' prior to the global. Second, they are reconstituted within the global, they are given a role to play and a space in which to play it that are contingent on and subordinate to the 'realities' of globality. This has been clearly expressed in the concepts of the 'enabling' and/or 'competition' state, the purpose of which is to facilitate 'enterprise' and 'competitiveness' and to provide little more than a basic 'safety net' for those unfortunate enough to be neither enterprising nor competitive.[71]

The strongly hierarchical relationship between the three elements constituting the contemporary state is obvious. The offshore economy provides a concrete institution of the global that demands the national economy be reoriented in the direction of the national private economy. By definition, the national private economy must then override the goals of social integration and universal welfare of the traditional national state and thus recognises the emergence of the anti-economy.

Yet it is precisely the non-homogeneity of globalisation which plays the significant constitutive role. For if it was the case that globalisation as presented in its simplified form was a fact, then frankly there would be little for the state to do. The state would just wither away, dissolve into the universal and homogenous global, and that would be that.

As we have demonstrated, however, the state has very specific and important roles to play in relation to the global economy. First, the state remains the ultimate guarantor, and indeed *creator*, of property titles that are exchanged in the market. It has been demonstrated that the state never held a monopoly over these functions in the past – not least because of the existence of powerful, private, transnational institutional structures such as the *lex mercatoria* – nor has it wholly lost them in the present.[72] Second, notwithstanding the emergence of structures of 'global govern-ance', the state remains central to the reproduction of capitalism and is therefore still responsible for the important functions of education, health, infrastructure, defence, regulation, and so on. Were the state to wither away, responsibility for these reproductive functions would fall to capital itself, a responsibility it is incap-able of performing without destroying the very structure of difference, hierarchy and variety which provides the lubricant for its dynamism. Rather than undermine the state, therefore, the purpose of re-describing and re-configuring the content of the state is to further ensure redistribution in the direction of capital *without* killing the goose that lays golden eggs.[73]

All this implies that as much as the reflexive reconstitution of the state through discourses of globalisation is a process of 'detraditionalisation', so it is also a powerful process of *retraditionalisation*, or, as Lash puts it, 'reflexive traditionalization'.[74] The result is the production of a conceptual 'map' of the state which, paradoxically, simultaneously locates and dislocates the state in relation to the global. The state and the national economy are both transgressed and rebuilt through a series of discourses (Thrift's 'rhetorics') that purport to describe a social reality that they in fact create. Contrary to many of the common assumptions about the global, this new map does not eliminate the state or the national economy (in many ways it strengthens them) but ascribes different functions, different spaces, and different historical tra-jectories to a variety of 'economies' and populations within and across states.

NOTES

1 Michel Foucault, *Les Mots et les Choses: Une Archéologie des Sciences Humaines* (Paris: Editions Gallimard, 1966) and Thomas Kuhn, *The Structure of Scientific Revolutions* (Chicago: Chicago University Press, 1970).
2 Ed Soja, *Postmodern Geographies: The Reassertion of Space in Critical Social Theory* (London: Verso, 1989); Kate M. Kirby, *Indifferent Boundaries: Spatial Concepts of Human Subjectivity* (London: The Guilford Press, 1996); Nigel Thrift, *Spatial Formations* (London: Sage, 1996); Scott Lash and John Urry, *Economies of Signs and Space* (London: Sage, 1994); Paul Q. Hirst, *From Statism to Pluralism: Democracy, Civil Society and Global Politics* (London: University College of London Press, 1997); and David Held, Anthony McGrew, David Goldblatt, and Jonathan Perraton, *Global Transformations: Politics, Economics and Culture* (Cambridge: Polity, 1999).
3 Kirby, *Indifferent Boundaries*.
4 Anthony Wilden, *System and Structure: Essays in Communication and Exchange* (London: Tavistock Publications, 1972).
5 Benedict Anderson, *Imagined Communities: Reflections on the Origin and Spread of Nation-alism* (London: Verso, 1991).
6 Pierre Bourdieu, *Language and Symbolic Power* (Cambridge: Polity 1991); Henri Lefebvre, *The Production of Space* (Oxford: Blackwell, 1991); and Thrift, *Spatial Formations*; Corne-lius Castoriadis, *The Imaginary Constitution of Society* (Cambridge, MA: MIT Press, 1987).
7 Mario Liverani, *Prestige and Interest: International Relations in the Near East 1600–1100 B.C.* (Padova: Sargon Sri., 1990) and Michel Foucault, *Discipline and Punish: the Birth of the Prison* (London: Allen Lane, 1977).

8 Nigel Thrift, 'Soft Capitalism', in *An Unruly World? Globalisation, Governance and Geography*, eds. Andrew Herod, Gearóid Ó Tuathail, and Susan Roberts (London: Routledge, 1998), 25–71.

9 Thrift, 'Soft Capitalism', 60.

10 Roger Keil, 'Globalisation Makes States: Perspectives of Local Governance in the Age of the World City', *Review of International Political Economy* 5, no. 4 (1998): 616–46.

11 Jamie Peck, 'From Federal Welfare to Local Workfare? Remaking Canada's Work-Welfare Regime', in *An Unruly World?*, 95–115.

12 Kenichi Ohmae, *The Borderless World* (London: Collins, 1990) and Kenichi Ohmae, *The End of the Nation State* (New York: Free Press, 1995).

13 Anthony Giddens, 'Living in a Post-Traditional Society', in *Reflexive Modernization: Politics, Tradition and Aesthetics in the Modern Social Order*, eds. Ulrich Beck, Anthony Giddens, and Scott Lash (Cambridge: Polity, 1994), 56–109.

14 Ibid., 107, emphasis in original.

15 Ibid., 107.

16 David Held, *Democracy and the Global Order: From the Modern State to Cosmopolitan Governance* (Cambridge: Polity, 1995); Daniele Archibugi, David Held, and Martin Köhler, eds., *Re-Imagining Political Community: Studies in Cosmopolitan Democracy* (Cambridge: Polity, 1998); and *Global Transformations*.

17 Ronen Palan and Jason Abbott with Phil Deane, *State Strategies in the Global Political Economy* (London: Cassell, 1996) and Thrift, 'Soft Capitalism'.

18 Peter Dicken, Jamie Peck, and Adam Tickell, 'Unpacking the Global', in *Geographies of Economies*, eds. Roger Lee and Jane Wills (London: Arnold, 1997), 158–66.

19 Peck, 'From Federal Welfare'.

20 A. Claire Cutler, 'Artifice, Ideology and Paradox: The Public/Private Distinction in International Law', *Review of International Political Economy* 4, no. 2 (1997): 261–85 and Gunther Teubner, ed., *Global Law Without a State* (Aldershot: Dartmouth, 1997).

21 Julian Saurin, 'Globalisation, Poverty and the Promises of Modernity', *Millennium: Journal of International Studies* 25, no. 3 (1996): 657–80.

22 Nicos Poulantzas, *State, Power, Socialism* (London: New Left Books, 1978).

23 Ibid., 104

24 Ibid., 105.

25 Michel Foucault, *The Archeology of Knowledge* (London: Tavistock, 1972).

26 Zygmunt Bauman, *Intimations of Postmodernity* (London: Routledge, 1992).

27 Ibid., 6.

28 There are, of course, nations without states and multi-national states: both types are defined, however, as exceptions to the rule, discovered in the very practice of the nation-states system. Nations without states and multi-national states are therefore defined in relation to the accepted norm of nations with states.

29 Gérard Maitret, *Les Principes des Souvereignté: Histoire et Fondement du Pouvoir Moderne.* (Paris: Gallimard, 1997), 97.

30 Bauman, *Intimations*, 6.

31 'The nations are the concepts which the spirit has formed itself', G. W. F. Hegel, *Lectures on the Philosophy of World History, Introduction: Reason in History* (Cambridge: Cambridge University Press, 1975), 51. For a discussion of the concept of the 'people', the 'Volk', discovers *en-route* great historical experiences; see Johann G. Fichte, *Discours à la Natione Allemande* (Paris: Aubier, 1981). So, for example, France discovered its origins variously in the misty days of the destruction of Troy, the German Romantics rediscovered their medieval 'Teutonic' roots and both have at different times claimed to be the true inheritors of Imperial Rome.

32 'The worth of individuals is measured by the extent to which they reflect and represent the national spirit, and have adopted a particular station within the affairs of the state as a whole... the individual's morality will then consist in fulfilling the duties imposed upon him by his social station'. Hegel, *Lectures on Philosophy*, 80.

33 Talcott Parsons, *The Social System* (New York: Tavistock, 1952).

34 The marginalists in the nineteenth century defined the economy in terms of efficiency of resource allocation. David Easton, *The Political System* (Chicago: University of Chicago Press, 1953).

35 Walt W. Rostow, *The Stages of Economic Growth: A Non-Communist Manifesto* (Cambridge: Cambridge University Press, 1971).

36 Humberto R. Maturana and Fransisco J. Varela, *Autopoiesis and Cognition: The Realization of the Living* (Dordrecht/Boston: Reidel Publishing Co., 1975).

37 Stephen Gill, 'New Constitutionalism, Democratisation and Global Political Economy', *Pacific Review* 10, no. 1 (1998): 23–40.

38 Manuel Castells, *The Rise of the Network Society*. vol. 1 of *The Information Age: Economy, Society and Culture* (Oxford: Blackwell, 1996), 376.

39 Ohmae, *Borderless World* and *The End of the Nation State*.

40 Paul Q. Hirst and Grahame Thompson, *Globalization in Question: The International Economy and the Possibilities of Governance* (Cambridge: Polity, 1996).

41 Ronen Palan, 'Trying to Have Your Cake and Eating It: How and Why the State System Created Offshore', *International Studies Quarterly* 42, no. 3 (1998): 625–44 and Sol Picciotto, 'Offshore: The State as Legal Fiction', in *Finance Centres and Tax Havens*, eds. Mark Hampton and Jason Abbott (Basingstoke: Macmillan, 1999).

42 Ronen Palan, 'Offshore and the Symbiotic Theory of the State and Globalisation' (paper presented to the British International Studies Association Annual Conference, University of Leeds, 15–17 December 1997).

43 Gary Burn, 'The State, the City and the Euromarkets', *Review of International Political Economy* 6, no. 2 (1999): 225–61.

44 Walter Diamond and Dorothy Diamond, *Tax Havens of the World* (New York: Matthew Bender Books, 1997).

45 Marcel Cassard, 'Offshore Banking; International Banking', *IMF Working Paper* WP/94/107, 1994.

46 International Labour Organisation, *Labour and Social Issues Relating to Export Processing Zones* (Geneva, 1998).

47 Helen Thanopoulou, 'What Price the Flag? The Terms of Competitiveness in Shipping', *Marine Policy* 22, no. 4–5 (1998): 359–74.

48 Hence, proposals are put forward to establish the moon and artificial satellites as offshore 'locations'. See, for example, 'Off-Planet Banking?', *Offshore and Privacy Secrets*, [http://permanenttourist.com/offshore-011.html] (14 April 1999).

49 Palan, 'Trying to Have Your Cake'.

50 Lash and Urry, *Economies of Signs and Space*.

51 Philip McMichael, *Development and Social Change: A Global Perspective* (Thousand Oaks, CA: Pine Forge, 1996).

52 Phil Cerny, *The Changing Architecture Of Politics: Structure, Agency and the Future of the State* (London: Sage, 1990).

53 Paul Krugman, 'Competitiveness: A Dangerous Obsession', *Foreign Affairs* 73, no. 2 (1994): 28–44.

54 Palan and Abbott, *State Strategies*; Peck, 'From Federal Welfare'; and Michael Webber, 'Producing Globalisation: Apparel and the Australian State', in *Unruly World*.

55 Nigel Dodd, *The Sociology of Money: Economics. Reason and Contemporary Society* (Cambridge: Polity, 1994), 90.

56   Fernand Braudel, *Civilisation and Capitalism Fifteenth to Eighteenth Century*, vol. 3: *The Perspective of the World* (London: William Collins and Sons, 1984), 24.

57   General Agreement on Tariffs and Trade (GATT), *Uruguay Round Final Act* (Geneva, 1994) XII, 1, emphasis added.

58   Ibid., XVI, 4.

59   Cutler, 'Artifice, Ideology and Paradox' and Teubner, *Global Law Without a State*.

60   John Lovering, 'Globalisation, Unemployment and "Social Exclusion" in Europe: Three Perspectives on the Current Policy Debate', *International Planning Studies* 3, no. 1 (1998): 35.

61   Friedrich Hayek, *Full Employment at Any Price?* (London: Institute of Economic Affairs, 1975); Stanley Aronowitz and William DiFazio, *The Jobless Future* (Minneapolis: University of Minnesota Press, 1994); Jeremy Rifkin, *The End of Work: The Decline of the Global Labour Force and the Dawn of the Post-Market Era* (New York: G. P. Putnam, 1995); John Grieve Smith, *Full Employment: A Pledge Betrayed* (Basingstoke: Macmillan, 1997); and Lovering, 'Globalisation, Unemployment and "Social Exclusion"'.

62   Useful accounts of the rise of the concept of social exclusion can be found in, for example, Rosemary Crompton and Phillip Brown, eds., *A New Europe? Economic Restructuring and Social Exclusion* (London: University College London Press, 1994); Ali Madanipour, Goran Cars, and Judith Allen, *Social Exclusion in European Cities: Processes, Experiences and Responses* (London: Regional Studies Association, 1998); Graham Room, ed., *Beyond the Threshold: The Measurement and Analysis of Social Exclusion* (Bristol: Policy Press, 1995); Hilary Silver, 'Social Exclusion and Social Solidarity: Three Paradigms', *International Labour Review* 133, no. 5–6 (1994): 531–78; and Ruth Levitas, *The Inclusive Society? Social Exclusion and New Labour* (Basingstoke: Macmillan, 1998).

63   Ruth Levitas, 'The Concept of Social Exclusion and the New Durkheimian Hegemony', *Critical Social Policy* 16 (1996): 5–20.

64   Jochen Clasen, Arthur Gould, and Jill Vincent, *Voices Within and Without: Responses to Long-term Unemployment in Germany, Sweden and Britain* (Bristol: Policy Press, 1998); and Jordi Gual, ed., *The Social Challenge of Job Creation: Combating Unemployment in Europe* (Cheltenham: Edward Elgar, 1996).

65   Deborah S. Johnson, 'Constructing the Periphery in Modern Global Politics', in *The New International Political Economy*, eds. Craig Murphy and Roger Tooze (Boulder, CO: Lynne Rienner, 1991), 149–70.

66   Scott Lash, 'Reflexivity and its Doubles: Structure, Aesthetics, Community', in *Reflexive Moderization*, 133.

67   Thrift, *Spatial Formations*, 47.

68   See also Lovering, 'Globalisation, Unemployment and "Social Exclusion"' and Zygmunt Bauman, *Work, Consumerism and the New Poor* (Buckingham: Open University Press, 1998).

69   Jeanette Money, *Fences and Neighbors: The Political Geography of Immigration Control* (Ithaca, NY: Cornell University Press, 1999) and Roula Khalaf, 'Lure of a New World Leaves Morocco's Children Old Before their Time', *Financial Times* (24 March 1999): 3.

70   Peck, 'From Federal Welfare', Lovering, 'Globalisation, Unemployment and "Social Exclusion"'; and Bauman, *Work, Consumerism and the New Poor*.

71   Cerny, *The Changing Architecture of Politics*.

72   Cutler, 'Artifice, Ideology and Paradox' and Teubner, *Global Law Without a State*.

73   Palan, 'Trying to Have Your Cake'.

74   Lash, 'Reflexivity and its Doubles', 126.

10

Debordering the World of States: Toward a Multi-Level System in Europe and a Multi-Polity System in North America? Insights from Border Regions

Joachim K. Blatter

Introduction: Debordering the World of States – Toward New Kinds of Polities?

The Westphalian system – as a conceptual template – "refers to the organization of the world into territorially exclusive, sovereign nation-states, each with an internal monopoly of legitimate violence" (Caporaso 1996: 34). Even though such an idealized model has never been completely realized in practice, it continues to dominate our thinking about polities and institutional change at the turn of the millennium. This might also be a result of the fact that the most far-reaching transformations beyond the Westphalian system have occurred in Europe. But since the process of European integration is becoming embedded in a wider discourse on globalization and regionalization, we are witnessing a new flurry of conceptual approaches for capturing the institutional transformations beyond the Westphalian system.

The discourse on European integration has been centered on two questions: first, does the EU still represent an inter-governmental regime dominated by the executives of the nation states or has it evolved beyond such a state-centered system? The debate has been framed in terms of "state-centric versus multi-level governance" (Marks et al. 1996) and is still heated. The second question, closely related, does not concentrate on the "nature of the beast" (Risse-Kappen 1996), but tries instead to disentangle the driving forces of European integration: can the process of integration be explained by the rational strategies and grand compromises of national political leaders, or must we employ functionalistic explanations with their emphasis on functional necessities, sectoralism, gradualism and "spill-overs" between different political fields? Both ways of framing the debate have limited our thinking about institutional transformation beyond the Westphalian system. What all of these debates have in common, however, is that they envision the "deterritorialization" and "unbundling" of politics (Elkins 1995). The modern Westphalian system is characterized by the fact that internally there exists a clear hierarchy of political authority/loyalty, with the nation-state taking center stage. Identities and political tasks/

responsibilities are "bundled" on a territorial basis. This means that other identities are subordinate to national identity. Furthermore, the territorial state is – ideally – an "all-purpose" organization. Political boundaries are congruent; that is, all specific functional jurisdictions occupy the same territory. With unbundling, however, the path is made clear for "territorial communities" to be supplemented by "non-territorial communities." What is missing, however, is a convincing classification of types of non-territorial communities (for attempts to provide these, see Agnew 1999: 504–7 and Ferguson and Mansbach 1996: 391–2; see also the editors' introduction to this volume for more extended discussion).

Overall, thinking on polities beyond Westphalia has been strongly influenced by the example of European integration, which has led to a focus on "multi-level governance" – a concept which is still inclined to the notion of "territoriality." Recently, this narrowness has been overcome by scholars from very different schools. Whereas public-choice scholars are challenging the assumption of the primacy of territorially based communities from an individualistic perspective, historical institutionalists are making clear that territorial contingency is just one possible way to establish political identity and authority. From the governance literature the concept of "policy networks" has been brought into the study of international relations (IR) (Risse-Kappen 1996). Furthermore, the aspects of the identity of, loyalty to, and legitimacy of polities are moving into the foreground (e.g., Laffan 1996), complementing the instrumental governance debate. The next step has to be the development of a variety of clearly defined polity concepts and the exploration of which kinds of polities are actually emerging. This article is an attempt to contribute to such an endeavor. By doing so, it transcends various disciplinary boundaries. The theoretical concepts are drawn not from the IR literature, but rather from political and organizational theory, and the empirical examples focus on subnational regions in the borderlands of nation-states and not on supranational levels of integration.

This paper proceeds as follows: first, I argue that insights from border regions are useful contributions to the debate on "debordering the world of states." Next, the notion of "political institution-building" is introduced for comparing and analyzing transformations of political structures. On the basis of such an understanding, I develop a classification of political institutions for cross-border cooperation by using various insights of "neo-institutionalism." I use four ideal types of cross-border political institutions – that is, commissions, connections, coalitions, and consociations – as my heuristic devices.

Equipped with these conceptual tools, I analyze the institution-building processes in four border regions. Two regions in Europe and two in North America, one on each continent with high material (socioeconomic and environmental) interdependencies and one on each continent with low interdependencies, make up my table of cases. Furthermore, on each continent one cross-border region (CBR) has been chosen with strong asymmetries between the political systems of the involved nation-states (France–Germany–Switzerland; USA–Mexico) and one with rather low asymmetries (Germany–Switzerland–Austria; USA–Canada). Despite these differences between border regions on the same continent, it turned out that the major differences in cross-border institution-building exists between the two continents. Based on these case studies, a speculative hypothesis is developed: the European path of debordering the world of states is indeed fairly accurately described as a "multi-level system" – since the emerging CBRs are developing into another "soft" but "comprehensive" institutional layer within the European multi-level-polity – while neither on the US–Mexican nor on the US–Canadian border is such an encompassing, territorially defined cross-border regional polity developing. Here, non-territorial institutions (utilitarian exchange networks at the southern border, and ideological coalitions at the northern border) complement the institutions of the nation-state(s), which remain(s) the single, almost uncontested territorial polity concept on this continent.[1] These non-territorial political institutions do not challenge the nation-state polity directly since they are not the same kind of polities. However, they provide examples of new kinds of polities that call into question traditional conceptions of polity systems.

Border Regions as Transformational Laboratories and Representations of Emergent Polity Concepts

Searching for emerging polities "beyond Westphalia" in the borderlands, in subnational CBRs, might seem inappropriate, since the most important developments which challenge the nation-state have certainly occurred on the supranational, continental, and global levels. Nevertheless, looking at the borderlands, the "front lines" of territorially demarcated modern states, provides numerous opportunities to discover alternative political forms. The various paths of cross-border political cooperation and integration in European and North American borderlands reveal a broader range of political orders "beyond Westphalia" than just the European Union (possibly complemented by NAFTA). This finding certainly does not diminish major insights gained by studying supranational integration processes, but may contribute to the development of a more comprehensive conceptual framework for the analysis of future political orders. Finally, the comparison on which this paper is based has shown so far a close connection between institution-building processes on the supranational level ("macro-integration") and the process of "micro-integration" in the borderlands (Blatter 2000). This suggests that the two developments are part of a broader development in the nature of political orders on both continents.

Two additional arguments can be offered to justify the study of institution-building in borderlands. First, seen as peripheral parts of the state territory, border regions are normally not the forerunners in the processes of "glocalization." Indeed, as Saskia Sassen (1996) has pointed out, it is "global cities" that are the most important places to become globally linked and disembedded from their national environment. Nevertheless, other proponents of the "rise of the regional state," like Kenichi Ohmae (1993), take CBRs as examples for a future characterized by the declining importance of the nation-state and the increasing relevance of "regions" that are being shaped by intensive socioeconomic interdependencies. Furthermore, many border regions are no longer at the "periphery"; quite often they are witnessing economic prosperity above the national average. At least in North America and in western Europe – and after the fall of the Iron Curtain, in central and eastern Europe as well – border regions are changing (or at least complementing) their character from "front lines" of sovereign states to socioeconomic "contact zones" for neighboring societies (Ratti 1993). Second, these regions were especially "bounded worlds" during the heyday of the sovereign state. If the postulated transformations "beyond Westphalia" are really taking place, we expect to encounter dramatic changes, since both elements of "glocalization" join forces in the borderlands: transnational integration and domestic decentralization/regionalization are challenging the dominance of national administrations in governing CBRs.

Regional Cross-Border Cooperation as Political Institution-Building

Since neo-institutionalism is comprehensive enough to capture a wide range of forms of cooperation and to provide an explanation of these forms, it provides *prima facie* a solid foundation for an analysis of cross-border cooperation. In this context the analytical distinction between instrumental and symbolic or identity-providing institutions becomes crucial. For example, Göhler (1996) developed an institutional theory based on the work of anthropologist Arnold Gehlen, who distinguished two fundamental dimensions of political institutions: the instrumental and the ideational.

The *instrumental* dimension sees institutions as mechanisms of control. Such a conceptualization starts with the assumption that there is a material interdependence between social actors and that institutions are created to serve specific purposes. Göhler calls the second dimension of political institutions the *symbolic* dimension and cites Gehlen, who described "ritual" as symbolic activity without a specific purpose (*zweckfrei*), but effecting mutual obligations among the members of a group. In other words, political institutions based on symbolic actions influence the identities of political actors. Therefore, I call institutions which are primarily based on symbols "identity-providing institutions." Such a conceptualization assumes that the identities and preferences of individuals are not exogenously defined, but endogenously influenced by institutionalized interaction. The "interaction orientation" is not individualistic but relativistic: actors discriminate between those who belong to the group, as here solidarity (or even altruism) prevails, and those who do not belong to the group, since competition (or even hostility) is here the dominant "interaction orientation" (Scharpf 1997: 84–9).

Table 10.1 sums up the differences between instrumental and identity-providing institutions. Whereas the instrumental perspective is based on an objective-materialist

Table 10.1 Differences between "instrumental" and "identity-providing" institutions

	Instrumental	Identity-providing
General function	Serving specific purposes: problem solving, control, enhancing utility (welfare)	Sense making: orientation, belonging, identity
Specific function	Reduction of uncertainty	Reduction of ambiguity
Motivation for institution-building	Material interdependencies: positive/negative external effects; synergies	Idealistic ties: mutual affection and shared values
Formation of actor's identities and preferences	Exogenous	Endogenous
Interaction orientation	Objectivistic/individualistic	Relative/comparative
Crucial element for collective action	Rules for interaction, (especially) for decision making	Strength of ties, (especially) mobilizing effect of symbols

worldview and tends toward functional and rational conceptions of human behavior, the identification view is based on a subjective-idealist ontology and has affinities to constructivist approaches in the social sciences.

Formal (Tightly Coupled) and Informal (Loosely Coupled) Institutions

There is a growing paradigm shift in the social sciences from concern with formal organizations (hierarchies) toward informal, interorganizational networks (heterarchies). Renate Mayntz (1993), describing this transformation as the latest step in a dialectical process of modernization, distinguishes forms of governance on the basis of their "structural coupling." Markets are characterized by no structural coupling, hierarchies by tight coupling, and networks by loose coupling. First, formal organizations (hierarchies) have replaced pre-modern "quasi-groups," and now hierarchies are being supplanted by heterarchies.

In their presentation of the *basic forms of social coordination*, Mayntz and Scharpf (1995) distinguish forms of *structural coupling* according to the degree of individual autonomy on the one hand, and the capacity for collective action on the other. The two variables correlate negatively, although there exists a continuum between the extremes. Mayntz and Scharpf furthermore introduce *modes of interaction* in order to determine the intensity of structural coupling (1995: 61, 62). Scharpf (1997: 46, 47) examines four modes of interaction: unilateral action, negotiated agreement, majority vote, and hierarchical direction. Four different *institutional settings* are characterized by these modes of interaction and are called: anarchic field, network, association, and organization. The relationship between the mode of interaction and institutional setting is not, however, a function of a single mode of interaction. Rather, institutional settings are characterized by their capacity to support different modes of interaction. While "organizations" are able to support all four modes of interaction, a self-organizing network can only support the reaching of agreement by negotiations and is open for unilateral activities. It can support neither the exercise of hierarchical authority nor decisions taken by majority vote.

Other authors, particularly those applying network analysis to structural patterns and to the transformation from hierarchies to networks, utilize a different set of criteria for classifying these institutional forms. For example, Kenis and Schneider (1991: 25) develop a concept of networks different from the classical definition of *formal hierarchies* provided by Herbert Simon. Simon (1962: 477) held "that hierarchies have the property of near-decomposability. Intra-component linkages are generally stronger than inter-component linkages." Networks are dominant in those cases where "near-decomposability" is lacking. This means that horizontal links to actors outside the unit are present to such an extent that they cannot be ignored. These horizontal links supplement/ignore the vertical links to the upper layer of the organization. The top level of the organization – in hierarchical organizations the only legitimate point for outside contacts – is bypassed. Defining *structural coupling* in terms of patterns of interaction means that *tight coupling* is primarily *rigid coupling*, because the links between actors are defined by formal lines of contact and not by the intensity of the links.

It is exactly the intensity of interdependencies/interactions which other authors place at the center of their analyses. Williamson (1991: 278, 279) points to the duration, frequency, and consequentiality of interdependencies when he differentiates between the adaptive advantages of *hierarchies* and *markets*. Hierarchies are favorable if there is a long-term interdependent relation and if the need for coordination increases in frequency and consequentiality. This suggests that political institutions with a high interaction intensity will perform tasks in many or in all policy fields, as has been the case (at least ideally) with the nation-state and the (European) city. Both political institutions "bundle" tasks and responsibilities in (almost) all policy fields on the basis of a congruent territorial space with clear-cut geographical boundaries. During the last few decades, however, we have witnessed a process of "unbundling" on various levels. On the metropolitan level, the city is not being transformed into a larger "metro-city" as envisioned in the 1960s and 1970s. Instead, many single-purpose governmental units are spreading throughout the region. Based on the concept of "variable geometry," this trend is leading to a "fragmented regionalism" (Bollens 1997). On the national level we also find an increasing relevance of "policy networks" in specific policy sectors, in contrast to earlier comprehensive policy approaches (Marin and Mayntz 1991). Similarly, in the international realm, states are increasingly enmeshed in a web of international institutions described as "dynamic sectoral legal regimes" (Gehring 1990).

The common features of these "new" forms of governance are: they focus on a specific function, policy issue or policy field; in comparison to the state or the city, they are less formalized; and finally, they include private as well as public actors. The boundary between the public and the private sector is becoming blurred at the same time as the territorial boundaries between traditional political units are being transcended (Kenis & Schneider 1991).

Until now, our indicators for distinguishing between tightly coupled and loosely coupled institutions have been drawn from the governance literature, which basically employs an instrumental view of political institutions. However, as I have argued above, political institutions have a further dimension: they shape identities. By analogy to the differentiation of tightly and loosely coupled institutions in the instrumental dimension, we can distinguish institutions that influence identities comprehensively on the basis of a territorial definition of community from those that activate identities in a non-comprehensive, more specific way. The former rely heavily on affective and emotional ties that are created and sustained by symbols and foster belief in a "natural community" (see table 10.2). The most important

Table 10.2   Differences between formal (tightly coupled) and informal (loosely coupled) institutions

	Formal institution, tight coupling	Informal institution, loose coupling
"Frontier" mode of interaction	Hierarchical order or majority vote	Negotiated agreement or unilateral action
Pattern of interaction	Vertical links	Horizontal links
Intensity/frequency of interaction	High (all/many tasks)	Low (one/few tasks)
Institutional loci	Territorial	Functional
Forms of idealistic ties	Affective-holistic (nationalism, regionalism)	Value-specific (ideology, e.g., liberalism)

community of this kind during the last few centuries has been the nation (in the modern, non-ethnic sense in which nationhood and citizenship are defined, e.g., in France). The latter institutions are not as holistic in their approach to shaping identities, but provide orientation in various policy disputes. As in Sabatier's conception of "advocacy coalitions" (1993), the members of such an institution share a certain "belief system." The core of such a "belief system" comprises fundamental normative and ontological axioms. Belonging to such a coalition reduces ambiguity for the individual in a world of paradoxes and competing values.

Ideal Types of Cross-Border Political Institutions

As a next step I combine the two analytical dimensions and distinguish four ideal types of cross-border political institutions (see figure 10.1).

Commissions

Following Swanson, the first ideal type of cross-border cooperation is labeled *commission*. Swanson (1978) compiled a comprehensive overview of the contacts between US American states and Canadian provinces, and distinguished commissions from committees. The former are formally created by an international treaty which clearly defines their specified tasks, competencies, and geographic scope. They are characterized by a scientific, technical, or judicial approach in order to "depoliticize" cross-border issues and disputes (Swanson 1978: 145, 146).

Such institutions are set up as formal instruments of the nation-states to solve problematic cross-border interdependencies. This means that the interests of the parties are aggregated along vertical lines, with national governments representing these interests in international negotiations. Indicators for such institutions are national delegations and voting procedures. The members of a commission are

	Formal/ tightly coupled	Informal/ loosely coupled
Instrumental/ control	**COMMISSIONS** Correct knowledge/rules; Experts: engineers, lawyers	**CONNECTIONS** Useful knowledge/resources; Broker:planners/developers
Identificational/ orientation	**CONSOCIATIONS** Emotional symbols; Integrators: leading regional politicians	**COALITIONS** Values, ideologies; Mobilizers: party and interest group representatives

Figure 10.1 Ideal types of cross-border political institutions

appointed by national governments, and the delegations are typically organized by
the national foreign ministry. Ideally, a commission can be used for all or at least for
a broad range of issues in the border area.

Commissions are set up by international treaty; goals, tasks, competencies, and
territorial scope are regulated in detail. They use decision mechanisms based not on
unanimity – typically, a neutral arbitrator fulfills this role. If a strong element of
hierarchy is not included, other mechanisms for finding joint solutions are created
that follow the logic of deduction. Leading members of commissions are typically
engineers or lawyers, experts whose interest it is to deduce the "best possible,"
"necessary," or "appropriate" measures and projects on the basis of scientific-
technical knowledge or the principles of international law. Finally, commissions
quite often become corporate actors, since they are assigned financial resources and
personnel. These organizational capacities are employed for fact finding and monitoring.

Connections

Connections, like commissions, are instruments created to serve specific purposes.
But they do not attempt to solve the problems of collective action by deducing the
"correct" solution with the assistance of scientific-technical or judicial expertise.
Instead, connections help to overcome obstacles preventing the exploitation of
positive externalities and synergies. In this case, information does not indicate the
"objective necessity" for coordinated action, it rather reduces transaction costs
(e.g., for finding exchange partners and calculating the benefits and costs of a
joint project). Resources are used not for controlling and monitoring, but
for transforming joint activities into positive-sum games. Typical actors, therefore,
are not technical or legal experts, but instead "brokers," such as planners and
developers. Trust and informal norms and rules develop in the course of ongoing
exchange relationships. This means that only a few people can be involved in such
an exchange network and that connections typically concentrate their activities in a
specific policy field. Connections are focused on specific tasks and projects;
therefore, their geographical space is determined by functional considerations and
not by clear-cut territorial lines of demarcation.

According to the practical, bottom-up approach of including all actors with
relevant resources, subnational administrative units and private actors are incorporated into connections on an equal basis. This means that horizontal linkages
between various actors dominate. Connections are informal and loosely coupled
institutions – they have no or only a weak legal basis and few internal regulations
and procedures. There is no explicit mechanism of decision making or it is based on
consent (unanimity).

Coalitions

In contrast to Keohane and Nye's concept of transgovernmental *coalitions* (1974),
my definition does not put primary emphasis on the resources of the allies in a

coalition and their desire to join forces in battles with other actors. Instead, I want to follow Sabatier's *advocacy coalition* approach, wherein political actors choose coalition partners not on the basis of material interdependencies or by calculating the most profitable interaction, but on the basis of idealistic affinity. A shared belief system is the glue that holds together the allies within a coalition; they share an ideological orientation. Typical actors within coalitions are representatives of political parties and interest groups.

Based on such premises, choosing sides and building institutions are seen to result from normative-cognitive affinities. We can expect that political actors will build coalitions even for projects in which the cross-border situation is not a positive-sum game. Thus solidarity with the partners on the other side of the border can lead political actors to activities where they bear the costs and the partner takes the profits. Nevertheless, actors within cross-border coalitions behave strategically – what counts is the common results against ideological rivals.

Apart from this basic difference, coalitions have many commonalties with connections: they are dominated by horizontal linkages between various partners (public and private actors). The focus for institutionalizing their interaction is not territorial, but a common idea (ideology, belief system). There are no or only minor rules and regulations for interactions, and the organizational capacity of the joint institution is only minimal.

Consociation

The fourth ideal type of cross-border institution combines idealistic interdependencies with strong formalization (a tight coupling). In accordance with Duchacek (1984: 9; 1986: 103), we will call this form of cross-border collaboration *consociation*.

A consociation influences individual behavior by symbolizing polity ideas which shape identities and preferences. Typical symbols are flags, logos, maps, and names for the common region. In contrast to coalitions, consociations "formalize" their identity-facilitating ties by creating and presenting such symbols. This formalization aims at mobilizing public and private actors for cross-border activities. Therefore, rather than technocrats, leading regional politicians are the major actors in cross-border consociations. The common identity of the members of such institutions is based on a territorial demarcation – the ideology of a consociation is a sort of cross-border regionalism.

The pattern of interaction is characterized by predominantly vertical lines of interaction, since the various interests become aggregated and are represented in the cross-border interaction by the political leaders of the subregions (e.g., governors or mayors). Nevertheless, the pattern of interaction is not as strongly dominated by vertical lines of interaction, since the hierarchical aggregation takes place not on a national basis, but on a subnational one. This is one major difference from commissions; moreover, compared to coalitions, the most important actors within consociations are "territorial representatives," politicians as delegates of a territorially defined constituency. Since this usually means that consociations are concerned with a broad range of policies, they are not limited to concrete projects or focused on specific goals (values).

Not only is the pattern of interaction less hierarchical than in commissions, but also the mode of interaction differs. Whereas commissions employ a sort of hierarchical order, consociations ideally use the rule of majority vote for decision making. A consociation is not based on an international treaty but is instead created by a highly visible symbolic event. Both can overlap, of course, but what matters primarily for consociations is not detailed prescriptions of the rights and duties of the parties, but the public visibility and signaling function of the founding procedure (and the following meetings). Financial and personnel resources are invested in the production and distribution of identity-facilitating symbols and not in investigation and monitoring, as is the case with commissions.

Political Institution-Building in European and North American Border Regions

The following section presents some results of a comparative study of cross-border institution-building in four border regions throughout the twentieth century (Blatter 2000).[2] Two of these are located in western Europe. One is the Upper Rhine Valley with the neighboring states of France, Germany, and Switzerland. This CBR is characterized by strong socioeconomic interdependencies and the fact that quite different political systems are involved. A second CBR is the Lake Constance region, where the federal states of Germany, Switzerland, and Austria share a border. Here, we find very low socioeconomic interdependencies. The other two border regions are located on the West coast of North America. One region will be referred to as "The Californias," a cross-border interaction space on the US–Mexican border centered on the San Diego–Tijuana agglomeration. This border region features strong socioeconomic interdependencies, but very distinct political systems. The other region is called "Cascadia" and includes various initiatives across the US–Canadian border in the Pacific Northwest – centered on the Cascadia corridor from Vancouver to Seattle and Portland. As in the Lake Constance region, the situation in Cascadia is characterized by low socioeconomic interdependencies, but it has comparatively similar political systems. After briefly describing the institutional profiles of the four border regions in words and symbols, we concentrate on the differences between the European and the North American institutions.

Institutional Profiles of Four Border Regions

In all border regions we have found a variety of cross-border institutions, each of which can be classified according to the typology for cross-border institutions developed above. Limited space makes it necessary to present summarized results for the four border regions. The following description refers to the situation in the mid-1990s.

(1)   In the *Upper Rhine Valley* there is a broad variety of active cross-border institutions. There are inter-governmental commissions (e.g., Oberrhein-

Ausbaukommission[3]), coalitions (e.g., Badisch-Elsässische Bürgerinitiativen[4]), connections (Begleitausschüsse für die EU-INTERREG programme[5]), and consociations (e.g., Regiorat[6], Oberrheinkonferenz[7]). How strongly this CBR has been institutionalized is expressed by the creation of a cross-border parliament (Oberrheinrat) whose members are elected indirectly. All these institutions operate with very divergent logics of interaction and possess quite typical features of the institutional ideal types defined above. Nevertheless, in comparison to other border regions, a regulatory and rather centralized element still dominates the overall cross-border cooperation. The national governments have created a detailed framework for cross-border cooperation on a subnational level with an international treaty ("Karlsruher Übereinkommen") signed in 1998, and in addition, in all cross-border institutions we find relatively differentiated, explicit rules and regulations.

The output and impact of the various cross-border institutions are also quite impressive and comprehensive. They include the joint construction and management of hydroelectric plants, the cleaning up of the Rhine river, the facilitation of socioeconomic exchanges in a highly integrated region, the creation of an integrated public-transport system, and the foundation of a variety of joint institutes (like the Centre Européen de Management in Colmar and the Institute for Regional Cooperation and European Administration in Kehl). Cooperation has also gone beyond projects with direct impact fostering mutual identification. This feature became apparent when a common economic regional development strategy was developed and German regional leaders strongly opposed any national/local retaliation when firms moved from the German side of the border to the French side to take advantage of high French subsidies. They argued both on the basis of self-interest ("Better they go to Alsace than to Poland") and on that of a common identity ("If we take the common CBR seriously, we cannot object to such a move") (translations from Blatter 2000: 255).

(2) The *Lake Constance region* also has a broad variety of cross-border institutions, but here the variation is not as broad and the overall characteristics have a different focal point. In the Lake Constance area there are also Commissions (e.g., Internationale Gewässerschutzkommission Bodensee[8]), Coalitions (e.g., Umweltrat Bodensee[9], Arbeitsgemeinschaft Wasserwerke Bodensee–Rhein[10]), and connections (Begleitausschüsse für die EU-INTERREG programme), but all of these institutions show strong elements of consociations in their actual performance. The strongest indicators for such a consociational core of cross-border cooperation are the comprehensive *Leitbilder* (development programs) produced in 1982 by the joint Raumplanungskommission (land-use planning commission) and 1995 by the Internationale Bodenseekonferenz, the cross-border institution of the government leaders from the *Länder* and cantons around the lake. These comprehensive development programs proved early on to be extraordinarily powerful symbols for a common identity within the CBR.

Regional cross-border cooperation at Lake Constance has led to one of the first and certainly most successful water conservation regimes in the world. In addition, it has resulted in the production of joint infrastructure even when a pressing need was not existent.[11] The politicians around the lake not only set up a highly attractive cross-border train service and financed a new ferry, they also induced stronger economic integration by providing information and platforms like the "Electronic Mall Bodensee."

(3) The cross-border cooperation among *The Californias* is based almost entirely on an instrumental logic. Formal commissions like the International Boundary and Water Commission (IBWC) are complemented by informal connections like the San Diego–Tijuana Binational Planning & Coordinating Committee. The twin institution Border Environmental Cooperation Commission/North American Development Bank (BECC/NAD-Bank), which has been created by side-agreements to NAFTA, is also a mixture of commission and connection. The task of this twin institution is to improve the environmental infrastructure in the border region. Relevant coalitions could not be established due basically to the weakness of the Mexican civil society. Attempts to create consociations failed; these institutions adapted to the situation and were transformed into connections. The San Diego Dialogue, for example, had to abandon its initial goals of instituting a regulatory border authority and creating a common identity in the cross-border metropolis and has shifted its center of activity toward the production and distribution of information for the business community.

Due to national legislation, but also to the many informal connections in a region "where North meets South" (Herzog 1990), there has been a phenomenal economic boom in the border zone. Thousands of *maquiladoras*, or twin-plants,[12] have been created despite the fact that efforts to construct joint infrastructure have been hampered by distrust and anxiety. After decades of negotiation, a joint sewage-treatment plant has been built under the auspices of the IBWC.

(4) *Cascadia* also lacks a comprehensive set of cross-border institutions. Only to a very limited extent have coalitions like the Pacific Northwest Economic Region (PNWER),[13] the Cascadia Project,[14] the British Columbia–Washington State Environmental Cooperation council, and the Sounds and Straits Alliance[15] developed into connections and consociations as was originally envisioned. Nation-state-dominated commissions have been ignored in recent times (e.g., the International Joint Commission (IJC)) or show serious malfunctions (e.g., the International Pacific Salmon Fisheries Commission).

The influence of transnational coalitions has been especially obvious in the joint struggle of environmentalists against the timber-harvesting practices in the forests of British Columbia. Environmentalists have joined forces in other conservation efforts as well (Levesque 2001). But the free traders have also been able to help each other in domestic policy struggles. For example, on both sides they were able to block a proposed border-crossing fee. But neither of these coalitions has been successful when it comes to conflicts with material cross-border interdependencies. Neither the environmentalists nor the free traders have been able to overcome the national cleavages in the field of salmon fishery. Instead, the conflict over salmons turned into a "fishery war" and interrupted all attempts to build a common CBR.

In line with the importance we ascribe to symbols in this study, the differences between the four regions is presented in a visualized form (Figure 10.2). The four institutional profiles are not only defined by their location within the matrix of institutional ideal types, they are also highlighted by symbols which represent these profiles.[16] The almost comprehensively institutionalized cross-border Upper Rhine region is shown as a square (the center still lies slightly within the upper-left field). Cross-border cooperation in the Lake Constance region, characterized by harmony and a common identity, is represented by a circle. The political cooperation in the San Diego–Tijuana region (The Californias), with its clear focus on instrumental institutions, is typified by a semi-permeable rectangle; and for the antagonistic coalitions in Cascadia the form of a wedge has been chosen.

The analysis of cross-border institution-building processes can be further disaggregated. First, I focus on the aspects of unbundling and de-territorialization. Second, I take a closer look on the "functional" ties which bind political actors in non-territorial "spaces of flows" – the two North American CBRs provide quite contrasting examples.

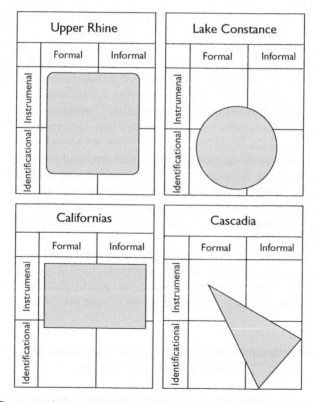

Figure 10.2 Dominant characteristics of the institutions of cross-border cooperation in the four border regions

Deterritorialization? Differences between Europe and North America

To what extend does cross-border political collaboration contribute to a development called unbundling and deterritorialization (Elkins 1995)? My discussion
below focuses on (1) the logics of representation, (2) the territorial demarcation,
(3) the scope of goals and tasks, and (4) the *leitmotivs* guiding cross-border institution-building,[17] in order to tackle this question.

Divergent logics of representation

For a discussion of the deterritorialization thesis, the question of primary interest
with regard to the logics of representation is this: are the members of the institutions territorial representatives (e.g., government leaders, parliamentarians,
mayors) or non-territorial representatives (e.g., representatives of interest groups,
scholars)?

There are clear differences between European and North American cross-border
cooperation in this respect: whereas in Europe the most important institutions
(Oberrheinkonferenz, Bodenseekonferenz) are purely inter-governmental and complemented by institutionalized meetings of parliamentarians, North American institutions are much more open for direct involvement by private actors: the
Commission of the Californias does not consist of parliamentarians, but it does
include a broad array of appointed representatives; the PNWER has both a public
and a private council and had to switch its predominant center of activity from the
former to the latter. In contrast to the steering committees of the INTERREG
programs, the Border Environmental Cooperation Commission not only cooperates
intensively with private actors, but also includes non-state members on its board of
directors. Comparing the cross-border associations on a local level, we get the same
picture. Although in all institutions we find territorial and non-territorial representatives, in the Regiorat (Upper Rhine Valley) and in the Bodenseerat politicians
clearly dominate. In contrast to this, the politicians in the San Diego Dialogue and
the Cascadia Project reduced their activity significantly after an initial euphoric
start, and these institutions rely much more on activists from the academic and
business spheres.

We can conclude that in Europe cross-border cooperation is still dominated by
territorial representatives (but national representatives have been replaced and
supplemented by regional ones), whereas in North America institutionalized
cross-border cooperation relies much more on private involvement.

Territorial demarcation: clear-cut geographical definitions and congruence versus fuzziness and overlaps

With respect to this indicator, the strongest differences appear between the European and the North American border regions as well. Whereas all European insti-

tutions have defined their geographic scope of activity, this is not the case with some North American institutions (e.g., San Diego Dialogue, Cascadia Project). Furthermore, in Europe the various institutions within a CBR share a common geographical definition of the border region (except for the INTERREG programs, which were introduced "top-down" by the EU), and the geographic spaces reclaimed by more local initiatives add up to the geographic spaces of the wider regional institutions (at least in the Upper Rhine Valley). In contrast, in the North American border regions we find geographical overlaps and no congruence between the various institutions. For example, the Mexican state of Baja California Sur is a member of the smaller Commission of the Californias, but not a member of the more encompassing Border Governors Conference (BGC). In Cascadia, the various institutions do not resemble each other geographically as is the case in Europe, in that the sum of the smaller units is equal to the larger unit, but they follow the logic of "concentric circles": the smallest institutions (in terms of geographical scope) focus on Mainstreet Cascadia (the metropolitan corridor of Vancouver, Seattle, and Portland), the Pacific Northwest Economic Partnership includes British Columbia and Washington State, whereas the PNWER embraces Alaska, British Columbia, Alberta, the Yukon Territory, Washington, Oregon, Montana and Idaho.

Universal versus specific goals and tasks

Another indicator which points to differences between European and North American ways of cross-border institution-building is the breadth of goals and tasks ascribed to any one cross-border institution (intersectoral integration). Here, the variance is most obvious when we examine developments over time. Whereas in Europe subnational cross-border institutions have developed almost encompassing programs and activities in many policy fields (e.g., in the 1990s the Bodenseekonferenz widened its scope of activities from mainly water-oriented policies toward economic and cultural activities), the corresponding institutions in North America (BGC, San Diego Dialogue, PNWER, Cascadia Project), which all started with similar broad aspirations, had actually to narrow their activities to offering basic services for economic development and business contacts.

The nation-states in Europe created commissions for their border regions with encompassing tasks and responsibilities (in terms of policy fields) in the 1970s (following a recommendation of the First Meeting of the Ministries responsible for Regional Planning under the auspices of the Council of Europe). The commissions in North America (IJC and IBWC), on the other hand, have only marginally expanded their fields of activity to include a broader array of environmental problems (the IJC has been much more open to this than the IBWC; this is one reason why a new institution has been created here: the BECC/NADBank); in these border regions no single institution has been created which can potentially address issues in all policy fields. Lastly, the same picture emerges if one looks at the policy scope of the INTERREG programs in comparison to those of BECC/NADBank. The former has been steadily expanded to include almost all possible policy fields and all kinds of projects, whereas the latter is restricted to environmental and health infrastructure.

Visions and leitmotivs: European spaces of place and North American spaces of flows

Last but not least, we find quite different visions and *leitmotivs* in the discourses on cross-border institution-building in Europe and North America. In the regions of west-central Europe, cross-border institution-building is guided by concepts based on territorial identities and encompassing, multi-functional polities. Following Castells we call this a logic of *spaces of place* (Castells 1996). In North America, cross-border institution-building follows much more the logic of *spaces of flows*, which means that non-territorial interdependencies and identities are primary *leitmotivs* for creating cross-border institutions. Here, these institutions are much narrower in focus and more fluid in respect to space and time.

The different logics of spaces of place and spaces of flows can be shown in the concepts and activities of environmentalists. In the Lake Constance region environmentalists evaluate a broad array of policies of the riparian municipalities. Based on this evaluation an "environmental capital city of the Lake Constance region" is chosen every year. Here, a holistic, intersectoral approach is combined with a territorial definition of the relevant space. This pattern differs quite remarkably from the bioregional concepts found in North America. Bioregions are demarcated according to specific natural flows like watersheds or the migratory routes of salmon or other wildlife. Examples of institution-building based on such a concept include the Georgia Basin Initiative, launched by the government of British Columbia, and the Georgia Basin–Puget Sound Task Force, created under the auspices of the British Columbia–Washington State Environmental Cooperation Council. The relevance of such a perspective is suggested by further cases. The environmental organization Northwest Environment Watch demarcated the boundaries of the Pacific Northwest on a watershed basis (Northwest Environment Watch 1994), and the Internet magazine *Cascadia Times* defines its area of concern in terms of the migratory space of salmon.

Those differences can not only be traced by comparing the concepts of environmentalists, but show up in a similar way if we look at the discourses of business groups and developers. Whereas in Europe developers describe their CBRs as *a place in the center of Europe*, North Americans talk about *ports of entry, corridors*, and *gateways*.

The limited sectoralized approach which accompanies the notion of spaces of flows contrasts sharply with the encompassing holistic approach based on spaces of place. The following quotation is typical for the thinking of the believers in cross-border cooperation in North America:

> Cascadia is neither a place nor a feeling. It is a rite of passage, a sign of maturity. To see this braver, newer world, a British Columbian would look not on a map, not in his shrivened or competitive heart, but in his bank account – economic man's most sacred place. (*British Columbia Business*, September 1992: 37)

Quite contrasting are the following statements from the conferences where the BODENSEERAT (Council of Lake Constance) was founded:

> Professor Timmermann has shown the interdependencies between the economic, political and socio-cultural spheres. In the long run it is impossible to adjust only one sphere to Europe. (Thomas Onken; Member of the Swiss Upper House (Ständerat); in Maus et al. 1990: 181; my translation).

> The Lake Constance region [should] develop into a common unit of the Alemans within Europe, that is taking part in creating Europe from the bottom up. We have found that there are already a multiplicity of cross-border institutions, attesting to the proclaimed Spirit of Lake Constance. [...] What is missing is a focal point, the *bundling* into a common voice, into a common organization. (Robert Maus, chief executive of the country of Konstanz and member of parliament in Baden-Württemberg; initiator of the Council of Lake Constance; in Maus et al. 1990: 187; my translation).

In sum, the proposed trends toward unbundling and deterritorialization are rather limited – basically to North America. In Europe, the cross-border institution certainly has an element of unbundling, since another layer of political decision making and identity formation is created, but this layer is again territorially defined and quite comprehensive in respect of policy goals and tasks and institutional variety. The North American border regions, in contrast, show much stronger elements of unbundling and deterritorialization. The territorial dimension of politics is weak because of the strong influence of private actors and because the institutions do not have clear-cut territorial demarcations. Furthermore, we can discover elements of unbundling, because only very limited tasks and goals are institutionalized at the cross-border level. Finally, the *leitmotivs* of the advocates of cross-border cooperation point toward a logic of "spaces of flows" as the guiding idea behind processes of micro-integration on this continent.

Beyond Unspecified "Functions" and "Spaces of Flows"

The empirical case studies make it quite obvious that we have to overcome unspecified notions like "from territory toward function" and to look more closely at the specific ties and links which are crucial for defining the new polities based on the logic of spaces of flows. The two North American border regions represent quite different alternatives to the "territorial imperative" as a basis for creating social cohesion and for building political institutions:

- socioeconomic exchanges and ecological interdependencies (*material flows*), or
- shared visions, beliefs, and ideologies (*flows of ideas*).

The Californias (the San Diego–Tijuana region) is a primary example of a polity that is highly integrated in a very selective way (only by many public–private networks for economic development) and shows a high degree of material flows. Nevertheless, all attempts to widen this selective path of micro-integration into a more comprehensive political region (including identity-facilitating institutions) failed. Neither on the US nor on the Mexican side has the idea of a common identity of this cross-border metropolis gained enough support to overcome long-standing negative attitudes. Therefore, cooperation can only emerge in those cases in which the enormous material profits gained by synergetic exchanges can overcome all barriers. Nevertheless, this selective form of integration has tremendous outputs and impacts.[18] It serves as one of the most dynamic economic development poles for North America, and the "exchanges" within the connections are significantly altering the involved nation-states. The impact on the Mexican side is already quite revolutionary: the capitalist spirit and the money which accompanied the *maquiladora* boom in the borderlands led to the growth of a middle class, which in turn proved to be the basis for the rise of the opposition party PAN. PAN started its successful contest with the oldest ruling party in the world, the PRI, at the end of the 1980s in the border cities (e.g., Tijuana), then won governorships in several border states (the first was Baja California). In the year 2000, finally, the election of PAN candidate Vincente Fox as president of Mexico represented the peak of revolutionary transformations in this nation-state. The USA, however, also faces tremendous challenges caused by the flows of people across the US–Mexican border (this flow is supported and sustained by the cross-border connections). It took a long time, but in the 1990s the *cultural browning* of the American southwest (Fernandez 1989: 30) was followed by elements of *political browning*. The Mexamericans can no longer be ignored by political parties and candidates and play an increasingly powerful political role in the border states. This has led to some talk (in the east) about a Mexican *reconquista* (*Atlantic Monthly,* November 1996: 68). In sum, the US–Mexican border *Connection* neither has a common identity, nor has it turned into a formal political institution, but it is already a structure with extraordinary political consequences.

In sharp contrast, the CBR called Cascadia has until now been integrated almost exclusively by shared ideas. Here, visions of the "rise of the region state" (Ohmae 1993) have found intellectual harbingers and have taken root in the political process on both sides. Two antagonistic worldviews with distinct ontological bases have been developed and publicly expressed in a radical and single-minded way which is probably unique. The *free traders* propose a borderless society in order to adapt to the globalized economy (Bluechel 1991); the *bioregionalists* advocate local communities which adapt to their natural environments (Mazza 1995). Both visionary coalitions are united in downplaying the modern, sovereign nation-state and have been able to mobilize people and resources on both sides of the border to further their goals in domestic policy processes. Furthermore, this CBR with its visionary ideas is a fertile ground for new social/political actors and concepts which are moving the world into a postmodern era. Cascadia has seen not only the most sophisticated elaborations of "bioregional governance" (Mazza 1995), but also the founding of Greenpeace in Vancouver. Washington State-based Boeing Aircraft and Microsoft are not only two of the most important global companies, their products are major facilitators of the process of globalization. Last but not least, it seems no accident that the most successful mystery series on TV, *The X-files*, which is a permanent attack on the modern belief in instrumental rationality and state control, is produced in Vancouver (with American investment). Nowhere are the fundamental ideas of the two cross-border coalitions, the free traders and the bioregionalists, more clearly and radically articulated than in the Pacific northwest. And – making Cascadia a politically relevant "space of flows" – these ideas refer to flows (free trade, natural flows) that are specified in the CBR in the northwest (by maps, concepts, governmental programs, thinktanks, and political institutions) but also have wider implications beyond the CBR, since the anti-modernist ideas produced in the Pacific northwest have been spread around the world (by actors and products like Greenpeace, Microsoft, and *The X-Files*). These coalitions have not been able, though, to overcome territorial identities and loyalties in policy disputes which are characterized by high material interdependencies (e.g., in the case of the salmon fishery).

In sum, both CBRs in North America are quite limited polities in respect of the scope of their social and political functions. Both are only able to invent and implement "developmental policies" (positive-sum games), whereas both are unable to fulfill (re)distributive tasks. Nevertheless, once again the logic of functional differentiation and specialization seems to work: the functional specialization of the polities has led to "high performance" in their specific fields, which seems to outweigh the total failure with respect to cross-border cooperation in fields with (re)distributive effects. The dynamic which is provided by such specialized polities might make them a viable alternative to the comprehensive polities we are witnessing in Europe.

Conclusion: Divergent Paths into a Debordered World – A Multi-Level System in Europe and a Multi-Polity System in North America?

In the four border regions in Europe and North America there is indeed a trend toward "debordering the world of states." The institutionalized links between subnational actors (governmental and non-governmental) and the official inclusion of subnational actors in cross-border institutions are undermining the exclusive gatekeeper role which national executives held during most of the twentieth century.

Territory is no longer the only imaginable basis for creating and defining primary political communities and institutions. Nevertheless, it would be too easy to "write off" the nation-state or the territorial basis of politics in general. In Europe, the process of regional cross-border institution-building shows the quite typical modern features of institutions with a rather clear-cut geographic basis and multi-sectoral goals and tasks. The European system of "multi-level governance" is being complemented by another – rather weak but comprehensive[19] – layer of institutions of governance and identity formation.

In contrast, in North America regional cross-border cooperation follows much more the logic of spaces of flows – but the new, quite "fluid" institutions in respect of geographic space and time are not strong enough to play a significant role in policy conflicts with distributive consequences across the national border. In these cases the "old" territorial identities and loyalties prevail. Therefore, here "debordering the world of states" means complementing the single territorial polity (nation-state) with non-territorial polities (transnational socioeconomic exchange networks or transnational ideological coalitions) which are relevant only in specific policy dimensions but have a significant mobilizing capacity. Such a system of "multi-polity governance" does not question the Westphalian system of sovereign states directly, since the states are not challenged by similar territorial units (same kind of polities), but presents a much more radical path of system change.

The hypothesis that we are witnessing divergent paths of polity change in Europe and North America might be challenged by the observation that the current state of affairs in the border regions in North America resembles the situation in western Europe at the end of the 1960s and the beginning of the 1970s when the first limited cross-border linkages emerged. A functionalist would assume that North America will catch up and that soon we will see the development of a full-blown, territorially based polity in North America on the continental and the borderlands levels. Those who ascribe a fundamental relevance to "ideas" would insist on the divergence of the emerging polity systems beyond Westphalia.

ACKNOWLEDGMENT

I would like to thank Katrin Auel, Sandra Lavenex, and the anonymous reviewers of the *European Journal of International Relations* for helpful comments on earlier drafts of this paper. A further thank you belongs to James Brice for language assistance and to Ingo Schnelle for technical assistance.

NOTES

This is a version of the paper previously published in *European Journal of International Relations* 7(2): 176–209.

1   The separatist movements in Quebec do not undermine this hypothesis, since such movements do not challenge the concept of sovereign nation-states. All that these separatists want is their own independent nation-state, neither a multi-level system nor a multi-polity system.

2   The hundreds of sources and references cannot be presented in this article – only the most important references are included.

3   The Oberrhein-Ausbaukommission was created in 1969 by the French and German governments in order to build and regulate joint power plants on the Rhine river.

4   The Badisch-Elsässische Bürgerinitiativen is the umbrella organization of environmental NGOs from the German border region of Baden and the French border region of Alsace.

5   The Commission of the European Community in 1990 launched a Community Initiative INTERREG to promote cross-border collaboration. The border regions are obligated to formulate a joint development program and must create steering committees for these programs. These committees comprise administrative representatives from the European Commission and the national and regional governments.

6   The Regiorat is a public–private organization established by the Swiss, French, and German "regio-associations" with a broad political agenda, but territorially limited to the southern part of the Upper Rhine Valley (the region around Basle).

7   The Oberrheinkonferenz is the successor of the Swiss–German–French intergovernmental commission for border affairs which was created in 1975. Nowadays, it

is dominated by the regional executives and includes representatives of the larger municipalities. The national governments have been retreating into the role of observers.

8   The International Commission for Water Conservation, established in 1960.

9   The Umweltrat Bodensee is the umbrella organization of the environmental NGOs located around the lake.

10 The Arbeitsgemeinschaft Wasserwerke Bodensee–Rhein is an international lobbying organization of waterworks around Lake Constance and along the upper Rhine valley.

11 The search of cross-border institutions for highly visible signs which symbolize the common cross-border regional identity can be seen as a major factor in explaining the success in regulating and protecting the water quality of the second largest lake in western Europe.

12 The term "twin-plant" signifies that the labor-intensive plants on the Mexican side are usually complemented by a headquarters unit on the American side of the border.

13 PNWER is an organization set up by parliamentarians and business groups from the Canadian provinces of Alberta and British Columbia and the US states of Washington, Oregon, Idaho, Montana, and Alaska. It was able to officially integrate the governments of these provinces and states as members of this organization; nevertheless, after the government from British Columbia withdrew its support, PNWER had to turn to the private sector as its primary supporter and to focus its attention on promoting free trade.

14 The Cascadia Project is a public–private initiative set up by academics and politicians focusing on "the Four T's" – transportation, trade, tourism and technology – throughout the corridor from Vancouver to Seattle and Portland (Schell and Hamer 1995: 154).

15 The Sounds and Straits Alliance is a coalition of environmental NGOs (Alper 1996).

16 To obtain these profiles, each cross-border institution was located in this matrix. A line was then drawn around these individual institutions and the result slightly modified to obtain the symbolic forms presented above. This rule of aggregation is a compromise between quantitative and qualitative approaches.

17 These elements refine the two dimensions used to distinguish formal and informal political institutions (see table 10.2).

18 Such a narrow institutionalization of the CBR with the predominance of utility-maximizing connections prevents the border region from confronting the economic boom's negative side effects (environmental degradation). Thus intervention by nation-states becomes necessary again, but the border regime's financial and regulatory environmental regime is narrowly limited and institutionally separated from the border connections.

19 "Comprehensive" means that all four types of cross-border institutions do exist in these regions and that the institutions of the executive and the private groups are being complemented by some kind of "representative assembly" like the Oberrheinrat or the Bodenseerat.

REFERENCES

Agnew, J. (1999) "Mapping Political Power Beyond State Boundaries: Territory, Identity, and Movement in World Politics," *Millennium* 28(3), 499–521.

Alper, D. K. (1996) "The Idea of Cascadia: Emergent Trans-border Regionalism in the Pacific Northwest–Western Canada," *Journal of Borderland Scholars* 11(2), 1–22.

Blatter, J. (2000) *Entgrenzung der Staatenwelt? Politische Institutionenbildung in grenzüberschreitenden Regionen in Europa und Nordamerika.* Baden-Baden: Nomos.

Bluechel, A. (1991) "Reaping Profit from a New World Order," *Journal of State Government* 64(1), 18–21.

Bollens, S. A. (1997) "Fragments of Regionalism: The Limits of Southern California Governance," *Journal of Urban Affairs* 19(2), 105–22.

Caporaso, J. A. (1996) "The European Union and Forms of State: Westphalian, Regulatory or Post-Modern?," *Journal of Common Market Studies* 34(1), 29–51.

Castells, M. (1996) *The Rise of the Network Society.* Oxford: Blackwell.

Duchacek, I. D. (1984) "The International Dimension of Subnational Self-Government," *Publius* 14(4), 5–32.

Duchacek, I. D. (1986) *The Territorial Dimension of Politics. Within, Among, and Across Nations.* Boulder, CO: Westview.

Elkins, D. J. (1995) *Beyond Sovereignty. Territorial and Political Economy in the Twenty-First Century.* Toronto: University of Toronto Press.

Ferguson, Y. H. and Mansbach, R. W. (1996) *Polities: Authority, Identities and Change.* Columbia, SC: University of South Carolina Press.

Fernandez, R. A. (1989) *The Mexican–American Border Region. Issues and Trends.* Notre Dame, IN: University of Notre Dame Press.

Gehring, T. (1990) "International Environmental Regimes. Dynamic Sectoral Legal Systems," *Yearbook of International Environmental Law* 1, 35–56.

Göhler, G. (1996) "Institutions in Political Theory: Lessons for European Integration," in D. Rometsch and W. Wessels (eds) *The European Union and Member States: Towards Institutional Fusion?*, pp. 1–19. Manchester: Manchester University Press.

Herzog, L. A. (1990) *Where North Meets South: Cities, Space and Politics on the U.S.–Mexico Border.* Austin: University of Texas Press.

Kenis, P. and Schneider, V. (1991) "Policy Networks and Policy Analysis: Scrutinizing a New Analytical Toolbox," in B. Marin and R. Mayntz (eds) *Policy Networks*, pp. 25–59. Frankfurt: Campus-Verlag.

Keohane, R. O. and Nye, J. S. (1974) "Transgovernmental Relations and International Organizations," *World Politics* 27(1), 39–62.

Laffan, B. (1996) "The Politics of Identity and Political Order in Europe," *Journal of Common Market Studies* 34(1), 81–105.

Levesque, S. (2001) "The Yellowstone to Yukon Conservation Initiative: Reconstructing Boundaries, Biodiversity and Beliefs," in J. Blatter and H. Ingram (eds) *Reflections upon Water: Emerging Perspectives on Transboundary Conflict and Collaboration*, pp. 123–62. Cambridge, MA: MIT Press.

Marin, B. and Mayntz, R. (1991) "Introduction: Studying Policy Networks," in B. Marin and R. Mayntz (eds) *Policy Networks*, pp. 11–24. Frankfurt: Campus-Verlag.

Marks, G., Hooghe, L., and Blank, K. (1996) "European Integration from the 1980s: State Centric v. Multi-level Governance," *Journal of Common Market Studies* 34(3), 341–78.

Maus, R., Ritscherle, W., and Sund, R. (eds) (1990) *Aufbruch nach Europa. 1. Bodensee-Forum 1989.* Konstanz: Universitäts-Verlag.

Mayntz, R. (1993) "Policy-Netzwerke und die Logik von Verhandlungssystemen," in A. Héritier (ed.) *Policy-Analyse: Kritik und Neuorientierung*, PVS-Sonderheft 24/1993, pp. 39–56. Opladen: Westdeutscher Verlag.

Mayntz, R. and Scharpf, F. W. (1995) "Der Ansatz des akteurzentrierten Institutionalismus," in R. Mayntz and F. W. (eds) *Gesellschaftliche Selbstregulierung und politische Steuerung*, pp. 39–72. Frankfurt: Campus-Verlag.

Mazza, P. (1995) *Lifeplace or Marketplace?: Bioregions, Region States and the Contested Turf of Regionalism* (http://www.tnews.com/text/lifeplace_marketplace.html; 11/13/1996).

Northwest Environment Watch (ed.) (1994) *State of the Northwest.* Seattle, WA: Northwest Environment Watch.

Ohmae, K. (1993) "The Rise of the Region State," *Foreign Affairs* 72(1), 78–87.

Ostrom, E. (1990) *Governing the Commons. The Evolution of Institutions for Collective Action.* Cambridge: Cambridge University Press.

Ratti, R. (1993) "Spatial and Economic Effects of Frontiers: Overview of Traditional and New Approaches and Theories of Border Area Development," in R. Ratti and S. Reichman (eds) *Theory and Practice of Trans-border Cooperation*, pp. 23–54. Basel: Helbig and Lichtenhahn.

Risse-Kappen, T. (1996) "Exploring the Nature of the Beast: International Relations Theory and Comparative Policy Analysis Meet the European Union," *Journal of Common Market Studies* 34(1), 53–80.

Sabatier, P. A. (1993) "Advocacy-Koalitionen, Policy-Wandel und Policy-Lernen: Eine Alternative zur Phasenheuristik," in A. Héritier (ed.) *Policy-Analyse: Kritik und Neuorientierung*, PVS-Sonderheft 24/1993, pp. 116–84. Opladen: Westdeutscher Verlag.

Sassen, S. (1996) *Metropolen des Weltmarketes. Die neue Rolle der Global Cities.* Frankfurt: Campus-Verlag.

Scharpf, F. W. (1997) *Games Real Actors Play. Actor-Centered Institutionalism in Policy Research.* Boulder, CO: Westview Press.

Schell, P. and Hamer, J. (1995) "Cascadia: The New Binationalism of Western Canada and the U.S. Pacific Northwest," in R. L. Earle and J. D. Wirth (eds) *Identities in North America. The Search for Community*, pp. 140–56. Stanford, CA: Standford University Press.

Simon, H. A. (1962) "The Architecture of Complexity," *Proceedings of the American Philosophical Society* 106(6), 467–82.

Swanson, R. F. (1978) *Inter-governmental Perspectives on the U.S.–Canada Relationship.* New York: New York University Press.

Williamson, O. E. (1991) "Comparative Economic Organization: The Analysis of Discrete Structural Alternatives," *Administrative Science Quarterly* 36, 269–96.

11

Rethinking Globalisation: Re-articulating the Spatial Scale and Temporal Horizons of Trans-Border Spaces

Ngai-Ling Sum

Introduction and Overview

Scholte (1997) suggests that 'globalisation' can refer to an increase in: (a) cross-border relations (or internationalisation); (b) open-border relations (or liberalisation); and (c) trans-border relations (or the relative uncoupling of social relations from territorial frameworks). I agree with Scholte that the third meaning is the most distinctive and useful starting point. Some scholars of globalisation in this third sense focus on the growing importance of 'the space of flows' due to, for example, the growth of global finance and trade (Corbridge and Thrift 1994; Agnew and Corbridge 1995) or the advance of information technologies (Castells 1996). Others focus on its relation to external 'threats' to sovereign 'nation-states' and their traditional *modus operandi*. There are strong and weak versions of this more 'state-centred' account. The strong version (e.g. O'Brien 1992) links this threatening 'outside' to the capacity of global finance to undermine states' monetary and fiscal powers. Scholars favouring a 'weak globalisation' (but strong internationalisation) thesis (e.g. Hirst and Thompson 1996) claim only that states' traditional roles *qua* sovereign powers or economic managers have been attenuated.

These 'space of flows' and 'state-centred' accounts have certainly enriched understandings of aspects of globalisation. But they also distract attention from the multiple and heterogeneous processes involved in the current re-articulation of spatial scales and temporal horizons (Mitchell 1997: 104); as well as from the role of other scales (and their spatio-temporal interlinkages) in the global–local interactions. Accordingly my chapter seeks to rethink globalisation in terms of a complex, tangled dialectic of changes in temporal horizons (such as the compressed-time and memory time of nations) and in spatial scales (such as global, regional, national and local scales). Such changes are especially prevalent in the making of trans-border spaces – which thereby reveal the complexities of this general form of globalisation. To this end, this chapter introduces the middle-range concepts of time-space governance and its associated capacities and tensions; it then applies these concepts to the trans-border space of 'Greater China'. This combination of theoretical and empirical analysis permits some more general conclusions on the multiscalar and multitemporal nature of globalisation.

A Multitemporal and Multiscalar Approach: Tendencies towards Time-Space Governance

This agenda requires examining four issues: the variability and multiplicities of time, space, and scales; the re-articulation, in the wider context, of the spatial scales and temporal horizons involved in making trans-border spaces; trends towards reflexive time-space governance for managing the spatial-temporal dimensions of trans-border social relations; and tensions and reimaginations involved in the (re)-making and time-space governance of trans-border spaces.

Time-space governance and its different moments

The concept of time-space governance focuses on the strategic networks of trans-border actors (both public and private) involved in coordinating and stabilising divergent trans-border modes of growth and their capacities to manage self-reflexively the material, social, discursive, and time-space dimensions of these modes of growth. These networks typically seek to promote global–regional–local competitiveness by shaping/disciplining/controlling the time-space dimensions of production and exchange (Gereffi and Korzeniewicz 1994; Adam 1994). These dimensions include the emerging temporalities-spatialities associated with 'electronic space' and the compression of social time through information and communication technologies. This approach can be developed by examining four key aspects of time-space moments in capitalist restructuring: finance, industry, commerce and culture.

First, the financial time-space moments are structured by the practices of networks of multinational banks, other financial intermediaries, and translocal organisations. Their operations are premised on 'de-nationalised' or 'stateless' funds which are pooled and managed in an allegedly 'borderless world' (Ohmae 1990). Fund movement is coordinated virtually instantaneously in and through 'electronic space' and 'electronic time'. Temporally, such operations are oriented to the nanoseconds of computer operations; speed is related in turn to profitability and global competitiveness (Adam 1994: 100–3). Spatially, they are mediated in 'electronic space' through telecommunication practices, ranging from the humble fax through electronic data interchange to an ever more mundane Internet and electronic conferencing (Poster 1995: 26). The so-called 'information superhighway' (albeit still partial and limited) plays an increasingly important role in transmitting information and knowledge. This does not nullify social space, for global/regional/national actors from the private and public realms typically need to meet face-to-face to develop trust, establish networks, form partnerships, settle differences, engage in mutual learning and interaction (Granovetter 1985; Jarillo 1988; Camagni 1991; Conti 1993; Mayntz 1993; Storper 1997).

Second, technological/industrial time-space moments are shaped by global networks of multinational firms interacting with regional and more locally based firms within the evolving regional division of labour/knowledge. Their operations are premised on trans-border cost differentials and/or technological complementarities that affect global-regional competitiveness (Simon 1995: 4). Temporally, such networks aim to produce goods in time, on time, and every time to customers wherever they may be located in the global market. To speed up innovation, reduce lead times, and coordinate time-bound schedules, firms within and beyond the region join forces in subcontracting activities, joint ventures, strategic alliances, etc., to produce just-in-time in 'regional factories'. Likewise, since production must be closely coordinated in trans-spatial and time-bound/compressed-time schedules, new institutional and technical forms of integrating activities emerge in both social and 'electronic space'. In social space, new spatial forms cut across borders and are mediated by dense networks of private-to-private and private-to-public alliances based on complex relations of trust, competition, and policy support (Jarillo 1988; Camagni 1991, Conti 1993; Mayntz 1993; Huber 1994). These networks are also shaped by their strategic calculations of how to produce and reproduce labour across borders through skilled commuter workers, guest and/or migrant labour. Besides social space, these links are reinforced by emerging practices in 'electronic space' whereby relevant industrial/technological information is exchanged about R & D and stages of the production process from design to manufacturing (Howell 1993). The sites which emerge in this new discourse/identity are 'regional blocs', 'growth triangles', 'growth circles', 'sub-regional economic zones', 'offshore production sites', and 'learning/technological regions' linking the regions with the global and other regional circuits (Boisier 1994; Florida 1995).

Third, commerce is influenced by networks of multinational service firms and their regional/local counterparts located in 'global-gateway' cities. These provide producer and distributive services and logistics information (i.e. insurance, legal services, consultancies, logistic management, transportation, retail) that 'facilitate all economic transactions, and the driving force that stimulates the production of goods' within the 'regional chain' (Riddle 1986: 26). Such networks coordinate the time-space of global–regional and regional–local production and distributive chains. Temporally, service firms engaged in the 'supply pipeline' are managing information flows that balance cost options as well as lead- and transit-time in time-bound projects. This is increasingly coordinated in 'electronic space'. One recent development here is 'virtual ports' offering 'virtual terminal services' with papers cleared and permits issued within minutes of arrival. Increasingly, information is substituted for inventory (i.e. 'virtual inventory') at the centre so that 'quick responses' can be made directly into the replenishment systems through local outsourcing or procurement (Christopher 1992: 108–24). Thus social space remains important in developing trust, forming liaisons with local subcontractors and management, and tapping local information flows to enhance customer service.

Fourth, cultural time-space moments are influenced by social practices embedded in networks of intra- and/or cross-cultural ties. Intra-cultural practices and norms embedded in common linguistic, familial, clan, and communal ties often help to 'grease the functioning of the social networks' through practices such as gift exchange and banqueting so as to generate familial/clan/communal loyalty. This intensification of social space may help to speed up the border-crossing time across private and public spaces. Cross-cultural subjectivities and networks emerge through the consolidation of practices and norms that reduce border-crossing time between cultural spaces. This is illustrated by global entrepreneurialism, multiculturalism, and even global post-colonialism.

These time-space moments help constitute the complex terrain in which networks of agencies struggle to construct new identities and to re-order their time and space across borders. New time-space and private–public practices may consolidate into a new form of geo-economic coordination, which can be termed time-space governance. This is defined as a mode of coordination that is mediated by a multilayered network of social relations that cuts across discursive-material, time-space, private–public, and global–regional–national–local dimensions of production and exchange.

Time-space governance: objects and capacities

Discursive-material dimensions

- As circumstances change, networks of actors struggle over the best way to define objects of governance (e.g. growth and competitiveness) despite differences in their respective spatio-temporal horizons of action;
- these struggles involve re-ordering available symbols and codes and lead to new identities, interests, and strategies; and
- these generate in turn new temporal-spatial moments in social relations.

Time-space dimensions

- 'Electronic space' and its related social practices are developed by networks of multinational banks and other financial intermediaries to pool and manage trans-spatial funds fast-in-time and fast-in-space for global competitiveness;
- practices in social and 'electronic space' coordinate networks of production-service firms to plan and manage time-bound and compressed-time projects just-in-time for global competitiveness;
- 'electronic space' and its related social practices help networks of service firms to reduce lead- and transit-time of production and distribution; and
- cultural/social practices/norms emerge to reduce the border-crossing time between cultural and/or private–public spaces.

Private–public dimensions

- These networks often link the private and public spheres to coordinate the use of their respective economic and political resources and thereby enhance the synergy of these resources within and across each of these spheres (e.g. combining disparate but complementary forces and resources for investment, labour power, information, knowledge, subsidies, etc.); and

- these often involve new scales of activity that lie beyond sovereign states (e.g. trans-local, local–regional, and local–global arrangements).

Global–regional–national–local dimensions

- Networks of global–regional–national–local actors develop mechanisms and strategies to coordinate production, finance, and trade practices across borders (e.g. strategic alliances, joint ventures, subcontracting, and foreign aid);
- these networks contribute to a specific regional division of labour/knowledge based on cost differentials and technological complementarities;
- certain nodal points (such as global-gateway cities) have a key role here in providing complex services to bridge time-space gaps in this global–regional–national–local complex of production, finance, and trade;
- specific cross-border migratory/labour flows, labour processes, and modes of (inter-as well as intra-generational) social reproduction of labour power also emerge; and
- so do trans-border social blocs which accept, support, and carry the discourses and practices beyond elites.

Such strategic networks for trans-border time-space governance could enhance: (a) joint decision-making based on information-sharing, trust, and commitment; (b) the privileged role of business and industrial interests in formulating policy; (c) capacities to deploy economic and political-bureaucratic resources, such as grants or loans (for infrastructure), authority, organisational intelligence, technology and manufacturing know-how; (d) capacities to reduce lead-times and so increase global competitiveness; (e) interactive learning among private–public actors and institutions; and (f) negotiation systems conducive to societal guidance in the region. On the other hand, such networks and structures do not arise just because they are needed; nor, once they have emerged for whatever reason(s), do they always operate beneficially. They develop in quite specific conditions and cannot be created at will through specific policy initiatives. Moreover, once developed, they may face various coordination problems and other challenges (in short, tensions) from within and beyond the networks.

Time-space governance tensions

Such tensions are rooted in trans-border strategic practices and identities. In examining them, we must first note that not all logically possible sets of trans-border regions are likely to develop into regional modes of growth. In particular, the network of private–public actors might fail to coordinate the economic spaces in which they are located because they are too similarly endowed to permit economic complementaries. Moreover, even if conditions are initially favourable, they may change, e.g. the rising costs of particular host economies or the 'leapfrogging' behaviour of subordinate partners in a system of technology transfer. These could create tensions for the host economies/dominant partner(s) in the time-space governance network. This may prompt problems regarding information-sharing, communication, trust, and cross-cultural understanding in strategic partnerships. However, this does not mean that such networks are thin and lack the capacities to learn: they may reorganise and/or combine with other existing networks to search for a new regional division of labour/knowledge.

As for time-space governance networks based on trans-local linkages, the politics of scale may involve conflicts over national sovereignty/security, local autonomy, and corruption at different levels. Moreover, given the socially embedded character of such networks, they are also linked to other geometries of power. For example, the geo-economic identity of a trans-border space may be intercepted by global–regional hegemons, which showcase it as a geo-political hub for 'democracy' and/or a 'nationalist' powerhouse. The co-existence of geo-economic and other geometries of powers may even de-stabilise a region through a contest of different identities, which cut across a thick network of economic relations. This can be illustrated, in a preliminary way, from the development of 'Greater China' as a trans-border space.

The Making of 'Greater China' as a Trans-Border Space

This section examines how trans-border actors construct and re-articulate the temporal and spatial horizons of the trans-border space. It starts with the global–regional–national contexts of the 'open door' discourse in the PRC [People's Republic of China].

Global–regional–national contexts of the 'Open Door' discourse in the PRC

The emergence of 'Greater China' as a trans-border space is articulated to a wide range of global–regional changes. Globally, techno-economic changes related to the rise of information technology, international competition based on shortened product life cycles and rapid dissemination of information have influenced the rise of the 'global factory' and the expansion of specific commodity chains (Dicken 1998; Gereffi and Korzeniewicz 1994). Transnational producers from the USA, Germany and Japan coordinate diversely skilled members working simultaneously to produce a good across many sites. Such international division of labour has created opportunities for outsourcing for cheap (un-)skilled labour, component parts and raw materials. These production and exchange activities also enable private–public actors in newly-industrialising countries (e.g. Hong Kong, Singapore, Taiwan and South Korea) to explore new time-space coordinates that cut across the global–regional–national–local domains.

These economic changes are also linked to the end of the Cold War, the re-emergence of China as a regional hegemon, and changes in its own internal politics. Despite struggles over China's identity after Mao's death, its leaders (especially Deng) did succeed during the 1970s in constructing a new hegemonic project to 'build socialism with Chinese characteristics'. This created the discursive space to re-make China's time-space meanings. The 'open door' narrative introduces the global–regional into China's own national–local spaces in and through localised experiments drawing on foreign direct investment (FDI) and/or 'special domestic' investment (a term used by China to refer to capital originating from Hong Kong and Taiwan) to expand and develop new production platforms and markets. Certain pioneering sites in China came to combine socialist-capitalist subjectivities and practices in new and productive ways. These imaginative experiments won support from key party elites and coastal-provincial actors in Guangdong and Fujian. The latter actors began to demand 'special/flexible measures' to create new geo-economic time-space forms to reconnect China to the regional and global system(s).

The Party Central Committee responded in 1979 with a decentralisation strategy permitting Guangdong and Fujian to adopt 'special policies and flexible measures'. The most notable measures include: (a) commercial reform that allows enterprises or business units under central control (except those in certain areas) to be managed by the province and to enter contracts (subject to central approval) with incoming investors valued up to $3 million (extended to $10 million in 1985, $30 million in 1988); and (b) fisco-financial reform enabling provinces such as Guangdong to retain 70 per cent of export earnings after paying 30 per cent of them to central government. These reforms were especially significant for the Special Economic Zones (SEZs) in Guangdong and Fujian, Shenzhen, Zhuhai, Shantou and Xiamen. These zones are the interface of an emerging socialist-capitalist and global–regional economy. They are the 'windows' and 'laboratory' for learning advanced technology and managerial skills as well as attracting foreign investment. Foreign investment in these zones enjoys various tax incentives and exemptions, etc. Moreover, given their headstart, the provincial and local governments in Guangdong above all had great incentives to open southern China.

In response to the above emerging discourse/opportunities within China, the rise of Western protectionism, the USA's granting of the Most Favoured Nation (MFN) trade status to mainland China, and increases in domestic costs for land and labour in Hong Kong, investors from the latter were searching for new outlets. Their search was influenced by strategic images of 'Greater China'. An increasing body of literature deploys ideas about 'Greater China' (e.g. 'Chinese Economic Circle', 'South China Economic Circle', 'Chinese Economic Community', 'Coordinating System of Chinese Economies') to present an image of vibrant economic interactions in the economically, culturally, and linguistically compatible area which map Hong Kong, southern China and Taiwan as part of an imagined community of 'Greater China' (Huang 1989; Cheng 1992; Fang 1992; Fu 1992). This project relates Hong Kong/Taiwan's time and space to Chinese strategies for growth and reunification. It remaps Hong Kong and Taiwan by, firstly, encouraging 'patriotic ethnic Chinese' (huaqiao) to 'invest in the motherland'. This pragmatic approach consolidates Hong Kong as a 'gateway' to China, 'Greater China', and the rest of the world. It enables China to stress the spatial coherence of the region and its competitiveness in relation to global restructuring; and to ground narratives of a common 'economic future' in pragmatic networking practices without having to confront, at least in the short term, the problematic relation between nationalism and politics.

Building and consolidating time-space governance capacities in 'Greater China'

Hong Kong is now by far the biggest investor in Guangdong province, supplying 80 per cent of the FDI. The Pearl River Delta is now a major production base for its more labour-intensive products. Almost 25,000 Hong Kong manufacturing enterprises, mostly in textiles and clothing, toys and consumer electronics, have moved there to exploit low labour and rent costs. They directly employ about 3 million workers, i.e. three times the total manufacturing labour force left in Hong Kong.

Unlike Hong Kong, the Taiwanese government in the early 1980s saw few advantages and many serious Cold War risks in trading with the mainland. Commercial links were first established in 1979 but were conducted through Hong Kong. However, the appreciation of Taiwanese currency from 1986, the rising cost of land, and the high standards set by the 1984 Basic Labour Law have all made the Chinese market increasingly attractive to Taiwanese businesses. Fears of an investment strike by Taiwan capital prompted the KMT government to replace restrictions on trade/investment with more positive state guidance. In particular, legalisation of travel and liberalisation of foreign exchange sharply accelerated the growth in trade and FDI between the two economies. In 1988, the Chinese State Council promulgated a set of 22 measures to encourage investment from Taiwan. Taiwanese capital is treated as 'special domestic capital' and can pursue business not open to foreign capital, such as banking, wholesale and retail. In January 1993, the Taiwanese government began allowing Taiwanese companies to invest not more than US$1 million in China without going through a third site. Five million Taiwanese have since visited China and 9,300 Taiwanese firms have moved production facilities there with investment of $8.6 billion at the end of 1993 (Cheng 1992: 102–5). However, for security considerations, Taipei requires that trade and movement of factors of production pass through a third site. Thus, whilst seeking to maintain its own competitive edge, Taiwan is adopting a gradual and selective 'open door' policy on cross-Strait economic exchanges.

Despite security apprehensions, Guangdong and Fujian, as FDI hosts, possess cheap labour and land; they also offer ready access to a vast and rapidly growing Chinese market. These coastal provinces also share a similar cultural background and common language. These cultural traits and decentralisation/coastal strategies have combined to consolidate a privileged set of networks that cross-cuts public–private, central–provincial–local, and global–regional domains within China and the 'Greater China' region. This meta-network has a key role in the emerging time–space governance of this cross-border region.

The emergence of cross-cutting networks in China

The 'open door' policy has unleashed new central–provincial–local forces in China itself. They are mediated by a network of public, quasi-public and private institutions aiming to expand foreign economic relations and development. At the centre, they include the Ministry of Foreign Economic Relations and Trade (MOFERT) which is responsible for managing the introduction of foreign investment, new trading arrangements, and new joint ventures. The provinces of Guangdong and Fujian followed the policy of the centre in setting up their own province-level functional and line ministries. These ministries were empowered in 1985 to administer and monitor incoming investments worth less than $3 million. Unsurprisingly, local functionaries often manipulate these policies to enable them to retain the benefits of inward investment.

On this issue, I will concentrate on the emergence of elites in 'special economic zones' or 'development zones' (Nee 1992: 1–27). They largely comprise state/party officials who control township-village enterprises (TVEs) around the coastal regions. They are termed 'cadre entrepreneurs' because they serve both as managers-executives of the TVEs and party-state functionaries at the same levels (Zweig 1995: 268; Goodman 1995: 136–8; Heberer 1995: 59). They mediate private and public interests. Such cadre entrepreneurs are eager to attract overseas Chinese investment to their counties, townships or villages. Often, they encourage inward investors from Hong Kong and Taiwan to 'unbundle' their investment so that its artificially constructed component parts each fall below the threshold which would trigger central–provincial monitoring and administration. This 'unbundling' tactic enables local elites to bypass higher tiers of government and network with inward investors on their own terms.

Their networking capacities are reinforced by decentralisation/coastal strategies. These have devolved ownership rights (including utilisation and return rights) from the central to provincial and local levels. This empowers cadre entrepreneurs to network with Hong Kong and Taiwanese investors through: (a) transfer of 'utilisation rights' of assets (such as taxes, land, labour, loans, power supply, import/export licences, etc.) to the local level, where these rights enable local players to deal more flexibly with Hong Kong/Taiwanese investors; (b) transfer of rights to revenue from the utilisation of state assets to the local level also permits unofficial 'second budgets' as cadre entrepreneurs creatively shift 'taxable' items away from the central–local budgetary accounts (Oi 1992: 100; Wang 1994: 99); and (c) fiscal softness at local level due to such 'second budgets' also enables local governments to 'experiment' with new local 'growth projects', external linkages, and central–local relations. These new capacities enable the coastal provinces, their cities and counties, as well as special economic zones, to compete more effectively for Hong Kong and Taiwanese investment.

The formation of strategic networks in 'Greater China'

Capitalising on these new capacities/opportunities, Taiwan and Hong Kong traders-cum-producers are sourcing for potential Chinese partners. They draw on their linguistic affinities and kinship ties to build socio-economic connections in the region (see Kong, [1999]). They also enter strategic networks with various local Chinese public, quasi-public, and private agencies in the region and consolidate them through the socio-cultural practices of '*guanxi*' (relationship). When such preexisting relationships are absent, it may take time to cultivate new linkages and this will often involve exchanging material/informational gifts (Smart and Smart 1991; Yang 1989 and 1994; Yan 1996), taking potential partners out for dinner, karaoke, or other entertainment, inviting them to ceremonial banquets/meetings, and making donations to the community (Zhao and Aram 1995: 360). These practices are often symbolised as gestures/signs of friendship, loyalty, mutual trust and 'giving face' (a code that communicates a sense of social importance in the network). The active exchange of these gifts/favours gives boundaries and significance to *guanxi* networks. These consolidate a reliable and effective social space of relatives, friends, and business partners to be called upon for utilitarian purposes. A reliable and effective network can speed up the border-crossing time between the private and public spaces as the latter becomes more permeable to private interests. For example, pre-existing good *guanxi* can expedite access to licences, loans, raw materials, etc., from public or quasi-public organisations.

Thus the cultural time-space aspects of 'Greater China' involve the steady rise of a strategic group of actors/institutions organised in a loosely-hierarchical network that spans the private–public divide as trans-local domains. These trans-border networks are quite different in form, scope, actors, aims, and modus operandi from the transnational networks formed among Hong Kong multinationals and their economic partners in the ASEAN region or elsewhere (see Dicken and Yeung, [1999]). Thus the networks at the centre of my analysis involve municipal authorities specialising in Hong Kong/Taiwan investment, county-township cadre entrepreneurs, as well as small- and medium-sized firms from Hong Kong and Taiwan. They draw on pre-existing *guanxi* to build a flexible and open system of networking relations which allows them to build trust, obtain advice, communicate demand and gain resources at below-market prices. The form of interaction tends to be group- and not firm-based: local state-party officials, semi-public TVE, and incoming firms from Hong Kong and Taiwan all play important roles. However, this is not a horizontal market connection because it does not involve links between legally equal individuals; it involves power asymmetries between actors and institutions. Nor do these networks resemble hierarchical command-economy linkages because exchanges are not mediated through authority relations between superiors and subordinates: rather, they involve informal material and administrative exchanges from which actors can exit when desired. For example, local party-state officials still control resources such as land, labour, capital and regulations; semi-public enterprises command information and contacts; and private firms control capital, managerial skills and market outlets. Given this interdependence, these public–private networks tend to form clientelist alliances that operate an interactive process of 'steering' and societal guidance. This may consolidate as a pattern of open regional collaborative networks that guide learning within 'Greater China'.

Consolidating a trans-border division of labour/knowledge in 'Greater China'

These strategic networks represent a coalition/alliance of local party/administrative officials, their entrepreneurial affiliates, and Hong Kong and Taiwanese capital. They form the social bases of support for a trans-border division of labour/knowledge for export processing in the 'Greater China' bloc. Hong Kong and Taiwan are moving up the industrial technology ladder by shifting their labour-intensive industries to low-wage and cheap-land localities in Southern China. Labour has been made available through rural de-collectivisation since 1984 and it is estimated that there are 100–150 million migrants (Wolf 1996: 14) from the inland areas. To compete for capital from Hong Kong and Taiwan, coastal communities undercut each other by providing low-cost and low-protection labour systems. Most workers, especially in the Pearl River Delta, are engaged in what one can call a highly 'flexible-taylorised' process whereby production is minutely divided, e.g. sewing, button-holing and button-stitching in the garment industry. The flexibility of this form of organisation of the labour process is further secured by adjusting hours, wage rates, a capital-controlled hire-and-fire procedure and lax interpretation of labour standards/laws in the region (Sum 1994: 90–3; 1998: 66–8). The resulting 'workhouse regions' also reproduce labour through their use of workfare shelters based on dormitory-type accommodation, subsidised meals and a trip back home for the Chinese New Year.

In response to the availability of a new labour regime in the region, 80 per cent of Hong Kong's manufacturing industries (e.g. simple electronics, toys, leather, shoe-making and watches) have moved to southern China. In the 1990s, a second wave of relocation has involved moving low-skilled white-collar work (e.g. telephone enquiry/paging service) to southern China. However, manufacturing relocation is still predominant in southern China. Because Hong Kong's manufacture is largely oriented to export-processing, its transfer to southern China promotes entrepot trade between the two regions.

As for Taiwan, investments before 1990 were mostly in manufacturing especially in labour-intensive industries. It was reported that Taiwan's traditional industries – for instance, 80 per cent of handbag production, 90 per cent of shoemaking, and over 90 per cent of umbrella-making – have been transferred to southern China. These goods are mainly exported and some are even sent back to Taiwan. Since 1989, Taiwan's investment has included petrochemicals and machinery. Given that Taiwanese investment needs to involve a third area, most of the flows of material, people, and money targeted on southern China pass through Hong Kong. In this regard, Hong Kong is a principal trade and capital dispatch centre for Taiwanese investment in China (Sung 1997: 61–6).

The shifting of labour-intensive processes to the Pearl River Delta not only consolidates Hong Kong's entrepot role but also enhances its capacity, as a global-gateway city, to coordinate investment, trade and services in and beyond the 'Greater China' region. Thus the region's international subcontracting chain is mediated by a more complex network of relations within and beyond the 'Greater China' bloc that comprises: global/regional buyers, Hong Kong and/or Taiwan-owned firms, China's quasi-state trading firms in Hong Kong, state-owned firms or county/township-village enterprises in China, provincial and local governments and their subsidiaries, and local branches of ministries and their affiliates. This strategic network is coordinated by subcontracting management based in Hong Kong which involves re-articulating time-space dimensions of trans-border production and trade.

More specifically, subcontracting management involves sourcing, production, authority and distribution management. Producers-cum-traders from Hong Kong/Taiwan locate Chinese partners through formal contacts as well as informal kinship and communal ties. Exchanges of visits and/or gifts help to consolidate reliable and effective *guanxi*. This intensification of the social space helps to speed up the border-crossing time across the urban-rural as well as the ethnic divide within the subregion; and also to build the mutual trust needed for future contracts or longer-lasting arrangements (such as subcontracting partnerships and joint ventures). The latter can involve more complex services related to legal services on production-sharing contracts, etc. After establishing the sourcing networks, the Hong Kong/Taiwan traders-cum-producers then engage in production management across time and space. This production process involves the coordination and supervision of time-bound projects dispersed over several sites with the more skill-intensive sub-processes in Hong Kong/Taiwan and the more labour-intensive ones in southern China. Production managers and quality-controllers from Hong Kong/Taiwan are at the forefront here in re-articulating spatial scales and temporal horizons in realising time-bound projects. These often involve more intensification of production practices such as finer differentiation of pre-production planning and more intensification of production schedules and monitoring. For example, Hong Kong or Taiwan-based managers make frequent visits to production sites to ensure their conformity to production schedules (Chan et al. 1991: 189); and quality controllers often get based in China to tighten monitoring procedures. Such practices build the capacity to coordinate trans-border production processes so that goods reach the global market just-in-time.

Also essential to this time-space governance network is the building of good relations with local/central officials and cadre entrepreneurs in China. Such strategic networking is important in reducing the border-crossing time between the private–public as well as the urban–rural divides. Here producer-cum-traders from Hong Kong/Taiwan intensify the social space through practices such as entertaining the authorities and making donations to the community. After all, these authorities still control enormous resources such as land, labour, capital and regulations. In addition to production and authority management, finished goods in the 'supply pipeline' need to be exported/distributed to the global market. Distribution management, then, involves the re-articulation of factory time and global lead time through the activities of service-based firms in the region as well as trading and customs authorities. This trans-border private–public network is coordinated in the 'electronic' and 'social space' that synchronises transport schedules, export procedures of import/export licensing, customs liaison, packaging and logistic management, etc., so that goods can be delivered just-in-time and 'right-in-place' for global/regional buyers. Practices of these kind help to speed up the transit-and pipeline-time crucial to time-bound projects. This phenomenon was described by one Hong Kong managing director of a multinational as being the three T's: time, trust and truth (personal communication). They form the basic ingredients, in the ideal case, for producing and reproducing this strategic private–public network both in social and electronic space. It is this capacity that enables Hong Kong to consolidate its emerging position as a global-gateway city providing trading and producer services (logistics, insurance, legal, banking, accounting expertise, etc.).

Similarly, the setting up of factories in southern China has gradually turned Taiwan into headquarters for higher-end production (e.g. computer monitors, desk-top and portable personal computers, motherboards, keyboards and PC mice), R & D activities, receipt of overseas orders, materials procurement, and provision of technical assistance and personnel training for plants in China. Economic and technological/financial complementarities between the partners include: (a) southern China's cheap land, trainable cheap labour, raw materials, negotiable investment packages and culturally-affiliated and FDI-friendly local cadre entrepreneurs; (b) Hong Kong's role as an entrepot and global-gateway city with good global–regional connections and knowledge in finance, trade, and production management; and (c) Taiwan's capital, applied technology on electronics, synthetic fabrics, plastic materials and the experience in administration and marketing of products (Xu 1994: 151; Chung 1997).

'Time-space governance tensions' and scale politics in 'Greater China'

My discussion of strategic cross-border networks in 'Greater China' would be incomplete without examining the tensions in this emerging form of time-space governance. But editorial constraints mean I will focus only on tensions related to the politics of scale in relation to the central–local, trans-national, and trans-local interfaces.

First, tensions may emerge between local development communities (led by cadre entrepreneurs) and the centre. Decentralisation has changed central–local fiscal relations. It weakens the fiscal leverage of central-level government over local government by reducing the latter's dependence on central revenues and investment funds relative to revenues generated by local investment and economic growth. Thus local party-state officials are less inclined to comply with superiors' wishes regarding economic activities (Wong 1991: 691–3; Walder 1994: 306). This weakening of central government is far from complete because it still controls 'recentralisation' levers, such as tightening macro-economic control, reorienting national economic policy, renegotiating resource-sharing and controlling personnel appointments. Similarly, local authorities have devised various coping strategies to deal with the centre, such as lobbying for central support, creatively interpreting central policies, flexibly implementing central measures and withholding as many funds as possible from central extraction. The use of these bargaining instruments in the tug-of-war between the central and local government is interpreted by Howell (1993) in terms of cycles of decentralisation and recentralisation in China since 1978. This rivalry is especially intense when the size of the fiscal and economic 'pie' is shrinking. On the other hand, the central and local governments are also willing to cooperate as partners when they anticipate rapid expansion in foreign trade. In such cases, localities may encourage local enterprises to accept the centre's rules of the game in order to achieve their mutual goal of expanding exports. Thus, in the case of trade, if the goal is to build export bases for raw material production, both sides would work together to establish a joint venture.

Such central–local tensions indicate the possibility of Guangdong/southern China regional challenges to the centre. Issues may include the share of tax revenue owed to Beijing, growing independence in foreign trade and conflicts between TVEs and state-owned enterprises. Following factional struggles in the central party elite, measures were taken in 1994 to alter central-provincial relations. These comprised fiscal and investment reforms, including closer scrutiny on local government's power to grant tax exemption and to reduce both central and shared taxes. Provinces and regions responded differently. Guangdong interpreted these measures as a 'conspiracy' of state-sector interests to favour state-sector dominated provinces such as Shanghai and weaken it and southern China more generally (Cannon and Zhang 1996: 90–4). Whether or not this is so, the central government is certainly promoting new centres of economic gravity in central and northern China, e.g. Shanghai-Pudong, Bohai Region, and Dalian.

As indicated earlier, central–local conflict not only raises the question of regional challenges but is also fuelling the debate among Chinese elites over possible path(s) of reform and over continued one-party domination. For example, the tendencies towards regionalism and coastal developmental communities intensify the conflict between the reformer-cosmopolitan and reformer-nativist factions within the central elites (Ling 1996: 17). This involves struggles over China's future identity as having an economy based on 'market socialism'/ 'socialism with Chinese characteristics'. Such tensions have also fuelled debates on the disjuncture between market and administrative reforms, the conflict between TVEs and state-owned enterprises, problems of corruption, etc.

Technology transfer in a regional division of labour/knowledge is also a site of tensions. This involves TVEs and their Hong Kong and/or Taiwanese counterparts. The latter typically import low-tech second hand equipment that is no longer profitable (or deemed too polluting) in Taiwan or Hong Kong. Unsurprisingly, the TVEs are demanding a deepening of technology transfer and the regional division of labour/knowledge. But Hong Kong and Taiwan are worried about the consequences for a 'hollowing out' of their own economies because of the relocation of more high-tech industries (e.g. computer manufacturing from Taiwan) and service sector (e.g. backroom banking services) to China. One way forward has been to re-think the future regional roles of Hong Kong and Taiwan (see below).

Private–public coordination of the different scales of action often takes the form of quasi-public people-to-people diplomacy (Clough 1993). This has generated new tensions because such trans-border networks also challenge specific identities and interests rooted in other geometries of power and time-space calculations (e.g. geo-political and nationalist ones). Thus Hong Kong not only has a geo-economic role as a 'global-gateway' for Beijing and Taiwan to attract 'huaqiao' investments to the 'motherland', but is also presented, within Anglo-American geo-political strategic discourse, as a 'democratic hub' to be contrasted with mainland China. Chris Patten had a key role here during his Governorship but local democratic groups continue to articulate the spatio-temporal perspectives of the American hegemon and present China as a 'risk' to other nation-states in the region as well as to 'democracy', 'human rights', and other Enlightenment values (Pollock 1993: 76; Sum 1996a: 215–20 and 1996b: 55–9). Matters are further complicated by Taiwan's security concerns, the fear of over-dependence on China, and the USA's geo-political linkages with the KMT and democracy movement in the island. This can be seen in the continued lease/sale of arms to Taiwan, open support by some senators for the Taiwanese democracy movement, permission for President Lee's unofficial visit to USA in 1995, and so forth. These geo-political partnerships between US, UK, Hong Kong (e.g. Democratic Party), Taiwan (e.g. Democratic People's Party) and the geo-economic network centred on China have clearly confronted social forces at different scales with crucial tensions/dilemmas on their identities/interests (Sum 1998).

The resulting politics of scales and identity struggles not only mark the emerging trans-border space as a contested space; they also open it up as a space for re-imaginations and re-visioning. This helps guide in turn the design of institutions to recode/redirect/remap time-space governance patterns. In the 1990s, the reconstruction of 'Greater Shanghai' as a new object of governance has affected the mode of time-space governance coordination within 'Greater China'. New repositionings and re-negotiation of identities are occurring within the region (Sum 1998).

Conclusion

My case study of 'Greater China' as a trans-border space offers a preliminary account of some complex issues in transnationalism. It departs from the 'space of flows' and 'state-centred' approaches noted above and proposes a rethinking of globalisation in terms of the complex, tangled dialectic of changes in temporal horizons (such as compressed-time and memory time of nations) and spatial scales (such as global, regional, national, and local scales). Such changes are most prevalent in the making of trans-border spaces and it is here that the latter crystallise some of the complexities of this process. To capture these complexities, this chapter introduces the middle-range concept of time-space governance which draws on insights from the new regional geography, discourse analysis, institutional economics/sociology and governance theory. The concept of time-space governance helps to explore articulatory practices across different sites and scales. It also highlights the strategic terrains on which new subject positions are re-imagined. In short, the chapter emphasizes contingencies, the politics of scales between the global-regional–national–local nexus, the re-ordering of time and space in remaking social relations in the trans-border space, and the role of reflexive time-space governance and reimagination that help to sustain these relations.

REFERENCES

Adam, B. (1994) *Timewatch*, Cambridge: Polity.

Agnew, J. and S. Corbridge (1995) *Mastering Space: Hegemony, Territory, and International Political Economy*, London: Routledge.

Boisier, S. (1994) 'Regionalization Process: Past Crises and Current Options', *CEPAL Review*, 52: 177–88.

Camagni, R. (1991) *Innovation Networks: Spatial Perspectives*, London: Belhaven Press.

Cannon, T. and L.-Y. Zhang (1996) 'Inter-Region Tension and China's Reforms' in I. Cook, M. Doel and R. Li, eds, *Fragmented Asia*, Aldershot: Avebury, 75–101.

Castells, M. (1996) *The Rise of the Network Society*, Oxford: Blackwell.

Chan, J., Sculli, D. and Si, K. (1991) 'The Cost of Manufacturing Toys in the Shenzhen Special Economic Zone in China', *International Journal of Production Economics*, 25: 181–90.

Cheng, C. Y. (1992) 'Greater China Common Market', *World Journal*, 26 July, C 2-4 (in Chinese).

Christopher, M. (1992) *Logistics and Supply Chain Management*, London: Pitman Publishing.

Chung, C. Y. (1997) 'Division of Labour Across the Taiwan Strait: Macro Overview and Analysis of the Electronics Industry', in B. Norton, ed., *The China Circle*, Washington, DC: Brookings Institution Press, 164–209.

Clough, R. (1993) *Reaching Across the Strait: People-to-People Diplomacy*, Boulder: Westview Press.

Conti, S. (1993) 'The Network Perspective in Industrial Geography', *Geografiska Annaler*, 75 B: 115–30.

Corbridge, S. and Thrift, N. (1994) 'Money, Power, and Space: Introduction and Overview', in S. Corbridge, R. Martin, and N. Thrift, eds, *Money, Power and Space*, Oxford: Blackwell, 1–25.

Dicken, P. (1998) *Global Shift: Transforming the World Economy*, third edition, London: Paul Chapman.

Dicken, P. and H. W.-C. Yeung (1999) 'Investing in the Future: East and Southeast Asian firms in the Global Economy', in K. Olds, P. Dicken, P. F. Kelly, L. Kong and H. W.-C. Yeung, eds, *Globalisation and the Asia Pacific: Contested Territories*, London: Routledge, 107–28.

Fang, S. (1992) 'A Proposal for Establishing a Mainland–Taiwan–Hong Kong Economic Commission', *Jinji Ribao*, 24 June: 4 (in Chinese).

Florida, R. (1995) 'Toward the Learning Region', *Futures*, 27 (5): 527–36.

Fu, L. (1992) 'Hong Kong-Macao and both Sides of the Taiwan Straits: A Chinese Economic Sphere', *Journal of Beijing University, Social Science Edition*, 5: 85–92 (in Chinese).

Gereffi, G. and Korzeniewicz, M., eds (1994) *Commodity Chains and Global Capitalism*, London: Praeger.

Goodman, D. (1995) 'New Economic Elites' in R. Benewick and P. Wingrove, eds, *China in the 1990s*, Basingstoke: Macmillan, 132–44.

Granovetter, M. (1985) 'Economic Action and Social Structure: The Problem of Embeddedness', *American Journal of Sociology*, 91: 481–501.

Heberer, T. (1995) 'The Political Impact of Economic and Social Changes in China's Countryside', *China Studies*, 1 (Autumn): 49–92.

Hirst, P. and Thompson, G. (1996) *Globalization in Question*, Cambridge: Polity.

Howell, J. (1993) *China Opens its Doors: The Politics of Economic Transition*, Hemel Hempstead: Harvester Wheatsheaf.

Huang, C.-L. (1989) *Hong Kong into the Twenty-First Century*, Hong Kong: Chung Wah Publishing (in Chinese).

Huber, T. (1994) *Strategic Economy of Japan*, Boulder: Westview Press.

Jarillo, J. C. (1988) 'On Strategic Networks', *Strategic Management Journal*, 9: 31–41.

Kong, L. (1999) 'Globalisation, Transmigration and the Renegotiation of Ethnic Identity', in K. Olds, P. Dicken, P. F. Kelly, L. Kong and H. W.-C. Yeung, eds, *Globalisation and the Asia Pacific: Contested Territories*, London: Routledge, 219–37.

Ling, L. (1996) 'Hegemony and the Internationalizing State: A Post-Colonial Analysis of China's Integration into Asian Corporatism', *Review of International Political Economy*, 3 (1): 1–26.

Mayntz, R. (1993) 'Modernization and the Logic of Interorganization Networks' in J. Child, M. Crozier, R. Mayntz et al., *Societal Change Between Market and Organization*, Aldershot: Avebury, 1–17.

Mitchell, K. (1997) 'Transnational Discourse: Bringing Geography Back In', *Antipode*, 29 (2): 101–14.

Nee, V. (1992) 'Organizational Dynamics of Market Transitions: Hybrid Forms, Property Rights, and Mixed Economy in China', *Administrative Science Quarterly*, 37: 1–27.

O'Brien, R. (1992) *Global Financial Integration: The End of Geography*, London: Pinter.

Ohmae, K. (1990) *Borderless World*, New York: Harper Perennial.

Oi, J. (1992) 'Fiscal Reform and the Economic Foundations of Local State Corporatism in China', *World Politics*, 45 (Cot.): 99–126.

Pollock, J. (1993) 'The United States in East Asia: Holding the Ring' in Conference Papers on *Asia's International Role in the Post-Cold War Era*, Part I, Adelphi Paper 275, London: International Institute of Strategic Studies, 69–82.

Poster, M. (1995) *The Second Media Age*, Cambridge: Polity.

Riddle, D. I. (1986) *Service-Led Growth: The Role of Service Sector in World Development*, New York: Praeger.

Scholte, J. (1997) 'Global Capitalism and the State', *International Affairs*, 73 (3): 427–52.

Simon, D. F., ed. (1995) *Emerging Technological Trajectory of the Pacific Rim*, Armonk: M.E. Shape Inc.

Smart, J. and Smart, A. (1991) 'Personal Relations and Divergent Economies: A Case Study of Hong Kong Investment in South China', *International Journal of Urban and Regional Research*, 15 (2): 216–33.

Storper, M. (1997) 'Territories, Flows, and Hierarchies in a Global Economy', in K. Cox, ed., *Spaces of Globalization: Reasserting the Power of the Local*, New York: Guilford, 19–44.

Sum, N.-L. (1994) *Reflections on Accumulation, Regulation, the State, and Societalization: A Styled Model of East Asian Capitalism and an Integral Economic Analysis of Hong Kong*, Ph. D. Dissertation submitted to the Department of Sociology, University of Lancaster.

Sum, N.-L. (1996a) 'Strategies for East Asia Regionalism and the Construction of NIC Identities in the Post-Cold War Era' in A. Gamble and A. Payne, eds, *Regionalism and World Order*, Basingstoke: Macmillan, 207–46.

Sum, N.-L. (1996b) ' "Greater China" and the Global–Regional–Local Dynamics' in I. Cook, M. Doel and R. Li, eds, *Fragmented Asia*, Aldershot: Avebury, 53–74.

Sum, N.-L. (1998) 'The Making of the "Greater China" Subregion' in G. Hook and I. Kearns, eds, *Subregionalism and World Order*, Basingstoke: Macmillan, 197–222

Sung, Y. W. (1997) 'Hong Kong and the Economic Integration with the China Circle', in B. Norton, ed., *The China Circle*, Washington, DC: Brookings Institution Press, 41–80.

Walder, A. G. (1994) 'The Decline of Communist Power: Elements of a Theory of Institutional Change', *Theory and Society*, 23 (2), April: 297–324.

Wang, S. (1994) 'Central–Local Fiscal Politics in China' in H. Jia and Z. Lin, eds, *Changing Central–Local Relations in China: Reform and State Capacity*, Boulder: Westview, 91–112.

Wolf, M. (1996) 'A Country Divided by Growth', *Financial Times*, February 20: 14.

Wong, C. P. W. (1991) 'Central–Local Relations in an Era of Fiscal Decline: The Paradox of Fiscal Decentralization in Post-Mao China', *The China Quarterly*, 128: 691–715.

Xu, X. (1994) 'Taiwan's Economic Cooperation with Fujian and Guangdong: The View from China' in G. Klintworth, ed., *Taiwan in the Asia-Pacific in the 1990*, St. Leonards: Allen and Unwin, 142–53.

Yan, Y. (1996) *The Flow of Gifts*, Stanford: Stanford University Press.

Yang, M. (1989) 'The Gift Economy and State Power in China', *Comparative Study of Society and History*, 31: 25–54.

Yang, M. (1994) *Gifts, Favours, and Banquets: The Art of Social Relationships in China*, Ithaca: Cornell University Press.

Zhao, L. and Aram, J. (1995) 'Networking and Growth of Young Technology-Intensive Ventures in China', *Journal of Business Venturing*, 10 (5): 349–70.

Zweig, D. (1995) ' "Developmental Communities" on China's Coast: The Impact on Trade, Investment, and Transnational Alliances', *Comparative Politics*, 27 (3): 253–74.

Part III

Reshaping Political Spaces

12

Remaking Scale: Competition and Cooperation in Pre-National and Post-National Europe

Neil Smith

Introduction

The geography of Europe only two decades ago was broadly conceived as a stable hierarchy of places at different spatial scales: Eastern and Western blocs, discrete nations, subnational regions, and local and urban communities. The disruption of this "given" postwar geography in the intervening two decades and of the political, economic and cultural assumptions that went with it could barely have been predicted in the early 1970s (but see Mandel 1975, 310–42 for a prescient discussion; Rowthorn 1971; Murray 1971). Certainly the development of a "European Economic Community", equalizing conditions of trade in several commodities between six countries beginning in the early 1950s, and the steady growth of a more fully fledged "Common Market" served notice that some disruption of the traditional economic geography (at least at the national scale) was afoot. Nonetheless, the reconstruction of Europe at all spatial scales that would follow the 1970s economic depressions in the West and the post-1989 implosion of official Communist Party rule in the East was quite unforeseeable. Thereby, the largely economic evolution of the Common Market into the European Community in the 1970s and 1980s and now into the more politically inspired European Union was bound up with a much more complex and halting entanglement of social, cultural and political as well as economic restructurings.

In the mountains of commentary about a "New Europe" – some optimistic to the point of fantasy and some so pessimistic that they depict a negative fantasy of apocalypticism – the shifting geography of Europe and especially the radical reorganization of the geographical scale of various kinds of societal activity has either been neglected or treated as a series of disparate but hardly connected events. The restructuring of geographical scale, however, has been at the centre of the political, economic and social redefinition of the "New Europe". The politics of scale, it turns out, not only helps to provide a theoretical perspective on the hotly contested questions of competition and cooperation but gives a certain fix on the direction of change in a remade Europe.

Theories of Geographical Scale

In order to deal more effectively with the implications of a remade Europe from the vantage point of scale, it is necessary to consider existing theories of scale – or more properly, the social production of scale. Geographical scale is traditionally treated as a neutral metric of physical space: specific scales of social activity are assumed to be largely given as in the distinction between urban, regional, national and global events and processes; and analysts choose specific scales as appropriate for examining specific questions. There is now, however, a considerable literature arguing that the geographical scales of human activity are not neutral "givens", not fixed universals of social experience, nor are they an arbitrary methodological or conceptual choice (Taylor 1981; Smith 1984; 1992; Marston 1990; Paasi 1991; Herod 1991; 1992; Jonas 1994). Rather, scale should be seen as materially real frames of social action. As such, geographical scales are historically mutable and are the products of social activity, broadly speaking.

To illustrate this simply, it is only necessary to compare the classic European walled city of the medieval period with the contemporary conurbation of Los Angeles or Sao Paulo. Both the walled and the contemporary city symbolize what we take to be the urban, but the scale of urban life in walled London is radically different from that of Sao Paulo today. This leads us to a refinement of the axiom that scale is a materially real frame of social action: geographical scale is socially produced as simultaneously a platform and container of certain kinds of social activity. Far from neutral and fixed, therefore, geographical scales are the product of economic, political and social activities and relationships; as such they are as changeable as those relationships themselves. At the very least, different kinds of society produce different kinds of geographical scale for containing and enabling particular forms of social interaction. The medieval city is the locus of feudal commerce and simultaneously a place to be defended from external military attack, while the modern metropolis is much more the expression of an expansive capitalism premised on large scale production, widespread financial, service and communication networks, and mass consumption. Scale is the geographical organizer and expression of collective social action.

If this is a reasonable way of rendering scale a simultaneously historical and material artefact, the next set of questions presumably focuses around the ways in which scales are actually set or fixed amidst the flux of social interaction. Here I think geographical scale is best conceptualized as the *spatial* resolution of contradictory social forces; in particular the resolution between opposing forces of competition and cooperation (Smith 1984). Take, for example, the nation-state. The boundaries of the nation-state represent a *geographical* bounding between those places and actors who are prepared to cooperate vis-a-vis certain social requirements and those with whom competition is the determining relationship. In the most immediate sense, most national boundaries were the product of political and/ or military contest, but they were drawn precisely as a means to establish and defend territorial units of a specific economic and cultural definition. Within the nation-state, corporations cooperate broadly in the construction of governmental apparatuses determining conditions of work, legal systems, conditions of private and public property holding, infrastructure for commerce, travel to work and communications, national defence. At different scales, these same corporate entities may well compete over customers, product identity, technological advantage, markets, etc. The boundaries of nation-states became the geographical demarcation of the compromise between competition and cooperation.

Scale then can be both fluid and fixed – materially as well as conceptually. "The language of scale," Jonas suggests, "is an anticipation of the future"; "future scales eventually become the 'scale fixes' to existing and imposed scale constraints, if only to create new constraints and opportunities for domination/subordination" (Jonas 1994, 262). The *production of scale*, therefore, is a highly charged and political process as is the continual reproduction of scale at established levels (e.g., defence of national boundaries, community tax base, regional identity). Even more politically charged is the reproduction of scale at different levels – the restructuring of scale, the establishment of new 'scale fixes' for new concatenations of political, economic and cultural interchange. Newly fixed scales of social intercourse establish fixed geographical structures bounding political, economic and cultural activity in specific ways; highly contentious and contested social relationships become anchored if not quite in stone at least in landscapes that are, in the short run, fixed. In geography, political difference is fossilized, as it were, naturalizing whole realms of contestable social organization. "Jumping scale" – the reorganization of specific kinds of social interaction at a higher scale and therefore over a wider terrain, breaking the fixity of "given" scales – is therefore a primary avenue to power. This applies whether we are considering national claims to empire, a city's efforts to annex surrounding suburbs, or feminist efforts to dissolve the boundaries between home and community (Marston 1990; Saegert and Leavitt 1990). Thus, the demarcation of scale should be seen as absolutely central to the processes and politics of uneven geographical development.

Most significantly, it is the scale of the nation-state that is being restructured as part of the new Europe, and it is this scale that occupies us here. As Gupta has pointed out, "the nation is so deeply implicated in the texture of everyday life and so thoroughly presupposed in the academic discourses on 'culture' and 'society' that it becomes difficult to remember that it is only one, relatively recent, historically contingent form in organizing space in the world" (Gupta 1992, 63). Indeed it is only one scale at which the world is organized even now. Whereas the local scale can be conceived as expressing the geographical range of daily reproduction activities (e.g., the journey to work) and the regional scale as an increasingly relict subnational expression of the geographical coherence (or otherwise) of distinct production systems, the scale of the nation-state springs more from the global circulation of capital. With the internationalization of commercial capital in the seventeenth and eighteenth centuries, the question of coordinating competitive and cooperative relationships between capitals became increasingly vital. The nationalization of capital, simultaneous with and as part of the internationalization of capital, was the solution that emerged historically (see Hobsbawm 1990; Nairn 1977). National capitals and their attendant political frameworks in the nation-state emerged as a vital geographical means for coordinating and arbitrating economic competition between capitals at the global scale. National capitals are in effect different national "laws of value" in a wider global market, and they remain coherent to the extent that the nation-states devised for the purpose succeed in protecting the gamut of social, economic and cultural conditions that sustain individual national capitals. That is, the functions of the state which were in earlier times attached to lower spatial scales of territorial control – city states, duchies, kingdoms, etc. – are, with the advent of capitalism, reconstituted at the scale of the nation.

Two caveats are important here. First, it would be a mistake to overgeneralize and assume a complete congruence of political and economic interests. From the American Civil War and the Paris Commune to the fate of the Hapsburg Empire and the failures of Versailles, there are abundant illustrations of the contentious fit of economic and political interests in the geographically absolute territorialization of the nation-state. These struggles took place along class and race lines or resulted from intraclass conflicts, as much as they were bound up with cultural and economic definitions of various nations in birth. Ongoing as such contests are, they did not prevent the emergence of the nation-state as the appropriate geographical scale and political means for arbitrating the division of capital.

Second, although I have stressed here the economic and political relationships that lead to the pupation of specific geographical scales, it is important to realize that the production of scale is also a cultural event. Individual and group identities are heavily tinctured by attachments to place at different scales. At the national scale, nation-states may be an expression of competing capitals in the world market, established, defended and expanded by military as well as political and economic means, but they also involve an extraordinarily deepseated identity creation (Anderson 1983). Nationalism is a cultural and ideological force in its own right which helps sculpt the spatialization of social relations from the start, and which represents at times a decisive force in any restructuring of scale.

A Post-National Europe?

It is commonly understood that the origins of the "New Europe" lie first and foremost in the altered relationship between the various national economies of Europe and the international market. At the simplest level, three interconnected kinds of shifts beginning in the postwar world but quickening in the 1970s led to the current restructuring of Europe.

First, economic globalization. Although a world market in commodity extraction and exchange was largely in place by the nineteenth century, the globalization of other aspects of the economy had to wait until quite recently. The great depression of the 1920s and 1930s, with somewhat coordinated crashes in Europe and North America and attendant effects throughout the world, provoked the realization of a global financial system already partly realized. The establishment of various international financial organizations in the wake of World War II – the IMF, World Bank, GATT etc. – represented an attempt at global regulation of this emerging reality. Until the 1970s, however, no matter how global (or at least international) the commercial and financial systems had become, economic production remained largely contained within pre-existing national boundaries. Only with the combined disinvestment and reinvestment that marked the global recession of the early 1970s did economic production begin in any small degree to transcend national boundaries and the national scale of political economic organization. In its most common form, the internationalization of production involves the manufacture of component parts in several different countries and their assembly at one central location. Even in the 1990s, the internationalization of production has affected only certain well publicized sectors of production – automobiles, textiles, electronic goods, for example – and even there only partially. Along with this emerging globalization of production came a dramatic increase in international labour migration and the emergence of a more accomplished international division of labour than in any previous era (Froebel et al. 1980).

The emerging globalization of production and finance as well as commerce should not be exaggerated, however. Many production activities remain local and regional or are still organized at the national level (as indeed is true with commercial and financial activity – cf. local commodity markets, local money lending, and local mortgage companies). And it is also true that amidst this internationalization a new (not just relic) level of local and regional production has at times emerged, although too much is often made of this as in the fabled case of the Third Italy (Piore and Sabel 1984). The connections between such cases of relict and new localization in production and the internationalization of the economy are complicated and cannot be investigated here. Suffice it to say that while globalization necessarily implies the corollary of localization, a clear trajectory of change toward a more accomplished internationalization (and at times globalization) of most functional sectors of the economy has emerged.

But why did such an internationalization take place? This leads us to consider the second shift that occurred in the postwar period: the increased scale of capital accumulation. Capitalist economies carry within them an inherent tendency toward an increased level of capital accumulation. This argument is probably best theorized by Marx and marxist economists at the level both of individual and collective capitals, but it is recognized equally in the neo-classical economic dictum that a healthy economy is a growing economy; a no-growth economy is an economy in crisis – in fact, a long-term impossibility given capitalist conditions of production. There is no absolute necessity for a growing national or international economy to translate into the need for an expanded scale of accumulation at the level of individual capitals, but there is a compelling logic behind such a centralization and concentration of capital (Marx [1867 (1967)], chs 23–5; Smith 1984). And indeed this is what happened in the postwar world. In the European automobile industry, for example, production for individual national markets was clearly an unprofitable prospect by the 1960s, and by the 1970s a series of automobile plants were established by all the major producers with a Europe-wide or at least multi-national market in view. This expansion of the scale of accumulation is precisely what drove the internationalization of production in the first place and further enhanced the internationalization of markets.

The third shift that took place beginning in the 1970s involved the unprecedented transnationalism of labour in the world economy. Not only the production functions themselves were increasingly internationalized but the labour force available for production was increasingly international. This is true not just in terms of the numerically more prevalent cases of unskilled and semi-skilled labour from outside Europe and even the peripheries of Europe, but also with more skilled labour.

Together and in myriad different ways, these three shifts have dramatically expanded the scale at which the command functions of the economy operate. As a result, the geographical congruence between economic and political functions expressed in the nation-state became more and more tenuous. Nationally established states became less useful and less convenient to internationally mobile capital; were less and less willing to expand regulations or even sustain existing regulations over capital; were less able, and despite shrill national outcries often less interested in, controlling the immigration of cheap foreign labour; and therefore found themselves more and more able to relinquish some of the national state's traditional regulatory role in social reproduction. Displaced increasingly from the national to the international scale in the world market, *economic* competition between *politically defined* and territorially fixed nation-states intensified dramatically in the 1970s. Ironically, of course, this occurred at the precise moment when the reality of "national capitals" was diffusing – precisely when the territorial definition of ruling economic and political interests was diverging. Necessity, then, was turned into virtue, and the privatization of various economies in the 1980s, as well as dramatic cuts in social services, housing and welfare provisions from Britain and the U.S. to the Netherlands and even Sweden, has to be seen in this context.

If the political crises of privatization and service cuts since the 1980s are in every way a social crisis of the internationalization of capital, they should also be seen as rather desperate responses by national state governments to [the need to] retain and redefine a political role for themselves at a time when their economic functions were increasingly subordinated to the global economy and even emerging aspects of a global state, especially the IMF. The power of the IMF, the World Bank and the United Nations is routinely used to discipline the states of the developing world, but in Europe the political assertion of the world market is more gingerly applied. Britain in the late 1970s felt the squeeze of the IMF as indeed does most of Eastern Europe now.

The much vaunted obsolescence of the national state therefore represents a very real trajectory of change and is of course central to the emergence of the "New Europe." In this respect, we can see clear connections between economic internationalization and the emergence of what might be called a "post-national Europe." The argument of a post-national world has been put forward more broadly by Appadurai (1993). And of course very similar forces of "scale jumping" are afoot in the tripartite ratification of NAFTA – the North American Free Trade Agreement – which will begin to provide a framework for and help routinize a pattern of transnational economic and labour movements between Mexico, the US and Canada that has been emerging at least since World War II but more intensely since the 1970s. More recently, the Southern Common Market has been ratified for South America.

The Politics of "Integration"

If the national scale of social, political and economic organization, represented a solution to a specific problem, namely how to arbitrate contradictory requirements for competition and cooperation in the economic sphere, it is important to make clear that this was not a universal problem even if it might be considered global. By this I mean that in the seventeenth to nineteenth centuries, it was specifically the commercial classes and emerging capitalist interests across the world who faced the problem of arbitrating competition and cooperation and establishing the political conditions under which capital accumulation should proceed. The organization of competing capitals was hardly an inherent problem for peasants, workers or even the petit bourgeoisie and only impinged on the aristocracies to the extent that the latter conjoined their traditionally landed wealth with commercial production capital. The emergence of the nation-state and the national scale of political and economic organization therefore represented in the first place a solution to a strictly class problem. This is obviously not to deny that the national framework of laws, infrastructure and economic development and the other accoutrements of national development, established primarily out of the political and economic aspirations of the emerging bourgeoisie, affected (sometimes but by no means always beneficially) other classes and groups as well – sometimes sooner, sometimes later. The ingenuity of the national state as a territorial form of governance is precisely that it tied clear class economic interests to limited promises of democratic participation and the dissolution of earlier forms of oppressive absolutism. Nor is it to deny that aspirations for such benefits led to the inclusion of various groups and classes in the nationalist movements of the time. Rather it is to recognize the bourgeoisie as a progressive force in this period, and to recognize that this class succeeded in generalizing its own agenda as a broader docket for social change, directing historical change toward a national division of economic, political and social interests.

Likewise today, as that system of national states no longer serves the purposes for which it was established, the struggle over the political geography of a "New Europe" involves clear social divisions of class, gender and race entwined within and between the filaments of national interest. After 1992, when the European Community took a further step toward economic unification, declaring in theory if not always in practice that neither capital nor labour mobility would be restricted by national boundaries, "integration" became the watchword in public debate over the "New Europe." With unification of Europe now seemingly a reality, public discussion, mirroring the discussions in Brussels and in every national capital, turned to methods and strategies of "integration." This discussion in turn has revolved around the different ways of retaining local and "national" competitiveness within a much enlarged "post-national" territory, an estimate of winners and losers in distinctly national terms, and unabashedly nationalist jousting over particular treaties, agreements, clauses and exceptions.

The language of "integration" is self-evidently technocratic. It takes as its starting point the technocratic optimism of Maastricht, namely the assumption that European unity is a virtually accomplished fact and an unquestioned good leaving only the details to be managed into place. But more important, the integrationist perspective takes as its unexamined point of departure the perspective of capital. Whether this treaty or that treaty is preferable, whether this clause or that clause should be included – these have become questions to be arbitrated according to national economic advantage insofar as the economic elites of the different countries cannot immediately agree, or, insofar as ruling class unity prevails, they are issues to be resolved as instances of national cooperation. The Maastricht agreement was a clear case of the latter in which means of economic, financial and political integration were agreed by the functionaries of the twelve member nations without serious consideration of the political opposition that such "integration" would face among the populace. As even the language of "treaties" suggests, the earlier struggle between local capitals to forge national unities is at the end of this century being substantially rerun at a higher scale. With the geographical core of the "New Europe" now substantially defined, "integration" is the rubric under which the new conditions of cooperation vis-a-vis competition are set. The largely unstated qualifier to "integration" is *economic* integration; integration is the solution to problems set by the unification of markets (including labour and financial markets) and conditions of production. Only at the margins is it a debate about social or cultural integration or the integration of environmental goals across Europe; indeed, local social, cultural and environmental differences are to be retained even highlighted within European unity, not only as nostalgic reminders of what differentiates Europe from the world outside, but as the primary commodities of the tourist industry.

It is hardly surprising therefore that opposition to a united Europe has focused on questions of jobs and social welfare, refusing implicitly or explicitly to accept the class-specific agenda denoted by economic integration. This opposition represents a very rational response to European unity, especially given the close connections between post-nationalism and the retrenchment of national governments against the provision of social services. The latter constitute a clear attack along class, gender and racial lines against those populations most dependent on social services but who have been pushed to the periphery of European unity. And yet at the same time, this opposition is at times driven by a narrow nationalism, especially in the discussion of jobs – a localism that itself indulges an appeal to national and at times racial exclusivity. "Save British jobs" and "Save British industry" are a dangerous response to European unity and no response at all to the class specific agenda of "integration."

Pre-National Europe?

A very different kind of response to the fragmentation of nationalisms is emerging elsewhere in Europe. Although the precipitous disintegration of the Soviet Bloc after 1989 was in the first case a political event, substantially removed from the dilemmas facing Western Europe, these two sets of experiences are not now as disconnected as they might once have seemed. In the first place, the Soviet Union after 1917, and Eastern Europe to a more limited extent after 1945, represented significant if ultimately failed experiments at a post-national economic and political structure, albeit somewhat removed from direct capitalist forms of production and social reproduction. The dilemmas of the European Community in the latter part of the twentieth century were to a significant degree anticipated in 1917 even as the Soviet Union fought at the same time to escape the central political and economic dynamic of capital accumulation that would bring the situation to a head in the West.

In the second place, the return to regional, religious and variously "ethnic" definitions of nationhood that have especially marked the remaking of the erstwhile

Soviet Union and Eastern Europe (but have also appeared in the West) have also brought about a remaking of scale intricately connected to the reassertion of various "subnationalisms." In this case, however, the remaking of scale is in large part a response not only to the "post-nationalism" of communist government but also to the earlier national state formation of capitalist governments. The baseline for the Armenian struggle with Azerbaijan, the division of Czechoslovakia into a Czech and Slovak Republic, the multifaceted fissures between Serbs, Croats, Bosnians, Christians and Muslims in the ex-Yugoslavia, the Serbian ethnic cleansing in the genocidal war in Bosnia, the reassertion of Cossack identity in Russia and of monarchical claims in Romania – the baseline for all of these struggles lies less with the recent past than with the enforced nationalisms that took place in an earlier era. In retrospect, the 1919 Versailles Peace Treaty begins to appear as, among other things, a tragically unsuccessful enforced territorialization of many smaller European nationalisms, judged to occupy the periphery of an effectively complete system of European states by 1919. It is this same core, of course, that is disintegrating in the opposite direction with "European unity."

In this sense, the reassertion of pre-national regional identities in Eastern Europe (nationalisms that predate the nation-state, that is) also represent a competitive response not just to European unity but to a longstanding globalization of capital. In most cases, pre-national regionalism has taken the form of a particularly reactionary reassertion of local identities. Nor is it restricted to Eastern Europe, as for example the case of Scottish nationalism makes clear. The visceral emotional appeal to Scottish nationalism over the last two decades may not have achieved such a politically charged or as violent a reaction to globalization and enforced nationalism as is now evident in much of Eastern Europe, but it springs from many of the same concerns. It is every bit a pre-national reassertion of regionalism vis-a-vis a British state officially dominated by England since the early eighteenth century, and is rooted in a quite mythical history of national unity prior to Union. What distinguishes Scottish nationalism in recent years is the somewhat novel attempt to use the "New Europe" as an appropriate venue for advancing its claims, thus vaulting over the scale of national government. That at least might be considered progressive. Such a tactic is only partly successful, of course. The central national government in London has not only limited severely the extent to which it will allow the borders of Britain to be made more porous. It has also in part succeeded in deflecting the challenge of Scottish nationalism into a marketing device; the kilt, Scotch whisky and the Scottish Highlands are now ready symbols for a *British* tourist industry capitalizing upon "regional diversity." The same point applies to the repackaging of Breton claims of national difference into celebratory symbols of *French* uniqueness. As the nation goes multinational, the region in different ways makes claims for the national (jumping scale) or is made to stand in for it.

Politics, Geography and the Periphery

Marx concluded the first volume of *Capital* with a chapter on colonization which, though much misunderstood, makes the powerful point that the social relations of capitalism are more clearly and sharply observable at the periphery of the system than at the centre. The same lesson may well apply in the context of a "New Europe" and the "integration" which is being led from the conservative core of Brussels and Bonn, London, Paris and the Hague. So evident is this locus of power that [...] peripheral "regions", from the Celtic and Nordic to the Eastern and Southern European find themselves forced to consider competitive responses. It would be a mistake, however, to accept the terms of this challenge in the national and often nationalist garb in which they are dressed. As the Scottish example suggests, it is at the periphery where the contradiction between a pre-national and a post-national Europe is most intensely felt. On the one hand, a pre-national regionalism is not only quite unrealistic insofar as fragmented pre-national regions would lack the power to compete under the economic conditions that have led in the first place to the diffusion of the power of national state boundaries and the entertainment of transnational possibilities. But on the second hand, it is difficult to imagine that such a pre-national regionalism could be a progressive historical force. Rather, such a fragmentation would in all likelihood set off a dangerous economic and cultural competitiveness between regional states defined through their appeal to a quintessentially *local* exceptionalism buttressed by historically partial reinscriptions of past calumnies.

If pre-national regionalism is no realistic option, nor is simple acquiescence to the intensified peripheral exploitation and marginalization that is likely to result from integration into a post-national Europe. Much as Marx argued about European-held colonies, the sharp differences of interest (in class, race and gender terms) pertaining to European unity are most sharply visible at the periphery where the conservatism of core governments is less commanding. And yet the social democratic opposition to the European Union, which pays lip service to such social differences, has hardly been more realistic. Swedish and Finnish integration into the European Union is indeed likely to involve a dilution or even dissolution of progressive social welfare systems (especially affecting women), somewhat protective labour legislation (affecting workers, especially migrant workers), and emerging environmental gains in those countries; it will also extend the penetration of privatization and commodification into the rhythms of daily life, much as social democrats have argued. The unspoken corollary of this prediction, however, is that it will be difficult for peripheral capitalisms outside the EU to sustain their previous systems of social services. Privatization and the dismantling of the social welfare systems in Britain or Sweden may have been the work of especially ideological conservatives, but they also represented a response to economic globalization, post-nationalism, and the precarious position in which the national state found itself. Even social democratic governments outside the EU have been forced to initiate or sustain austerity cuts. Reversing this movement will take a more profound political shift than that implied by inclusion in the EU.

In a quite pessimistic assessment of Europe and the Left, David Marquand's (1994, 24–6) only allowance to optimism is that at least European Unity is controlled by political rather than economic means and this may afford the Left some kind of entre. Too many on the Left, he says, have put "the cart of economics" before "the horse of politics":

There is, in short, a contradiction between the monetary ambitions of the Union [for monetary unity] and its territorial divergences. Unless and until that contradiction is resolved, the Union is as likely to move backward as forward. And the contradiction can be resolved only by and through political institutions.

But it may be Marquand who has the cart of a defeated pessimism before the horse of politics. What else is one to make of his resignation to the idea that the contradiction between economics and geography will only be resolved via the institutional structures of the Union? For no other alternative is proposed. In the first place, as the earlier discussion of scale suggests, post-nationalism may not be inevitable but it is backed by a powerful logic of the political economic geography of capital accumulation which, far from being comprehensible in terms of forward and backward, is multifaceted. Second, in recognition of this historical restructuring in the geographical scales of social organization, an internationalist response to the ongoing formation of a new Europe is imperative. But such a response involves a more ambitious mix of *political* competition and cooperation than Marquand envisages: competition to ruling agendas for economic restructuring, guided first and foremost by the dictates of profitability; cooperation across national boundaries between political movements with an inherently *social* (rather than economic) vision of different possible futures.

If, as many geographers have been arguing for two decades, it is appropriate to see social geographical forms as the temporary fossilization of social relationships, and vice versa, then the reterritorialization implied by a New Europe must be seen as equally a new socialization in which reinscribed relations of class, race and gender are re-etched as new structured geographies of social difference. That the accomplishment of a New Europe is likely to lead to an exacerbation of existing patterns of uneven development, notwithstanding new pockets of development taking advantage of cheap labour and EU subsidies applied to the poorer periphery, is a more appropriate entrée for an internationalist Left opposition than existing political institutions. Where Marquand's pessimism may be intuitively justified is that the progress of European unity on a broadly capitalist basis has dramatically outstripped any internationalist response from feminist and green, socialist and anti-racist movements.

The size of this task should not be underestimated. The power of the ruling classes to dictate the agenda for European integration has been considerable; they have already jumped scales, leaving any possible internationalist opposition to begin almost from the beginning. They have successfully cast their own economic interest for profits in terms of jobs and thereby significantly fragmented increasingly conservative and isolated union movements along national lines. That the task now of asserting popular interests seems so great is in many ways the direct result of the missing networks of crossnational grassroots political organization. To the extent that such modest networks now emerging can have a significant effect on the conditions of European integration, they will express popular social interests in global interconnectedness rather than the economic interests of ruling elites. A more egalitarian social geography of Europe should be the political goal of these movements.

REFERENCES

Anderson, B. (1983), *Imagined Communities*, Verso, London.

Appadurai, A. (1993), 'Patriotism and its Futures', *Public Culture* 5, 411–30.

Froebel, F., Heinrichs, J. and Kreye, O. (1980), *The New International Division of Labour*, Cambridge University Press, Cambridge.

Gupta, A. (1992), 'The Song of the Nonaligned World: Transnational Identities and the Reinscription of Space in Late Capitalism', *Cultural Anthropology* 7, 63–79.

Herod, A. (1991), 'The Production of Scale in US Labour Relations', *Area* 23, 82–8.

Herod, A. (1992), *Towards a Labor Geography: The Production of Space and the Politics of Scale in the East Coast Longshore Industry, 1953–1990*, Unpublished Dissertation, Department of Geography, Rutgers University.

Hobsbawm, E. (1990), *Nations and Nationalism Since 1780*, Cambridge University Press, Cambridge.

Jonas, A. (1994), 'The Scale Politics of Spatiality', *Environment and Planning D: Society and Space* 12, 257–64.

Mandel, E. (1975), *Late Capitalism*, New Left Books, London.

Marquand, D. (1994) 'Reinventing Federalism: Europe and the Left', *New Left Review* 203, 17–26.

Marston, S. (1990), ' "Who are the People?": Gender, Citizenship and the Remaking of the American Nation', *Environment and Planning D: Society and Space* 8, 449–58.

Marx, K. (1867), *Capital* vol. 1, International Publishers (1967 edn.), New York.

Murray, R. (1971), 'Internationalization of Capital and the Nation State', *New Left Review* 67.

Nairn, T. (1977), *The Break-Up of Britain*, New Left Books, London.

Paasi, A. (1991), 'Deconstructing Regions: Notes on the Scales of Spatial Life', *Environment and Planning A* 23, 239–56.

Piore, M. and Sabel, C. (1984), *The Second Industrial Divide*, Basic Books, New York.

Rowthorn, R. (1971), 'Imperialism: Unity or Rivalry?', *New Left Review* 69.

Saegert, S. and Leavitt, J. (1990), *From Abandonment to Hope*, Columbia University Press, New York.

Smith, N. (1984), *Uneven Development: Nature, Capital and the Production of Space*, Basil Blackwell, Oxford.

Smith, N. (1992), 'Geography, Difference and the Politics of Scale', in J. Doherty, E. Graham and M. Malek (eds.) *Postmodernism and the Social Sciences*, Macmillan, Houndsmills, 57–79.

Taylor, P. (1981), 'Geographical Scales in the World Systems Approach', *Review* 5, 3–11.

13

The National and the Regional: Their Autonomy Vis-à-Vis the Capitalist World Crisis

Alain Lipietz

Social Relations and Space: Some Definitions[1]

From the modes of production to space-in-itself

Each social formation is a complex structure of social relations intertwined at the economic, politico-juridical, and ideological instances. It presents itself as an articulation of modes of production: typical mixtures of social relations such as capitalism, petty commodity production, and domestic production. This articulation, however, represents something more than a mere combination of these relations.

On the one hand, the form of existence of each of the forms of production depends largely upon the role attributed to it by the reproduction of the dominant mode in the social formation (i.e., capitalism). On the other hand, the conditions of existence of the dominant mode of production itself presuppose the presence of other modes of production, serving, for example, as reserves of labor power and outlets.

If, a priori, each mode of production has its own developmental dynamics and logic, which is generally in contradiction to that of the other modes, the dominance of the capitalist mode of production imposes on the whole structure its unity (i.e., its mode of functioning), which thereby manifests itself as a coherent whole. Thus, every practice and social relation figures within a concrete totality that is always already given and that determines that relation as its condition of existence. This totality, to the extent that it has materiality, carries a spatial dimension, for example, the separation of the producer from his/her means of production and the division of labor. As soon as this separation is realized – becomes physically established – it allows for the reproduction of the relation and, consequently, of the separation itself. Though all relations contribute to the constitution of social reality, every singular practice takes social reality – and hence spatiality – for granted. This is what may be called the "ecological paradox": for although the socioeconomic space is a product of practices, it appears, however, as somehow externally given for each individual practice or interaction (Lipietz 1989).

In other words, to the extent that it is not a historical transformation of the conditions of existence (i.e., of a revolutionary or long-term nature), the material existence of social reproduction also plays the part of a "social mold" determining the "habitus" (Bourdieu [1979]), anticipations, behavior, and opportunities of the social formation as a whole. The social space, therefore, is one of the dimensions (the spatial dimension) of this social mold that one could call "the habits of history" (Lipietz 1987). In this light, social space should not be comprehended as the reflection (or support of the reflections) of social relations that would exist "elsewhere"; nor should it be perceived as a milieu, a field of deployment of regular practices constituting these relations. But in social reproduction the material space appears either as a result or as a determinant of these relations and practices. One can state that the social space is a "moment" of social reproduction. In this respect – and in this Hegelian terminology – the social "space-in-itself" is a "reflection" of social relations. This space-in-itself is the objective foundation of the empirical space in which social practices seem to take place, are embedded, and deployed[2].

From hegemony to space-for-itself

It is to the merit of Antonio Gramsci to have made, within the Marxian approach, significant progress in reflecting on the passage from "society as a field of relations" to "society as an agreement or struggle for the conservation or the establishment of a field of relations."[3] He did so precisely on the issue of the regional and national question, suggesting the notions of "social bloc" and "hegemonic bloc." A social bloc is a convergence of social groups or fractions belonging to certain groups.[4] A hegemonic bloc is the social bloc capable of representing or dictating (i.e., imposing) its project as that of society as a whole.[5] A space-for-itself is the spatial dimension of a social bloc, of its hegemony, or of the open struggle between such blocs.

Spaces-for-themselves might include such cases as the following: a nation, recognized or seeking to be recognized (e.g., Palestine or Sahara); or a more restrained space, still affirming its specificity (a region defined by a regional movement); or a wider space materializing in a community seeking a certain mode of life ("the Umma," the "Free World"). Notice first that a space-for-itself can as easily express positions of either a conservative, modernist, reactionary, or progressive nature. And second, a space-for-itself may be defined in any instance (e.g., economic, ideological, religious, political, and linguistic options). Hence conflicts of legitimacy and the possibility of shifts: One can experience oneself as a Yugoslavian (against Stalin) and then as a Croatian (as a Catholic); one can experience oneself as an Arab nationalist, but also as Lebanese, and, then again, as a Sunni; and so forth. Notice finally that, as a result, the borders of a space-for-itself do not necessarily coincide with the space-in-itself proper to a particular social relation, nor with the language community or the citizenship.[6] In contrast, few social movements exist without a spatial dimension, whether nationalist or regionalist. Conversely, a region that acquires a consciousness-of-itself cannot avoid having an ideological dimension: elegy for a re(li)gion, writes Francisco de Oliveira (1977) speaking of the northeast of Brazil.

Economic regions, regional armatures, nation-states

An homogeneous area consisting of an articulation of modes and forms of production will be defined henceforth as an "economic region."[7]

"Homogeneous" here should not imply that we disregard subregional differences, the most evident of which are urban–rural divisions, or that we neglect economic and social divisions in the urban spaces or urban hierarchies within the region. Considering the totality of these relations (urban and rural; workers and bourgeois neighborhoods), it may be said that the form of articulation of these relations "individualizes" the region. In an economic region, a definite subregime of accumulation evidently exists that maintains relations with its exterior. The choice of scale (i.e., of the social relations under consideration) can be somewhat artificial; the "Industrial North," for instance, is a global economic region, whereas the Great West of France and the northeast of Brazil form economic regions within national spaces.

Yet such illustrations of space-in-itself do not necessarily provide a sufficient basis for the articulation of a space-for-itself. For example, while the North-Western part of the world and the Brazilian *nordeste* provide illustrative cases, for the time being at least, the Great West of France does not. Evidently, there is some question as to the existence of the hegemonic social bloc and the institutional forms that grant a space for its personality. And it is precisely at this point that the question of the state can no longer be avoided: the state as "the apparatus by which society equips itself in order that the different groups of which it is constituted do not exhaust themselves in a struggle without end," as Marx and Engels defined it in *The German Ideology*. The topology of state relations – i.e., the topology of relations of sovereignty (or national borderlines) – relentlessly divides the scale of spaces among the national, the local, and the global.

We will call "regional armature" a space-for-itself where the dominant classes of the hegemonic bloc mobilize ideological and political apparatuses enabling the appropriate regulation at this level of some aspect or another of the socioeconomic conflict. Several regional armatures can divide an economic region, and certain parts of an economic region can appear as deprived of a significant regional armature. (Think of the specificity of Wales in relation to Sussex, for example.) Yet, the regional armature must be sharply distinguished from the nation-state, the territory of which is characterized by the universality of law (social law in particular), the uniqueness of its currency, and the monopoly of legitimate violence (sovereignty).

Let us limit ourselves to the economic aspects. It is only at the national scale that a policy of social compromise can become durably stable. For it is only within the totality of a state that social reproduction – and, in particular, the regime of accumulation – can make use of all the forms of compensatory mechanisms and of monetary, nonexchange transfers (e.g., taxes and social revenues). It is the privilege of the state to issue the general equivalent: the national currency that each holder of an income can exchange for an output realized at every location in the national territory, in an expedient fashion for both the individual and society. But this is also its limit. The exterior or balance of trade constraint requires that a distributed income exchanged for a foreign output should almost simultaneously have its counterpart in an equivalent exportation. A region (subnational), in contrast, does not face an exterior constraint.[8] This fundamental difference between the national and the local inevitably leads to political consequences; struggles and compromises can only be settled at the national level or, more precisely still, can only be settled at the level of regional armatures at the mercy of conditions warranted at the national level. A regional armature can extract the conditions for local compromises from the rest of the nation (in France, for example, le Midi Viticole, the industrial regions in decline). But it is certainly a national compromise (the maintenance of a "culture of the vine," of industries unprofitable from a capitalist point of view), at the charge of the nation, to make this compromise respected within the context of its exterior constraints.

But what about supranational spaces-for-themselves? Are there supranational forms of regulation, embedded in an international consensus among classes? Of course such forms exist, but until recently they have been rather weak forms of implicit hegemony, such as the dollar standard and "virtuous configurations" of complementarity between the national regimes of accumulation (Lipietz 1987). I will return to this issue later, when dealing with the European question.

Interregionality

First of all, a fundamental point needs to be clarified: the statute of interregionality in the definition of regions. In other words, one must ask: Is a region defined by itself, by the type of articulation of social relations that characterize it (see the definition above), or in relation to the others by the relation that opposes it to the other regions? Or yet more problematically: Is this "homogeneity" ascribed to the economic regions solely the product of the history of socioeconomic relations in these regions, or is it the impact of the position that regions take in an interregional division of labor? In brief: Is the interregionality derived from the regions, or vice versa? This is a decisive theoretical question for the problem at hand, irrespective of the degree of autonomy of the space-for-itself that grounds the economic region under investigation. If one adopts a global or an international theoretical perspective, then the potential for recognition of local, regional, or national socioeconomic transformations is very small. If, however, one adopts a regional standpoint, then everything evidently changes.

Despite the decisive nature of this issue, the answer will be voluntarily ambiguous.[9] First of all, it is evident that there exists a spatial division of labor internal to the economic region and that this very division in turn defines the subspaces (e.g., urban–rural). On the other hand, it is evident that there exists at the supraregional level a de facto spatial division of labor between the economic regions as soon as they become articulated among themselves: different-type regions neither produce nor exchange the same things. The only question lies in knowing whether the difference between regions (i.e., between the types of internal articulation that characterize them) is the product of different internal (genealogical) causalities, or whether it is the outcome of interregional relations. To this specific question, I answer: Both at the same time, according to a varying importance, and depending upon the topology proper to the division of labor corresponding to the most developed forms of contemporary capitalism, but leaving to internal causation an irreducible importance that always conserves its primacy in the case of a space identified with a given nation-state. To put things differently, the interregional division of space develops in correspondence with the current tendencies of the capitalist division of labor and on the basis of a checkerboard of regions having their internal "Okinawa"-social features inherited from the past (this is the "coarseness" or rather the "viscosity" of space, as evoked by Milton Santos, [1979]). Thus, the development of the interregional division of space also takes into account the possibilities and willingness of the hegemonic social bloc in the concrete regions to adapt or resist. More simply still: The interspatial relations of the center–periphery type are the results, not the causes, of the socioeconomic characters of the peripheral spaces. The ultimate causes should be traced back to the internal dynamics of peripheral spaces, in the understanding that the forms of colonization should be considered as a part of these internal dynamics, and that the relations between the internal hegemonic bloc and the exterior weigh heavily on its proper dynamics.[10]

The Crisis of Fordism

Let us briefly review the notion of Fordism – the regime of intensive accumulation with mass consumption under monopolist regulation – that dominated in the North-West of the world from 1945 to 1970.

As a regime of accumulation, Fordism is based upon an organization of labor that combines Taylorism (separation of conception and execution, parceling and standardization of tasks) and mechanization (by incorporating the social know-how systematized in the machine system). The consequence of this process is a rapid growth of the apparent productivity of labor and of fixed-capital per capita. The outlets for this increased productivity are established through this same growth of per capita capital, on the one hand, and an increase in the real wage level corresponding to gains in productivity, on the other. Regulation of this regime of accumulation is in the first instance based on regulation of the wage-labor relation: coercive institutional forms (generalized collective agreements, growing minimum-wage levels, the welfare state) controlling parallel growth of demand stemming from the wage-laborers and capitalist production. To these one must add the consolidation of a pure credit currency with legal tender, issued in function of the involvements of private capital.

The spatial arrangement of triumphant Fordism

There is an immediately striking and intimate relationship between Fordism and national space. Never before has the space of capital been so closely identified with the national framework, characterized by the validity of the legal-tender credit-currency and the redistribution of revenues in the welfare state. It was in the mid-1960s that the relation between exports and the domestic markets for manufactured goods reached its historical depth in most capitalist countries. Still, the exchange flows took place most essentially inside supranational continental blocs (e.g., the EC, USA–Canada). After that date, these exchanges tended to intensify and, as such, badly affect the efficiency of national regulation.

During the "Golden Age" of Fordism, the interregional division of labor forming the regional spaces tended to modify itself. In the preceding stages of capitalism these relations corresponded essentially to the spatial dimension of exchange relations between modes of production (external articulation) or between sectors of economic activity. It was the classical spatial division of labor between primary goods and manufactured products that also held sway in the international domain.

But Fordism allowed for a spatial disjunction, a new topology of its own productive process, according to the tripartition of:

1   Tasks of conception
2   Skilled tasks of production
3   De-skilled tasks of assembly

This disjunction did not necessarily adopt an interregional dimension, but could only do so once the firms found, within the old division of labor, the pools of labor power differentiated according to skills, costs, traditions of struggle, and – in the corresponding regional armatures – the social forces available to support such an industrialization strategy. Of course, during the two decades after World War II, this "new interregional division of labor" modified the regional armatures themselves.

The crisis of Fordism

Nevertheless, after the mid-1960s. Fordism began to run out of breath. The Fordist operational modes engendered declining productivity gains while the technical composition of capital increased. This resulted in a fall of profitability that simultaneously diminished the capacity to accumulate; at the same time, accumulation led to less and less employment. As a consequence, the financing of the welfare state went into crisis. This, in turn, also decelerated the rhythm of accumulation.

The first reaction of firms was to counter the fall in profitability and the increase in the cost of the welfare state by seeking to implant "type III" activities in the economic regions external to the national Fordist social-formations in southern and eastern Europe and in the Latin American or East Asiatic Third World. This strategy, which extended the Fordist interregional division, succeeded all the better as it matched the division of local hegemonic blocs. Therefore, this strategy is called "primitive Taylorization" (cf. Lipietz 1985). But this strategy, in effect, served also to accelerate the internationalization of production and markets, and in this way it paralyzed the national monopolistic regulation to an increasingly greater degree. The external constraints entered into contradiction with the principles of the monopolist regulation of the wage-labor relation: In order to be competitive, the domestic wage-labor costs needed to be compressed. But what was consequently a cost to the domestic market could not automatically be regained through growing exportations.

In a first configuration of the crisis (1974–1979), the internal stimulation of the central markets continued to prevail by means of the credit system and gave certain newly industrialized countries access to a form of "peripheral Fordism" (Lipietz 1987). But more fundamental, within the industrialized countries themselves the wage-labor relation had to face two important inflections, the first one being regressive, the second one potentially progressive.

First of all, conditions for the reproduction of labor power were challenged. During economic growth, the coupling of productivity and wage level to one another had played the principal part and the welfare state a supportive part. As the welfare state continued to develop, securing for the wage-laborers and their families a kind of permanent income, enterprises tried to get rid of the heavy contractual bonds that were linking them directly to their wage-laborers. The "hard core" of labor (the permanent workers) began to break down, while a world of statuteless, low-paid, short-term, and part-time workers began to develop. These workers live primarily on the welfare state and only occasionally on a salary. This peculiar form of wage-labor relation, being an attractive solution to each individual enterprise, became a burden upon population and enterprise as a whole, for, in fact, social security and payroll taxes increased substantially. Moreover, this evolution even further disarticulated the consensus on Fordism. The last remainders of "statute" or "craftsmanship" disappeared among the young, condemned as they were, upon entry into the job market, to "bit (odd or small) jobs" and welfare.

The second tendency, evidently more interesting, was the search for new deposits of productivity. These sources were looked for within the work process itself, in the promising potential of the electronic "technological revolution" and the challenge to Taylorist principles: redefining tasks, and individual or collective involvement (through the "quality circles") of producers in search of efficiency.

But these germs of the future, just like Taylorism before them, could only develop in a favorable macroeconomic and social framework. This was clearly rejected by the monetarist shock. At the end of the 1970s, the social hegemonic bloc in the North-West of the world openly [abandoned] policies aimed at stimulating domestic demand. The restriction on credit and the challenge to social legislation drove this economic region into a succession of sharp business cycles resulting by 1979 in industrial stagnation. This contraction of credit and outlets by the "Center" has had disastrous effects on the whole of the old periphery, but it hit certain countries of peripheral Fordism particularly hard.

It is as if, having correctly identified the origin of the crisis in the fall of profitability, the world hegemonic bloc confined the search for its solution to a technological revolution liberated from the obstacles of national monopolistic regulation, and social legislation in particular. Yet, one should think more carefully about the real contribution of the technological revolution. Between technology and the model of development are a series of linkages established throughout social relations: from technology to technical operationalization and direct production relations (i.e., who decides how the collective work process will be organized?); and the overall socio-economic relations from production to the economy (i.e., will there be enough consumers or, conversely, investors? what will they produce? which form of full employment?). In other words, a new regime of accumulation and a new mode of regulation, especially with respect to the wage-labor relation (or other relations of production), remain to be invented. In addition, the development should also be compatible within some new international configuration. I will briefly examine these three series of problems.

The great liberation of the 1980s?[11]

What does informatics offer? It offers not so much a gain in productivity per second of utilized machine-time, but rather the possibility of making full-time use of the machines on the workfloor and also of making that workfloor more flexible (Coriat 1984). A Fordist plant, based on the double-specialization of machines and people, makes uneconomic use of their time, for example, waiting-times between two operations, intermediary buffer stocks that pile up, and the impossibility of balancing work positions. The automatic control of a workfloor allows for a leap forward in the flexibility of the production process and hence for the economic use of constant capital. This is the large source of profitability that informatics offers. Information systems are quite expensive in initial investments, yet these investments can be used at full capacity.

There is more to consider. Electronics, especially, allow for increased flexibility in the system of machines. It was indeed a long while ago that the principle of automation entered the workshop: people created machines that, by themselves, would repeat their movements, such as in production lines in automobile processing or in print shops. But in order to produce the same uniform product, these enormous machineries could only perform a well-defined series of movements. In contrast, the robot can adapt itself and shift from one task to another by means of rapid reprogramming. As such, the robotized workshop can adapt itself to a fluctuating demand, jumping from one small series of tasks to another.

First bifurcation
Two evolutionary axes open up for the post-Fordist reorganization of the labor process. Automating the administration of the production process opens the temptation to separate still further the theoretical concept of the process from the executing acts of the collective worker. The operating workers would then become mere flesh and blood in the automated process of production. A majority of US as well as some European plants, especially in Spain, France, and the UK, follow this path. In contrast, however, automation can give rise to a partial reskilling of the collective worker, the practical knowledge of the operators having not only a real-time involvement in the process itself, but also in the permanent tuning of the equipment. This route seems to be being pursued by the majority of Japanese and European plants, especially in Germany and Scandinavia (Aoki [1984]). This bifurcation is the scene of an immense social struggle over a new social compromise dealing with worker involvement and distribution of increased gains in productivity.

Second bifurcation
One should also know how these gains in productivity are to be utilized. The first variant in the post-Fordist alternative will mobilize even more capital than the aging Fordism itself. Productivity gains will be reserved as profit, and final demand will

not grow. The flexibility, in itself, of computerized processes allows for the profitability of large-scale investments – by a succession of limited series of products – meant for segmented and capricious consumption by well-to-do clients. But these gains in productivity, in the absence of an extension of mass consumption, will also entail the growth of unemployment and the risk of a three-tiered division of society: a dominant class benefiting from the new gadgets of the electronic revolution; a stable but limited core of permanent employees; and a growing mass of increasingly more precarious wage-laborers marginalized by significantly weakened social protection, and finding only provisional access to service jobs during cyclical upswings. This seems to be the route being followed at present in the United States.

The other trajectory is the negotiated redistribution of gains in productivity, with mass access to the new consumption commodities that themselves require consumption time (e.g., cultural, optical, and acoustic hardware, home computers). These low-cost commodities (in comparison to automobiles) call for a division of gains in productivity in the sense of a substantial decrease of working time. Of course, a development model based on mass extension of nonpecuniary activities (e.g., leisure, creative activities, or intellectual enrichment) risks becoming translated into greater uncompetitiveness (in terms of the hourly wage-labor cost) compared to a model based on the intensification of labor without redistribution of gains in productivity. Yet, this way is being followed by Germany, Scandinavia, and, lately, even Japan. Consequently, there is a new bifurcation: Do the configuration of the world economy, the choices of the most powerful states, and the forms of interregional and international regulation leave certain spaces-for-themselves (regional armatures or nation-states) sufficient degrees of autonomy to explore new social relations? This question leads to the core of the subject, and the experience of previous years already gives some indication as to future possibilities.

The Autonomy of Spaces in Crisis

A little more theory

In order to face a crisis of the regime of accumulation and/or the mode of regulation at the local, national, or world level, it is important to understand that the social formation breaks down into not two but at least three basic postures that, in turn, can give birth to social blocs:

1 Defenders of the prevailing order up until the crisis itself (i.e., the conservative bloc);
2 Advocates of change in the capitalist hegemonic system (i.e., the modernist bloc);
3 Protagonists of a profound revolutionizing of existing social relations (i.e., the radical bloc); and also, in most cases, a fourth posture:
4 Those favoring a return to the mythical "golden age" preceding the regime in crisis (i.e., the reactionary bloc).

This very general typology is concretely materialized by ideological currents and social movements that combine these four postures in an often inextricable manner. Moreover, social classes are themselves divided between these different postures, hesitating as they are between the different routes and between the different blocs being formed and aspiring to hegemony.

It would be easy to illustrate this phenomenon of typological breakdown in its political reality.[12] But what about its spatial dimension in terms of spaces-for-themselves? At the regional as at the national level it can happen that the brutality of the transformations turns the whole of participating parties in the old bloc (of the exploiters as well as the exploited) against the project of monopolistic capital and of the centralized state (as in the case of declining regimes). The projected modernist space seems to enter openly into conflict with the old concrete regional space; the modifications of the juridical space, implied by the new project, appear despoiled, while the new classes fostering the changes appear as invaders. In these circumstances, the struggle between classes assumes a very distinct form: It opposes, at least initially, the defenders of the "old space" to the "new space" (or to the new mode of development), which is perceived as imposed by the "foreign state" and rejected as a whole. This is a phantasmagoric figure, where the whole population of a real, concrete space fights a virtual and abstract space.

In correspondence with the facilities they apparently offer, these struggles raise very difficult problems of hegemony in the social movement. At first they appear as indeed legitimate and unanimous – legitimate because humans must fight to save a land they have modeled with their own hands and also for the right to live and work in this country; unanimous because the enemy is elsewhere, at a distance, foreign and abstract. And additionally, as the enemy is monopoly capital and the state that regulates it (in the case of regional struggle) or, more precisely still, multinational capital, one could think that these struggles automatically embody the possibility of forming a radical, anticapitalist social bloc. But it is not so simple. For the old space is itself the very space that articulates social relations, which are themselves relations of exploitation. The regional social armature (or the national state) is de facto under the hegemony of the social conservative bloc. The legitimacy of the struggle may therefore only be the legitimation of the old way of exploitation, and the unanimity of the struggle may mask the direction of the struggle by the old exploiters belonging to the regime in crisis, or even to the preceding regime of accumulation. These are typical cases of nationalist or regionalist reactions, where radical and conservative or even radical and reactionary aspirations become mixed up with one another.[13]

There also exists an inverted image of this mix of reactions. A project of local, regional, or national compromise is difficult to accomplish within the existing interregional and/or international relations. It unites the radical refusal of the old order and the modernist aspirations of the new elites. The opposition between projected and real space then adopts the form of a progressive nationalism or regionalism that perceives exterior dependence as an obstacle to progress. This latter form generally covers situations in which the new seeks to be born, while the former mix of radical and conservative reactions refers back to situations in which the old dies out. In this way, the developmentalist nationalism of Europe and Latin America in the 1950s combined the search for social conquests guaranteed by the state and the more or less successful establishment of the Fordist regime of accumulation. Today's regionalist struggles against industrial restructuring or for protectionist maintenance of social gains in a national support system combine the workers' refusal to be treated as chess pieces and the conservative reaction of state functionaries, the employers' associations, and labor unions belonging to the Fordist compromise. The liberal-modernist current presently affecting the North-West of the world combines the libertarian refusal of the heavy forms of state administration in the Fordist compromise and the projects of multinationalization of a capital disembodied from social legislation.

This observation helps in understanding the absurd polarization that is tearing apart the left in Western industrialized countries, divided as it is between attachment to social-democrat compromises that have become conservative, on the one hand, and a subordinate affiliation to a new modernist bloc, on the other. The conservative avenue is by definition without outlet, even if it remains a feasible practice in the medium term.[14] It is economically condemned by the crisis of Fordism and its forms of national regulation, and, since the mid-1960s, politically rejected by the potentially progressive forces, even before the opening of the economic crisis. But is the modernist solution, as presented by the liberal orthodoxy, really a solution? This will now be briefly examined in order to stress the spatial aspects of the problem.

The shortcomings of modernist liberalism and the question of the spaces of regulation

The thrust of the liberal-modernist current lies in the first instance in the more or less theorized weakness of the Fordist modes of regulation, and especially of the national welfare state. Although too expensive for the productive system, the state organizes for its beneficiaries an economy of distribution in the absence of production. Moreover, the bureaucratic regulations, satisfactory to pilot the capital-widening growth of mass production and free of major innovations, are incapable of detecting and putting into operation the strategic lines of a new productive model still to be discovered. This exploration needs total flexibility and is stimulated by the largest possible competition, at the same time without really knowing if flexibility is required only in the exploratory stage or if it actually constitutes a durable feature of the future model.

The weakness of this current of thought is its total silence with respect to regulation, or rather that global competition would play the part of regulation. For neoliberalism, the future regime of accumulation would be already inscribed in the germs of the "third industrial revolution," and the individual agents (the firms) would adapt, on their own, through a process of struggling for their own existence and natural selection. The spatial consequence would be a reshuffling of the hierarchy of spaces (worldwide/national/local) that Fordism would have concentrated, now more than ever, at the national level. Schematically, the economic would be played out more directly at the world level, and the administration of the social (i.e., of the reproduction of labor power, whether in capitalist employment or otherwise) would be played out at the local level. Less schematically, the local would also have a role as the breeding ground for new productive forces. In a poorly defined continuum, the region would simultaneously be the site of the self-organization of survival through the mechanisms of civil society (e.g., the family, the informal economy) and of the emergence of innovative enterprises (corresponding to the myth of the replicability of Silicon Valley). The role of the state would not disappear; it would assist national firms in facing the world scene. From an organizer of society, it would become a cooperative or a syndicate in the service of local coalitions of private capital in the midst of worldwide competition. But this new role granted to the national state definitely discards the old distinction between nationalist and internationalist fractions of dominant classes. In the countries that became "central Fordisms" during the 1950s and 1960s – thanks to their developmental nationalism – the cooperative state reconciles matters between those advocates of a retreat of the welfare state and those defending state support of industry.[15] In newly industrialized countries led to peripheral Fordism by dictatorships, the democratic pressures stemming from the workers as well as from the interior bourgeois sometimes dissolve into the ascension to power of very moderate social democrats pursuing modernization without necessarily jumping ahead to the welfare state. In fact, these social democrats refuse to sacrifice the internal conditions for external competitiveness.[16]

Obviously, this model shows weaknesses on both sides. At the world level, at least without reservations too numerous to ignore, the argument is full of sophisms: In order to move away from the crisis, each national economy would merely have to become more competitive. This is the illusion of a world market that would function as a thermostat, capable of absorbing all the outputs, as if the competitiveness of some would not subtract from that of the others. The 1982 and 1991 economic slumps and the latent debt crisis of the worldwide economy have, however, demonstrated the instability resulting from an uncontrolled coupling of national economies. At the local level, new responsibilities assigned to civil society bypass by far what is possible within a regional armature devoid of a political apparatus; these include the disaggregation of the family and the local communities as well as the incapacity of the informal economy to provide the professional training corresponding to the proclaimed needs of the technological revolution. If the capacities of local regulation are not reinforced (i.e., if a local political society is not constituted), all of these allow one to foresee a disappearance of the social rather than its regeneration at the local level. As a result, the mode of regulation implicit to this model (within the bifurcation tree originating from the technological revolution outlined earlier) privileges the most regressive sides: aggravation of the separation, internationally as well as interregionally, between designers and executing manual workers; and aggravation of the social dichotomy between the beneficiaries of gains in productivity and the rejected economic agents now oscillating between the regular domestic economy and the bit (small) jobs. In this way, the spatial displacement of the instances of regulation can turn out to determine the evolution of the work process and the regime of accumulation.

Still, it is undeniable that – at the regional as well as at the national level – social blocs and political projects exist that proclaim themselves as "free trade" while still promoting progressive compromises between workers and management and, with respect to the command of technical change, pretend to search for a means for the local administration of the social, the forms of which would be mutually beneficial to society and the individual (e.g., think of the behavior of the Communist Party in

Emilia-Romagna). But the success obtained by these modernist blocs often trans-lates into the opposite of what liberal ideology would like to demonstrate. Spaces-in-themselves that are particularly well organized, equipped with intense internal forms of regulation without market character and practicing a protectionism more efficient than it is tacit ("cultural," as one says of Japan), often reveal themselves as the best adapted to world competition. In any case, these spaces (regions or nations) remain reliant on the global economic conjuncture upon which they themselves have no impact, whence the appeal to the national as the only space of explicit regulation possible at present, or the appeal to a supranational, worldwide, or continental (European) regulation.

In this fashion, the shortcomings of modernist liberalism and its economic defeat in the 1980s tend to revive two spatial instances that have had their time of glory but at the moment are doubtless facing a new youth: the federal state and the multi-national bloc. These instances oblige us to refine the spatial scale suggested in the first part of this chapter.

By federative state we do not mean so much a juridical form of the state (although it is necessary) but a form of articulation of the national hegemonic system. Since the state cannot seek to assure everywhere the same form of macroeconomic regulation (and because this is not even desirable), the issue is to equip the regional armatures with more powerful instruments of economic and social regulation and to reserve for the nation-state the administration of the external relation (support to industries, administration of foreign exchange). In comparison to Fordism, which is above all and by definition "national," this new division of capacities between the national and the regional means a contraction of the national legislation and collective agreements and a larger variability for the regional armatures in their choice of the social protection level, as, for example, in Ronald Reagan's United States. With respect to peripheral Fordism, this development means that certain regions are abandoned to underdevelopment while others situate themselves for a globally oriented form of modernization (e.g., Brazil and China could follow this route). At the other side of the national level, a multinational bloc confers certain attributes of overall macroeconomic administration on supranational authorities, translating transnational compromises between forces that can themselves be trans-national, multiregional alliances. The creation of the European Economic Commu-nity has typically represented the constitution of such a bloc. It translated not only the hegemony of the Fordist national blocs of all its participants, but also foresaw forms of collective regulation of the articulation of the modes of production (e.g., the Common Agriculture Policy) and compromise measures for transnational forms of particular regional armatures (e.g., the Mediterranean Programs).

In any case, the crisis of Fordism makes the radical insufficiency of the European Economic Community overt. Being a free-trade zone without common social policy (e.g., there is only the implicit common engagement in the treaty of 1957 to assure interregional equilibrium through an accelerated growth in the standard of living), its institutions condemn the different nations in the community to administer against each other their external constraint by a competitive stagnation resulting in an extended general stagnation. No internal policy – and the social-communist French experience of 1981–1984 is the best example thereof – can escape this iron law.[17] Orchestrated stimulation policy and the coordinated reduction in work time seem to be dictated by common sense, but they imply societal choices, among which are the formation of true hegemonic systems equipped with attributes of sovereignty: something approaching the constitution of a European nation that would eventually adopt the form of a federal state. But the experience of Italian or German unification shows that a nation is not formed coldly and objectively, without civil and foreign wars, even in the favorable case of the language community. In contrast, the experiences of Austria-Hungary or the US Civil War show the great instability of a federal, yet regionally differentiated, state when it is not bound together by a common hegemonic system. Therefore, the purely technological European undertakings, such as the Eureka Project, incur the same risk as the "Parallel Action" in Musil's novel.[18] And the "cold revolution" of European unification through the Maastricht Agreement could eventually lead to similar tensions and outcomes, as in the cases of past unifications such as Yugoslavia or Czechoslovakia.

Conclusion

The articulation of the spatiality proper to the Fordist regime, centered on regulation of the nation-state with its virtuous international configuration and its internal differentiations in regional armatures, is at present as outmoded as the corresponding regime of accumulation. The spatiality corresponding to the modernist-liberal ideological current, based upon the coupling of the worldwide or the local with a national state carrying reduced responsibilities, appears at the same time macro-economically unstable as well as socially regressive. The amendments that the formation of federative states and multinational blocs could offer appear themselves as fragile and unstable. But are all these reasons sufficient to reject such improvements in a progressive strategy?

The problem, as we have seen, is the lack of specialized sovereign authorities to guarantee the compromises institutionalized in the core of a hegemonic system. Whether one likes it or not, struggles and fundamental social compromises are still settled at the national level. But it is not necessarily desirable that the nation-state should keep the quasi-monopoly of the stabilization process and control of historical and social innovations.

For precision's sake, it is important to form an idea of an up-to-date and progressive solution to the crisis. In the absence of credible revolutionary perspectives, it would consist of a form of compromise equivalent to the social-democratic compromise facing the crisis of the 1930s (but necessarily different), more or less opening the road to radicalization. The latter would entail the increased capacity of the administration by the producers and the citizens of their way of life and work, while still pushing back alienation as much as possible through market exchange and forms of state exploitation and oppression, be it capitalist or in a family setting. Such compromises would orient the technological revolution toward increased skills and mastery as well as more conscious cooperation by participants in the productive process, increased control of the social consequences of technical change, and, in particular, of the distribution of gains in productivity in the form of a substantial reduction of work time. In the same sense, while maintaining or improving the level of social protection, such a compromise would seek to increase productivity (in terms of use-value) of the welfare state's funds. The latter would serve to finance alternative (e.g., community-wide, cooperative) forms of collective goods and services, to the detriment of moonlighting and the exploitation of women.

It is clear that such a model, which implies a "reterritorialization" of the relation between skills and jobs and between production and social use, will need nonmarket, democratic forms of regulation, as close as possible to the grassroots and thus regional levels. These forms will imply (while the converse does not) the gradual federalization of the nation-state. The central state should keep its responsibility to lay the minimum thresholds for regional social legislation and guarantee a general realignment of social welfare in order to limit the perverse effects of competition among regions. At the international level, the formation of multinational blocs matching their nonrecessive, macroeconomic policies, bringing together scientific and technical means, and allowing for social innovation, can only play a beneficial role in the continuation of national progressive experiences.

But a reasonable skepticism excludes the possibility that the different nations of a bloc adopt straightaway the same social compromises. Moreover, this is probably not desirable. In a progressive alliance between Europe and certain nations in the Third World, the first may allow the reduction of working time while the others opt to maximize production. One should rather aim at institutional forms within the bloc that would allow or even encourage the social advances, even if they are insulated from each of its members (a kind of Pareto optimality principle), without, however, excluding the coordination of progressive politics.[19] But the political willingness can only be imposed through social movements that are themselves transnational and through social experiences that are themselves regionalized.

NOTES

[. . .]

1   This theoretical part, as in the next one on Fordism, repeats, summarizes, and develops considerations presented earlier within the context of my work on space and the crisis of the regime of accumulation (see Lipietz 1977, 1987). I repeat intentionally each time when possible my initial formulations relative to both conceptual fields, in order to explore their compatibility.

2   The concepts of "space-in-itself" and "space-for-itself" are developed along lines similar to those found, for example, in the master/slave dialectics of Hegel's *Phenomenology of Mind* and in Marx's early writing. A space-in-itself would be purely objective (empirical) and prereflective conditions, as determined by the mode of production, whereas space-for-itself would imply a subjectively self-conscious region both in terms of territory and goal-oriented praxis ([original] editors' comment).

3   Society is not just the automatic reproduction of a structure of relations. These relations are relations of practices that, in addition to their routine character, can have an innovative ambit and, to the extent that the relations are contradictory (i.e., opposing individuals and the groups to one another at the same time as unifying them), can even carry a

revolutionary or at least transformative vocation. The political is exactly the instance whereby this dialectical reproduction/transformation is condensed; and the ideological is the instance in which this tension is represented.

4   Or, more precisely, defined in themselves by the socioeconomic relations centered upon the project of maintaining or modifying the form of the existing relations.

5   Notice that a social class in itself can be divided among several competing blocs, and that inside a bloc the materiality of the convergence of interests inherent to one group with the interests of the bloc in general may be either more or less disputable. Therefore, it is necessary to distinguish between ruling groups and allied or related groups (Poulantzas 1973).

6   See on this point the criticism by E. Terray (1973) against the empiricist definitions of the nation (for example, Stalin's definition).

7   I intentionally use the vague term "form," first to leave room for the forms of production that the reader would refuse to acknowledge as a real mode of production, but also to take into account that every mode has adopted and adopts a number of forms, which can [be rivals] on the same territory.

8   This is a very important point. The "purchasing power" of a region against the overall product of an economic whole is certainly limited by the sum of the budgetary constraints (and the credit capacity) of its members, but this sum can be totally different from the "exportable" production of the region, if the interregional transfers are sufficient.

9   This is the criticism that D. Massey (1978) has addressed to me since the beginning: "The definition of the regions by Lipietz (1977) oscillates between that constructed through historical analysis and that relevant to the actual spatial division of labor."

10 This is the thesis that I defend (1987) in the case of international relations. The example of USA-Mexico relations (two spaces created by colonization; then both become politically independent in the same period) is particularly illustrative. The analysis "starting from internal causes" sketched by Octavio Paz (1985) seems much clearer to me than the powerless invocation to "dependence."

11 I repeat here the conclusion in Lipietz (1984b). More recent developments are found in Leborgne and Lipietz ([1988]) and Lipietz (1989).

12 One can, for example, think of the breakup of the old Roosevelt alliance in the US Democratic party in 1984 between Jackson, Hart, and Mondale, representing roughly the three basic attitudes. [. . .]

13 The rise of Muslim integrism can often be interpreted as a "radical-reactionary" reaction to the development of primitive Taylorization or peripheral Fordism. It has all the more success because the secular "radical-modernist" alliances of the preceding period (e.g., Nasserism) pretended that modernization and "progressism" are foreign aggressions.

14 One can interpret the decline of Great Britain and Argentina during the years 1950–1970 as the result of incapability to "modernize" their hegemonic system, facing the growing success of Fordism. Notice that now the conservative route can be embodied by labor or social-democratic parties (in the North) or by "developmentalist" parties (in the South).

15 I have analyzed, under the name "Saint Simonisme" (1984a) the strength of this current in France, well represented by A. Minc (1982) and his formula: "less state-protector (for the wage-labors), more state-shield (for industry facing worldwide competition)."

16 Rereading Poulantzas in the light of the theory of peripheral Fordism, I have called the leading class of this regime of accumulation "interior bourgeoisie." I have analyzed (1987) its hegemony over the democratic transition in Southern Europe in the seventies and in Brazil and Korea at present.

17 See Lipietz (1984b, 1989). One finds more and more analyses of this "perverse effect" in terms of game theory (cf. "prisoner's dilemma") [...]

18 In *The [Men] Without [Qualities]*, intellectuals from Austria-Hungary seek to riposte by a "parallel action" to the growing prestige of ally-rival Prussia. Their wild imaginings end in an order by the Austrian army to the merchants of Prussian guns.

19 More details on these dreams are in Lipietz (1989).

REFERENCES

Aoki, M., ed. 1984: *The Economic Analysis of the Japanese Firm*, New York: Elsevier Science.

Bourdieu, P. 1979: *La distinction: critique sociale du judgement*, Paris: Editions de Minuit.

Coriat, B. 1984: *L'atelier et le chronometre: essai sur le Taylorisme, le Fordisme, et la production de masse*, second edition, Paris: C. Bourgeois.

Leborgne, D. and Lipietz, A. 1988: 'New technologies, new modes of regulation: some spatial implications', *Environment and Planning D: Society and Space*, 6, 263–80.

Lipietz, A. 1977: *Le capital et son espace*, Paris: Maspero.

Lipietz, A. 1979: *Crise et inflation: pourquoi?*, Paris: Maspero.

Lipietz, A. 1984a: *L'audace ou l'enlisement*, Paris: La Découverte.

Lipietz, A. 1984b: 'La mondialisation de la crise générale du Fordisme: 1967–1984', *Les Temps Modernes*, 459, 696–736.

Lipietz, A. 1985: *Mirages et miracles: problems de l'industrialisation dans le Tiers Monde*, Paris: La Découverte.

Lipietz, A. 1987: *Mirages and Miracles: The Crises of Global Fordism*, London: Verso.

Lipietz, A. 1989: *Choisir l'audace*, Paris: La Découverte.

Massey, D. 1978: 'Regionalism: Some current issues', *Capital and Class*, 6, 106–25.

Minc, A. 1982: *L'après-crise est commencé*, Paris: Gallimard.

Oliveira, F. 1977: *A Economia da Dependencia Imperfeita*, Rio de Janeiro: Graal.

Paz, O. 1985: *Semana Cultural de La Nacio*, Buenos Aires: La Nacion.

Poulantzas, N. 1973: *Political Power and Social Classes*, London: New Left Books.

Santos, M. 1979: *The Shared Space: The Two Circuits of the Urban Economy in Underdeveloped Countries*, London: Methuen.

Terray, E. 1973: 'L'idée de nation et les transformations du capitalisme', *Les Temps Modernes*, 324, 492–508.

14

The Invention of Regions: Political Restructuring and Territorial Government in Western Europe

Michael Keating

What Is a Region?

For several years now regionalism has been back in fashion in Europe, in both the scholarly and the political domains. There are books and articles about the new regionalism, the Europe of the regions, multilevel government, the third level. Some even talk as if the nation state itself were being replaced by a new level of government. While this is good news for those of us who have a vested interest in the phenomenon, it is well to be cautious. The nation state never monopolized political action in Europe in the past; and in the present it remains a powerful actor. The political, economic, cultural and social meaning of space is changing in contemporary Europe. In some ways, politics, economics and public policies are deterritorializing; but at the same time and in other ways, there is a reterritorialization of economic, political and governmental activity. The new types of regionalism and of region are the product of this decomposition and recomposition of the territorial framework of public life, consequent on changes in the state, the market and the international context. There is no new territorial hierarchy to replace the old one, but a diversity of new forms of territorial action. The territorial principle in politics is ever-present but often elusive. It takes a variety of forms and structures social relations even where it does not give rise to regionalist political movements.

So, while it might seem logical to start a paper on regional government with a definition of the word region, this must be the outcome of the analysis and not the start. The word takes on a variety of meanings in the various social science disciplines and the historical traditions of European countries and is politically loaded and sensitive, since the very definition of a region as a framework and a system of action has implications for the distribution of political power and the content of public policy.[1] Certainly, there is agreement that the word region refers to space, but the notion of space itself can take various meanings: territorial space; political space and space of social relationships; economic space; functional space. A region is constructed from the confluence of these differing concepts of space. It is also an institutional system, either in the form of a regional government or as a set of institutions operating in a territory. Finally, it may constitute itself as an actor in national and external politics. In the remainder of the paper, the idea of region is discussed in the broad sense, not simply as an institutional system, but as a set of social and economic relationships underlying institutions, and as a system of action. It is only by appreciating the conjunction of these different logics within a territory that we can understand the regional phenomenon and its importance. Before proceeding to this, however, we need to analyse the historic construction of the ideas of region and of regionalism and its relationship with the process of nation- and state-building, and particularly with the development of the postwar interventionist welfare state. Then regionalism is examined as a contemporary phenomenon, in the context of continental integration and the changes being experienced by the west European state.

The State and the Regions, or Top-Down Regionalism

The premodern state was a highly differentiated polity in which territories of various types and extents and corporate groups would share a common suzerain but each would have its own specific relationship to the central power (Tilly, 1990; Tilly and Blockmans, 1994; Majone, 1995). There were overlapping spheres of authority in the governmental, ecclesiastical and economic domains and relationships, depending not merely on military force, but on complex compacts and customs. The nineteenth century modernizing and consolidating state generally had little time for these principles or for regions, regarding them as obstacles to the forging of national identity and to the building of a modern and effective state. Bureaucratic administration, education, unified legal systems and military service were all used to break down territorial and other barriers. Nowhere was this entirely successful, and territorial management continued to be one of the primary tasks of statecraft (Keating, 1988). In France under the monarchy, an extraordinary array of territorial institutions mediated between the central power and local society (Braudel, 1986) and even the republican regime had to tolerate a system in which the state's orders were modified at the periphery. The German empire had to recognize the federal principle and the autonomy of the federated units in much internal policy. The Spanish state was forced to recognize the Basque *fueros* until the 1870s and even after that had to concede them a special fiscal regime. The United Kingdom was a union, with a single source of political authority, but in which a territorially differentiated civil society maintained a high degree of autonomy from the state (Paterson, 1994). This need to accommodate to territorial distinctiveness was widely seen, by modernizing liberal politicians, by the radical left, and by many social scientists (such as Deutsch, 1966), as a mere transitional phase towards a world of homogeneous nation states [(Finer, 1974; Blondel, 1973)].

After the second world war, and especially from the 1960s, European states started to take regions more seriously, as part of their projects for modernization. In Germany, federalization was imposed by Allied pressure as well as the desire on the part of Germans to immunize themselves from the excesses of Nazi centralization; but the form was shaped by German federalist traditions. In the other European states, regionalism stemmed from functional needs and the necessities of territorial management. In several states, notably France, Italy and the United Kingdom, the region emerged as a key level of action for the state. Territorial disparities were recognized as a problem (albeit marginal and temporary) which resisted the macroeconomic management of the Keynesian era, and the region was chosen as the most appropriate level to address them. Starting with general policies of industrial diversion, states proceeded, with more or less success, to more detailed intervention in the form of regional planning, growth poles, coordination and that untranslatable form of integrated spatial intervention which the French call *aménagement du territoire*. States also used regions as a framework for cultural policies, with more or less generous concessions to the cultural particularities of particular regions (for example in Belgium and Great Britain). In some cases, administrative deconcentration and executive agencies were used by states to enhance effectiveness and coordination at the regional level (as in France and the UK).[2] Successive French governments sought to reinforce the power of the prefects in territorial coordination, efforts which continued into the 1990s with the Pasqua law of 1993.

Although early regional policies were administered by the state with little local input, states came to seek collaborators on the ground, to help implement regional development policies and ensure their coherence with the actions of local governments and the private sector. In some cases, the state's aim was to renew the local political class, either for partisan reasons as in Italy with the arrival of the centre-left in the 1960s or in France with the consolidation of Gaullism at the same time, or because the old elites and their networks of influence were insufficiently committed to modernization (Biarez, 1989). Where existing territorial elites were considered obstructive, or too committed to the old logic of distribution or clientelism rather than the new logic of modernization and growth, states would sometimes by-pass them by setting up new regional institutions; this was particularly so in southern European countries, where it is difficult to reform the existing system of local government (notably in France). In Spain, the new technocrats of the 1960s, such as Lopez Rodó, were less successful in their efforts to undermine the apparatchiks of the Francoist *Movimiento*. In Italy, the establishment of regions, although provided for in the constitution, was postponed until 1970, when national political conditions were more favourable (Pastori, 1980).

This top-down modernizing regionalization was presented in a technocratic mode and largely depoliticized, but the political implications of state intervention in regions soon became apparent. In Spain, the paranoia of the Francoist regime about anything which smacked of regionalism prevented the elaboration of coherent regional policies (García, 1979; Cuadrado, 1981). In the democratic countries, state intervention often served to destabilize traditional systems of territorial representation. The process rapidly politicized as regions came to be contested by the state; the traditional elites and notables; and the new modernizing elites from the regions themselves. Issues came increasingly to be perceived in a regional focus and the very definition of the region as well as the policy content of regional action became matters of political competition. This politicization was further reinforced by the increased mobilization of actors within the regions themselves.

Regional Mobilization, or Bottom-Up Regionalism

Regionalism, as a political movement and set of demands, has taken a great many forms and at one time or another been linked to just about every other ideology, from the extreme right to the extreme left, via liberalism, social democracy and christian democracy. To simplify, let us take six ideal types, whose characteristics can be mixed and matched in individual cases.

First, there is a conservative regionalism, anchored in the idea of affective community, resisting modernization, especially where this takes the form of the uniformizing and secular state. In the nineteenth century, regionalism, especially in France, was often regarded as reactionary and opposed to progress (Mény, 1982).[3] The early demands of the Basque movement were for a return to the *fueros*, based on traditional authority and compact, rather than the recognition of a distinct nation (De La Granja, 1995). In the twentieth century, regionalism has been an element of christian democratic thought, a way of reconciling tradition with modernity, as well as a way of operationalizing the principle of subsidiarity. It is not, however, one of the base principles of christian democracy (Durand, 1995) and has often been subordinated to the tactical needs of political parties, as in Italy after 1948, or even in the age of Sturzo after the first world war, or exploited for clientelistic ends (Barbera, 1985).

Also on the right, one might recognize a 'bourgeois regionalism' in industrialized and economically advanced regions. In these cases, a dynamic bourgeoisie seeks to free itself from the shackles of an archaic state, or strives to create more modern administrative and political structures to favour industrial development. A historic example would be the Catalan movement in its 'regionalist' phase in the late nineteenth century, when it sought to modernize Spain by 'catalanizing' it (Oltra et al., 1981; Vicens, 1986). A contemporary example might be found in German *Länder* like Baden-Württemberg, or even contemporary Catalonia, with their links to the 'Four Motors of Europe'. In 1960s Italy, the employers' organization *Confindustria* recognized the modernizing potential of regional government (Rotelli, 1973).

Another type of modernizing regionalism is more technocratic and depoliticized, less linked to specific class or sectoral interests. As mentioned above, this type of regional approach was much favoured by central states in the postwar ear, but on the ground there is also found a technocratic element, often tied to public sector management and to the planning profession both in government and in universities.

On the left, there is a progressive regionalism. Even in the nineteenth century, there were regionalist movements which stressed the themes of progress, democracy, reform of the state and equality, for example the ephemeral *Félibrige Rouge* in France (Touraine et al., 1981), the progressive movements in Scotland (Keating and Bleiman, 1979) and Wales (Morgan, 1980) or the *Meridionalismo* of Dorso and/ or Salvemini (Galasso, 1978). From the 1960s, there was a new regionalism linked to the libertarian new left, to ecological movements and to popular struggles against plant closures (Keating, 1988; 1992). This regionalism borrowed from earlier Gramscian ideas and contemporary national liberation movements in the third world, stressing uneven development and internal colonialism (Lafont, 1967). It remained rather weak, however, because of the heterogeneity of its constituent elements and the difficulties of building an alternative paradigm of economic development. Social democratic movements also contained within them a historic regionalist stream, though this was for many years subordinated to the needs of jacobin state-building and centralized economic and social management. From the 1960s, this stream slowly expanded and by the 1980s was an important element. The conversion of the social democratic parties to regionalism, however, had to await the foundering of the old social democratic model of centralized state management under the impact of globalization.

A right-wing populist regionalism is directed against the centralized state, sometimes against fiscal transfers to poorer regions, and often against immigrants, whether these are from other parts of the state or abroad. One thinks, for example, of the Liga Nord (Biorcio, 1991) or the Vlaams Blok; some of the French regionalist movements have also ended up on the populist extreme right (Keating, 1985; 1988).

Finally, there are 'nationalist' movements in some of the historic territories of Europe. The division between nationalism and regionalism here is by no means clear, and is becoming less so as the state reconfigures (Keating, 1996b). The most important separatist movements – if one excludes the Northern Irish case, since it is irredentist rather than separatist – are in Scotland and the Basque Country.[4] In Catalonia and the Belgian regions there are strong nationalist/regionalist movements which generally aim for a new distribution of power within the state and in Europe rather than for the establishment of their own state in the classic sense.

It is from the dialectic of these different regionalisms with the state that the dynamics of political regionalism are made. Each movement contains a mixture of distinct elements. Each state provides a distinct opportunity structure and set of incentives and constraints. Regionalism is not necessarily autonomist. There are integrative regionalisms, seeking the full integration of their territories into the nation and the destruction of obstacles to their participation in national public life. There are autonomist regionalisms seeking a space for independent action; and there are disintegrating regionalisms, seeking greater autonomy or even separation. Poor regions have often preferred centralization, especially when this is accompanied by good lines of access to the central state. For example, the Spanish regions of Andalusia and Extremadura, enjoying privileged links with the PSOE government in Madrid in the 1990s, were very cautious about further decentralization, especially in fiscal matters. When rich regions dominate a central state, of course, they too are liable to be centralist, as in France and the United Kingdom. By contrast wealthy regions which are not politically dominant are likely to be decentralist, as in Lombardy or Catalonia.[5]

There is no consistent relationship between the placement of regionalisms on the left–right scale and the degree of integration or disintegration which they seek. Generally speaking, regionalism has since the 1960s moved to the left, though there are exceptions such as the christian democracy of the Catalan CiU or the right-wing populism of the Lega Nord. Rather than being associated with reaction and resistance to modernization, it tends now to be seen as a form of democratic maturation (Sharpe, 1993). Similarly, the relationship between social class and territory has changed as capital has internationalized while labour has increasingly fallen back upon locally based forms of resistance.

So the European state never succeeded, *pace* the diffusionist and assimilationist school, in eradicating territorial specificities. Instead, it has managed them. From time to time, states have experienced a crisis in territorial management; from the regional end this manifests itself as a crisis of territorial representation (Keating, 1988). There are examples of this in the late nineteenth century, around the time of the first world war, briefly after the second world war, and again in the 1970s.[6] After each such crisis, the states of western Europe succeeded in re-establishing a territorial equilibrium. In the 1960s and 1970s several states recognized the political dimensions of regionalism and moved from regional administration to regional government. At the same time, they accommodated and encouraged the more integrative types of regionalism; for example in France and Italy the existing territorial elites, tied into the central state, were effectively given control of the regionalization process. At the end of the twentieth century, however, states face a new wave of territorial mobilization, which this time puts into question the whole tradition of territorial management by taking it out of the exclusive framework of the nation state.

The New Regionalism

Regionalism, after an active phase in the late 1960s and early 1970s, stagnated after the crisis of the mid 1970s. The French regions set up in 1972 were weakly institutionalized and not until 1986 did they become full local governments, directly elected. In the UK, the devolution projects for Scotland and Wales failed and the English regional planning councils were abolished in 1979. The institutional development of the Italian regions after the law of 1977, expanding their functions, was disappointing. In Belgium and Spain, pressures from minority nationalist and linguistic movements ensured a continued progress to regionalization and, indeed, federalization of the state. Yet even in Spain, where regional autonomy had been an integral part of the transition to democracy, the LOAPA law of 1981 represented an attempt on the part of the state to recover powers.

From the late 1980s, however, there has been a new wave of regionalism, impelled by economic restructuring; globalization; the transformation of the nation state; and above all by European integration. The international market, modern communications technology and the individualization of social life are sometimes presented as destroyers of territory as a principle of organization (Badie, 1995). Yet at the same time they encourage the invention of new forms of space (Keating, 1996a; Amin and Thrift, 1994). Economic restructuring follows two complementary logics, global and local. It is guided by factors like the investment decisions of multinational corporations and international capital flows; but the impact of these is mediated by local factors and even global effects are felt as local ones. Globalization creates a tension between the aspatial rationality of the transnational corporation, with its multiple branches and ability to move investment around, and the spatially bound rationality of communities which depend on these investments (Keating, 1991). So firms escape territorial influences, while territories become more dependent on firms. Given global constraints, states are no longer able to manage their spatial economies by diversionary regional policies or strategic placing of public investments. Yet at the same time, it is increasingly recognized that economic development and the insertion of territories into the global economy depend on specific characteristics of territories. So modern development policies put more emphasis on indigenous growth, or the attraction of investment by qualities linked to the region like the environment, the quality of life, a trained labour force, rather than on investment incentives provided by the central state (Stöhr, 1990; Gore, 1984). Scholars have rediscovered the classic notion of the industrial district, characterized by networks of territorial interdependence (Dunford and Kafkalis, 1992; Morgan, 1992). Development itself is defined more broadly, to include quality of life issues. The new development paradigm gives an important role to the construction of identities, of territorially based systems of action, and territorial solidarities. These new regional systems of action are now placed more directly in confrontation with the international market (Courchene, 1995) because the intermediary role of the state has been severely attenuated.

Much has been written on the crisis of the state and the end of sovereignty (Camilleri and Falk, 1992). It would be a mistake to exaggerate the decline of the European state, since it retains a formidable arsenal of powers and resources. It is also important to avoid falling into the analytical trap of contrasting a mythical past state, all-powerful, monopolistic and sovereign, to a modern state which is weakened, pluralist and forced to share its powers with supranational, subnational and private sector agencies. As already noted, these tendencies have always been present. Nonetheless, there has been an important transformation in the state and a disarticulation of the various spheres of social, economic and political action which it formerly encompassed. There is a gap between the system of representation, through state institutions, and decision-making, which has retreated into territorial and social networks. Consequently, the divorce between politics and policy is growing. This division of the social reality can have pernicious effects, not only for governmental efficiency but also for democracy and social cohesion (Touraine, 1992a, 1992b). Human beings are rarely content to be ruled by mere mechanical principles, and there is a reaction on the part of those who wish to re-establish a public space. This new public space, however, has now to be constructed at various territorial levels, and not merely that of the state.

European integration has had important effects on regions and regionalism (Bullman, 1994; Jones and Keating, 1995). Market integration may increase economic disparities, while depriving states of their traditional means of dealing with these in the form of tariffs and subsidies (Dunford, 1994). In the single market, regions are in competition for inward investment and markets, as the other example of a large single capitalist market, the United States, shows. European Union policies have varying effects on the different regions (Molle and Cappelin, 1988). The construction of the Community and the Union has modified the political relationships between states and regions. In the early years, it was used to justify the centralization of powers in the hands of central governments, with the doctrine that Community matters were foreign affairs and thus an exclusive central competence.[7] Peripheral regional interests, for their part, tended to cleave to the central state, fearing the effects of market integration and the dismantling of protectionist measures. Now there has been a shift, at least in some prominent cases, from resistance to constructive engagement. Since the Single European Act, regions have increasingly insisted on their right to be heard, both by EU institutions and by national governments, in the preparation of European policies. The EU's own regional policy, started in the 1970s as a mere inter-state transfer mechanism, was transformed in the 1980s into an instrument of genuine policy (Marks, 1992; Hooghe and Keating, 1994). The structural funds were doubled, and now represent the second largest item in the budget, accounting for a quarter of spending. The Commission insisted (with varying degrees of success) on the principles of additionality and transparency, to ensure that the regions, and not state treasuries, are the beneficiaries. A system of planning was put in place, with partnerships among the regions, states and the Commission allowing direct links between regions and the EU. While it remains true that states are still the prime actors, these EU interventions into the regions have nonetheless encouraged a powerful mobilization on the ground and the emergence of new territorial actors, in a manner reminiscent of the impact of nationally based regional policies in the 1960s and 1970s. Some countries, like Ireland (Holmes and Reese, 1995), have had to establish regional structures in order to qualify for funds. In others the needs of European competition in the single market have put on the agenda the issue of reinforcing regional institutions, or redrawing regional boundaries ([...] Benz, 1992).

The new European and international context has had important effects on the representation of regional identity, taking it out of the framework of the state and encouraging a process of imitation and learning among regions in different states. Regional identity is sharpened by the comparison and its content is changed. Competition within Europe has consolidated regional identities and solidarities as political competition within territories is partially displaced by competition between them.

There is thus a recomposition of political space in western Europe, in which regions are emerging in two senses. They are political arenas, in which various political, social and economic actors meet and where issues, notably to do with economic development, are debated. At the same time, they are constituting themselves as actors in national and now European politics, pursuing their own interests. We cannot, however, merely talk of regions emerging or re-emerging. The region is not a natural entity, but a social construction, in a given space (Agnew, 1987; Balme et al., 1994). Its definition, as noted at the outset, is difficult and politically contentious. One way to approach this is to see regions as constructions formed by the confluence of various economic, social and political processes in territory. As also noted earlier, a region is a space, but this space can be understood in several senses, and the coincidence or otherwise of these is critical to the invention of a region.

Regional Space

We can talk of regional space in several senses: as territorial space; a functional space; as political space.[8] Generally, regions have arrived rather late on a crowded institutional scene but where there is a space to insert themselves they can institutionalize themselves, become political arenas and constitute themselves as actors.

Territorial space

A region is, of course, a territorial entity,[9] but the definition of this territory varies greatly from one case to another. One way to define the regional space is negatively, as intermediate between the state and central government, although even here there are exceptions.[10] Where there is a tradition of strong and autonomous municipal government, combined with a unitary state, as in the Netherlands or the Scandinavian countries, there is little space for regions. Elsewhere, regions can exist at several territorial levels. There are metropolitan regions, built around big cities with their hinterlands, unified by economic linkages, transport, and systems of functional interdependence. There are provincial-scale regions, drawn on the map of the whole state. Some of these cover vast areas while others are drawn on the basis of smaller historic units and others again are the leftovers from the construction of neighbouring regions. Even in the same country, regions may exist at different levels. In Germany, there are the *Flächenstaaten* (which themselves range from North Rhine Westphalia to the Saar) and the *Stadtstaaten* of Hamburg, Bremen and Berlin. In Spain, there are large regions like Catalonia and Andalusia, and simple provinces turned into autonomous communities, like La Rioja and Cantabria. Even at the European level, there is no consistent territorial definition of a region. The EU Commission uses the NUTS system, with three levels, but these are mere aggregations of national units and in the implementation of its own regional policies it uses a whole range of territorial units according to the task at hand (Hooghe and Keating, 1994).

Functional space

It is equally difficult to generalize about what functions are proper to regions. As might be expected for a level which is intermediary in both the territorial and the functional sense, regions usually have powers in planning and programming. They are also important for economic intervention, in the new conditions described above. The new models of economic development, with their emphasis on professional training, construction of networks and circuits, external economies of scale, local firms (especially small and medium sized ones), environment and quality of life, indicate a regional rather than a state-wide level of intervention. At the same time, the need for coordination in planning and policy in travel-to-work areas, and the desirability of avoiding beggar-my-neighbour competition for investment,[11] suggest something larger than the local level. There is a tendency in several countries to devolve manpower training to the regional level in order to exploit its links with local and regional development policies.

Regions often have powers in culture, especially where there is a cultural or ethnic specificity. On the other hand, it is not easy to territorialize the management of linguistic or cultural minorities, since the groups concerned are rarely concentrated within boundaries which correspond to regions in other functional senses. So only a minority in Wales is Welsh speaking; the same is true of Brittany and the Basque Country. In Belgium, regionalization and cultural autonomy are linked only indirectly since territorial regions have been established for territory-based functions and linguistic communities for person-based ones; they coincide only in the executive of the Flanders region (Hooghe, 1991).

In general, regions do not have important functions in social solidarity. The welfare state remains the responsibility of national states, while solidarity on the ground is managed by local governments.

Regional governments may also establish themselves where there is a lacuna in the institutional or functional coverage of the state. Where regions are weakly institutionalized, lacking, for example, elected governments, they may become a kind of constitutional no man's land. In this free space where there is neither hierarchical bureaucratic control, nor horizontal control by elected governments, corporate interests may establish themselves. Examples would be the quangos in the United Kingdom, especially in England, colonized by the technocracy (Hogwood and Keating, 1982), at least before being brought more directly under central control by the Thatcher government (using a mixture of hierarchical control and patronage appointments). In several countries, economic development agencies were insulated from political control precisely to allow them to respond to market demands, although in some cases, notably Italy, they were then colonized by political parties and used for clientelist ends. States may also assign social policy functions to the regional level in order to insulate them from political pressures, especially in matters where it is difficult to control expenses such as health services (Sharpe, 1993).

Regions also have an important role as intermediaries, in both the territorial and the functional sense. The French CODER [Commissions de dévelopment économique régional] and British REPBs [Regional Economic Planning Boards] brought together regional interests and encouraged a dialogue with central government. Similarly, the system of regional deconcentration in both countries, with the prefects and regional offices respectively, was intended to improve coordination of central government's own actions on the ground. Unfortunately, this idea of coordination was too often understood as a technical rather than political matter and consequently failed. The German system of cooperative federalism provides a model of territorial coordination which is both more politicized and more institutionalized but is not easily exportable to countries which lack a tradition of consensus and political bargaining.

Political space

A region is a political space where it provides an arena for political debate, a frame for judging issues and proposals, and a space recognized by actors as the level where decisions may legitimately be taken. This does not necessarily correspond with governmental institutions. For example, Scotland constitutes a political space, with an internal debate and its own political agenda, although it lacks political autonomy.[12] The French and Italian regions, on the other hand, while they have elected governments, are not political spaces but rather links in partisan national systems, or federations of local units. The German Länder, Belgian regions (more and more) and the Spanish autonomous communities (especially the three historic nationalities) are both political spaces and self-governing regions.

The constitution of a political space depends on a number of factors. One is a sense of identity, which may itself be the product of ethnic or linguistic solidarity, or be founded on institutions and civic cooperation. Regional identity is not to be seen as a competitor to national identity, except in rather rare cases of minority nationalism. Instead it is an additional identity, to be mobilized and exploited for specific purposes. There is undoubtedly a historic dimension to this, but sense of identity is not merely a historic given, which persists independently of institutions. Even in historic nations like Catalonia and Scotland, a process of nation-building is still at work, to adapt historic identities to the needs of the contemporary world. In other regions, such as Brittany, there is a rich historical tradition which finds adaptation more difficult (Guillorel, 1991). In the German *Länder*, mostly devised artificially after the second world war, a sense of identity has been constructed by political institutions. In Italy there is a strong sense of local identity but much less identification with the administrative regions, even among supporters of the Lega Lombarda (Woods, 1995). The conditions for the production and reproduction of territorial identity are still poorly understood, in large part because of the weight of the diffusionist model of nation-building, which assumed that they were only transitional and would disappear with modernization. Much also depends on the constitution of the regional civil society (see below).

The party system plays an important role in the construction of political space. Where there are separate parties, or the state-wide parties adapt themselves to the local situation, as in Catalonia, the Basque Country, Scotland or Corsica, political issues and debate may be regionalized. In France, the party system is not regionalized, except in Corsica. In Italy, the regional structures of the parties in the former regime of the *partitocrazia* were weak compared to the provincial structures (Dente, 1985). In Spain, by contrast, regional political elites are strengthening their influence within the national parties and a regionally based political class may be emerging. In the Italy of the 'first republic', electoral behaviour was markedly regionalized and increasingly so in the 1980s, but territory served as a resource in clientelistic linkages to the centre, rather than the basis for a political regionalism or autonomism. The Lega Lombarda/Lega Nord explicitly introduced regionalist themes into the Italian political debate and challenged the territorial basis of centralized power; but these themes soon foundered in a generalized populism (Schmidtke, 1993) and a pronounced anti-government rhetoric (Savelli, 1992).

In those cases where there are elected governments, the regional electoral system is also important. A system such as the French, proportional representation based on departmental lists, makes the construction of governing majorities difficult and favours the expression of departmental demands rather than a debate on regional priorities. The existence of regional media is another element which helps the construction of a regional political space. Of course, the existence of distinct regional issues favours a debate focused on the region, but even matters of central government or EU competence are perceived differently in some territories. Regions may also be used by new social movements, either because their concerns are linked to territory, or because the region, as a new arena, is not strongly colonized by existing political movements. The obvious case of this is the environmentalist movement but one could cite others.

A region is a construction, of history and of present-day actions. Its invention depends on the confluence of these distinct meanings of space. We must also distinguish between two dimensions of region-building. A fully articulated region is a functional and political system, a place where decisions are made. This involves governmental institutions and also the constitution of a territorial civil society. Secondly, regions may constitute themselves as actors in the state, EU and international systems. As actors, they possess a measure of autonomy, conditioned not merely by their relationship to the state but by a wider set of relationships. Finally, we can consider the question of regional power as the capacity to mount a territorially based development project.

Regions as Systems of Action

Regional government

Just as there is a variety of regionalisms, so there is a variety of types of regional administration. In some cases, it is no more than deconcentrated administration of the central state. In the United Kingdom, the territorial administrations in Scotland, Wales and Northern Ireland are part of the central government, and headed by national ministers. In France, a system of state regional administration coexists with that of the regional councils themselves. Regional administration may also consist of ad hoc agencies whose directors are nominated by the state, the social partners or local governments – this model is also common in the UK.

If we are to talk of regional *government*, however, this should be restricted to autonomous institutions elected by universal suffrage. Here too there are several models. The strongest is represented by federalism, as in Germany, Austria, Belgium or Switzerland; Spain may also be evolving in a federal direction. In a federal system, competences are guaranteed constitutionally, and the federated units have the right to participate in national politics through territorial second chambers of the legislature, or systems of institutionalized cooperation. Then there are systems of strong regionalism, as present-day Spain. During the second republic (1932–39), Spanish governments, seeking a formula to reconcile the need to accommodate the historic nationalities with their desire for unity, and to avoid a federalization which would have weakened the central state, invented the formula of the *Estado Integral* (Hernández, 1980).[13] The same compromise between unity and diversity also underpins the present Spanish constitution, with its *Estado de las Autonomías*[14] In France and Italy, there are much weaker regions, with limited competences and autonomy. There is also the formula of asymmetric regionalization, adopted by some unitary states in order to respond to demands from specific territories, while retaining a unitary constitution. Italy and France have special status regions (Sicily, Sardinia, Val d'Aosta, Trentino-Alto-Adige, Venezia-Friulia-Giulia, Corsica). In the United Kingdom, Northern Ireland had its own parliament from 1922 to 1972 and the Labour Party is committed to special status for Scotland and Wales.

The institutionalization of regions depends not merely on their constitutional status, but also on the institutional context. Where municipal governments are strong or constitutionally guaranteed, they present an institutional competitor to regions. In France, regions are faced with competition from the departments and the big cities, who were the main winners from the decentralization programme of the 1980s. There is a rivalry between the Generalitat of Catalonia and the city of Barcelona. In Italy, regions have found it very difficult to insert themselves in the space remaining between the communes, the provinces and the state (Cassese and Torchia, 1993). In spite of the Europeanization of regions, state traditions still play an important role. In France, Italy, Spain and the United Kingdom, there are strong traditions of centralization, rooted in political practice and the state bureaucracy. Certainly there exists a territorial basis to power, especially in France, but this is less of an autonomous power than a resource to be used in national politics. In France, regions have to coexist with a parallel state administration, with which they share competences. In line with French administrative tradition, public policies are contractualized between the state and the region, with the result that regions often end up not only adopting national priorities but even subsidizing activities which are officially the responsibility of the national government, like universities and railways. The interlinking of state and regional actions continues all through the implementation process, and only a personalized power focused on the territorial notables can overcome this institutional weakness. In Italy, the state possesses important parallel competences and continues to legislate in detail on matters of regional responsibility (Ministro per gli affari regionali, 1982). Relationships between state and region are sectoralized, with detailed intervention by sectoral ministries (Merloni, 1985).

In Germany, by contrast, the national government does not have a territorial administration of its own, except in narrowly defined spheres like military matters, and so depends on the *Länder* for the administration of national as well as regional policies. According to German tradition, public policies are negotiated between the federal government and the *Länder*, whose power is institutional rather than, as in southern Europe, personal or partisan. The *Länder* retain an important degree of autonomy as to the details of administration, prompting some people in Spain[15] to advocate a similar system of a single administration there.

Regions as civil society

Regions do not exist merely in the sphere of government but can also be a principle for the organization of civil society. Given the retreat of the state and its diminished ability to represent on its own the principle of territorial unity, a greater weight falls upon civil society. There is some evidence that the two are linked in that regional government operates best where there is a well-developed civil society, a sense of identity, civic traditions, an associative life, and relationships of confidence and exchange within the territory (Putnam et al., 1985; Putnam, 1993).[16] The origins of this civil society and the mechanisms for transmitting it across history are less clear.[17] Only in France has there been a serious effort to trace continuities and discontinuities in political and social behaviour within particular places across time.[18] While it is obvious that the conditions for the institutionalization of regions are better in some places than others, there is nonetheless always a margin of manoeuvre for political entrepreneurs in the construction of new systems of action.

Piattoni (1996) shows how, *pace* Putnam, it was possible to effect a transformation in a southern Italian region by political action. I have already mentioned the cases of Scotland and Catalonia, where elites are in the process of building identity or, as Jordi Pujol puts it, *fer pais*. In Wales, a new identity may be replacing the old, oriented more to economic development and the insertion of the territory into Europe than the old historic and cultural issues (Jones, 1996). In Wallonia, a sense of identity and political movement were constructed after the second world war (Hooghe, 1991).

In some territories, the institutions and practices important for identity formation and representation are regionalized – for example sports and recreation bodies, cultural activities. Interest groups may be regionalized, encouraging sectoral or other interests to be cast in a territorial frame. This may modify the expression of class interests in important ways. It is not that regional identity and organization necessarily attenuates class conflict, as many on the left used to fear, but where employers and unions have a territorial basis for organization they may add a territorial dimension to their demands. Class interests, recognizing the new opportunity structures created by the opening of territorial politics, may in turn be encouraged to adopt a regional dimension to their own action. So there is again a dynamic process in which identity is constructed by action and this in turn reinforces identity.

Regions as Actors

In the reconstruction of political space, regions may constitute themselves as actors, able to pursue defined interests. Where they do so, they face an opportunity set which has been modified considerably by the changes in the political and economic context. This affects the understanding of autonomy, and of the power of regions as actors in complex systems.

Regional autonomy

Traditionally, regional autonomy was considered as a question of the bilateral relationships between the regions and the state in a zero-sum game. Nowadays, the game is more complicated, as regional space has been opened up by economic and political change.

Firstly, with the European Union, there is a third level of politics (Bullman, 1994) and a set of triangular relationships among the regions, the states and the decision-making organs of the EU (Jones and Keating, 1995; Petschen, 1993; De Castro, 1994). Regions seek to influence the policies of the EU by direct contacts; by using their influence within their own states; through inter-regional lobbies; through the partnerships established by the Commission for the implementation of its regional policies; and in the new networks created by EU activities (Keating and Hooghe, 1996; Engel, 1994). At one time, some regions believed that it was possible to compensate for an exclusion from influence in domestic politics by establishing direct links with the Commission and thus by-passing the nation state. The evidence, however, shows that it is those regions which are best integrated into national circuits of influence who have most influence in Brussels. Power resources are cumulative and it is not easy for regions to substitute one for another. Europe, however, has opened up territorial politics to new influences so that regional politics is increasingly Europeanized, while national politics is both Europeanized and regionalized. Discussions about politics at the regional level are now usually replete with references to the European dimension and the internal market.

A second influence which has opened up regional politics is the relationships among regions in different states, particularly but not exclusively border regions. Regions seek external links for a number of reasons (Córnago, 1996). The most important considerations are economic. Regions seek investment, markets and technology for their development. In some cases, there are cultural motivations linked to the recognition and diffusion of minority cultures. Finally, there are political motives, as regional elites use the external projection of the region as a means to construct an identity back home, postulating a common regional interest and raising their institutional profile. Of course, this often serves equally to raise the profile of the regional leaders themselves. There is often a high symbolic content in all this, and inter-regional competition is more difficult than appears at first sight. There is a functional logic pointing to cooperation in order to exploit comple-mentary skills and resources. On the other hand regions are in competition for markets, for investment, and for technology and this makes cooperation very diffi-cult. External policy has nonetheless changed the issues in regional politics and given it another dimension. Traditional roles and relationships have been changed in important ways (Hocking, 1996) and again autonomy is no longer a matter of bilateral exchange.

The third element transforming our understanding of autonomy is the relation-ship between the region and the market. In an open economy, regions depend on the continental and global market for investment, markets and resources. The paradox of institutional decentralization is that, the more autonomy regions gain from their own states, the less they are protected from the market and thus the more dependent they become upon the market. Even for states, there is no real independ-ence nowadays; rather there are strategies for managing interdependence. The relationship with the market varies widely from one region to another according to its resources, its ability to attract investment, its level of economic development and its technological and human assets.

In this new context, rather than talking of regional autonomy as a bilateral relationship, or merely reformulating it as a trilateral or multilateral one, it is better to talk of governmental capacity at the territorial level (Keating, 1991), that is the capacity to formulate and implement a developmental and social project. The nature of the development project differs from one region to another, according to the balance of social forces. In one place, there is a project geared to the inter-national market, in another one with a higher social content, seeking to influence the impact of the market on the region. In one place, there is an emphasis on cultural development; in another an effort to use culture as an instrument of collective action. In regions with strong regional governments, where there is a political and functional space, and a capacity to reach legitimate decisions, the leadership of the project may be assumed by political forces. Elsewhere, it may be determined by a combination of internal pressures, from firms, unions, social movements, and external constraints. In some limiting cases, the external context may even be determinant, leaving no room for regional politics. In all cases, the implementation of a regional project is dependent on the constitution of a regional power.

Regional power

The invention of regions is thus a complex process, depending on the coincidence or otherwise of a number of forces. Territory is being reconstituted, but not in the same way everywhere. We can even say that regions, in the full sense indicated earlier, only exist in some places. Elsewhere, power is weakly territorialized, or concentrated at national state, or municipal level. Where there are regions, we can analyse the extent of regional power across seven dimensions.

Institutions
Institutions here include not only political and governmental bodies, but also those of civil society and the economy. Amin and Thrift [(1994)] introduce the idea of 'institutional thickness' to measure the density of these institutions and their interactions.

Capacity to formulate a policy
There are regions with a political system, a decision-making capacity, and the ability to define a legitimate 'regional interest'. Others lack this unity of action and are reduced to simple linkages in other systems of action.

Competences
Obviously, the competences attributed to regional governments are an asset, especially where they come with real decisional autonomy. When competences are fragmented and shared with the state, instead of being devolved in large blocks, the role of the region may be subordinated to that of the state, as in France or Italy.

Power of integration
Regions are intermediary level, both territorially and functionally, and their power depends on their ability to integrate various levels of action. This depends in turn on their knowledge and mastery of decision-making networks. Regions can position themselves strategically in relation to these, or they can be marginalized. The power of integration depends also on the existence of partners at the regional level within civil society. Where there are regional organizations of business or unions then forms of concerted action are possible, although a real regional corporatism may be impossible because of the weakness of the actors (Anderson, 1992), all the more so in a world of diffused authority.

Financial resources
Regions need resources to pursue policies, but also a margin of freedom in their allocation. Tax-raising powers give them a greater freedom in those cases where they have a substantial tax base. Otherwise, freedom to levy taxes merely reinforces

their dependence on the market as they are obliged to maintain their tax base by attracting investment. It is not necessary for regions to dispose of large financial resources. Big budgets may even be a source of weakness if they are accompanied by heavy administrative burdens and subject regions to pressures from clients. The power to integrate often depends on the ability to allocate resources at the margin and influence other actors. In the absence of their own tax base, regions are obliged to play in the intergovernmental system.

The intergovernmental system

This refers to the relationships with the state and the European Union. In some cases, this is a relationship of dependence, but in others regions can influence national and even European policies. There are institutional relationships, as in Germany; personal relationships, as in southern Europe; partisan links, as in Spain, the UK and Belgium; and the French *pouvoir notabiliaire*, product of a complex process of legitimation combining territorial, personal, institutional and partisan elements.

Relationships with the market

Regions depend on the market for one of their prime tasks, economic development. They cannot direct the market, but they may be able to manage the precise terms of their insertion into the global market place.

Conclusion

There is no regional level of government in Europe, since such a level, in the traditional sense of government, is not possible in a world where the link between territory and political power has been so attenuated. This link is characteristic of the nation state in its classic era. Since then, as before it, power is dispersed in networks and multiple spheres of authority (Badie, 1995; Keating, 1996a; Camilleri and Falk, 1992: Lenoir and Lesourne, 1992). Yet, there is a reinvention of political space, as the European state restructures. Collective identities are reforged. New systems of collective action emerge in state and civil society. New forms of both autonomy and dependence come about.

In some cases, there emerge powerful regions, with political institutions and a vibrant territorial civil society. Here the regional principle imposes a territorial order and structures social relations. Regions constitute themselves as actors to intervene in the new complex systems of production and distribution. In other cases, large cities play this role.

Elsewhere, strong states may survive, albeit in competition with new territorial and sectoral powers and penetrated by them. Finally, there are territories where there is no capacity to impose a territorial logic and which are disaggregated or reduced to dependants of the state or the international market. Territory either becomes a link in a chain of dependent relationships, as in the old clientelist systems of Italy (1870–1922 and 1946–92) or Spain under the Restoration; or else territory as an element in social organization is destroyed altogether. The invention of regions is thus a sporadic and partial process, not a wave sweeping across Europe and transforming the architecture of politics in a uniform manner.

NOTES

1   As Anderson (1994, p. 6) puts it, 'From the outset, the term was highly indeterminate – floating between the specifically territorial and the generically sectoral, and lending itself to any number of metaphorical applications or extensions.'

2   Leading Crowther-Hunt and Peacock (1973) to commit the analytical error of believing that a regional level of government existed already in Great Britain (Keating, 1979).

3   Many French intellectuals still regard the word as politically incorrect, being charged with anti-republican connotations.

4   It is not widely known in Europe that the separatist party with the largest proportion of its local vote is the Scottish National Party (22 per cent at the General election of 1992 and 33 per cent at the European elections of 1994).

5   Though even Catalonia has always sought to balance autonomy with access to the centre, most recently in the pact between its governing party CiU and the minority socialist government in Madrid, between 1993 and 1995.

6   As always, there are cases which escape these generalizations, such as the territorial crisis of the Spanish state during the Civil War.

7   This was the general conclusion of the studies in Keating and Jones (1985).

8   There is also economic space, which is important in the constitution of a region as a system of action; but a discussion of this would be beyond the limits of this paper. For discussions of the concept of space in social science see Gore (1984, ch. 6, 'Space and Explanation in Regional Development Theory') and Agnew (1987).

9   When I presented an earlier version of this paper in French in 1995, a member of the audience asked if we could not consider the internet too as a region. I insisted on the territorial dimension as fundamental!

10   The recently abolished regions in Scotland were local governments.

11   The evidence, such as it is, generally suggests that small investment subsidies, such as local governments routinely give in the United States, may influence the choice of location within a region (where other costs of production are constant) but are less effective in attracting investment across regions, since distance makes other factors more important. So in the absence of regional coordination, local governments are tempted to attract investment by giving subsidies and other benefits, which benefit shareholders at the expense of taxpayers but have no impact on employment at the level of the region or metropolitan area.

12   This has produced a crisis of legitimacy for government in Scotland (Keating, 1996a).

13   Their model was the German Weimar Republic.

14   Article 1.2 sums it up as follows: *La Constitución se fundamenta en la indisoluble unidad de la Nación española, patria común e indivisible de todos los españoles, y reconoce y garantiza el derecho a la autonomía de las nacionalidades y regiones que la integran y la solidaridad entre todas ellas.*

15   Most prominently Manuel Fraga, president of Galicia and a convert to regionalism when he changed his role from centre to periphery.

16   The origins of this idea of the reciprocal relations between government and civil society go back at least to the Scottish Enlightenment thinker Adam Ferguson (1966).

17   Putnam for his part loses himself in a historic reductionism (in fact an ahistoric procedure) in searching for a specific time for the origin and holding evolution constant, rather than following the true historical spirit by examining evolution over time.

18   For example in the work of *annalistes* like Braudel (1986) or, in a more quantitative vein, Le Bras (1995). For Europe as a whole there is Todd (1990).

REFERENCES

Abélès, M. (1989), *Tranquille jours en '89*. Paris: Odile Jacob.

Agnew, J. (1987), *Place and Politics. The Geographical Mediation of State and Society*. London: Allen and Unwin.

Amin, A. and Thrift, N. (1994), 'Living in the Global', in A. Amin and N. Thrift (eds.), *Globalization, Institutions, and Regional Development in Europe*. Oxford: Oxford University Press.

Anderson, J. (1992), *The Territorial Imperative. Pluralism, Corporatism and Economic Crisis*. Cambridge: Cambridge University Press.

Anderson, P. (1994), *The Invention of the Region, 1945–1990, EUI Working Paper EUF No. 94/2*. Florence: European University Institute.

Badie, B. (1995), *La fin des territoires. Essai sur le désordre international et sur l'utilité sociale du respect*. Paris: Fayard.

Balme, R., Garraud, P., Hoffman-Martinot, V. and Ritaine, E. (1994), *Le territoire pour politiques: variations européennes*. Paris: l'Harmattan.

Barbera, A. (1985), '1970–85; como superare le insufficienze del decentramento', *Democrazia e diritto*, XXV.1.

Benz, A. (1992), 'Redrawing the Map? The Question of Territorial Reform in the Federal Republic', *German Politics*, 1.3: 38–57.

Biarez, S. (1989), *Le pouvoir local*. Paris: Economica.

Biorcio, R. (1991), 'La Lega come attore politico: dal federalismo al populismo regionalista', in R. Mannheimer (ed.), *La Lega Lombarda*. Milan: Feltrinelli.

Blondel, J. (1973), *Comparative Legislatives*. London: Prentice Hall.

Braudel, F. (1986), *L'identité de la France. Espace et histoire*. Paris: Arthaud-Flammarion.

Bullman, U. (ed.) (1994), *Die Politik der dritten Ebene. Regionen im Europa der Union*. Baden-Baden: Nomos.

Camilleri, J. and Falk, J. (1992), *The End of Sovereignty? The Politics of a Shrinking and Fragmenting World*. Aldershot: Edward Elgar.

Cassese, S. and Torchia, L. (1993), 'The Meso Level in Italy', in L. J. Sharpe (ed.), *The Rise of Meso Government in Europe*. London: Sage.

Córnago, N. (1996), *Acción Exterior y Paradiplomacía. La Poyección Internacional de los Mesogobiernos*, Doctoral Thesis, Universidad del País Vasco.

Courchene, T. (1995), *Celebrating Flexibility: An Interpretative Essay on the Evolution of Canadian Federalism*, C. D. How Institute, Benefactors Lecture, 1994, Montreal.

Crowther-Hunt, Lord, and Peacock, A. (1973), *Volume 11 Memorandum of Dissent*. Royal Commission on the Constitution, 1969–73, London: HMSO.

Cuadrado Roura, J. (1981), 'La política regional en los planes de desarrollo', in R. Acosta España (ed.), *La España de las Autonomías* Tomo 1. Madrid: Espasa-Calpe.

De Castro Ruano, J. L. (1994), *La emergente participación política de las regiones en el proceso de construcción europea*. Vitoria: Instituto Vasco de Administración Pública.

De La Granja, J. L. (1995), *El nacionalismo vasco: un siglo de historia*, Madrid: Tecnos.

Dente, B. (1985), *Governare la frammentazione*. Bologna: Il Mulino.

Deutsch, K. (1966) *Nationalism and Social Communication: An Inquiry into the Foundations of Nationality*, Cambridge, MA: MIT Press.

Dunford, M. (1994), 'Winners and losers: the new map of economic inequality in the European Union', *European Urban and Regional Studies*, 1.2: 95–114.

Dunford, M. and Kafkalas, G. (1992), 'The global–local interplay, corporate geographies and spatial development strategies in Europe', in M. Dunford and G. Kafkalis (eds.), *Cities and Regions in the New Europe*. London: Belhaven.

Durand, J.-J. (1995), *L'Europe de la Démocratie chrétienne*. Paris: Editions Complexe.

Engel, C. (1994), 'Regionen im Netzwerk europaïscher Politik', in U. Bullman (ed.), *Die Politik der dritten Ebene. Regionen in Europa der Union*. Baden-Baden: Nomos.

Ferguson, A. (1966), *An Essay on the History of Civil Society, 1767*. Edinburgh: Edinburgh University Press.

Finer, S. E. (1974), *Comparative Government*. Harmondsworth: Penguin.

Galasso, G. (1978), *Passato e presente del meridionalismo*. Naples: Guida.

García Barbancho, A. (1979), *Disparidades Regionales y Ordenación del Territorio*. Barcelona: Ariel.

Garside, P. and Hebbert, M. (1989), *British Regionalism 1900–2000*. London: Mansell.

Gore, C. (1984), *Regions in Question: Space, Development Theory and Regional Policy*. London: Mansell.

Guillorel, H. (1991), 'The social bases of regionalism in France: the Breton case', in J. Coakley (ed.), *The Social Origins of Nationalist Movements. The Contemporary West European Experience*. London: Sage.

Harvie, C. (1994), *The Rise of Regional Europe*. London: Routledge.

Hernández, A. (1980), *Autonomía e integración en la segunda república*. Madrid: Encuentro.

Hocking, B. (1996), 'Regionalism: an international relations perspective', in M. Keating and J. Loughlin (eds.), *The Political Economy of Regionalism*. London: Frank Cass.

Hogwood, B. (1995), ['Regional administration in Britain since 1979: trends and explanations', *Regional and Federal Studies*, 5.3: 267–91.]

Hogwood, B. and Keating, M. (eds.) (1982), *Regional Government in England*. Oxford: Clarendon.

Holmes, M. and Reese, N. (1995), 'Regions within a region: the paradox of the Republic of Ireland', in B. Jones and M. Keating (eds.), *The European Union and the Regions*. Oxford: Clarendon.

Hooghe, L. (1991), *A Leap in the Dark: Nationalist Conflict and Federal Reform in Belgium*, Cornell University, Western Societies Program, occasional paper no. 27. Ithaca: Cornell University.

Hooghe, L. and Keating, M. (1994), 'The politics of EU regional policy', *Journal of European Public Policy*, 1.3: 368–93.

Jones, B. (1996), 'Wales. A developing political economy', in M. Keating and J. Loughlin (eds.), *The Political Economy of Regionalism*. London: Frank Cass.

Jones, B. and Keating, M. (eds.) (1995), *The European Union and the Regions*. Oxford: Clarendon.

Kantor, P. (1995), *The Dependent City Revisited. The Political Economy of Urban Development and Social Policy*. Boulder: Westview.

Keating, M. (1979), 'Is there a regional level of government in England?', *Studies in Public Policy* no. 49. Glasgow: Centre for the Study of Public Policy, University of Strathclyde.

Keating, M. (1985), 'The rise and decline of micronationalism in mainland France', *Political Studies*, XXX111.1: 1–18.

Keating, M. (1988), *State and Regional Nationalism. Territorial Politics and the European State*. London: Harvester-Wheatsheaf.

Keating, M. (1991), *Comparative Urban Politics. Power and the City in the United States, Canada, Britain and France*. Aldershot: Edward Elgar.

Keating, M. (1992), 'Do the workers really have no country? Peripheral nationalism and socialism in the United Kingdom, France, Italy and Spain', in J. Coakley (ed.), *The Social Origins of Nationalist Movements*. London: Sage.

Keating, M. (1996a), *Nations against the State. The New Politics of Nationalism in Quebec, Catalonia and Scotland*. London: Macmillan. Version française, Presses de l'Université de Montréal, 1996.

Keating, M. (1996b), 'The political economy of regionalism', in M. Keating and J. Loughlin (eds.), *The Political Economy of Regionalism*. London: Frank Cass.

Keating, M. and Bleiman, D. (1979), *Labour and Scottish Nationalism*. London: Macmillan.

Keating, M. and Hooghe, L. (1996), 'By-passing the nation state? Regions in the EU policy process', in J. J. Richardson (ed.), *Policy Making in the European Union*. London: Routledge.

Keating, M. and Jones, B. (eds.) (1985), *Regions in the European Community*. Oxford: Clarendon.

Lafont, R. (1967), *La révolution régionaliste*. Paris: Gallimard.

Le Bras, H. (1995), *Les trois France*. Paris: Odile Jacob.

Lenoir, R. and Lesourne, J. (eds.) (1992), *Où va l'état?*. Paris: Le Monde Editions.

Majone, G. (1995), 'Unity in diversity, competition with cooperation: Europe's past as its future', Florence European University Institute, mimeo.

Marks, G. (1992), 'Structural policy in the European Community', in A. Sbragia (ed.), *Euro-Politics. Institutions and Policymaking in the 'New' European Community*. Washington: Brookings.

Mény, Y. (1982), 'Introduction', in Y. Mény (ed.), *Dix ans de régionalisation en Europe. Bilan et perspectives*. Paris: Cujas.

Merloni, F. (1985), 'Perché è in crisi il regionalismo', *Democrazia e Diritto*, 1.

Ministro per gli affari regionali (1982), *Rapporto 1982 sullo stato delle autonomie*. Rome: Istituto Poligrafico e Zecca dello Stato.

Molle, W. and Cappelin, R. (eds.) (1988), *Regional Impact of Community Policies in Europe*. Aldershot: Gower.

Morgan, K. O. (1980), *Rebirth of a Nation. Wales, 1880–1980*. Oxford: Oxford University Press.

Morgan, K. (1992), 'Innovating by networking: new models of corporate and regional development', in M. Dunford and G. Kafkalas (eds.), *Cities and Regions in the New Europe*. London: Belhaven.

Némery, J.-C. (1993), 'Les institutions territoriales françaises à l'épreuve de l'Europe', in J.-C. Némery and S. Wachter, *Entre l'Europe et la décentralisation. Les institutions territoriales françaises*. Paris: DATAR/éditions de l'aube.

Némery, J.-C. and Wachter, S. (1993), *Entre l'Europe et la décentralisation. Les institutions territoriales françaises*. Paris: DATAR/éditions de l'aube.

Oltra, B., Mercadé, F. and Hernández, F. (1981), *La ideología nacional catalana*. Barcelona: Anagrama.

Pastori, G. (1980), 'Le regioni senza regionalismo', *Il Mulino*, 268: 204–26.

Paterson, L. (1994), *The Autonomy of Modern Scotland*. Edinburgh: Edinburgh University Press.

Petschen, S. (1993), *La Europa de las regiones*. Barcelona: Generalitat de Catalunya.

Piattoni, S. (1996), 'Local political classes and economic development. The cases of Abruzzo and Puglia in the 1970s and 1980s', in M. Keating and J. Loughlin (eds.), *The Political Economy of Regionalism*. London: Frank Cass.

Putnam, R. (1993), *Making Democracy Work. Civic Traditions in Modern Italy*. Princeton: Princeton University Press.

Putnam, R., Leonardi, R. and Nanetti, R. (1985), *La pianta e le radici. Il radicamento dell'istituto regionale nel sistema politico italiano*. Bologna: Il Mulino.

Rotelli, E. (1973), 'Dal regionalismo alla regione', in E. Rotelli (ed.), *Dal regionalismo alla regione*. Bologna: Il Mulino.

Savelli, G. (1992), *Che cose vuole la Lega*. Milan: Longanesi.

Schmidtke, O. (1993), 'The populist challenge to the Italian nation-state: The Lega Lombarda/Nord', *Regional Politics and Policy*, 3.3: 140–62.

Sharpe, L. J. (1993), 'The European Meso: an appraisal', in L. J. Sharpe (ed.), *The Rise of Meso Government in Europe*. London: Sage.

Stöhr, W. (1990), *Global Challenge and Local Response. Initiatives for Local Economic Regeneration in Europe*. London: Mansell.

Tilly, C. (1990), *Coercion, Capital and European States*, AD 990–1990. Oxford: Blackwell.

Tilly, C. and Blockmans, W. (eds.) (1994), *Cities and the Rise of States in Europe, AD 1000 to 1800*. Boulder: Westview.

Todd, E. (1990), *L'invention de l'Europe*. Paris: Seuil.

Touraine, A. (1992a), *Critique de la modernité*. Paris; Fayard.

Touraine, A. (1992b), 'L'état et la question nationale', in R. Lenoir et J. Lesourne (eds.), *Où va l'état?*. Paris: Le Monde Editions.

Touraine, A., Dubet, F., Hegedus, Z. and Wieviorka, M. (1981), *Le pays contre l'état. Luttes occitanes*. Paris: Seuil.

Vicens Vives, J. (1986), *Los catalanes en el siglo XIX*. Madrid: Alianza.

Woods, D. (1995), 'The crisis of center–periphery integration in Italy and the rise of regional populism: the Lombard League in comparative perspective', *Comparative Politics*, 27.2: 187–204.

Zaggario, V. (1981), 'La tradizione meridionalista e il dibattito sulle autonomie nel secondo dopoguerra', in G. Mori (ed.), *Autonomismo meridionale: ideologia, politica e istituzioni*. Bologna: Il Mulino.

15

Globalization Makes States: Perspectives on Local Governance in the Age of the World City

Roger Keil

This essay explores several perspectives on local (state) agency in the age of the global city and demonstrates various ways in which globalization "makes states." On the one hand, the national state is being "hollowed out," as its central functions continue to exist nominally even as its sovereign capacities are increasingly being limited through a complex replacement of state power(s) through (globalized) market powers and supranational governance institutions. On the other hand, national states themselves have become protagonists of globalization. The "national competition state" emerges from the ruins of the Fordist state structure (Hirsch 1995, 1997; Panitch 1994). The state is not "withering away" but is being reincarnated in myriad forms on many sociospatial levels. Many traditional functions of national states are now displaced into lower or superordinate state institutions that are wholly new or else have been fundamentally altered thereby. This does not mean that the "state" is everywhere nowadays or that all politics occurs inside states. There is also an important role for civil society on different scales.

Globalization makes states but these differ from those with which we are familiar. This paper focuses on new forms of governance that emerge on the level of the urban, particularly in global or world cities. For this, I draw on the literature on world and global cities, for example, the thirty-plus urban centers that are linked in a network that spans the globe as the skeleton of the globalized economy. Such world cities are places where this newly globalized economic world has a tangible, concrete reality. Global flows of capital and labor move through world cities and are controlled from there. This gives civil society and politics in such places a specific role: they are not just *products* but also *producers* of these seats of seemingly universal power.

My argument is a plea to recognize the urban as a relevant and important site of the political in the era of globalization. Global cities pose the challenge of a "governance of complexity." Analytically, it is most fruitful to combine urban regime theory, urban-scaled regulation theory, and discourse theory to understand the various dimensions of the governance of complexity. I see urban politics as connected with – but not subjected to – the complexities, institutions, and discourses of the local state that I consider the historico-geographic product of the dialectics of state and civil society.

Local states have come to be seen as increasingly important interfaces of different scales of governance in the global order. Three recent developments in local state theory are relevant to my project. First, capitalism's uneven spatial development necessitates states at different levels (Duncan and Goodwin 1988); local states are part of the tendency to form an urban "structured coherence" (Harvey 1989) or regional mode of regulation (Goodwin, Duncan and Halford 1993). Second, the local state has to be understood as occupying "an indistinct but important place in the relations between the state, economy and civil society" (Kirby 1993: 102) and the municipality is located "at the boundary between the state and civil society" (Magnusson 1996: 302). Third, building on earlier work (1985), Magnusson has proposed a fundamental rethinking of politics and opted for decentering the state. This inevitably puts the local state into focus as an alternative political space and organization. Despite its historical marginalization in real politics and political science, urban politics in its limited sovereignty has now become a salient site of the governance of globalization. All three approaches help us to counter the "spatial amnesia" (Duncan and Goodwin 1988) of much of political science literature on states; they point to the inherent significance of civil society in constituting the political and the local state but do not entail a simplistic concept of civil society; and they agree on the local state's key position in globalization processes, because the urban (Lefebvre 1991, 1996) becomes an important site of conflict and integration of scalar governance. The urban is the medium of the global and the private (Schmid 1997) and the space of the everyday practices of political action (Kipfer 1997). Moreover, insofar as local states display non-state features, my essay title needs qualification. Globalization makes states, but the local state is neither a closed system in the sense of a governmental-administrative institution nor simply a derivative of the nation-state. Rather, the local state has perforations at its interface with the dynamized, global, city civil society – perforations that provide openings for resistance and alternatives to hegemonic globalization.

Globalization

Robertson and Khondker claim that the concept of globalization has become so slipshod and ideological that it is becoming harder and harder to use the term rigorously (1998: 27). To overcome this they argue for analytic strategies of "complexification" rather than simplification by presenting "as fully as possible the extent of the complexity before we begin to engage in practices of simplification" (1998: 27). Their own approach orders the globalization debate into "four, empirically overlapping, types of globalization discourse": "clusters of regional and civilizational discourses," "disciplinary discourses," "ideological discourses," and "shifting female and male discourses" (1998: 33). They argue that applying theoretical and ideological critique to these discourses is a better way of rescuing the concept of globalization than resorting to the more usual sorts of simplification.

The concept of globalization has *ideological* and *analytical* dimensions (Kipfer and Keil 1995). The former dimension usually appears in the guise of neo-liberal "theories" that treat globalization as a natural constraint rooted in the market. Over the past two decades, neo-liberal governments have contributed substantively

to practical globalization by tearing down international barriers to trade, deregulating national economies, and attempting to break local resistances wherever
possible. Globalization is being sold by these forces as unqualifiedly beneficial to
the world's societies and peoples. There seem to be fewer boundaries to the
glorification of everything global than there are to the process of globalization itself.
For the neo-liberal worldview builds on the sovereignty of the individual as the core
of the social as well as the engine of globalization of economy, society, culture, and
politics. For, as Magnusson notes, only "if the world as a whole is open to us all can
we be as free as possible individually – or so it is claimed" (1996: 105). The
dominant world of images surrounding globalization is still the world of the dominant. Yet the hegemony of globalization rests on the capillarization of global images,
processes, and structures through social and cultural diversity, differentiation, and
fragmentation (Hall 1997; Robertson 1997; Appadurai 1990). This dialectics of
globalization often escapes those critics in science and politics who assume a too
linear trajectory of globalization and who make the paper tiger of globalization into a
nasty and invincible golem. Indeed, as Robertson and Khondker observe, many
leftists have participated in this by rationalizing the world historic role of a global
economic system on the path to liberation or demonizing globalization as disabling
of local movements (Robertson and Khondker 1998: 37). Simplifying depictions
fall for the deceptions and tricks of neo-liberal propaganda, with potentially devas-
tating consequences for political counter-strategies.

The *analytical* dimension of globalization is mostly studied by political economy,
with authors from all political camps describing it as a top-down process. Thus
globalization is seen as a combination of partial processes of migration, the movement of capital, world trade, and cultural change – all of which gain shape "above
and seemingly outside of national, regional, and urban scales" and flow into the
empty receptacles of local places (Kipfer and Keil 1995: 62). Nonetheless, as these
accounts generally adopt economistic approaches to development, they tend to
neglect or marginalize cultural aspects of globalization. More recent analytical
work, however, warns of too flippant a use of the term. For example, Hirst and
Thompson (1996) argue that the world economy is less open now than before 1914
and that foreign direct investment and world trade are concentrated almost
exclusively in the triad formed by North America–Europe–Japan. Others have
argued that, rather than deploying a "global–local" opposition, research should
focus on "glocalization" (Swyngedouw 1997); that globalization is a complex,
spatially differentiated process of territorialization and deterritorialization (e.g.,
Storper 1997; Cox 1997); and that it involves complex processes of rescaling
(Brenner 1997, 1998; Todd 1997). Indeed, Jessop argues that globalization
involves a relativization of scale since no single scale can any longer be regarded
as primary (Jessop 1997a).

In contrast to the analytical and ideological uses of the term, my own approach
treats globalization as *an ensemble of reconstructable and tangible material processes and
accompanying discursive formations in areas as diverse as fashion, music, art, products of
everyday use, etc.* These processes and formations are characterized by social
conflicts, class struggles, political dispute, and all manner of cultural wars; they
are complexes of social relationships and political forms of governance on all spatio-
social scales (Kipfer and Keil 1995: 62). This view rejects any economist's tale – of

the right or left – of these processes and engages cultural, ecological, and spatial dimensions with classical political economy. It also emphasizes the importance of agency as well as structure. Thus, as Robertson and Khondker argue, we should bring spatial, synchronic considerations firmly into our thinking and consider fully the spatiality of particularism as well as the tendency toward homogenizing universalism (1998: 28). It follows that the large transnational city, the world or global city, should be seen a key site for the intersection of globalization processes that can be observed at once synchronically and spatially.

This altered view of globalization puts new issues at the heart of the research agenda. The incongruence of the processes occurring on different levels/scales in market, state, and society creates *points of friction* for the analysis of the globalized world and obstacles for political agency (Altvater and Mahnkopf 1996: 29–30). The intersections and nodal points of the diverse dynamics move to center stage in many research projects (including my own). "Articulation" is an important concept here. For Altvater and Mahnkopf, articulation signifies "that very diverse, even contrary tendencies are in effect: those mechanisms of the freeing (*Herauslösung*) of economic processes from social and political constraints ('disembedding mechanisms') on the one hand, and the production of new constraints ('networks') at specific locations on the other hand, clash in the activities of social actors" (Altvater and Mahnkopf 1996: 30). Globalization is crystallized and articulated in concrete material processes, where the practices of social collectives and the politics of place play an important role (Kipfer and Keil 1995; Swyngedouw 1997). Articulation also has a clearly spatial connotation. Friedmann notes that world cities articulate larger national, international, and global economic units with one another and are embedded themselves in a "hierarchy of spatial articulations" (Friedmann 1995: 23–4). Indeed, Jessop (1997b) has coined the term "glurbanization" to denote this spatially bound process of multiple intersections. "Glocalization" ultimately proves to be insufficiently complex as it is a purely *quantitative* articulation of local and global dynamics (and conceivably any level in between) instead of capturing the *qualitatively* new forms of governance in the urban and through the urban. The urban is, in the sense of Henri Lefebvre, the scale of mediation of the global with the private and the space of agency of everyday practices of political actors (Kipfer 1997; Schmid 1997; Brenner 1997) and the space of the "politics of presence" of strategic actors in the globalization process (Sassen 1994; Phillips 1996).

A Weakening of the State or Reorientation of State Powers?

The common use of the concept of "globalization" rests on the assumption that states on all levels, from local community councils through the national state apparatus to supranational institutions, are being compromised by exogenous processes. Popular and scholarly treatments of the subject incline to the view that the state is "weakening." Mann notes four core theses of such positions: first, global capitalism is undermining the nation-state; second, the social and environmental problems of a global "risk society" exceed the reach of individual states; third, new identity-based movements compete with national and class identities and highlight demands originating in civil society; and fourth, the end of the nuclear confrontation of the world powers ends the sovereignty of individual nation-states (Mann 1997: 473–4).

Mann adds that these core theses tend to assume that relations of political power are relatively irrelevant and responds that state institutions "still have causal efficacy because they too (like economic, ideological and military institutions) provide necessary conditions for social existence" (1997: 474). He further argues that the variations among states "cause variations in other spheres of social life" and concludes that one should "establish *degrees* of relative causality: to what extent is the nation-state being transformed, to what extent is it declining – or even perhaps still growing?" (1997: 474). Accordingly, Mann distinguishes five "socio-spatial networks of social interaction in the world today": local networks; national networks; international networks; transnational networks; and global networks. He generally assumes that "[o]ver the last centuries, local interaction networks have clearly diminished in relative weight; while longer-distance networks... have become denser, structuring more of people's lives" (1997: 475). However, whilst Mann's critique of the "weakening state" thesis is plausible as regards the continued importance of the national state, his admonition not to pour the baby (or state) out with the bathwater of globalization has its own characteristic blind spots. Among these are the local state; the regulatory power of the urban; and the world city as a site of the post-national state.

I The Local State

First, Mann underestimates the role of subnational networks in globalization. His claim that the local is being increasingly replaced by supralocal networks ultimately involves a surprisingly linear and undialectical historico-geographical view, which almost posits a teleologically guided historical process and tends to equate spatial relationships with physical distance. The hierarchy of five networks is reminiscent of those Russian dolls which, upon opening, reveal an exact copy, albeit of smaller size, of themselves. This view of state levels and geographic scales is entirely insufficient. Indeed, as I will elaborate below, local states belong to the important foundations of the global order. *Globalization makes states and local states make globalization.*

Kirby (1993) has shown that the state is not a monolithic bureaucracy concentrated in a capital city but a fragmented set of institutions and processes that covers the entire territory. At the heart of this fragmentation lies the tension between the state and civil society and its expression in specific local states. This invalidates any simple historical or geographical generalization about the characteristics of the local state. Instead we can draw on three current theoretical strands. First, there are theories that start out from the contradictory character of the bourgeois state and explore its contradictions at the local level, with the form and functions of the state being regarded as expressions of historically changing relationships (Krätke and Schmoll 1987: 33). Since social relationships develop unevenly, different policies are required in different places (fashioned under the influence of locally specific politics); and locally specific institutions are required to implement them (Duncan and Goodwin 1988: 41). This argument is directed against the "spatial amnesia" of traditional state theory and emphasizes that uneven sociospatial development makes a geographically diversified analysis necessary to reveal how subnational variations in state structures follow therefrom. Thus the necessity of the local state is explained in terms of the global division of capitalist production and the subsequent spatial differentiation.

The insertion of the local sphere into the global economy is a conflictual political process precisely because the local state (and local civil society) has a certain autonomy vis-à-vis the national state and global capital. "The importance of this combination between particular spatial divisions of labour, civil society and im-agined communities in producing a particular spatial division of the state with distinctive local policies" has now been widely accepted (Duncan and Goodwin 1988: 78). Possible place-specific combinations are subject to rapid change, of course, but they also have a proactive stance in the global context (Duncan and Goodwin 1988: 82).

Almost all social processes are spatially differentiated and have local expressions. Space presents itself in a politically defined form. Specifically created state appar-atuses address the demands of spatial differentiation. Sometimes the fragmentation of the political form exacerbates and underlines the spatial fragmentation. The specificities of local processes combine to produce the general experience of social space. A separation of both levels appears as a confusion of mental processes of abstraction with real developments. States are always concrete and embedded in all kinds of contingent relationships, including spatial relationships (Duncan and Goodwin 1988: 56). Combining regulationist terms with Harvey's concept of "structured coherence," Goodwin, Duncan and Halford suggest that accumulation regimes and modes of regulation can be regarded "as an ensemble of relations and institutions that are anchored in particular places at particular times. Changes in the mode of regulation will necessarily involve changes in the spatial form and configur-ation of society" (1993: 73).

A second theoretical approach goes beyond noting the significance of spatiality and the social division of labor. Thus Kirby recently defined the local state as occupying "an indistinct but important place in the relations between the state, economy, and civil society and [. . .] also, as a jurisdictional unit, part of the state." Civil society and the state "crucially" come into existence together in the form of the local state (Kirby 1993: 102). In this view, spatiality and sociality emerge simultaneously in historically contingent processes of political institutionalization. This sees the "local state as being both within and beyond the state." "Political action within the local state is to bring together simultaneously [residents'] roles as citizens and as unencumbered individuals, roles within and yet beyond the state" (1993: 103). Magnusson, on whose analysis Kirby's theorization partly rests, talks similarly about a liminality and ambiguity of the municipality, which makes it a particularly significant political space. He argues that "[t]he municipality is at the boundary between the state and civil society, the centre and the locality, social disciplines and everyday life" (1996: 302).

Kirby treats the local state as one of the elements of the "state of chaos that defines a contradictory relationship between the state and its components" (1993: 136). This suggests that the current wave of flexibilization and globalization is increasing diversity and contradiction and that the resulting instability will lead to rather unpredictably diverse, contradictory, and unstable local state practices and also produce new contradictions in civil society (Altvater and Mahnkopf 1996: 51). Urban societies are currently experiencing a period in which the relative stability of the Fordist compromise of the post-World War II years is being replaced by new modes of regulation that are more locally diversified, more globally induced, and less long-term. Historically, it has been the state's role to act as an "apparatus that grapples with, and attempts to minimize, the differences extant within civil society" (Kirby 1993: xiii). It is largely in the institutions of the local state that this process of regulation of difference takes concrete shape.

Finally, following Magnusson (1985: 123), one can "conceive of the local state as encompassing only those agencies that are *physically present* in the local community and *specifically concerned* with its affairs." This excludes policies and agencies that have some effect on localities but are located outside the physical area of these localities and whose functional logic resides on a more than local level. Magnusson differentiates between "municipal politics," which refers to the business of local government, and "local politics," which includes struggles "related to the activities of special-purpose local governments" as well as struggles directed at "the local agencies of the central government" (1985: 124). Although he mainly conceives of the local state as a derivative – though not in the functionally dependent sense – of the central state, he also admits that there are "many local institutions that are at the boundary between the state and civil society" (Magnusson 1985: 122).

Magnusson's more recent work has attempted to develop a plausible theory of politics that escapes the confines of state-centric thinking. Thus he proposes a "decentring of the state" on the grounds that the state system is only one of many phenomena that have to be understood in a global context (1996: 35). The local state has historically played a subordinate or no role at all in political science; and in real politics the local state has been used to "provide an enclosure for popular politics, and so to render that politics safe for the state, the market, and the other forms of government to which we are subject" (Magnusson 1996: 10). Despite its historical marginalization and its continued dislocation and suppression as a site of serious politics, the municipality appears as a particularly important political space. Like Kirby, Magnusson sees the municipality as "identified with the local community, it is understood as an organization of civil society, and it is intended to provide ordinary people with a place to participate in the business of the state" (1996: 10). He argues convincingly that the traditional fixation of politics and political science on the alleged sovereignty of the national state is of little help in the era of the global city (1996: introduction). The modern state system fixes politics in a characteristic manner on "the sovereign institutions of the state. If we allow our own political understanding to be fixed in the same way, the opportunities and dangers of the present are likely to be profoundly misconceived, and we are likely to find ourselves acting to an old script that relegates most of us to the crowd scenes" (Magnusson 1996: 15–16). Magnusson, therefore, chooses to regard the city and the urban as an alternative site of political activity in the current period (1996: 16).

Urban politics is by definition not sovereign. Thus it can provide a model for a period when states themselves can no longer demand sovereignty and when state institutions "like the parliamentarian process with its legitimation-, decision-, and compromise-building processes lose in significance" (Hirsch 1995: 118; cf. Hirsch 1997). But urban politics carries with it the special capacity to withstand the enclosure attempts of the state system, to pass beyond itself and to spill over "the boundaries that contain it geographically and functionally" (Magnusson 1996: 23). This "passing beyond itself" is a consequence of the decentering of the state and of the lack of self-sufficiency on the part of the newly created political spaces, which are inevitably constituted by countless relationships to other spaces (Magnusson 1996: 302). At this point, we are led beyond classical political science's fixation with sovereignty and the state–society dichotomy to think about municipalities and movements as sites of political action (1996: 304).

These three views of the local state are relevant in our context in three ways. First, they share an emphasis on the spatial situatedness of politics in contrast to the "spatial amnesia" of much political science (Duncan and Goodwin 1988); second, they note the pre-eminent significance of civil society for the constitution of the political and the local state, yet do not succumb to the lure of the sort of simplifying concepts of civil society used in many current popular and scholarly debates; and, third, they ascribe the local state a key position in globalization by treating the urban as a major site of conflicts that define our current existence. I now turn to this third aspect.

2   Urbanization Makes States: The Regulative Power of the Urban

Mann underestimates the significance of the *state* as opposed to the institutions of *civil society* in globalization. His emphasis on the tenacity of the national state eschews the simple-minded conclusion that globalization undermines the state's legitimacy and control functions. But it also neglects the important role of the differently scaled social networks in the hierarchization of various state functions. Among these are the urban sociospatial modes of regulation including the urban itself. *Here I argue that (urban) society makes states.*

To emphasize that the state is grounded in civil society does not commit one to the normative ideal of a canonized civil society as a panacea of late and post-capitalist crises (for a critique, see Schmals and Heinelt 1997). Hirsch has correctly warned of the dangers of a naïve euphoria about civil society and a "totalitarianism of civil society" (1995: 156–70). In contrast to this normative (and naïve) ideal, I adopt a conflictual model of civil society. Thus, in my earlier work on Los Angeles, I proposed the historico-geographically specific term of an "urban civil society" and also introduced the idea of an "insurgent civil society" as an historical counter-model to bourgeois society, pointing beyond its boundaries (Keil 1993, 1998b, 1998a). This subaltern, subversive, and insurgent counter-strategy has historically been linked to a *popular civility* that questions the racism, the bigotry, the sexism, and the class rule that characterized the dominant model of civil society for the past two centuries (see Keil 1998a: ch. 3 for a longer discussion of civil society in Los Angeles). In short, my use of the term civil society borrows from the Marxian understanding of civil society and Gramsci's idea of civil society as a "permanently contested origin and foundation of bourgeois class rule" (Hirsch 1995) as well as a potential hearth of revolutionary action. Thus, consistent with but going beyond the redefinition of the local state as a locus of the historical clash of state and civil society, I propose giving special attention to the urban process.

The argument that the state becomes weaker in the globalization process usually coincides with the idea that cities become irrelevant in the global age. Thus, Touraine, in an article entitled "The End of the Cities?," argued that we "continue to believe we live in cities... But the city, which once grew around the important places of activity – the palace, the market, the cathedral – has long been a thing of the past" (1996: 24). Although Touraine concedes network functions to some cities in the global economy, he has little trust in the capacities of the urban to secure social integration. This observation certainly holds true insofar as it describes trends toward the internal dissolution of the urban fabric as witnessed worldwide: urban centers, particularly in North America, lose in significance relative to a continuously differentiated periphery; local elites distance themselves in their economic practices and life designs from the project of the urban as incorporated in specific place, while espousing a featureless cosmopolitanism; the informational city bases its power on increasingly place-*in*dependent and dematerialized exchange processes which are realized in the net and not in situ; and so forth (see also Altvater and Mahnkopf 1996: 125–6).

Yet, at second glance, the rhetoric of the end of the city is not very convincing. Sassen has already critiqued this discourse devastatingly in her work on the global city (1994), and so I will focus on the city's alleged incapacity for social integration. While there are some dangers in this depiction, I support Sassen's comment that the city as a real site concentrates social difference (1994: 122). Both the dominant economic culture and the multiplicity of cultures and identities are inscribed in its spaces. Sassen shows how global control functions are not entirely external to cities but must be produced *locally* via concrete material production processes. The production of the global economy involves more than just disembedded economic processes; it is grounded in multiple economies with roots in real places (1994: 123).

Due to its growing diversity and dynamics, urban society is becoming the most significant integrative mechanism of the global age. The challenges of globalized urban society call for new mechanisms of regulation and new forms of governance; these in turn produce new kinds of local states. In contrast to the common view that local states are corrupted by globalization from above, I posit that the conflictual self-regulating needs of local civil society help to produce a wide range of municipal state structures. But we need to look beyond the moment of globalization and acknowledge, as predicted by Lefebvre, that we live in an *urban* society that is a product of long-term processes of capitalist development (1991). Prigge reminds us, following Lefebvre, that urban politics reaches beyond city politics in its narrow sense and occurs in the intermediary space of civil society. Urban politics has no specific place without being utopian. It denotes a bundle of intermediary procedures through which globally induced problems are articulated as problems of the concrete place. Prigge continues: "Urbanity has always been structured in polarities, contained oppositions, which were integrated by it (proletariat and bourgeoisie in former times). The current social oppositions and fragments confront urban politics with new problems" (1995: 185). Sociospatial contradictions now need to be made public, need to be moderated, civilized, discussed, decentered. Urban politics, in this sense, breaks the institutional chains of municipal politics (as represented by local governments) and creates *urban* regulations and a new kind of urbanity linked to the "reflexive potential of modernization, democratization, and civilization of social contradictions" (Prigge 1995: 186).

Society makes states in the sense that globalization can be understood as a social movement that evokes state institutions. Focused on the urban, we can thus "think of urbanism as a social movement stretching across the centuries, in which people more or less consciously attempt to create a world for themselves" (Magnusson 1996: 304). This political auto-creation of urban society reveals a new quality in the period of global capitalism – a new quality that is particularly visible in those places that we call world or global cities.

3   The World City as a Site of the Construction of the Post-National State

Mann largely disregards the new state formations below the national level, particularly urban and regional governance. We can address this obvious defect by looking at world cities as sites of the construction of the post-national state. World city theory does not have a ready-made theory of politics. Yet, from the experience of European and North American world city formation, we know that local politics has become an integral part of this process (Schmid 1997; Kipfer 1997; Hitz et al. 1995; Keil 1998a; Ronneberger and Keil 1995; Keil and Lieser 1992; Todd 1997; Friedmann 1997). We must look elsewhere for clues to how politics contributes to world city formation. For world cities generate specific local or urban politics with distinctive arenas of social struggle and policy formation: growth and development; immigration and citizenship rights; identity and anti-racist politics; neighborhood versus "world class" culture; use and exchange value; new forms of class struggle; collective consumption; and sustainability (Keil 1998a, 1996). All these arenas are concrete spaces of mediation and negotiation where demands of actors from different levels of agency are mutually imbricated. Originally, Friedmann and Wolff (1982) had framed the characteristic structures of the world city in the terms "citadel and ghetto." We can now insist that the social contradictions created in world cities cannot easily be contained in such a polarity. The emergence of new global–local arrangements in the world city should be seen as a dynamic process of mutual definition of social forces and as the product of material power relations. We can distinguish two processes here: the globalization of the urban region, and the fragmentation of urban civil society and political sphere. Urban politics in the world city is the forum in and through which the nexus among various scales of globalization is being produced.

World city formation is a globally induced but locally contingent process in and through which globalization manifests itself as a contradictory relationship of the local political sphere. Globalization takes shape in the world city. Thus the articulation of specific places depends on local struggles and gives world city politics a place-specific nature. Due to this complexity, we cannot speak of the world city as a political unit. Only authoritarian fantasies can draw the image of a globalized urban region like Los Angeles, Toronto, or Berlin. The world city is an ideal field for the study of post-national state structures.

In the age of globalization, urban politics has often been portrayed as at best reactive to and at worst ineffective in the face of global pressures. Progressive agendas, above all, seem to have vanished almost entirely from urban politics. Alternatives to development schemes and regulation modes imposed on urban regions by internationalized urban growth machines are little understood theoretically, and few empirical studies exist that look into the actual workings of such politics. Much of the debate in the 1980s and early 1990s conveyed impressions of globalization and subsequent local disenfranchisement. Some authors argued that, in global capitalism, there would be a "relative decline of the relative autonomy of the state" vis-à-vis capital. The effects of the increased mobility of "footloose capital" hit hardest those regions threatened by capital flight (taking into account that, in world cities, capital typically flows both in and out). In this situation, the authors contend, the space wherein the local state makes decisions will become noticeably smaller. The implied loss of the relative autonomy of regions and cities was captured appropriately in the phrase "local planners – global constraints" (for a summary of this view, see Ross and Trachte 1990). Rather than the (local) state disappearing, however, I argue that a new kind of local state will emerge in the confluence of globalization dynamics and increased local political action based in civil society.

World City Governance

To understand these specific and distinctive processes, however, we must turn to three related approaches to the regimes, regulation, and discourses of urban politics. This can be justified on the grounds that world city politics is concerned with the governance of complexity, the elements of which are regime, regulation, and discourse. Much of this complexity derives from the articulation of different spatial scales (Brenner 1997, 1998; Jonas 1997). These scales differ in geographic, economic, social, political, and also ecological terms. The central problem of local governance under these conditions of complexity is the temporary stabilization of everyday actions and the transactions of individuals, collectives, and institutions whose productive and reproductive necessities and desires are not easily predictable.

Regime

The so-called urban regime theory of the American political economy school provides an excellent conceptual toolbox to understand the *complexities* of urban political decision-making and its associated social struggles. US scholars developed this theory in reaction to the problems of conventional pluralist and elitist theories of urban politics. Modeled after similar approaches in international relations, urban regime theory has developed a distinct body of literature that has usefully been applied in various empirical settings, mostly in North America. Particularly in the age of globalization, it seems that each urban situation is unique in its complexity of themes and actors. Different regimes relate differently to the demands of urban development planning and politics. Regime theory allows us to distinguish between periods of local politics using clearly defined typologies and criteria (Stone 1993).

This school has shown that urban development is a process that rests on *political* decision-making that involves distinguishable and significant alternatives. Local actors combine in governing regimes or coalitions in both formal and informal political arenas. They shape the history of the city in a controversial political environment, where different private and public sectors must cooperate (Kantor, Savitch, and Vicari Haddock 1997; Stone 1993; Lauria 1997). The political economy school is significant because it lends some structure to classical pluralist arguments; it furnishes the classically economist Marxist urban theory with politics; and it contradicts growth apologists like Peterson (1981), who argue that urban development was a consensual political project favoring everyone in a city.

Regulation

The French regulation approach has advanced our understanding of the modes of regulation, practices, and *institutions* of organization that can help stabilize capital accumulation for a certain time period. One can plausibly identify specifically urban or regional modes of production as well as the national territorial modes that have usually captured the attention of regulation theorists (Goodwin et al. 1993; Keil and Lieser 1992; Mayer 1995; Painter 1995; Peck and Tickell 1994). As Lipietz (1991) has shown, the structuring of space is one of the key dimensions of regulation. Urban regions (rather than nations) are the pivotal points of post-Fordist restructuring. The supporting elements of the new accumulation regime evolve in urban modes of regulation. Lipietz distinguishes two different dynamics. First, the neo-Fordist variant of development, which entails a return to urban agglomeration, is a heightened form of Fordist regulation that involves a remetropolitanization of urban forms and the emergence of megalopolises in a disorganized society. And, second, the post-Fordist variant rests on the "organized mobilization of the territory" and includes cooperation, based on negotiation, face-to-face relationships, and proximity, that amounts to a new kind of urban agglomeration, one which is based on negotiation and stable contractual links among institutions (Lipietz 1991: 133). Besides these tendencies of concentration, the post-Fordist variant mostly comprises organized networks of smaller local production systems that would form the basis of community democracy and inter-spatial solidarity (Lipietz 1991: 134–5).

The fundamental tendencies of after-Fordist local politics include the following: cities are – to differing degrees – marked by processes of social polarization, which have been exacerbated by the crisis of government finances since the early 1990s. The ubiquitous "budget crunch" has propelled existing attempts to replace a welfare state model of local politics with the modernization model of the "entrepreneurial city." Models of industrial management – such as lean production – are transposed onto urban institutions; monetarization or privatization of public services is rampant (Heinelt and Mayer 1992: 17–18). Such options complement entrepreneurial strategies that have marked urban politics since the 1980s: urban management, corporate identity politics, public–private partnerships, etc. At the same time, these restructurings imply a changing role for the municipality vis-à-vis local actors. Processes intended to promote moderation, consensus building, and cooperation are becoming more important (Selle 1996a, 1996b). "Selective" and "participatory" versions of post-Fordist local politics can be distinguished: the former trusts in economic prosperity and does little to integrate popular demands and needs into the new mode of regulation; participatory policies strive toward a broad mobilization of urban actors and toward minimizing marginalization (Heinelt and Mayer 1992: 24–5). This latter – political – aspect of urban development politics points beyond the material aspects of urban processes and foregrounds the discursive formation of urban politics in the age of globalization.

Discourse

Discourse analytical approaches have greatly clarified the mechanics and semiotics of *hegemony*. Goodwin and Painter (1997: 26) have noted that "a regulation theory based on social process, conflict, and strategy turns the spotlight on to discursive as well as material practices. In principle, the regulation approach has always been concerned with discourse." Yet, while they maintain that regulationist writers "have often repeated, mantralike, the claim that regulation is a social, political, and *cultural* process, ... substantive regulationist accounts have rarely considered the contributions of discourse to specific regulatory processes or, in the more usual terminology, modes of regulation" (Ibid.). More generally, it is ultimately also impossible to maintain an ontological position in which discourses are separate from or causally removed from material processes.

The political can best be understood in discursive as well as material terms (Harvey 1996: 78; see Harvey's ch. 4 for a fine discussion of the dialectics of discourse). Discourse analysis permits an examination of the structures of hegemonic regulation modes and urban regimes and also internal heterogeneities of discourses (Harvey 1996: 88). Equally, it allows slippages, ambiguities, and incoherences among and inside different discourses to be demonstrated (Harvey 1996: 89) that would be impossible to discern in a purely material analysis.

Complex(c)ities: Regime, Regulation, and Discourse

I propose that regime-, regulation-, and discourse-theoretical approaches be merged critically and selectively into a theory of local governance. Only such a comprehensive approach, it seems to me, can do justice to "the governance of complexity" (Jessop 1997c). This complexity is particularly present in the formation and regulation of world cities. Magnusson writes that "from an urbanist's perspective, city life is where the principles of state sovereignty – and the complementary principles of individual sovereignty – fall apart in the face of the complexities of human existence" (1996: 285). Kirby also argues that, historically, the growing complexity of civil society, which he equates with increasing spatiality, militates against the restrictive structures of states that attempt to capture conflicts inside its boundaries (1993: 136). In discussing complexity we must not rely on abstract formulae but identify the real processes that increase complexity and systematic differentiation (Hirsch 1995: 115). This is why we must root our analyses in the concreteness of the urban process. Urbanization brings a certain number of spatialized permanences in relation to each other (Harvey 1996: 419) and creates a continuously changing sociospatial complexity. In contrast to the regular and regulated politics of the liberal democratic state, the politics of complexity in the metropolis offers peculiar opportunities of destabilization through alternative designs of urbanity and sociality (Magnusson 1996: 285).

The question of how agency must be understood in the context of the governance of complexity poses a serious problem in a world where structural change seems to originate either abstractly in global flows of information and capital or concretely in the boardrooms of transnational corporations. Much of the current literature on world city formation still treats this process and its governance as mere derivatives of hegemonic material and discursive realms that are said to occur on the global level. This view of the political sphere of the world city is erroneous: for urban politics is also an important factor in world city formation (cf. Keil 1993, 1998a). Having said this, however, we are still left with the tension between the rational choice foundations of *regime theory*, in which purposeful actors make conscious decisions, and the more structuralist view of the *regulation approach* (Painter 1997: 133–43). In the tension between these two approaches, we may be able to isolate concrete modes of explaining political decision-making in the globalized city. We need a concept of political praxis and strategy that can guide analyses of urban politics "without contradicting the methodological stance of regulation theory" (Painter 1997: 134). Just how the rationalist and materialist premises of regime and regulation theories can be linked most productively is still up for debate. Painter approaches this question with Bourdieu's concept of "habitus," a term that is also important in Lipietz's work, and concludes with the question: "How is that particular form of political agency and political subjectivity generated that seeks to calculate its rational self-interest and aims to act strategically to enhance it?" (Painter 1997: 141). This question moves away from the rational choice basis of traditional regime literature and is more compatible with Jessop's neo-Gramscian formulations. Jessop develops the concept of "strategic selectivity" to refer to "the differential impact of the core structural (including spatio-temporal) features of the labour process, an accumulation regime, or a mode of regulation on the relative capacity of particular forces organized in particular ways to successfully pursue a specific economic strategy" (1997a: 63). He combines this structural undergirding of the rational actor model with the view of actors as reflexive and capable of reformulating their interests and identities (1997a: 63).

Painter also notes the problematic of regulation and counter-regulation (1997: 123). This way of thinking enables us to break from the hegemonic systems logic of the globalized urban growth discourse and to acknowledge and take seriously alternatives of urban development; it also enables us to foreground cultural, ideational, or environmental aspects in our analyses. This second aspect seems particularly relevant in the context of world cities with their dynamized cultural politics. Elsewhere Goodwin and Painter speak of "sites of regulation" and sites of "resistance and disruption" (1997: 22). The problem with these distinctions is that the authors argue as if each of these sites had a discrete nature (either regulatory or counter-regulatory), rather than seeing the sites as contested terrains themselves. It seems more useful to emphasize the role of counter-regulatory practices in shaping the governance of complexity and processes of regulation even in their oppositional negativity. In fact, it is exactly through their ability to impose part of their agenda on the hegemonic discourse that – short of political revolution – they are effective political actors in a world that seems so clearly structured against them.

While it makes sense to differentiate analytically between sites of resistance and sites of regulation, then, they cannot be separated empirically. The complexity of the world city is marked by a complete imbrication of hegemonic and resistant potentials that acquire reality in social struggles. Yet hegemonic urban politics aims to maintain the status quo or to continue it in different ways; as a rule, this limits and canalizes the horizons of urban political demands to a one-sided articulation of urban policy goals with the hegemonic project of globalization (economic growth), or even to a complete subjection of the social, ecological, and cultural to the demands of economic development. Nonetheless, most cases I have examined closely over the past years point in a different direction – beyond the narrow confines of the growth logic and administrative constraints. For forces of resistance tend to expand and explode the territorial, administrative, and jurisdictional boundaries set for them (Keil 1998b).

Concluding Remarks

Globalization makes states in various ways. This paper has focused on the creation of local state institutions that must accomplish two kinds of integration and articulation in the process of world city formation: the external integration of world city spatialities with other scales of the global economy, society, culture, and ecology; and the internal integration of fragmented societies. These local state institutions are under constant attack from the dynamized global city civil society, which formulates its demands on the co-creation of the world city politically. Local politics is inscribed as an integral moment of world city formation. Currently politics in the world city (particularly progressive politics) is mostly equated with defensive measures against the material bulldozer and ideological puppet of globalization. The alternative approach to local politics and local state agency, in terms of the governance of complexity, aims to break this defensive attitude and to recognize and articulate a new emancipatory politics in and against the hegemonic concepts of global urbanization. In this sense, this new way of thinking might create the precondition for creating "possible urban worlds" (Harvey 1996) in a globalized context.

REFERENCES

Altvater, E. and Mahnkopf, B. (1996) *Grenzen der Globalisierung: Ökonomie, Ökologie und Politik in der Weltgesellschaft*. Münster: Westfälisches Dampfboot.

Appadurai, A. (1990) "Disjuncture and Difference in the Global Cultural Economy," *Public Culture*, 2 (2), 1–24.

Brenner, N. (1997) " 'Trial by Space': Global City Formation, State Territorial Restructuring and the Politics of Scale," presented to ISA-RC21 Conference on "Cities in Transition," Berlin, 20–22 July.

Brenner, N. (1998) "Global Cities, Glocal States: Global City Formation and State Territorial Restructing in Contemporary Europe," *Review of International Political Economy*, 5 (1), 1–37.

Cox, K., ed. (1997) *Spaces of Globalization: Reasserting the Power of the Local*. New York: The Guilford Press.

Duncan, S. and Goodwin, M. (1988) *The Local State and Uneven Development*. Cambridge: Polity.

Friedmann, J. (1995) "Where We Stand: A Decade of World City Research," in P. L. Knox and P. J. Taylor, eds, *World Cities in a World-System*. Cambridge: Cambridge University Press. 48–62.

Friedmann, J. (1997) "The Common Good: Assessing the Importance of Cities." Unpublished paper, Melbourne: Royal Melbourne Institute of Technology.

Friedmann, J. and Wolff, G. (1982) "World City Formation: An Agenda for Research and Action," *International Journal of Urban and Regional Research*, 6 (3), 309–44.

Goodwin, M. and Painter, J. (1997) "Concrete Research, Urban Regimes and Regulation Theory," in Lauria 1997: 13–29.

Goodwin, M., Duncan, S. and Halford, S. (1993) "Regulation Theory, the Local State, and the Transition of Urban Politics," *Environment and Planning D: Society and Space*, 11 (1), 67–88.

Hall, S. (1997) "The Local and the Global: Globalization and Ethnicity," in King 1997: 41–68.

Harvey, D. (1989) *The Urban Experience*. Oxford: Blackwell.

Harvey, D. (1996) *Justice, Nature and the Geography of Difference*. Oxford: Blackwell.

Heinelt, H. and Mayer, M. (1992) "Europäische Städte im Umbruch – zur Bedeutung lokaler Politik," in H. Heinelt and M. Mayer, eds, *Politik in europäischen Städten. Fallstudien zur Bedeutung lokaler Politik*. Basel: Birkhäuser. 7–28.

Hirsch, J. (1995) *Der nationale Wettbewerbsstaat. Staat, Demokratie und Politik im globalen Kapitalismus*. Berlin: Edition ID-Archiv.

Hirsch, J. (1997) "Globalization of Capital, Nation-States and Democracy," *Studies in Political Economy*, 54, 39–58.

Hirst, P. and Thompson, G. (1996) *Globalization in Question*. Cambridge: Polity.

Hitz, H., Keil, R., Lehrer, U., Ronneberger, K., Schmid, C., and Wolff, R., eds (1995) *Capitales Fatales: Urbanisierung und Politik in den Finanzmetropolen*. Frankfurt: Rotpunktverlag.

Jessop, B. (1997a) "A Neo-Gramscian Approach to the Regulation of Urban Regimes: Accumulation Strategies, Hegemonic Projects, and Governance," in Lauria 1997: 51–73.

Jessop, B. (1997b) "New Geographies of Urban Governance: Discussant Paper", presented to ISA-RC21 Conference on "Cities in Transition," Berlin, 20–2 July.

Jessop, B. (1997c) "Capitalism and its Future: Remarks on Regulation, Government and Governance," *Review of International Political Economy*, 4 (3, Autumn), 561–81.

Jonas, A. E. G. (1997) "Regulating Suburban Politics: 'Suburban-Defense Transition,' Institutional Capacities, and Territorial Reorganization in Southern California," in Lauria 1997: 206–29.

Kantor, P., Savitch, H. V., and Vicari Haddock, S. (1997) "The Political Economy of Urban Regimes: A Comparative Perspective," *Urban Affairs Review*, 32 (3), 348–77.

Keil, R. (1993) *Weltstadt – Stadt der Welt. Internationalisierung und lokale Politik in Los Angeles*. Münster: Westfälisches Dampfboot.

Keil, R. (1996) "World City Formation, Local Politics, and Sustainability," in R. Keil, G. R. Wekerle, and D. V. J. Bell, eds, *Local Places in the Age of the Global City*. Montreal: Black Rose Books. 37–44.

Keil, R. (1998a) *Los Angeles: Globalisation, Urbanisation and Social Struggles*. Chichester: Wiley.

Keil, R. (1998b) "Greening the Polis or Policing Ecology? Local Environmental Politics and Urban Civil Society in Los Angeles," in J. Friedmann and M. Douglass, eds, *Cities for Citizens: Planning and the Rise of Civil Society*. Chichester: Wiley. 91–105.

Keil, R. and Lieser, P. (1992) "Frankfurt: Global City – Local Politics," in M. P. Smith, ed., *After Modernism. Global Restructuring and the Changing Boundaries of City Life* (Comparative Urban and Community Research, 4). London: Sage. 39–69.

King, A., ed. (1997) *Culture, Globalization and the World System: Contemporary Conditions for the Representation of Identity*. Minneapolis: University of Minnesota Press.

Kipfer, S. (1997) "Between Neo-Liberalism and Neo-Populism: Facing the Dilemmas of Progressive Urban Politics in Toronto," presented to ISA-RC21 Conference on "Cities in Transition," Berlin, 20–2 July

Kipfer, S. and Keil, R. (1995) "Urbanisierung und Technologie in der Periode des globalen Kapitalismus", in Hitz et al. 1995: 61–87.

Kirby, A. (1993) *Power/Resistance: Local Politics and the Chaotic State*. Bloomington: Indiana University Press.

Krätke, S. and Schmoll, F. (1987) "Der lokale Staat – 'Ausführungsorgan' oder 'Gegenmacht'?," *Prokla*, 68, 3072.

Lauria, M., ed. (1997) *Reconstructing Urban Regime Theory: Regulating Urban Politics in a Global Economy*. London: Sage.

Lefebvre, H. (1991) *The Production of Space*. Oxford: Blackwell.

Lefebvre, H. (1996) *Writings on Cities*. Oxford: Blackwell.

Lipietz, A. (1991) "Zur Zukunft der städtischen Ökologie," in M. Wentz, ed., *Stadt-Räume. Die Zukunft des Städtischen, Frankfurter Beiträge, Band 2*. Frankfurt: Campus Verlag. 129–36.

Magnusson, W. (1985) "Urban Politics and the Local State," *Studies in Political Economy*, 16, 111–42.

Magnusson, W. (1996) *The Search for Political Space*. Toronto: University of Toronto Press.

Mann, M. (1997) "Has Globalization Ended the Rise of the Nation-State?," *Review of International Political Economy*, 4 (3), 472–96.

Mayer, M. (1995) "Stadtpolitik im Umbruch," in Hitz et al. 1995: 123–36.

Painter, J. (1995) "Regulation Theory, Post-Fordism and Urban Politics," in D. Judge, G. Stoker and H. Wolman, eds, *Theories of Urban Politics*. London: Sage. 276–98.

Painter, J. (1997) "Regulation, Regime, and Practice in Urban Politics," in Lauria 1997: 122–43.

Panitch, L. (1994) "Globalization and the State," in *Socialist Register 1994*. London: Merlin Press. 60–93.

Peck, J. and Tickell, A. (1994) "Searching for a New Institutional Fix: The *After*-Fordist Crisis and the Global–Local Disorder," in A. Amin, ed., *Post-Fordism: A Reader*. Oxford: Blackwell. 280–315.

Peterson, P. E. (1981) *City Limits*. Chicago: University of Chicago Press.

Phillips, A. (1996) "Dealing with Difference: A Politics of Ideas, or a Politics of Presence?," in S. Benhabib, ed., *Democracy and Difference: Contesting the Boundaries of the Political*. Princeton, NJ: Princeton University Press. 139–52.

Prigge, W. (1995) "Urbi et orbi – zur Epistemologie des Städtischen," in Hitz et al. 1995: 176–87.

Robertson, R. (1997) "Social Theory, Cultural Relativity and the Problem of Globality," in King 1997: 69–90.

Robertson, R. and Khondker, H. H. (1998) "Discourses of Globalization: Preliminary Considerations," *International Sociology*, 13 (1), 25–40.

Ronneberger, K. and Keil, R. (1995) "Ausser Atem: Frankfurt nach der Postmoderne," in Hitz et al. 1995: 284–353.

Ross, R. and Trachte, K. (1990) *Global Capitalism: the New Leviathan.* Albany, NY: State University of New York Press.

Sassen, S. (1994) *Cities in a World Economy.* Thousand Oaks: Pine Forge Press.

Schmals, K. M. and Heinelt, H., eds (1997) *Zivile Gesellschaft. Entwicklung – Defizite – Potentiale.* Opladen: Leske and Budrich.

Schmid, C. (1997) "Globalisation, the Urban Region and the Question of Territorial Scales: The Case of Zurich," presented to ISA-RC21 Conference on "Cities in Transition," Berlin, 20–2 July.

Selle, K. (1996a) "Lokale Partnerschaften – Organisationsformen und Arbeitsweisen für kooperative Problembearbeitung vor Ort," in S. Müller, ed., *Die neuen Planungstheorien: Postmoderne, Regulation und Raumstrukturen. Ein Reader.* Dortmund: Universität Dortmund, Fakultät Raumplanung. 253–73.

Selle, K. (1996b) "An der Entwicklung der Städte mitwirken. Oder: vom Hang und Zwang zur Kooperation," in M. Wentz, ed., *Stadt-Entwicklung. Die Zukunft des Städtischen. Frankfurter Beiträge Band 9.* Frankfurt: Campus Verlag. 21–31.

Stone, C. N. (1993) "Urban Regimes and the Capacity to Govern: A Political Economy Approach," *Journal of Urban Affairs,* 15, 1–25.

Storper, M. (1997) "Territories, Flows, and Hierarchies in the Global Economy," in Cox 1997: 19–44.

Swyngedouw, E. A. (1997) "Neither Global nor Local: 'Glocalization' and the Politics of Scale," in Cox 1997: 137–66.

Todd, G. (1997) "Scaling Governance: Local Strategies, Global Accumulation, and Democracy," presented to ISA-RC21 Conference on "Cities in Transition," Berlin, 20–2 July.

Touraine, Alain (1996) "Das Ende der Städte?," *Die Zeit,* 23 (31 May), 24.

16

Cities and Citizenship

James Holston and Arjun Appadurai

[...] Since the eighteenth century, one of the defining marks of modernity has been the use of two linked concepts of association – citizenship and nationality – to establish the meaning of full membership in society. Citizenship rather than subject-ship or kinship or cultship has defined the prerogatives and encumbrances of that membership, and the nation-state rather than the neighborhood or the city or the region established its scope. What it means to be a member of society in many areas of the world came to be understood, to a significant degree, in terms of what it means to be a right-bearing citizen of a territorial nation-state. Undeniably, this historical development has been both revolutionary and democratic, even as it has also been conservative and exclusionary. On the one hand, for persons deemed eligible, nation-states have sought to establish citizenship as that identity which subordinates and coordinates all other identities – of religion, estate, family, gender, ethnicity, region, and the like – to its framework of a uniform body of law. Over-whelming other titles with its universal *citoyen*, citizenship thus erodes local hier-archies, statuses, and privileges in favor of national jurisdictions and contractual relations based in principle on an equality of rights. On the other hand, the mobilizations of those excluded from the circle of citizens, their rallies against the hypocrisies of its ideology of universal equality and respect, have expanded democ-racies everywhere: they generate new kinds of citizens, new sources of law, and new participation in the decisions that bind. As much as anything else, these conflicting and disjunctive processes of change constitute the core meaning of modern citizen-ship, constantly unsettling its assumptions.

Although one of the essential projects of nation-building has been to dismantle the historic primacy of urban citizenship and to replace it with the national, cities remain the strategic arena for the development of citizenship. They are not the only arena. And not all cities are strategic. But with their concentrations of the nonlocal, the strange, the mixed, and the public, cities engage most palpably the tumult of citizenship. Their crowds catalyze processes which decisively expand and erode the rules, meanings, and practices of citizenship. Their streets conflate identities of territory and contract with those of race, religion, class, culture, and gender to produce the reactive ingredients of both progressive and reactionary political move-ments. Like nothing else, the modern urban public signifies both the defamiliarizing enormity of national citizenship and the exhilaration of its liberties.

But if cities have historically been the locus of such tumult, they experience today an unsettling of national citizenship which promises unprecedented change. In some places, the nation itself is no longer a successful arbiter of citizenship. As a result, the project of a national society of citizens, especially liberalism's twentieth-century version, appears increasingly exhausted and discredited. In other places, the nation may maintain the envelope of citizenship, but the substance has been so changed or at least challenged that the emerging social morphologies are radically unfamiliar and force a reconsideration of the basic principles of membership. Such transformations have generated profound uncertainties about many aspects of citizenship which only recently seemed secure: uncertainty about the community of allegiance, its form of organization, manner of election and repudiation, inclusiveness, ethical foundations, and signifying performances; uncertainty about the location of sovereign power; uncertainty about the priorities of the right and the good; uncertainty about the role of cultural identities increasingly viewed as defining natural memberships.

It has become common in the literature on national identity to consider such transformations in terms of a dichotomy between the national and the global. Cities usually drop out of the analysis because this dichotomy tends to present globalization, especially of labor, capital, and communication, as neutralizing the importance of place, indeed of rendering it irrelevant. This [essay] proposes that such demateri-alization is mistaken, that place remains fundamental to the problems of membership in society, and that cities (understood here to include their regional suburbs) are especially privileged sites for considering the current renegotiations of citizenship. It regards cities as the place where the business of modern society gets done, including that of transnationalization.[...]

Our point is not to argue that the transnational flow of ideas, goods, images, and persons – intensified by recent developments in the globalization of capital – is obliterating the salience of the nation-state. Rather, it is to suggest that this flow tends to drive a deeper wedge between national space and its urban centers. There are a growing number of societies in which cities have a different relationship to global processes than the visions and policies of their nation-states may admit or endorse. London today is a global city in many ways that do not fit with the politics of the United Kingdom, just as Shanghai may be oriented to a global traffic beyond the control of the government of the People's Republic of China, as Mogadishu may represent a civil war only tangentially tied to a wider Somali politics, and as Los Angeles may sustain many aspects of a multicultural society and economy at odds with mainstream ideologies of American identity. Cities have always been stages for politics of a different sort than their hinterlands. But in the era of mass migration, globalization of the economy, and rapid circulation of rights discourse, cities represent the localization of global forces as much as they do the dense articulation of national resources, persons, and projects.[...]

The conventional distinction between formal and substantive aspects of citizenship is helpful in sorting out various dimensions of these proposals. In particular, it suggests why cities may be especially salient sites for the constitution of different citizenships, or at least for considering the exhaustion of national modes. If the formal refers to membership in the nation-state and the substantive to the array of civil, political, socio-economic, and cultural rights people possess and exercise, much of the turmoil of citizenship derives from the following problem: although in theory full access to rights depends on membership, in practice that which constitutes citizenship substantively is often independent of its formal status. In other words, formal membership in the nation-state is increasingly neither a necessary nor a sufficient condition for substantive citizenship. That it is not sufficient is obvious for many poor citizens who have formal membership in the state but who are excluded in fact or law from enjoying the rights of citizenship and participating effectively in its organization. This condition also applies to citizens of all classes who find that their preferences for a desirable or proper form of life – for example, with regard to sexual or religious practices – are not adequately embodied in the national-public sphere of rights even though the communities in which they live may overwhelmingly approve them. Moreover, it is now evident that a condition of formal membership without much substantive citizenship characterizes many of the societies which have experienced recent transitions to democracy and market capitalism in Latin America, Asia, and Eastern Europe.

That formal citizenship is less necessary for access to substantive rights is also clear: although it is required for a few rights (like voting in national elections), it is not for most. Indeed, legally resident noncitizens, and even illegally resident ones, often possess virtually identical socio-economic and civil rights as citizens. Moreover, the exclusive rights of citizens are often onerous, like jury duty, military service, and certain tax requirements. Thus, people tend to perceive them more as burdens than as rights. It is not surprising, therefore, that recent surveys indicate that many immigrants are not as anxious as they once might have been to embrace the citizenship of their new countries, thereby compromising their right of return.[...]

Such disjunctions between the form and substance of citizenship have made defining it in terms of membership in the nation-state less convincing and have thus devalued this form of association for both members and nonmembers alike. As a result, there have been two general responses. One tries to make citizenship more exclusive. Hence, we witness a host of reactionary movements: some aim to deny social services to various categories of noncitizens or to legislate the exclusive use of one language or another. Others employ urban incorporation to gain the powers of local government. Their objective is to privatize or dismantle public spaces and services and to implant zoning regulations which in effect keep the undesired out. Around the world, it is all too common to find homeowner associations using these powers and privileges of democratic organization to exclude, discriminate, and segregate. For example, in the Los Angeles Metropolitan Region alone there are over twenty-five such exclusive urban incorporations, and in São Paulo there are hundreds of so-called closed condominiums using somewhat different legal mechanisms to achieve similar ends. Other exclusionary movements (some militia-backed) attack federalism and the idea of national government itself, advancing the priority of local, small-scale communities.[1] All of these movements tend to emphasize private security and vigilantism as acceptable forms of self-determination. Most are tinged with racism if not outright violence.

The other kind of response has gone in the opposite direction. It tries to make citizenship more inclusive. It aims to reconceive citizenship in supranational and nonlocal terms in which rights are available to individuals regardless of national origins, residence, or place of work. Examples include movements for human rights, transnational citizenship, and continental associations (e.g., EEC, Nafta, and Mercosur). But if both types of response aim to reinvigorate citizenship, they both typically have their perverse outcomes: in the one case, localism can generate xenophobic violence; in the other, the elimination of local community as the ground of citizenship tends to preclude active participation in the business of rule. Instead, it leads to the replacement of that civic ideal with a more passive sense of entitlement to benefits which seem to derive from remote sources. Far from renewing citizenship, violence and passivity further erode its foundations.

As such erosion spreads, it threatens the very notion of a shared community and culture as the basis of citizenship. The extension of the shared beyond the local and the homogeneous is, of course, an essential part of citizenship's revolutionary and democratic promise. This extension of citizenship is corrosive of other notions of the shared precisely because its concept of allegiance is, ultimately, volitional and consensual rather than natural. Yet, one would be hard-pressed to find a major urban population today which felt compelled, except in extraordinary moments like war, by "a direct sense of community membership based on loyalty to a civilization which is a common possession," to use a phrase from T. H. Marshall's classic study of citizenship (1977[1949]:94). The exhaustion of this sense over the half century forces us to reconsider not only the national basis of citizenship but also its democratic ideals of commonwealth, participation, and equality.

The project of national citizenship depends less on the idea of the nation as a neutral framework for competing interests than on that of the nation as a community of shared purposes and commensurable citizens. Its working assumption is that this national community is committed to constituting a common good and to shaping a common life well-suited to the conditions of modernity. This notion requires a set of self-understandings on the part of citizens which lies at the core of the liberal compact of citizenship: it requires that people perceive, through a kind of leap of faith, that they are sufficiently similar to form common purpose. This perception is sustained in the long run through performances of citizenship. These determine, first, that there are meaningful common goods; second, that active participation rather than mere reception or inheritance establishes the fundamental claim to goods; and, third, that those who participate have equal – or at least fairly adjusted – rights regardless of other differences. This liberal compact is now under tremendous strain. With the unprecedented growth of economic and social inequalities during the last few decades in so many nations, the differences between residents have become too gross and the areas of commonality too few to sustain this compact. As a result, the social imaginary of a nation of commensurable citizens disintegrates. And the performances which sustain it fail. In the breach, the idea of a shared culture seems implausible.

One could argue that where liberalism encounters this failure – at different times in different places – its response has been to replace the teleological notion of common good and measure with the priority of right over good. In this more modern version, the nation of citizens is based not on constitutive ends but on procedural means of justice that ensure that no particular end (a vision of the good life) "trumps" any other, to use Dworkin's famous image.[2] Deriving from Kant, this liberal ethic asserts principles of justice that do not presuppose or promote any substantive conception of the good. Rather, they are supposed to enable citizens to pursue their own ends consistent with a similar liberty for all. In elevating the priority of right to a supreme value, it opposes the regulation of society in terms of utilitarian ends or communist needs that ultimately may sacrifice individual rights for the sake of the general welfare.

If this version of liberalism has triumphed globally in twentieth-century models of democracy and citizenship, it has also come under powerful attack. Critics across many spectrums – from Left to Right, from Islamic to American Fundamentalism, from Aztlan to Common Cause – argue that it relies in theory and practice on a notion of shared allegiance that it officially rejects. This notion derives from the argument that without prior formative attachments and commitments to family, culture, ethnicity, religion, and the like, people cannot achieve the very sense of moral depth and personhood that the liberal compact requires. However, it is precisely these kinds of prior affiliations that liberal citizenship refuses. Hence, liberalism in reality gives the lie to its official values; and yet, in insisting on them, it undermines the sense of community on which it actually depends. In effect, procedural liberalism leaves citizens more entangled in obligations they do not choose and less attached to common identifications that would render these obligations not just bearable but even virtuous. Thus, it produces citizens who are predominantly passive in their citizenship. They are, for the most part, spectators who vote. Yet, without active participation in the business of rule, they are citizens whose citizenship is managed, for better or worse, by an unelected bureaucracy.

Among the most vocal critics of liberal citizenship in this sense are groups organized around specific identities – the kind of prior differences liberalism relegates to the private sphere – which affirm the importance of these identities in the public calculus of citizenship. That is, they affirm the right to difference as an integral part of the foundation of citizenship. Feminism launched this critique by arguing that liberalism depends in fact on an ideology of difference because its supposedly universal citizen is, historically, of a particular type, namely, a white, European, propertied, male.[3] The ideology of universal equality arises because members of this referent group have never had to assert their difference, but only their equality, to claim citizenship. From the perspective of the rest who are excluded, this assertion looks like one of difference, not equality. In any case, it will not work for those not already equal in these terms. Hence, for the excluded, the political question is to change the terms. Therefore, the politics of difference becomes more important and potentially incompatible with that of universal equality as the real basis for citizenship.[4] [...]

[Many] distinguishing identities have given focus to organized groups who challenge established, difference-neutral conceptions of citizenship. These include national and cultural minorities, sexual-orientation groups, and racial, religious, and ethnic organizations.[5] They demand different treatment on the basis of their inalienable right to retain and realize their unique qualities, contributions, and histories. Their core argument usually entails the claim they have been denied respect and opportunity because they are different. That difference in fact constitutes their authentic and original character, which they have every right to develop to full capacity. Thus, they demand citizenship rights as persons who have authentic needs and interests which must be met if they are to live fully human lives. [...] Although this kind of demand would seem contradictory and incompatible with citizenship as an ideology of equality, there is nevertheless a growing sense that it is changing the meaning of equality itself. What it objects to is the equation that equality means sameness. It rejects citizenship as a homogenizing identity with the charge that homogenization reduces and impoverishes. Rather, it would take equality to mean equal opportunity. Thus, it would define citizenship on the basis of rights to different treatment with equal opportunity.

Identity politics of this sort is having a major impact because the identities of difference are competing more successfully for people's time and passion than the tired identity of formal, national citizenship. Without doubt, this impact is divisive. Identity politics tends to disrupt established ideologies of civic unity and moral solidarity in ways which often make people angry and anxious. For example, the politics of difference challenges the basic premise of liberal citizenship that the principles of justice impose negative restrictions on the kinds of goods individuals can pursue. Hence, when Muslim women in France demand the right to use the veil in public schools, or American Fundamentalists to include creationism in the curriculum, they contest that priority and the plural public sphere it supposedly creates. By demanding the right to pursue their definitions of the good and proper life in the public sphere, they challenge the liberal democratic conviction that the *res publica* should articulate all interests according to conditions which subscribe to none in particular. Precisely because their demands are opposed, they show that Western liberal republics neither achieve nor in fact subscribe to such a procedurally neutral articulation. Thus, they debunk a fundamental premise of liberal ideology. The politics of difference has become so intense precisely because it suggests a basic change in the historical role of citizenship: it indicates the increasing disarticulation of formal citizenship as the principal norm for coordinating and managing the simultaneity of modern social identities in highly differentiated societies. In that suggestion, it ignites deep anxieties about what form such coordination might take, both juridically and symbolically, if citizenship no longer has that primary role.

As nowhere else, the world's major cities make manifest these reconstitutions of citizenship. The compaction and reterritorialization of so many different kinds of groups within them grind away at citizenship's assumptions. They compel it to bend to the recognition that contemporary urban life comprises multiple and diverse cultural identities, modes of life, and forms of appropriating urban space (Hannerz 1992; Holston 1995). Immigration is a central link between classical issues of citizenship – imaged as a right-bearing form of membership in the territorial nation-state – and the city as this dense and heterogeneous lived space. Immigrants typically congregate and work in cities because the demands for their labor tend to be generated by urban commerce, infrastructure, and wage-differentiation. Moreover, immigrants tend to rely on previous networks of knowledge and affiliation for jobs and basic amenities. Thus, the politics of immigration is closely tied to the politics of cities, and the violence surrounding immigration is intimately connected with urban youth, gangs, slums, and politics. In the recent hunt for Islamic terrorists in the subways of Paris, or the recent expulsion of Bangladeshi immigrants from Bombay (which also involved the deportation of many Indian Muslims by "accident"), we see that in cities the politics of quality (in particular of difference) meets the politics of quantity (and of the anxieties of density). Immigration politics cannot be abstractly conducted evenly across all national space. It tends to be implosive (Appadurai [1996]), and its most intense points of implosion are cities.

Because of this volatile complexity, cities are especially sensitive to the peregrinations of capital and labor. When these produce sharp increases in socio-economic inequality, they affect citizenship profoundly because they provoke new notions of membership, solidarity, and alienage. That is, they generate new morphologies of social category and class which interact not only to shift sociabilities and cultures but also to transform the legal regimes of state and local community in keeping with these displacements. The politics of immigration largely concerns these shifting interactions between culture and law. Especially in the developing world, this dynamic of change seems extraordinary today because many cities are undergoing two kinds of localizations of capital and labor simultaneously. First, most cities are still in the grip of nationally oriented processes of industrialization, with corresponding commercial, financial, and bureaucratic consequences. Second, some cities have become, often at the same time, strategic and specialized sites for the operations of more globally oriented capital and labor.

In the first case, the great turmoil of citizenship in cities derives in large measure from new concentrations of wealth and misery among nationals related to industrialization. Where the shanties of migrants sprout next to the mansions, factories, and skyscrapers of industrial-state capitalism, new kinds of citizens engage each other in struggles over the nature of belonging to the national society. Such struggles are particularly evident in the social movements of the urban poor for rights to the city. They are especially associated with the emergence of democracy because they empower poor citizens to mobilize around the redistributive right-claims of citizenship.[6] These movements are new not only because they force the state to respond to new social conditions of the working poor – in which sense they are, indeed, one of the significant consequences of massive urban poverty for citizenship. They are also unprecedented in many cases because they create new kinds of rights outside of the normative and institutional definitions of the state and its legal codes. These rights generally address the new collective and personal spaces of the modern metropolis, especially its impoverished residential neighborhoods. They affirm access to housing, property, sanitation, health services, education, child care, and so forth on the basis of citizenship. In this assertion, they expand the scope and understanding of entitlement. Is adequate housing a right? Is employment? In this sense, the development of the economy itself fuels the growth of citizenship as new areas of social and economic life are brought under the calculus of right.

This expansion amounts to more than multiplying the number and beneficiaries of socio-economic rights, itself no small achievement. In addition, it changes the very conception of right and citizenship. Right becomes more of a claim upon than a possession held against the world. It becomes a claim upon society for the resources necessary to meet the basic needs and interests of members rather than a kind of property some possess and others do not. It is probably the case that this change applies mostly to socio-economic and political rights rather than to civil rights. In the emerging democracies of the developing world, the latter tend to remain decidedly underdeveloped. But in terms of rights to the city and rights to political participation, right becomes conceived as an aspect of social relatedness rather than as an inherent and natural property of individuals. This sort of claim is often based on the deeply felt capacity of new urban workers to contribute morally and politically to the public sphere because they do so economically. That is, even though poor, even if illegal squatters, they have rights because they are consumers and taxpayers. Moreover, in the development of this mode of reasoning, it is also possible to discern the beginnings of a more radical argument: people have rights to a minimum standard of living which does not depend on their relative economic or market worth but on their absolute rights as citizens to a measure of economic well-being and dignity. Potentially, this argument is radically redistributive of a society's wealth because it breaks down entrenched, elite-based explanations for relative worth and inequality.

Furthermore, as mobilizations for these rights are organized in relation to new conditions of work and residence, and concern people for the most part previously excluded from the resources of the state, they come to be based on specific claims which are generally not defined in existing constitutions or legal codes. Where there are urban housing problems on a massive scale, for example, movements arise which claim that property must fulfill a social function or risk expropriation and redistribution. This claim relativizes the traditionally positivist and absolute right to property. In many cases, such unprecedented claims are so strong that they succeed in producing new legal regimes in the form of new constitutional principles, and new legal codes in the form of new constitutions, as well as revising legal codes, and reforming judiciaries [...]. In terms of the last, they force isolated judiciaries to confront social and legal contradictions. They create new services which permit broader access to justice, especially in civil law. [...] Moreover, although such changes may be legislated from the top down, they often result from popular participation in constitutional congresses. In turn, they mobilize people into helping to frame legislation and government reform at the local level. In sum, as the social movements of the urban poor create unprecedented claims on and to the city, they expand citizenship to new social bases. In so doing, they create new sources of citizenship rights and corresponding forms of self-rule.

Many of these same cities around the world are now also sites of a second and more encompassing localization of capital and labor. Even as they undergo national industrialization, they have become strategic arenas in which global capital structures its operations, for these too require place (Appadurai 1990; Sassen 1991). The accompanying transnationalization of labor includes both highly skilled and unskilled immigrants: it produces a new set of class fractions in the city of high-income capital managers and the low-income manual and service workers who attend them. Increasingly, managers see the workers as marginal "others." Although this transnationalization generates its own forms of politics, these fractions are less likely to engage in struggles over the form and substance of national citizenship. Rather, they are more likely to produce new forms of overlapping citizenships and multiple jurisdictions for several reasons.

First, transnationalization initiates a new dynamic of inequality which significantly reduces the possibility of common allegiances and civilities, even of a mythological sort, between capital managers and others. Although they may both work in the transnational economy, their life-worlds are too different. Each world tends to its own promotion, delegitimizing if not criminalizing the other. Second, as mostly non- or postnationals (Appadurai 1993), neither feels much loyalty to the place in which they are perhaps only temporary transplants. They need state government for their economic activity. But they have reduced moral and personal commitments to it. Instead, they are likely to retain primary loyalty – at least in cultural terms – to diasporic identities. Third, transnationalization generates a new global network of cities through which capital and labor pass. The fluidity of this network causes nation-states to modify their organizational, and especially legal, structure to attract global resources. In particular, they change the legal regulation of borders and modes of association because it is through these that global capital and labor must flow. Also vulnerable are laws of monopoly over national resources. In addition, labor codes frequently suffer rewriting to meet the exigencies of international capital and its local partners. Thus, to mediate between national sovereignty and global economic interests, nation-states tend not only to produce new legal regimes but also to accept the legal authority of transnational regulatory bodies (e.g., of trade and banking) within their borders.

This new legal cocktail tends to give special privileges to the managers of global capital, in the sense that it absolves them from local duties and makes them immune to local legal powers. However, it tends to disempower labor. In part this is because it renders significant segments of the transnational low-income labor force illegal by using the system of national boundaries to criminalize the immigrants it attracts for low-wage work. Even though immigrant manual and service workers contribute substantially to the local community – and thereby should earn at least partial standing according to the modern calculus of citizenship – the local does not reciprocate by offering membership.[7] Rather, it tends to exploit the illegal status of workers, using the threat of deportation to keep wages low and workers from organizing. But since what brings these new class fractions together, the international market, has its own rules and networks which contradict national boundaries, both rich and poor immigrants also successfully evade state control to a significant degree. Therefore, even as their translocation to the city generates new legal regimes, it also propagates new and diverse forms of illegality. This unstable mix of the legal and the illegal, and of various forms of each, turns the city into a honeycomb of jurisdictions in which there are in effect as many kinds of citizens as there are kinds of law. Such multiplicity delegitimates the national justice system and its framework of uniform law, both hallmarks of national citizenship. Although, as we have seen, this urban multiplicity can spawn new and more democratic forms of citizenship, it also suggests the emergence of an almost medieval body of overlapping, heterogeneous, nonuniform, and increasingly private memberships.

To the extent that we have theories of citizenship that link these factors of globalization, economic change, immigration, and cities, they tend to focus either on the labor/immigration nexus or on the narrative of the erosion of Fordist ideas about industrial production. Yet, to deal with the range of cities in which dramas of citizenship are today played out, we need a broader image of urban processes that breaks out of the constraints of the Fordist (and post-Fordist) narrative. The histories of many cities in Africa, Asia, and Latin America have little to do with industry, manufacture, or production. Some of these cities are fundamentally commercial and financial, others are military and bureaucratic, and yet others are monumental and recreative of nationalist historiographies. This variety of cities generates a variety of dramas of citizenship, and in each of them the relationship between production, finance, labor, and service is somewhat different. We need more images and narratives of urban economies so that we can better identify the various ways in which such cities spawn class fragments, ethnic enclaves, gang territories, and varied maps of work, crime, and kinship. [...]

If the city is a special site for such formations and reformations of citizens, it can also be a special war zone, a space in which these processes find expression in collective violence. The city has always been a site of violent social and cultural confrontation. But in the contemporary world, the density of new social formations and the superimposition of diverse cultural identifications produce a corresponding complexity of violence: urban terrorism from the extreme right and left, racist attacks, Islamic bombings, gang shootings, death squads, riots, vandalism, human rights abuses, vigilante lynchings, political assassinations, kidnappings, police shootings, high-tech security harassments, private justice making, civil disobedience, shantytown eradication, and soccer hooliganism suggest the enormous range of contemporary forms of collective violence. How are these related to conflicts of citizenship and in what way is the violence of citizenship city-specific?

As we have suggested [...], citizenship concerns more than rights to participate in politics. It also includes other kinds of rights in the public sphere, namely, civil, socio-economic, and cultural. Moreover, in addition to the legal, it concerns the moral and performative dimensions of membership which define the meanings and practices of belonging in society. Undeniably, people use violence to make claims about all of these dimensions of belonging. In this sense, violence is a specific type of social action. Moreover, different social processes have their stock expressions of violence. This is not to say that industrialization features one repertoire of violence and globalization another. It is rather to suggest [...] that social processes instigate their own forms of violence in a given social and historical context, the meanings of which consolidate around specific problems, for example, of cultural identity, labor, or residence.

Thus, it is possible to observe that in many countries today democratization brings its own forms of violence. Moreover, as democratization is always a disjunctive process, in which citizenship rights expand and erode in complex arhythmic ways [...], it is possible to discern the effects of disjunction on the forms of violence. As discussed earlier, many transitions to democracy included a sustained expansion of political and socio-economic rights for the urban poor. Strikes which are violently repressed and turn into riots, land invasions and expulsions, destruction of public transportation, and political assassinations typically express the conflicts of this expansion. But even where the political and socio-economic components of citizenship are relatively consolidated in these transitions to democracy, the civil component which guarantees liberty, security, and above all justice is often inchoate and ineffectual. This disjunction is common to many countries undergoing democratization today. Where it happens, the majority cannot expect the institutions of state – the courts and the police especially – to respect or guarantee their individual rights, arbitrate their conflicts justly, or control violence legally. In this situation, violence takes a well-known course (Caldeira [2000]). There is a broad criminalization of the poor at the same time that social groups at all levels come to support the privatization of security and the extralegalization of justice as the only effective means to deal with "marginals." In other words, there is massive support for market forms of justice on the one hand (private security, vigilantes, enforcers) and, on the other, for extralegal and even illegal measures of control by state institutions, particularly the police (and related death squads) who kill large numbers of "marginals." This kind of violence further discredits the justice system and with it the entire project of democracy and its citizenship.

If there are, therefore, certain forms and meanings of violence associated with citizenship conflicts, how might they be specific to the city? To suggest such specificity is not to reduce violence to an overdetermining urban pathology. Nor is it to consider the city as a mere spatial metaphor of social relations. As we have argued throughout, the city is more important to the conflicts of belonging than these options indicate. Rather, we might say that the city both provides a map of violence and establishes its features. In this geography of violence, the city can be pretext and context, form and substance, stage and script. Of course, a great deal of collective violence has always been identity-based in ways which do not coincide with the administrative areas of city or nation – think of religious wars, anti-Semitism, the European witchcraze. Surely, violence is not city-bound. But coincidence does not have to be absolute or exclusive to establish correspondence. The point is that people use violence to make claims upon the city and use the city to make violent claims. They appropriate a space to which they then declare they belong; they violate a space which others claim. Such acts generate a city-specific violence of citizenship. Its geography is too legible, too visible to be missed in the abandoned public spaces of the modern city, in its fortified residential enclaves, its division into corporate luxury zones and quarantined war zones, its forbidden sectors of gangs and "armed response" security, its bunkers of fundamentalists, its illegally constructed shanties, its endless neighborhoods of unemployed youth.

With the breakdown of civility and nationality thus evident, many are seeking alternatives in the post-, trans-, de-, re-, (and plain con) of current speculations about the future of the nation-state. It is a heady moment, full of great creativity and uncertainty. Many proposals are circulating for new kinds of public spheres, third spaces, virtual communities, transnations, and diasporic networks. The results are surely contradictory. It may be that cybercitizenship draws some into a more tolerant and accessible public realm. But it also seems to drive others further into the recesses of the private and the market. The failure of nation-states to produce convincing fantasies of the commensurability of its citizens ("The People") compels some to imagine recombinant forms of nonterritorial, life-world sovereignties, while it forces others into even more primordial and violent affiliations of territory, religion, and race. The grand theories that were once used to explain pushes and pulls of such magnitude have themselves splintered, in keeping with the nations which gave them sustenance. Contemporary theory seems as displaced and dislocated, as hybrid and diasporic, as so many of the world's populations.

In all of this commotion, it is perhaps understandable to treat the city, that old form of human society, as irrelevant. But until transnations attain more flesh and bone, cities may still be the most important sites in which we experience the crises of national membership and through which we may rethink citizenship. It may even be, after all, that there is something irreducible and nontransferable, necessary but not quite sufficient, about the city's public street and square for the realization of a meaningfully democratic citizenship. If we support the latter, we may have to do much more to defend the former.

NOTES

1 Examples of these exclusionary movements include, respectively: California's Proposition 187, which passed overwhelmingly in 1994; French-only legislation in Quebec; urban incorporations in Los Angeles (Davis 1990) and closed condominiums in São Paulo (Caldeira [2000]); the bombing of the Oklahoma Federal Building; and recent opinions by Supreme Court Justice Clarence Thomas.
2 On this version of liberalism, several of the important discussions are Berlin 1969, Dworkin 1977, Sandel 1982, Rawls 1988, and Walzer 1983.
3 Feminist studies of citizenship include Pateman 1989, Dietz 1992, and Okin 1992.
4 For opposing views on this question of difference and equality, see Schlesinger 1992 and Scott 1992.
5 For examples, see Anzaldúa 1987, Kallen 1924, Ferguson et al. 1990, and Warner 1993.
6 For examples from Brazil, see Alvarez 1993, Caldeira 1986, and Holston 1989.
7 On immigration and the politics of citizenship, see Brubaker 1989.

LITERATURE CITED

Alvarez, Sonia E. 1993. "'Deepening' Democracy: Popular Movement Networks, Constitutional Reform, and Radical Urban Regimes in Contemporary Brazil." In *Mobilizing the Community: Local Politics in the Era of the Global City*, Robert Fisher and Joseph Kling, eds. Newbury Park: Sage Publications, 191–219.

Anzaldúa, Gloria. 1987. *Borderlands/La Frontera: The New Mestiza*. San Francisco: [Aunt Lute Books].

Appadurai, Arjun. 1990. "Disjuncture and Difference in the Global Cultural Economy." *Public Culture* 2(2): 1–24.

——. 1993. "Patriotism and Its Futures." *Public Culture* 5(3): 411–429.

——. [1996] *Modernity at Large: Cultural Dimensions of Globalization*. Minneapolis: University of Minnesota Press.

Berlin, Isaiah. 1969. *Four Essays on Liberty*. Oxford: Oxford University Press.

Brubaker, William Rogers, ed. 1989. *Immigration and the Politics of Citizenship in Europe and North America*. Lanham, Maryland: University Press of America.

Caldeira, Teresa Pires do Rio. 1986. "Electoral Struggles in a Neighborhood on the Periphery of São Paulo." *Politics and Society* 15(1): 43–66.

——. [2000] *City of Walls: Crime, Segregation, and Citizenship in São Paulo*. Berkeley: University of California Press.

Davis, Mike. 1990. *City of Quartz: Excavating the Future in Los Angeles*. New York: Vintage.

Dietz, Mary. 1992. "Context Is All: Feminism and Theories of Citizenship." In *Dimensions of Radical Democracy: Pluralism, Citizenship, Community*, Chantal Mouffe, ed. London: Verso, 63–85.

Dworkin, Ronald. 1977. *Taking Rights Seriously*. Cambridge: Harvard University Press.

Eisenstein, Zillah R. 1988. *The Female Body and the Law*. Berkeley: University of California Press.

Ferguson, Russell, Martha Gever, Trinh T. Minh-ha, and Cornel West, eds. 1990. *Out There: Marginalization and Contemporary Cultures*. Cambridge: MIT Press.

Hannerz, Ulf. 1992. *Cultural Complexity: Studies in the Social Organization of Meaning*. New York: Columbia University Press.

Holston, James. 1989. *The Modernist City: An Anthropological Critique of Brasília*. Chicago: University of Chicago Press.

——. 1995. "Spaces of Insurgent Citizenship." *Planning Theory* 13: 35–51.

[. . .]

Kallen, Horace M. 1924. *Culture and Democracy in the United States*. New York: Boni and Liveright.

Marshall, T. H. 1977. [1949]. "Citizenship and Social Class." In *Class, Citizenship, and Social Development*. Chicago: University of Chicago Press, 71–134.

Okin, Susan Moller. 1992. "Women, Equality, and Citizenship." *Queens's Quarterly* 99(1): 56–71.

Pateman, Carole. 1989. *The Disorder of Women*. Stanford: Stanford University Press.

Rawls, John. 1988. "The Priority of Right and the Ideas of the Good." *Philosophy and Public Affairs* 17: 151–176.

Sandel, Michael. 1982. *Liberalism and the Limits of Justice*. Cambridge: Cambridge University Press.

Sassen, Saskia. 1991. *The Global City: New York, London, Tokyo*. Princeton: Princeton University Press.

Schlesinger, Arthur. 1992. *The Disuniting of America*. New York: W. W. Norton.

Schuck, Peter H. 1989. "Membership in the Liberal Polity: The Devaluation of American Citizenship." In *Immigration and the Politics of Citizenship in North America*, William Brubaker, ed. Lanham, Maryland: University Press of America, 51–65.

Scott, Joan W. 1992. "Multiculturalism and the Politics of Identity." *October* 61: 12–19.

Taylor, Charles. 1992. "Multiculturalism and the Politics of Recognition." In *Multiculturalism and the Politics of Recognition*, Charles Taylor, edited with commentary by Amy Gutmann. Princeton: Princeton University Press, 3–73.

Walzer, Michael. 1983. *Spheres of Justice: A Defence of Pluralism and Equality*. New York: Basic Books.

Warner, Michael, ed. 1993. *Fear of a Queer Planet*. Minneapolis: University of Minnesota Press.

17

Citizenship, Territoriality and the Gendered Construction of Difference

Nira Yuval-Davis

What is citizenship? In the many articles written in the British press about Princess Diana's death and the radical changes as a result of public pressure which followed it in the behaviour of the royal family, one sentence kept on being repeated as an explanation of the change – 'the people behaved as citizens and not as subjects'. This concept of citizenship has very little to do with the right to vote or even to carry a passport of a specific state. It has to do instead with people's sense that they are members of a specific community and polity, and have a say in what the leaders of that community do and say. The French word *citoyen*, which emerged so powerfully after the French Revolution, has tended to express that meaning of citizenship most commonly.

In the ideology of the French Revolution and in the majority of literature on citizenship in political theory, either liberal or social democrat, the notion of citizenship is bound to that of the 'nation-state', as the state is the collective expression of the 'will of the people'. There is an automatic assumption that the boundaries of 'the people', 'the nation' or 'civil society' overlap the boundaries of the state. In the political reality at the beginning of the twenty-first century this is not true in the case of virtually all states, if it was ever true before. T. H. Marshall, the most important British theoretician on citizenship and the welfare state (1950; 1975; 1981), has defined citizenship as 'a full membership in the community' including rights and responsibilities. While Marshall did identify 'the community' with the 'nation-state', this definition can also be useful when we recognize that these days people are usually members in more than one community and polity – local, ethnic, national, state and cross/supra-state.

Elsewhere (Yuval-Davis, 1991; 1997; 1999) I have developed the notion of 'the multi-layered citizen', which follows such a recognition. Very often people's rights and obligations to a specific state are mediated and largely dependent on their membership of a specific ethnic, racial, religious or regional collectivity, although very rarely are they completely contained by it. At the same time, the development of ideologies and institutions of 'human rights' means that, ideologically at least, the state does not always have full control of the construction of citizenship's rights, although usually it is left for states to carry them out. It is important to remember that in this respect people are not positioned equally within their collectivities and states, collectivities are not positioned equally within the state and internationally, and states are not positioned equally with other states. However, citizenship is not just a question of being or not being a member in communities. Different social attributes would construct the specific positioning of people within and across the communities in certain social categories. The liberal/communitarian debate notwithstanding (Avineri and De Shalit, 1992; Daly, 1993; Mouffe, 1993), what follows is that citizenship cannot be analysed as either a completely individual or a collective phenomenon.

This chapter examines the territorial/spatial nature of contemporary citizenships and how these relate to ethnic/national collectivities, global cities and the construction of difference. In exploring these relationships the chapter explores the roles of women as symbols of collectivities, as symbolic border guards and as the bearers of 'the private' domain.

States, Nations and Territoriality

The state can be defined as 'a body of institutions which are centrally organized around the intentionality of control with a given apparatus of enforcement (juridical and repressive) at its command and basis' (Anthias and Yuval-Davis, 1989, p. 5). The reason we included the word 'intentionality' is that, although states claim to be the only legitimate power in control, very often this intention is not realized because smaller or larger parts of the state's territory include other polities which do not accept partially or wholly the legitimacy of the authority of the state (Joseph, 1993). In many Third World countries the state's penetration of its periphery would be partial at best, and although to a certain extent modern means of transportation and communication have increased central control, and there are probably no more *totally* isolated communities in the world (Lowenhaupt Tsing, 1993), there *are* communities in jungles or in the mountains organized by traditional tribes which have not been incorporated into the civil society of the state. Such territories may also be controlled by revolutionary guerillas attempting to establish a competitive social and political order in the state and/or drug barons.

However, communities which are not governed by the state do not necessarily have to be territorially remote. There are many cases of warlords in shanty towns or religious and other cults who are to a greater or lesser extent able to establish an alternative social and political order to that of the state, without the latter being able or willing to challenge them. Sometimes it is even desirable to those who control the state that there are enclaves within the state's territory which are to some extent outside their direct control: examples include the Bantustans in South Africa under apartheid, and the West Bank supposedly under the control of the Palestinian National Autonomy, where more than 70 per cent of the land belongs to the Israeli government.

In many other cases, a more or less centralized regional or federal regime does exist and central and local government share in the control of the territory. And in many other cases, as remnants of older political orders in the post-colonial, postwar world, as well as part of the new world order, one or more superpowers and/or UN forces have extra-territorial rights to use territory as military bases for their own strategic goals, as buffers between warring polities, and as facilities for the work of international agencies (Enloe, 1993).

If states do not always control their own territories, the relationships between nations and states is even more complicated. Gellner has defined nationalism as a 'theory of political legitimacy which requires that ethnic boundaries should not cut across political ones, and in particular, that ethnic boundaries within a given state ... should not separate the power holders from the rest ... and therefore state and culture must now be linked' (Gellner, 1983, pp. 1, 36).

Today there is virtually nowhere in the world in which such a 'pure' nation-state exists, if it ever did, and therefore there are always settled residents (and usually citizens as well) who are not members of the dominant national collectivity in the society. The fact that this automatic assumption about the overlap between the boundaries of the state citizens and 'the nation' still exists is one expression of the naturalizing effect of the hegemony of one collectivity and its access to the ideological apparatuses of both state and civil society. This constructs minorities into assumed deviants from the 'normal', and excludes them from important power resources. This, in turn, has crucial implications for the relations to space and territory of minorities as well as to states, and will be discussed again later on in this chapter.

Both ethnic and national collectivities are constructed around boundaries which separate the world into 'us' and 'them'. As such, both are the Andersonian 'imagined communities' (Anderson, 1983). Depending on the objectives of different ethnic and national projects involving members of the same collectivity, or people outside it, the boundary lines of these collectivities can be drawn in very different ways. One example, of course, is the debate over whether the English and the Scots or the 'Anglo' and the 'Francophone' Canadians are/ should be members of the same nation. Another is the difference between the Jewish Bund which saw itself as the national liberation movement of the Jews – but related only to the Jews of Eastern Europe – and the Zionist movement who included (in principle) in the boundaries of its imagined community Jews from all over the world.

What is specific to the nationalist project and discourse is the aim of a separate political representation for the collective. This often – but not always – takes the form of a claim for a separate state and/or territory, although some states are based on bi- or multinational principles (for example, Lebanon or Belgium) and some supra-state political projects like the European Union can, at specific historical moments, develop more state-like characteristics. Nationalist demands can also be aimed at establishing a regional autonomy rather than a separate state – such as in the case of Wales or Catalonia – or they can be irredentist, advocating joining a neighbouring state rather than establishing one of their own – such as the republican movement in Northern Ireland or the Kashmiri movement for unification with Pakistan. Although state and territory have been closely bound together, there have been cases of nationalist movements which called for the state to be established in a different territory than that in which they were active. Both the Jewish Zionist movement (which established the state of Israel) and the Black Zionist movement (which established Liberia) called for the mass emigration of their members from the countries in which they lived. Others have not articulated any specific territorial boundaries for their national independence. It is the demand for political sovereignty which separates the 'Black Nation' from other 'Black community' activists, and which separates those who call for the 'Khalipha', the global nation of Islam, from other committed Muslims. The Austrian Marxist Otto Bauer (Bauer, 1940; Nimni, 1991; Yuval-Davis, 1987a) called for the separation of nationalism and the state as the only viable solution to the hopeless mix of collectivities in the territories which constituted the Austro-Hungarian empire, and this might be the only viable long-term alternative to 'ethnic cleansing' in contemporary ethnic fundamentalist movements that have emerged with the fall of the Soviet empire and in many other places in the post-colonial world (for example, in Rwanda).

The separation of nationality and the state also takes other forms. In many parts of the world there exist immigrant communities which are culturally and politically committed to continue to 'belong' to their 'mother country' – or more specifically to the national collectivity from which they, their parents or their foreparents, have come. The rise of these 'committed diasporas' has been co-determined by several factors. First, technological advances in means of international travel and in media and communication have made the preservation of links with the 'homeland' much easier, just as they have made inter-generational cultural and linguistic reproduction easier. 'Ethnic videos', for example, is one of the largest video markets and is aimed at people who have very little or no access to the mass media of the countries where they live. Cable systems or satellite dishes have enabled, for many, direct access to their own national and ethnic media, as well as established new defused ethnic collectivities (for example, of an international South-Asian community).

At the same time, as a result of certain successes of the anti-racist and civil rights movements, there has been a certain shift in national ideologies in many western countries, and multiculturalism has, until recently, become an hegemonic ideology which, with all its problems, has somewhat eased the pressures on immigrants to assimilate. This has been aided by the fact that in the post-colonial world there are many ongoing nationalist struggles in which different collectivities compete not just for access to their states' powers and resources, but also over the constitutive nature of their states. One cannot imagine the continued nationalist struggles of the IRA, for instance, without the financial, political and other help of the Irish diaspora communities, especially in the USA. In the case of the Jewish diaspora – the oldest 'established' diaspora – the hegemony of Zionism has meant that many have transformed Israel into a 'post-factum homeland' even if they have never been, let alone lived, there, and international Jewish support has played a crucial role in the establishment and development of Israel (Yuval-Davis, 1987b). As Anderson has commented (1983), not enough recognition is given to the role of diaspora communities in contemporary nationalist struggles, although recently Robin Cohen (1997), for instance, has started to carry out such research.

However, the connections between diasporas and homelands or between associated diasporas do not solely depend on means of communication and political and economic assistance. The exchange of brides, which Levi-Strauss has seen as the basic cement of social cohesion (1969), is one of the major ways in which the close connections and the management of inclusionary relations within the imagined national community continue to operate between diasporas and homelands. This points to the important roles gender relations play in the construction of ideological and emotional attachments between territories, states and nations.

Women as Embodiments and Border Guards of 'the Nation'

The mythical unity of national 'imagined communities' which divides the world between 'us' and 'them' is maintained and ideologically reproduced by a whole system of what Armstrong (1982) calls symbolic 'border guards'. These 'border guards' can identify people as members or non-members of a specific collectivity. They are closely linked to specific cultural codes of style of dress and behaviour, as well as to more elaborate bodies of customs, religion, literary and artistic modes of production, and, of course, language. Because of the central importance of social reproduction to culture, gender relations often come to be seen as constituting the 'essence' of cultures as ways of life to be passed from generation to generation. The construction of 'home' is of particular importance here, including relations between adults and between adults and children in the family, ways of cooking and eating, domestic labour, play and bedtime stories, etc. Constructions of manhood and womanhood, as well as sexuality and gendered relations of power, need to be explored in relation to these processes (Yuval-Davis, 1997).

A figure of a woman, often a mother, symbolizes in many cultures the spirit of the collectivity, whether it is Mother Russia, Mother Ireland or Mother India. In the French Revolution its symbol was *La Patrie*, a figure of a woman giving birth to a baby, and in Cyprus a crying woman refugee on roadside posters was the embodiment of the pain and anger of the Greek-Cypriot collectivity after the Turkish invasion. In peasant societies, the dependence of the people on the fertility of 'Mother Earth' has no doubt contributed to this close association between collective territory, collective identity and womanhood. However, women also symbolize the collectivity in other ways. As Cynthia Enloe (1990) has pointed out, it is supposedly for the sake of the 'womenandchildren' that men go to war. Women are associated in the collective imagination with children and therefore with the collective, as well as the familial, future. But this does not only happen during wars. For instance, in the riots which flared among Muslim youth in Bradford, during the mid-1990s, one of the participants clarified the motivation behind their actions to the *Guardian* reporter: 'It's not about prostitution or unemployment or about all that nonsense of the Chief Constable. It's about the way two police officers treated one of *our* women' (Travis, *The Guardian*, 18 June 1995).

The 'burden of representation' on women for the collectivity's identity and future destiny has also brought about the construction of women as the bearers of the collectivity's honour. Manar Hasan (1994) describes how many Palestinian women have been murdered by their male relatives because in their behaviour they brought 'shame' on their families and community. Women, in their 'proper' behaviour, their 'proper' clothing, embody the line which signifies the collectivity's boundaries. Other women in many other societies have also been tortured or murdered by their relatives because of adultery, flight from home, and other cultural breaches of conduct which are perceived as bringing dishonour and shame on their male relatives and community (see Chhachhi, 1991; Rozario, 1991). A weaker version of retaliation against women who betrayed the collective honour was the mass shaving of women's heads in different European countries after the Second World War. These women were accused of befriending the occupying Nazi armies during the occupation (Warring, 1996). The flip-side of this is the use of systematic rape during war as a way of shaming the collective enemy. It is not incidental that, until the success of the feminist campaign in the 1994 UN conference on human rights, the Geneva Convention would not consider rape a war crime or a mode of torture [but a] 'crime against honour' – the honour not being that of the woman alone (Pettman, 1996; Zajovic, 1994).

The centrality of women in nationalist discourse is even more apparent when we examine their roles in national liberation struggles both pro- and anti-modernist. 'Women's emancipation' or 'women following tradition' (as has been expressed in various campaigns for and against women's veiling, voting, education, military service and employment) has been at the centre of most modernist and anti-modernist nationalist struggles.

Chatterjee (1986) observed that cultural decolonization has anticipated and paved the way for political decolonization – the major rupture which marked the twentieth century. This process involved not so much going back to some mythical golden age in the national past but rather a growing sense of empowerment, a development of a national trajectory of freedom and independence. A central theme in this process of cultural decolonization has been the redefinition and reconstruction of sexuality and gender relations. Franz Fanon (1952) encapsulated it for the black man [as 'reclaiming] his manhood'. As Ashis Nandy (1983) has argued, the colonial man has been constructed as effeminate in the colonial discourse, and the way to emancipation and empowerment is seen as the negation of this assertion. In many cultural systems, potency and masculinity seem to be synonymous. Such a perspective has not only legitimized the extremely 'macho' style of many anti-colonialist and black power movements, it has also legitimized the secondary position of women in these national collectivities.

And yet the 'emancipation of women' has come to signify much wider political and social attitudes towards social change and modernity in a variety of revolutionary and decolonization projects, whether in Turkey, India, Yemen or China (Kandiyoti, 1991). As Chatterjee (1989) has pointed out, because the position of women has been so central to the colonial gaze in defining indigenous cultures, it is here that symbolic declarations of cultural change have taken place. It has been one of the important mechanisms in which ethnic and national projects have signified – inwardly and outwardly – their move towards modernization. Similarly, the inclusion of women in the national liberation armies of countries such as Nicaragua, Eritrea and Libya has been a signifier not only of the incorporation of women as citizens of the nation, but also, if not more importantly, of the incorporation of the nation as a whole in the populist armed struggle. However, these changes did not lack ambivalence because at the same time they had to signify modernization and national independence. The process of mimicry was limited at best.

Because the hegemony of the modern nation state in the post-colonial world has often been very limited, being mostly confined to urban centres and the upper classes, the use of cultural and religious traditions as symbolic border guards has to a large extent enabled the continued co-existence of a 'modern' centre with pre-modern sections of society. At a later period, it has also enabled, in many cases, the rise of a new generation of leaders who could turn to those very customs and traditions and develop ethnic and national projects of a very different kind. In these projects, what formerly symbolized progress and modernity was now constructed as European cultural imperialism. As an alternative, a fundamentalist construction of 'the true' cultural essence of the collectivity has come to be imposed. These constructions, however, are often no more similar to the ways people used to live historically in these societies than the previous modernist 'national liberation' ones, nor have the fundamentalist projects abandoned modernity and its tools, whether they be modern media or high-tech weaponry (Sahgal and Yuval-Davis, 1992).

Once again, women occupy an important role in these projects. Rather than being seen as the symbols of change, women are constructed in the role of the 'carriers of tradition'. The symbolic act of unveiling which played centre stage in the emancipatory projects is now being surpassed by the campaigns of forced veiling, as happened, for example, in post-revolutionary Iran. Even practices such as Sati in India can become foci of fundamentalist movements which see in women following these traditions the safeguard of the national cultural essence, operating as a mirror mirage to the colonial gaze which focused on these practices to construct Otherness (Mani, 1989; Chhachhi, 1991).

Cultures, however, are not fixed essential entities. As the slogan of Southall Black Sisters and Women Against Fundamentalism challenged, when they chanted in anti-domestic violence demonstrations in Southall and in countering the Islamist anti-Rushdie demonstration, 'Women's tradition – resistance, not submission!'

Rather than a fixed and homogenous body of tradition and custom, 'cultural stuff', therefore, needs to be described as a rich resource, usually full of internal contradictions, which is used selectively by different social agents in various social projects within specific power relations and political discourses in and outside the collectivity. Gender, class, membership in a collectivity, stage in the life cycle and ability all affect the access to and availability of these resources and the specific positions from which they are being used.

Urban Space and the Construction of Difference

Migrant labourers and refugees, unless bound in particular labour contracts to particular geographical locations, tend to settle in metropolitan urban areas. This is where labour markets would be the largest and the most flexible (Castles and Miller, 1993). Familial and ethnic networks of support would develop so that later waves of immigration would tend to settle, if possible, near those who came earlier, and the growth of community religious and cultural services would reinforce this tendency. Sometimes, as happened in the Southall area in London, the high concentration of communal services and networks of support might counterbalance the attraction of upwardly mobile suburbs, and even people who could afford to move to more affluent areas would not do so, or would sometimes return after a period of moving out. Overall, however, like most other strata of population, the more settled and upwardly mobile the immigrant community, the more it transfers itself gradually from the inner city to suburbia, resisting the racism and other modes of exclusion which originally make such a move problematic.

Territorial concentrations in inner cities are almost never ethnically homoge-neous, unless this is decreed by law, as in the case of the Jewish ghettos under the Nazi regime. Socio-economic class factors such as prices of housing, places of work, transport facilities, etc. would tend, in the last instance, to determine the population character of a particular neighbourhood. Public housing policies would operate in similar ways.

Sharing public space in housing estates and neighbourhood streets does not necessarily break down boundaries. Phil Cohen (1997), for instance, has shown how male youth gang cultures develop in order to mark the territoriality of one 'community' in certain public spaces, with the tacit – and sometimes not so tacit – support of the older generations. Control of the behaviour and mode of dress of women and girls of the community is a major occupation of such gangs when they are not fighting (Patel, 1990).

Even when communal boundaries are not marked by open 'warfare', urban space is not considered to be 'a safe home', as there are no proper defences in it from the intrusion of 'the stranger'. Verity Staffulah Khan (1979) carried out a comparative study on women's purdah in Bradford in the UK and in Bangladesh in the villages from which the Bradford immigrants had come, and found the practice of purdah to be much more extreme and rigid in Bradford than in Bangladesh. This is but one facet of a more general defensive rigidity and 'freezing' of cultures which tends to take place in diasporic communities.

This is important, because the classical studies on 'the stranger' (Schutz, 1976; Simmel, 1950) have tended to consider the immigrant, the newcomer as 'the stranger'. But, of course, as John Berger (in his famous *The Seventh Man* [1982]) has pointed out, for 'the stranger', all the locals are strangers as well! As Therese Wobbe (1995, p. 92) has shown, the fear of the stranger is often specifically gendered. She argues that the gendered challenge that the stranger presents consti-tutes a physical-affective dimension which is central to the understanding of racist violence. It is structured around the common stereotype of the male stranger harassing, threatening or actually raping 'our women', whose honour has to be defended. On the other hand, she also argues that the constructed collectivity boundary 'between "us" and "them"' also indicates the limits and intersections of social obligations and social norms'. This is a central dimension in the understand-ing of actual racist violence and violence against women in everyday life, as the absence of social responsibilities towards the Others often implies the freedom to violate and attack. The targets for such attacks could be not only 'their' women, but also 'traitors', such as wives from mixed marriages.

Multiculturalism and its Dangers

The doctrine of multiculturalism has developed as an attempt to neutralize this sense of mutual threat and the exclusions and violence which develop as a result of it. Minh-Ha Trinh has commented (1989, pp. 89–90) that there are two kinds of social and cultural differences: those which threaten and those which do not. Multiculturalism is aimed at nourishing and perpetuating the kind of differences which do not.

Carl-Ulrik Schierup (1995) has claimed that multiculturalism is an ideological base for transatlantic alignment whose project is the transformation of the welfare state. It has been developed as a major form of accommodation to the settlement of immigrants and refugees from ex-colonial countries, the institutionalization of ethnic pluralism and the preservation of the cultures of origins of the ethnic minorities as legitimate parts of the national project. Multiculturalism, however, is problematic in several ways. As Andrew Jakubowicz concluded in relation to Australian policies of multiculturalism: 'Multiculturalism gives the ethnic communities the task to retain and cultivate with government help their different cultures, but does not concern itself with struggles against discriminatory policies as they affect individuals or classes of people' (Jakubowicz, 1984, p. 42).

A controversial, related question is the extent to which the conservation of collective identities and cultures is important as a goal in itself or has only become so as a result of collective will. John Rex (1995) argues that both are true, but this implies a homogeneous construction of both cultures and collective wills, and assumes that the attitudes of all members of a specific ethnic community to its 'culture' would be the same.

Moreover, it would be a mistake to suppose that those who support multiculturalism assume a civil and political society in which all cultural identities would have the same legitimacy. In all states in which multiculturalism is an official policy, there are cultural customs (such as polygamy, using drugs, etc.) which are considered illegal as well as illegitimate, giving priority to cultural traditions of the hegemonic majority. At the same time, in multicultural policies, the naturalization of the western hegemonic culture continues while the minority cultures become reified and differentiated from normative human behaviour.

The whole debate on multiculturalism stumbles on the fact that the boundaries of difference, as well as the boundaries of social rights, are determined by specific hegemonic discourses, perhaps using universalistic terminology, but definitely not universal. And universalist discourses which do not take into account the differential positionings of those they refer to often cover up racist (and one can add sexist, classist, ageist, disablist, etc.) constructions.

The construction of 'the community' in multiculturalism assumes a unified cultural or racial voice for each community. These voices are constructed to be as distinct as possible (within the boundaries of multiculturalism) from the majority culture in order to be able to be 'different'; thus, within multiculturalism, the more traditional and distanced from the majority culture the voice of the 'community representatives' is, the more 'authentic' it is perceived to be within such a construction. Such constructions do not allow space for internal power conflicts and interest differences within the minority collectivity, for instance conflicts along the lines of class, gender politics and culture. Moreover, they tend to assume collectivity boundaries which are fixed, static, ahistorical and essentialist, with no space for growth and change. When such a perspective becomes translated into social policy, 'authenticity' can become an important political resource with which economic and other resources can be claimed from the state as being the representative of 'the community' (Cain and Yuval-Davis, 1990). As Yeatman observes:

> It becomes clear that the liberal conception of the group requires the group to assume an authoritarian character: there has to be a headship of the group which represents its homogeneity of purpose by speaking with the one, authoritative voice. For this to occur, the politics of voice and representation latent within the heterogeneity of perspectives and interests must be suppressed. (Yeatman, 1992, p. 4)

This liberal construction of group voice, therefore, can collude with fundamentalist leaderships who claim to represent the true 'essence' of their collectivity's culture and religion, and who have high on their agenda the control of women and their behaviour (Sahgal and Yuval-Davis, 1992).

Multiculturalism can often have very detrimental effects on women in particular, as often 'different' cultural traditions are defined in terms of culturally specific gender relations and the control of women's behaviour (in which women themselves, especially older women, also participate and collude) is often used to reproduce ethnic boundaries (Yuval-Davis and Anthias, 1989). An example of such collusion, for instance, is the case in which the judge refused a request for asylum to an Iranian woman who had to escape Iran after refusing to be veiled because 'this is their culture' (case recounted by the solicitor Jacqui Bhabha). Another example is that of a young Muslim girl who fled her parents' home because of their restrictive control of her, and who was placed by the social services in another Muslim home, even more pious, against the wish of the girl and the advocacy of the Asian Women's Refuge (case recounted by the workers of Southall Black Sisters).

As Stuart Hall (1992; 1996) points out, cultural identities are often fluid and cross-cutting. Even more importantly, perhaps, they are not only multiple, but they are multi-layered. This does not mean only that boundaries of certain identities are by definition wider and inclusive of other more specific identities (local, regional, national, racial, etc.) but also that some identities which have no pre-fixed cohesion or assumption of common origin or even common destiny may co-exist within individual or communal subjective narratives. Those hyphenated identities have been theorized as hybrid identities located within the symbolic border (or, rather boundary) zone (Bhabha, 1990; 1994; Anzaldua, 1987).

Hybrids have been celebrated in post-modernist literature as the symbol of the time, and are seen as both evoking and erasing the 'totalizing boundaries' of their adoptive nations. Located within the context of globalization, hybrids, nomads (Bradiotti, 1993) and other 'travelling identities' have been celebrated by writers like James Clifford and Rosi Bradiotti. Talal Assad (1993, pp. 9–10), for instance, contrasts James Clifford's (1992) celebration of 'the widening scope of human agency that geographical and psychological mobility now afford' with the deep pessimism of Hannah Arendt (1951), herself a refugee from the Nazis, who spoke of 'the uprootedness and superfluousness which has been the curse of modern masses'. The difference, of course, is embedded in the construction of the notion of free agency versus what Amrita Chhachhi calls 'forced identities' (1991). Whoever watched the terrible sight of Rwandan refugees being taken back to Rwanda from Zaire would question the global validity of the celebration of the nomad.

The problems with the notion of 'the politics of border' and its associated constructions of the nomad, the hybrid and 'travelling cultures' are twofold (Brah, 1996; Welchman, 1996). First, its image of crossing boundaries, travelling and miscegenation relies upon a fixed notion of location and culture which brings back essentialism through the backdoor. Second, in the process of concentrating on the imagery, the signifier, the agency, all too often questions of political economy disappear. As a result, there is not enough attention to the differential power relations between the different cultures and locations which are supposedly hybridized or travelled. Carl-Ulrik Schierup (1995) and Aleksandra Ålund have called this mode of analysis and politics 'culturization' in which 'the cultural has colonized the social' (Ålund, 1995, p. 319).

The conflation of (territorial) borders and (identity) boundaries can have important political consequences. The politics of diaspora illustrate these particularly well. It is important to differentiate between what Avtar Brah calls the 'homing desire' and the 'desire for homeland' (1996, p. 180), as well as between 'diaspora communities' (Brah, 1996; Lavie and Swedenburg, 1996; Lemelle and Kelley, 1994) and political exiles. Political exiles are usually individuals or families who have been part of political struggles in the homeland and their identity and collectivity membership continues to be directed singularly, or at least primarily, towards it, with the aim of 'going back' the moment the political situation changes. For diaspora communities, on the other hand, participation in the national struggles in the homeland, including sending ammunition to Ireland or 'gold bricks' to build the Hindu temple in place of the Muslim mosque in Ayodhya which was burned in December 1992, can be done primarily within an ethnic rather than a nationalist discourse, as a symbolic act of affirmation of their collective identity. Their destiny is primarily bound up with the country in which they live and their children are growing up, rather than with their country of origin. Nevertheless, such acts of symbolic identification can have very radical political and other effects in the 'homeland', a fact which might often be of only marginal interest to the people of the diaspora. I came across this very clearly when I was speaking in the early 1970s in the USA on the effects American Jewry's support had had on the continued occupation by Israel of the territories after the 1967 war, and the resulting violations of human rights by Israel. I was speaking before a synagogue audience known for its liberal politics concerning Vietnam and civil rights in the USA, trying to dissuade them from continuing to send money to Israel as a means of pressure on Israel to end the occupation. 'You don't understand,' a woman from the audience explained to me. 'I'm not interested in what Israel is doing – for me the most important thing is that I support Israel because Israel is part of me.' The sentiments are not always so extremely clearcut, but this is definitely one illuminating example of the danger of under-emphasizing the difference between mythical desires for home and actual political realities, as well as the conflation of identification and participation (i.e. membership in the community, citizenship).

This example highlights the crucial importance of incorporating differential spatial relationships into the notion of citizenship and the ways in which living in the diaspora, living in metropolitan urban centres in the 'homeland' or living on the land might affect modes of participation in ethnic and national collectivities.

The Domains of the Private and the Public

When discussing issues of citizenship, space and gender relations vis-à-vis the spatial division of 'the private' and 'the public' as gendered and ethnocized, it is crucial also to discuss the spatial dichotomy which has been underwritten as the basis of the relationship of gender and citizenship – the domains of 'the private' and 'the public'.

The private/public dichotomy has been central to the theorization of gender relations (Pateman, 1988; Vogel, 1994; Lister, 1997) as well as political theory, citizenship and the state (Turner, 1990; Jayasuriya, 1990). Feminist theory has challenged this dichotomy in several different ways, claiming that 'the personal is political'; that 'the public' social/political 'contract' cannot be understood without including 'the private', 'sexual contract' into the story; and that the dividing line between 'the public' and 'the private' is itself politically, culturally and gender specific. Moreover, as I have argued elsewhere (Yuval-Davis, 1997), there has been a high degree of inconsistency in the ways in which different authors discuss the public/private boundary and its relationship to other concepts such as political and civil society, the family, the economy, the voluntary sector, etc.

In the way in which feminists such as Carol Pateman (1988), Rebecca Grant (1991) and Ursula Vogel (1991), for instance, talk about the public and the private spheres, it is clear that the public sphere is identical in their writings to the political sphere, while the private sphere relates primarily to the family domain in which women are mainly located. In contrast to this construction of the private as the domain of the family, in Jayasuriya's writings (1990), the private domain is that which is not financed and/or controlled by the state and includes, for example, religious institutions. Bryan Turner (1990) uses the public/private dichotomy as one of the axes for his typology of citizenship, and includes in the private domain self-enhancement and other leisure, as well as spiritual activities. Sylvia Walby (1994, p. 383) criticizes him for adopting 'the male viewpoint' by conflating two meanings of 'private' – one which relates to the autonomy of the individual, and one which relates to freedom from the interventions of the state. She argues that while the family can or cannot be free from the intervention of the state, it is not an autonomous and free space for women, nor has it a unitary set of interests because husbands and wives (and children and other relatives in cases of extended families) have different social positionings, powers and interests within the family.

If we accept the meaning of 'private' as that in which the individual is autonomous, then this can be exercised to a lesser or greater extent in all social spheres in which people – and not just women – can act both as part of social structures and collectivities, with all the constraints these provide, and as autonomous individual agents, whether it be in the family, in the civil or in the political domain. Similarly, depending on people's preferences and hobbies, leisure and self-enhancement activities can be spent with the family or other personal friends, with a trade-union, church or ethnic sports association, or as a councillor in the local government in the political domain. At the same time, especially in the modern welfare state, there is no social sphere which is protected from state intervention. Even in cases where there is no direct intervention, it is the state which has usually established, actively or passively, its own boundaries of non-intervention. In other words, the construction of the boundary between the public and the private is a political act in itself. Political power relations with their own dynamics exist in each social sphere. The most important contribution of feminism to social theory has been the recognition that power relations operate within primary social relations as well as within the more impersonal secondary social relations of the civil and political domains.

There is another meaning of 'the private', one which Sylvia Walby does not explore. This relates to the hidden, the unmarked, the anonymous. In the context of 'the global city', real and virtual, the visible and the invisible play particularly important roles. At the same time the imaginary geography of contemporary media and IT technologies has also helped to transform notions of intimacy, individual and collective.

Anonymity and visibility are context-dependent. The veiling of women in Muslim societies has been aimed at maintaining their anonymity in the public domain of the street. However, in western countries in which most women do not veil themselves or wear a headscarf, wearing one has the opposite effect of making one invisible – it makes a public statement about one's identity and usually (unless one is forced to this by others) one's identification with a particular cultural tradition, as part of a specific ethnic/political project. In the public debates about the 'headscarf affair', both in France and in Britain, newspaper articles continuously commented on the fact that the girls who insisted on wearing headscarves to school were anything but meek and subdued (Silverman and Yuval-Davis, 1997).

Ethnic, sexual and other minorities tend to gravitate to large metropolitan cities. Such cities can often offer two contradictory/complementary attractions relating to the private and the public. As Jeffrey Weeks explains:

> It was the growth of the city, with its physical density and moral anonymity, which provided the possibilities for lives lived at odds with the norms and values of the culture, both private in that they expressed personal needs and desires, and often had to be protected from the threat of exposure and possible social disgrace, and public in that new social spaces offered the chance for different ways of life. (Weeks, 1995, p. 147)

Here Weeks speaks of 'culture' in generic terms, but it is important to emphasize that the anonymity of the city can offer protection not only for those who 'deviate' from the hegemonic culture. It can also offer, probably even more so, the opportunity for members of ethnic minorities and other minority culture communities to escape from gendered social controls enacted upon them in efforts to reproduce the boundaries of their community of origin. Their 'deviancy' can be constructed in terms of assimilation into the hegemonic culture as well as in other urban subcultures.

Moreover, the sheer size, density and heterogeneity of human populations in global cities often also ensures that people in search of new social spaces can find others who share with them facets of identity and culture, such as the same myth of common origin, language etc., and with whom the anxiety and risk of facing the unknown, of often being doubly excluded from the hegemonic majority and from the established minority community, can be shared and mutually supported (examples include Jewish gays and lesbians, black feminists, Christian AIDS sufferers, etc.). At the same time the urban space can offer fluidity and temporality to these comings together, and people are freer to move on from these closures than in other social settings. Moreover, the involvement of people in the city in such communities on the marginal matrix of society (Evans, 1993) can be partial and can often remain detached from other facets of their lives at work and in the family.

Even more partial and hidden can be the membership of people in virtual communities, based on e-mail and the internet. However, as a transsexual Labour councillor explained recently to an interviewer on BBC Radio 4, such hidden communities can become invaluable sources of support and empowerment when those in the immediate physical spatial environment do not share, or have strong views against, people of particular social categories, identities or political views.

Conclusion

Physical and imaginary territories and boundaries construct the spaces in which citizenship practices and struggles are being carried out. As the boundaries of countries, nations and states do not usually overlap with each other, and as the individual boundaries of each country or nation are often contested, citizenship needs to be seen as a multi-layered construct, because people's membership in communities and polities is dynamic and multiple.

Ethnic, class and gender differences play particularly important roles in constructing and delineating the spaces, especially the urban spaces, in which the theatre of citizenship is taking place on a daily basis. One imaginary boundary whose tenacity is particularly vulnerable in such a context is the boundary between the private and the public.

New technologies, global markets and the changing international political context all affect specific constructions of citizenship. However, these effects are mediated via the specific gender, ethnicity, class and other intersecting categories of the social positioning from which people view the world, as individuals and as members in multi-layered communities.

BIBLIOGRAPHY

Ålund, A. (1995) 'Alterity in Modernity', *Acta Sociologica*, 38: 311–22.

Anderson, B. (1983) *Imagined Communities* (London: Verso).

Anthias, F. and Yuval-Davis, N. (1989) 'Introduction', in N. Yuval-Davis and F. Anthias (eds), *Woman-Nation-State* (London: Macmillan).

Anzaldua, G. (1987) *Borderlines/La Frontera* (San Francisco: Spinsters/Aunt Lute Books).

Arendt, H. (1951 [1975]) *The Origins of Totalitarianism* (New York: Harcourt Brace Janovitch).

Armstrong, J. (1982) *Nations Before Nationalism* (Chapel Hill: University of North Carolina Press).

Assad, T. (1993) *Genealogies of Religion* (Baltimore: Johns Hopkins University Press).

Avineri, S. and De Shalit, A. (eds) (1992) *Communitarianism and Individualism* (Oxford: Oxford University Press).

Bauer, O. (1940) *The National Question*, in Hebrew (Hakibutz Ha'artzi).

Berger, J. (1982) *The Seventh Man: A Book of Images and Words about the Experience of Migrant Workers* (London: Writers and Readers).

Bhabha, H. (ed.) (1990) *Nation and Narration* (London: Routledge).

—— (1994) *The Location of Culture* (London: Routledge).

Bradiotti, R. (1993) 'Nomads in Transformed Europe: Figurations for Alternative Consciousness', in R. Lavrijsen (ed.), *Cultural Diversity in the Arts* (Amsterdam: Royal Tropical Institute).

Brah, A. (1996) *Cartographies of Diaspora: Contesting Identities* (London: Routledge).

Cain, H. and Yuval-Davis, N. (1990) 'The "Equal Opportunities Community" and the Anti-Racist Struggle', *Critical Social Policy*, 29: 5–26.

Castles, S. and Miller, M. J. (1993) *The Age of Migration: International Population Movements in the Modern World* (New York: Guilford).

Chatterjee, P. (1986) *Nationalist Thought and the Colonial World: A Derivative Discourse* (London: Zed Books).

—— (1989) 'The National Resolution of the Women's Question', in K. Sangari and S. Vaid (eds), *Recasting Women, Essays in Colonial History* (New Delhi: Kali for Women).

Chhachhi, A. (1991) 'Forced Identities: the State, Communalism, Fundamentalism and Women in India', in D. Kandiyoti (ed.), *Women, Islam and the State* (London: Macmillan).

Clifford, J. (1992) 'Travelling Cultures', in L. Grossberg, T. Nelson and P. Treichler (eds), *Cultural Studies* (New York: Routledge).

Cohen, P. (1997) *Rethinking the Youth Question* (London: Macmillan).

Cohen, R. (1997) *Global Diasporas: An Introduction* (London: UCL Press).

Daly, M. (1993) *Communitarianism: Belonging and Commitment in a Pluralist Democracy* (Belmont, CA: Wadsworth).

Enloe, C. (1990) '"Women and Children": Making Feminist Sense of the Persian Gulf Crisis', *The Village Voice* (25 September).

—— (1993) *The Morning After: Sexual Politics At the End of the Cold War* (Berkeley, CA: University of California Press).

Evans, D. T. (1993) *Sexual Citizenship: The Material Construction of Sexualities* (London: Routledge).

Fanon, F. (1952 [1986]) *Black Skin, White Masks* (London: Pluto Press).

Gellner, E. (1983) *Nations and Nationalism* (Oxford: Basil Blackwell).

Grant, R. (1991) 'The Sources of Gender Bias in International Relations Theory', in R. Grant and K. Newland (eds), *Gender and International Relations* (Bloomington, IN: Indiana University Press).

Hall, S. (1992) 'New Ethnicities', in J. Donald and A. Rattansi (eds), *"Race", Culture and Difference* (London: Sage).

—— (1996) 'Who Needs "Identity?"', in S. Hall and P. du Gay (eds), *Question of Cultural Identity* (London: Sage).

Hasan, M. (1994) *The Murder of Palestinian Women for Family "Honour" in Israel* MA dissertation, Gender and Ethnic Studies, University of Greenwich.

Jakubowicz, A. (1984) 'State and Ethnicity: Multiculturalism as an Ideology', *Australia and New Zealand Journal of Sociology*, 17 (3).

Jayasuriya, L. (1990) 'Multiculturalism, Citizenship and Welfare: New Directions for the 1990s', paper presented at the 50th Anniversary Lecture Series, Department of Social Work and Social Policy, University of Sydney.

Joseph, S. (1993) 'Gender and Civil Society', *Middle East Report*, 183: 22–6.

Kandiyoti, D. (1991) 'Identity and its Discontents: Women and the Nation', *Millennium*, 20 (3): 429–44.

Lavie, S. and Swedenburg, T. (eds) (1996) *Displacement, Diaspora and Geographies of Location* (Durham, NC: Duke University Press).

Lemelle, S. and Kelly, R. (eds) (1994) *Imagining Home: Class, Culture and Nationalism in the African Diaspora* (London: Verso).

Levi-Strauss, C. (1969) *The Elementary Structures of Kinship*, ed. R. Needham, trans. J. H. Bell and J. R. von Sturmer, 2nd edn (Boston: Beacon Press).

Lister, R. (1997) *Citizenship: Feminist Perspectives* (London: Macmillan).

Lowenhaupt Tsing, A. (1993) *In the Realm of the Diamond Queen* (Princeton, NJ: Princeton University Press).

Mani, L. (1989) 'Contentious Traditions: The Debate on Sati in Colonial India', in K. Sangari and S. Vaid (eds), *Recasting Women, Essays in Colonial History* (New Brunswick, NJ: Rutgers University Press).

Marshall, T. H. (1950) *Citizenship and Social Class* (Cambridge: Cambridge University Press).

—— (1965 [1975]) *Social Policy in the Twentieth Century* (London: Hutchinson).

—— (1981) *The Right To Welfare and Other Essays* (London: Heinemann Educational Books).

Mouffe, C. (1993) 'Liberal Socialism and Pluralism: Which Citizenship', in J. Squires (ed.), *Principled Positions* (London: Lawrence and Wishart).

Nandy, A. (1983) *The Intimate Enemy: Loss and Recovery of Self Under Colonialism* (Oxford: Oxford University Press).

Nimni, E. (1991) *Marxism and Nationalism* (London: Pluto Press).

Patel, P. (1990) 'Southall Boys', in Southall Black Sisters (eds), *Against the Grain* (London: SBS).

Pateman, C. (1988) *The Sexual Contract* (Cambridge: Polity).

Pettman, J. J. (1996) *Worlding Women: A Feminist International Politics* (London: Routledge).

Rex, J. (1995) 'Ethnic Identity and the Nation State: The Political Sociology of Multicultural Societies', *Social Identities*, 1 (1).

Rozario, S. (1991) 'Ethnic-Religious Communities and Gender Divisions in Bangladesh: Women as Boundary Makers', in G. Bottomley, M. de Lepervanche and J. Martin (eds), *Intersexions: Gender/Class/Culture/Ethnicity* (Sydney: Allen and Unwin).

Sahgal, G. and Yuval-Davis, N. (eds) (1992) *Refusing Holy Orders: Women and Fundamentalism in Britain* (London: Virago Press).

Schierup, C-U. (1995) 'Multiculturalism and Universalism in the USA and EU Europe', paper for the workshop 'Nationalism and Ethnicity', March, Bern, Switzerland.

Schutz, A. (1944 [1976]) 'The Stranger: An Essay in Social Psychology', in A. Brodersen (ed.), *Alfred Schutz: Studies in Social Theory, Collected Papers II* (The Hague: Martinus Nijhoff).

Silverman, M. and Yuval-Davis, N. (1997) *Racialized Discourses on Jews and Arabs in Britain and France*, Research report submitted to the ESRC.

Simmel, G. (1950) 'The Stranger', in K. H. Wolff (ed.), *The Sociology of George Simmel* (New York: Free Press).

Starffulah Khan, V. (ed.) (1979) *Minority Families in Britain: Support and Stress* (London: Macmillan).

Trinh, Minh-Ha (1989) *Woman, Native, Other* (Bloomington, IN: Indiana University Press).

Turner, B. S. (1990) 'Outline of a Theory of Citizenship', *Sociology*, 24 (2): 189–217.

Vogel, U. (1991) 'Is Citizenship Gender Specific?', in U. Vogel and M. Moran (eds), *The Frontiers of Citizenship* (Basingstoke: Macmillan).

—— (1994) 'Marriage and the Boundaries of Citizenship', in B. van Steenbergen (ed.), *The Condition of Citizenship* (London: Sage).

Walby, S. (1994) 'Is Citizenship Gendered?', *Sociology*, 28 (2): 379–95.

Warring, A. (1996) 'National Bodies: Collaboration and Resistance in a Gender Perspective', paper presented at the *Women and War* session at the European Social Science History Conference, May, The Netherlands.

Weeks, J. (1995) *Invented Moralities: Sexual Values in an Age of Uncertainty* (Cambridge: Polity Press).

Welchman, J. C. (ed.) (1996) *Rethinking Borders* (Basingstoke: Macmillan).

Wobbe, T. (1995) 'The Boundaries of Community: Gender Relations and Racial Violence', in H. Lutz, A. Phoenix and N. Yuval-Davis (eds), *Crossfires: Nationalism, Racism and Gender in Europe* (London: Pluto).

Yeatman, A. (1992) 'Minorities and the Politics of Difference', *Political Theory Newsletter*, 4 (1): 1–11.

Yuval-Davis, N. (1987a), 'Marxism and Jewish Nationalism', *History Workshop Journal*, 24.

—— (1987b) 'The Jewish Collectivity and National Reproduction in Israel', *Khamsin*, special issue on *Women in the Middle East* (London: Zed Books).

—— (1991) 'The Citizenship Debate: Women, the State and Ethnic Processes', *Feminist Review*, 39 (Autumn): 58–68.

—— (1997) *Gender and Nation* (London: Sage).

—— (1999) '"The Multi-layered Citizen": Citizenship at the Age of "Glocalization"', *International Feminist Journal of Politics*, 1 (Autumn).

Yuval-Davis, N. and Anthias, F. (eds) (1989) *Woman-Nation-State* (London: Macmillan).

Zajovic, S. (ed.) (1994) *Women for Peace* (Belgrade, Women In Black).

18

Shadows and Sovereigns

Carolyn Nordstrom

One day the political scientist Ed Garcia showed me a letter he had received from a well-established group that had been fighting for autonomy against government repression for several decades. The authors explained that, as they did not constitute a state, they were cut off from many opportunities most take for granted. Without the status of state, they were not recognized by the other states of the world as a formal trade partner, as part of political and military associations, or as being a signatory in economic treaties. They were not represented in the international banking system, nor could they receive IMF state-based loans. They had no seat at the United Nations, no inviolable land to attract multinational businesses. Yet their people required food, clothing, household goods, jobs and cars like anyone else in the world. They required travel visas and the means to travel. They needed access to the resources to set up industries and exchange their products on the world's open market. Not an easy thing for a group at war with a state. The state-based nature of the world's politics and economy forced them to rely on non-formal markets. How, they wanted to know, would it be possible to function in the world's formal economy?

It will be obvious to note that as I read this letter, I saw the role of states in determining the kinds of political and economic access people and populations have in the world. But I was in fact struck by something more subtle: I saw the vast international machinery that kept this group clothed and fed and armed and in business for all these decades, a machinery that functions outside of the world's formal markets and politics – one invisible to government's formal policies but equally powerful in shaping the course of the world's progression, a machinery capable of sustaining entire populations and creating new nations.

This article will explore a series of shadow powers, international by definition, that – while capable of shaping world economies and policies – remain largely invisible to formal analysis. The heart of this study is ethnographic in nature. In the 15 years I have been conducting fieldwork in war zones,[1] I have charted the ways in which people gain the necessities to wage war and create peace – necessities that range from major weapons systems to basic medicines and goods. An equally important aspect of this equation concerns the ways in which people pay for these goods and services: gold, diamonds, drugs, precious metals, human labor, sex workers, timber and even seafood move out of war zones into world markets to purchase everything from AK-47s and M-16s to satellite-linked computer communications and weapons systems, from antibiotics to basic grains. A large part of this trade takes place outside formal state and legal channels. As war gives way to peace in the conflict zones in which I have worked, I have also charted the ways in which people begin to rebuild war-devastated economies. Here, too, people often rely on buying and selling the same goods they did during war, along the same non-state channels – both to gain life's necessities and to acquire the finances and supplies to rehabilitate livelihoods and industries. Those most successful at this non-state trade amass economic fortunes that can be translated into political power, fortunes that can reshape social, economic and political landscapes (Nordstrom, 1995, 1997; Nordstrom and Robben, 1995).

This study of the shadows is not merely a study of extra-state transactions. The finances and power wielded by these shadow networks challenge academics to rethink our theories on states, sovereignty and the loci of power. It is not the story of individual people operating in the shadows, but a study of the vast networks of people who move goods and services worldwide – networks that broker power comparable to, and in many cases greater than, a number of the world's states. I have come to this research through the study of war zones, where non-state actors and transactions are perhaps most visible. But, as this study will show, vast extra-state networks expand across war and peace, and across all the world's countries. I have chosen to use the word 'extra-state' in defining the shadows to underscore the fact that while these networks are not comprised by states themselves, neither are they entirely distinct from, or opposite to, states – they work both through and around formal state representatives and institutions. This point is critical to the theory developed here: states and shadow networks exist simultaneously, each phenomenologically different, each representing distinct forms of authority and politico-economic organization.

I use the term 'shadows' (rather than criminal or illegal) as the transactions defining these networks are not confined solely to criminal, illicit or illegal activities – but they do take place outside formal state institutions. The relationships of power and exchange I am concerned with here cross various divides between legal, quasi-legal, gray markets and downright illegal activities. I do not use the term 'informal', but instead use 'non-formal', as the former in many definitions, the International Labor Organization's included, refers expressly to small-scale, low-income, low-tech and subsistence level activities. Shadow should not be taken to mean insubstantial: these transnational networks, taken together, employ millions of people and generate more than a trillion dollars annually.

Shadow networks, licit or otherwise, are more than sprawling value-neutral international market networks (Appadurai, 1996). They fashion economic possibilities, they broker political power and, importantly, they constitute cultures, for these networks of power and exchange are governed by rules of exchange, codes of conduct, hierarchies of deference and power – in short, they are governed by social principles, not merely the jungle law of tooth and claw. Shadow networks, as I define them here, and as this article will develop:

- are more formalized, integrated, and bound by rules of conduct than studies of the gray and black markets that focus on high-risk items like armaments and drugs, or studies that focus on basic informal markets like foodstuffs, imply;

- are by definition international – they entail societal systems that cross-cut national, linguistic and ethnic collectivities;
- are not simply (shadow) markets or economies (Ayers, 1996) – but a compilation of political, economic and sociocultural forces;
- benefit from analyses like those of William Reno's (1995, 1998) that look at 'shadow states' – nation-based systems of power and patronage paralleling state power – but focus on a different, and more distinctly international, set of criteria that constitute a set of 'institutional frameworks' in their own right;
- are not marginal to the world's economies and politics, but central. While little in-depth work exists on estimates of the sums generated per year through extra-state activities, initial inquiries seem to place them in the trillions. To give some examples of how these figures add up, the following examples run from the tragically exploitative to the remarkably mundane. As much as 20 percent of the world's financial deposits are located in unregulated banks and offshore locations (Lopez and Cortwright, 1998). UN estimates of illicit drugs earnings run at US$500 billion a year (UNRISD, 1995). Illicit weapons sales are also placed at US$500 billion a year (Ayers, 1996; Castells, 1998). As a single country, India's black economy in the early 1980s was placed at more than US$60 billion, and has grown since then (Gupta, 1992). India is not unusual: in Peru, 48 percent of the economically active population works in the informal sector, and that figure rises to 58 percent in Kenya, and perhaps even higher in Russia (Greif, 1996). Prostitution brings in scores of billions of dollars annually, and people-smuggling brings in equally large amounts. In a study on money laundering, Pasuk Phongpachit of Chulalongkorn University in Bangkok estimated that people-smuggling earns US$3.2 billion a year in Thailand alone, and that solely from Thai women smuggled into Japan, Germany and Taiwan for prostitution. Profit to Chinese triads smuggling illegal immigrants into the USA alone is placed at US$2.5 billion a year (Strange, 1996). As to the more mundane, 1 million tonnes of oil was smuggled into China in the first six months of 1997: the standard savings to smugglers per single standard cargo of 30,000 tonnes amounts to US$1.8 million (Singapore Newsroom, 1997). Freon smuggling is a classic example of the mundane and often overlooked that reaps huge profits – in Miami alone, illegal freon smuggling has exceeded drug-trafficking in volume and may soon rival it in revenues (Tyson, 1995).

We do not know how these vast sums affect global (stock) markets, economic (non-)health and political power configurations. What we can surmise is that these extensive transnational transactions comprise a significant section of the world's economy, and thus of the world's power grids. If all these industries were to collapse overnight, the world's economies would be in chaos.

Ethnographic work on these networks prompts a reassessment of basic theoretical ideas concerning the nexus of legality/illegality, state/non-state and formal/non-formal power relations. Susan Strange writes that social scientists cling to outmoded and inappropriate theories that are rooted in a belief in a more stable and orderly world than the one we live in. Arguing that academics need to rethink the nature and sources of power, Strange (1996: 4) states:

The argument put forward is that the impersonal forces of world markets, integrated over the post-war period more by private enterprise in finance, industry and trade than by the cooperative decisions of governments, are now more powerful than the state to whom ultimate political authority over society and economy is supposed to belong.

Organized crime, for Strange, is an undeniable part of the world market. Sassen (1998), and Castells as well, find informal and criminal networks central to our understanding of global power. Castells (1998: 166) writes:

> Crime is as old as humankind. But global crime, the networking of powerful criminal organizations, and their associates, in shared activities throughout the planet, is a new phenomenon that profoundly affects international and national economies, politics, security, and, ultimately, societies at large.

Like Strange, Castells (1998: 167–8) notes that: 'There is a general acknowledgment of the importance and reality of this phenomenon, and a wealth of evidence. ... Yet the phenomenon is largely ignored by academics.'

Ethnographic interviews yielded another possible explanation for the dearth of formal research on illicit economies. When I was in southern Africa in the second half of the 1990s, I interviewed several leading United Nations Development Fund (UNDF) economists about why formal economic indicators did not take account of non-formal economies when they so significantly affected the outcomes of any policy, from development to peace accords. For example, in both Mozambique and Angola in the mid-1990s, fully half of the nations' resources were taken out of the country through extra-legal channels.[2] I asked the UNDF economists why these figures were seldom represented, even in passing, in formal research and policy documents. 'We cannot study this', the senior economist from a European office replied, 'it is not in our mandate.' I clearly did not understand, replying that retooling mandate priorities would be a good idea. After a few moments, the senior economist asked me to consider where all those millions of dollars worth of seafood goes – to whose factories and whose tables? Where do all the billions of dollars' worth of precious gems, gold and diamonds end up? They purchase hard currency, weapons and luxury items, from whom? 'The countries', he answered, 'who write our mandates.' Or, as he and his colleagues concluded, who write things out of the mandates.

Strange and Castells have explored the development of organized crime and the increasing numbers of alliances among major mafias, cartels and triads in the world; and Sassen looks at the increasing importance and complexity of informal markets in major cosmopolitan 'global cities' – and all chart the impact these activities have on global economic and political realities. My research both draws upon and supports these conclusions.

What is different in this study is the ethnographic component that demonstrates links across arenas of politico-economic activity that are traditionally divided in theory and analysis – links that show complex sociocultural and political as well as economic organization in these networks of exchange and association.

Linkages – Theoretical and Ethnographic

Theory has generally disaggregated:

- illegal and dangerous goods (drugs, weapons, mercenaries);
- illegal and immoral practices (child labor, sexual slavery, exploitation of non-legal immigration);
- illicit and non-dangerous goods (gems, precious minerals, entertainment electronics);
- non-legal and informal goods and services (clothing, food, basic supplies).

Analyses tend to concentrate on single discrete categories: there are studies that focus on mafias (Italy, the new Russian criminals); on drugs (narcotrafficking, the opium trade); on illegal immigration, forced prostitution or women's markets in Africa. These studies tend to be restricted to their field of inquiry: those investigating weapons transfers do not tend to look at the linkages with prostitution or immigration; those writing on narcotraficking do not tend to explore the links to informal market economies or illicit trade in minerals and high-tech electronics.

Each category tends to be approached as a distinct set of networks, and is ascribed a distinct ethical and politico-theoretical domain. The outcome is that it appears each network represents a different, closed and bounded, category – drug cartels are international criminal organizations; gem runners are international profiteers; and non-licensed clothing vendors operate in informal sectors that are neither as dangerous nor as ethically compromised as those of drug runners, nor as cosmopolitan and illicit as those of gem runners.[3] Each is taken as a distinct domain.

In reality, in markets, and in people's lives, these arenas of non-legal and extra-state activities are not so clearly disaggregated. For example, it is not enough to discuss the illegal arms trade as a distinct sphere of activity, separate from the lives of those who transport a weapon from point A to point B. To say only that the illegal arms industry generates US$500 billion worth of profits a year, and to discuss ways of curtailing this trade, gives the impression that these caches of weapons circulate as an indistinct mass through shadowy brokers to militias and criminals – and avoids the observation that each weapon exchanges hands, individual to individual, for very specific reasons. A criminal buying an illegal weapon to commit a crime is not equivalent to a hungry African woman who trades an AK-47 for a chicken to feed her family. Neither, my fieldwork has demonstrated, is the exception to the rule of illicit weapons transfers. Each, theoreticians can argue, belongs to a different moral universe. Both make up the arena of illegal sales of dangerous goods.

I am not arguing we collapse categories here, either morally or analytically – quite the opposite. I am arguing for a greater nuancing and understanding of complex international extra-state realities. The same complexities of analysis adhere to, by way of another example, the gem trade. While the illicit gem trade runs in the billions of dollars a year (Angola and Sierra Leone alone each generate US$500 million a year), it is not confined to a nebulous world of profiteer business people. Gem miners can be local families plying the only trade they can in a war-devastated economy; or, as Paul Richards (1996) discusses, men with university education who are unable to find any other work in conflict zones where unemployment can run at 50 percent. Gems don't flow in a vacuum – they flow along informal food and supply lines, along illegal drug and weapons routes, along undocumented immigration passageways, along legal diplomatic channels.

By uncritically disaggregating the various spheres of extra-state activities analyses not only miss the overlapping connections among the various networks, but also fail to add up the sum total of extra-state phenomena and their impact on global finances, security, politics and economic systems. Castells (1998) and Strange (1996) are both careful to point out that, while organized crime is not new to the world, the degree to which different organized crime networks in the world are creating alliances, partnerships and the non-legal equivalent of transnational corporate organizations is new, and is changing the face of international markets and state systems of authority. Networks overlap. The dangerously criminal, the illicit and the informally mundane cannot, in actual practice, be always or easily disaggregated. Castells (1998: 167) reminds us:

> In addition, is everything that receives added value precisely from its prohibition in a given institutional environment: smuggling of everything from everywhere to everywhere, including radioactive material, human organs, and illegal immigrants; prostitution; gambling; loan-sharking; kidnapping; racketeering and extortion; counterfeiting of goods, bank notes, financial documents, credit cards, and identity cards; killers for hire, traffic of sensitive information, technology, or art objects; international sales of stolen goods; or even dumping garbage illegally from one country to another (for example, US garbage smuggled into China in 1996).

What I want to add to Castell's equation are shadow goods, services, and networks that form not only because they are prohibited, but because they are basic to survival. Angola provides a good example. Large-scale illicit networks operate to bring military supplies into a country that has been at war for several decades, and pay for these supplies with luxury resources like gems. But also, because of the disruptions of war, 90 percent of Angola's economy, by UN estimates, is non-formal. Average people, to survive, must trade outside formal state channels. This, as the letter to Ed Garcia points out in the introduction to this article, is true of rebel groups and war zones worldwide.

Following the Complexities of the Shadows in the Example of Angola – From Informal Economies to Global Power

Angola has been at war for decades, first for independence from the Portuguese, and then in a civil war between the rebel forces Unita and the MPLA government (Maier, 1996; Human Rights Watch, 1994, 1999; Minter, 1994). Many people and countries worldwide have vested interests in the outcome of the war: Unita was long supported by the United States and by the apartheid South African Defense Forces; the MPLA by the socialist bloc of the Cold War. In addition, powerful international profiteers and transnational companies, ranging from interests in diamonds and oil to timber and seafood, have wild-catted enormous profits made possible by the political dislocations of war. The civil war has gone through cycles of peace accords and the re-eruption of war throughout the 1990s. At the turn of the century, the war has escalated dramatically: in 1999 there were 1.7 million internally displaced people inside the country, and hundreds of thousands more fled to other countries. Over a million people have been killed since hostilities began. In terms of governance, there are really two Angolas: the MPLA holds the major cosmopolitan areas and the major infrastructure (roadways, airports, oil production); Unita holds the rural areas and the food-producing regions. Thus people in the government areas have goods but suffer a lack of food while those in Unita-held zones have food but lack basic goods.

To focus on the highly profitable gem trade sustaining Savimbi's forces is to understand only a fragment of the complexities of extra-state networks. To understand the interconnections between power, politics, economics and survival that define Angola and its relationships within larger global systems it is critical to follow the complex linkages of state/non-state, legality/illegality and formal/informal *beyond* mere discussions of (a) large-scale gems and weapons networks; and (b) small-scale informal economies (Nordstrom, 1998).

First: *profitable trade in illicit and dangerous goods is intricately tied to informal trade.* Savimbi's weapons systems do not emerge out of a vacuum into the hands of his soldiers, nor do the gems and goods to pay for these flow straight from the mines into the hands of international smugglers. Each shipment is carried along a complex network of people – many, like the women who trade automatic weapons for food or the university graduates who work in the mines, do so in order to meet daily necessities. Savimbi's weapons and gems *depend* on these people, these linkages with informal networks. In war zones civilians and soldiers alike need food, clothing, medicines, daily supplies, etc., and supplying these requirements generally flows, like weapons and illicit goods, along extra-state routes – and often along the same extra-state routes. Like the harsh realities of survival, the complexities of trading illicit goods for survival are an ethically challenging issue for many of the people involved.

Second: *clear distinctions between legal and illegal, state and non-state, or local and international are often impossible to make.* Extra-state activities and the power politics that support them cannot be easily divided into opposing separate spheres of state/ legal and non-state/illegal. Like gems and weapons, everyday goods can follow international channels of production and distribution that may intersect with states, but are not bounded by them. They can partake of official channels, non-formal production systems, quasi-legal gray markets and downright illegal enterprises. A state actor can function simultaneously as a formally recognized official, a non-state actor (say, in his or her role as family member or service organization volunteer), a state-recognized manufacturer and a black-marketeer. A state actor can simultaneously vote sanctions into law and then ignore them for profit or power.[4] Disenfranchised civilians and wild-catting entrepreneurs bring everything from grains to industrial equipment through non-formal routes that link the cosmopolitan centers of the world with its hinterlands – hinterlands that may well be seen as the 'breadbaskets' of the world's states for precious minerals and fuels, food and timbers, labor and raw materials. As Strange (1996: 117) writes:

The fact is that while financial crime has grown enormously... it remains, legally and morally, an indeterminate gray area. The dividing line is seldom clear and is nowhere the same between transactions which are widely practiced but ethically questionable and those which are down right criminal.... The need to use such secret or covert financial channels is not only a prerogative of organized and economic criminal groups – but also of terrorist and revolutionary groups and indeed of many individuals and economic operators engaged in activities which are not necessarily illicit. Investigations into the biggest financial scandal of the last fifteen years, the bankruptcy of the Bank of Credit and Commerce international, showed that BCCI was engaged in 'reserved' or illicit financial services for a very varied group of clients, including Colombian narco-traffickers, Middle East terrorists and Latin American revolutionary groups, as well as tax evaders, corrupt politicians and several multinational companies [...].

These intersections of power, legality/illegality, non-legitimacy, and formality/non-formality are characteristic of shadow networks.

Third: *illicit and extra-state trade is, ironically, linked to development*. I have traveled to towns in the interior of Angola on several occasions. Many were among the most war-damaged I have seen in two decades of studying political violence. Roadways were heavily mined and beset by predatory armed bands, formal trade was virtually non-existent, banks were closed and state infrastructure was decimated. Yet in these besieged towns I found sophisticated electronic and computer equipment, transport vehicles, industrial supplies and other cosmopolitan goods. This involved trade that linked these remote areas to the major industrial centers of the world. It involved payments, not in the local Angolan kwanza (which does not trade on the inter-national market), but in convertible 'currencies' like gems, precious resources, luxury items like hardwoods and seafood, and possibly drugs and weapons. As dangerous and illegal as drug and illicit weapons trade may be, it is often the means by which citizens gain the currency to buy industrial necessities, agricultural supplies and development goods. Such illicit goods purchase hard currency, they broker power, they allow investments into land, legal industries and political part-nerships. They spawn and support subsidiary industries, both legal and illicit. And, of course, daily necessities like clothing, textbooks and medicines follow these same trading trajectories. If development is to take place without relying on illicit trade in dangerous goods, viable ways of making goods, services and payments available in these difficult circumstances need to be created.

Fourth: *illicit transaction and development link with political power*. The people in Angola who are adept at manipulating the junctures of licit/illicit markets to gain wealth often invest in legal enterprises in their countries. Illicit money, as Castells (1998) reminds us, must be laundered into legality. As business people amass economic power and status, they gain the ability to stand for political office. As influential business people, they may have the stature to work with international nongovernmental organizations, hold a position with the United Nations, consult for the World Bank. Business people who profit from shadow transactions are unlikely to give up shadow sources of power, profit and supply as they develop legitimate enterprises, and in fact, their success may depend on keeping these networks current.

Fifth: *the junctures of licit/illicit economy shape formal global markets*. In countries like Angola during the war, it may be impossible to conduct business without exploiting extra-state transactions. But it is important to remember all the goods that enter countries outside formal state channels constitute profits for legitimate businesses in industrial centers of the world. All US$500 billion worth of illicit weapons sold annually constitute a profit for legal arms industries in the industrial centers of the world. Angola is not unique: 50 percent of Italy's, 60 percent of Russia's, and up to 30 percent of the United States' economies are non-formal (Ayers, 1996). This vast set of global shadow exchanges affects global pricing, stock markets, interest rates and exchange rates, though these effects are as yet little researched or understood.

When we look at the networks that make such diamond/armament transfers possible, we are talking about thousands of people and billions of dollars annually, from a single diamond locale such as Angola alone. If we expand this to the other gem-producing regions of the world, and the armaments they purchase, the figures rise to millions of people and multi-billions of dollars. The number of people involved can rival populations of states. The revenues generated can far surpass the GNP of smaller nations. The power the leaders in these extra-state empires wield can rival that of state leaders. These vast networks shape the course of international affairs to as great a degree as the formal state apparatuses of some countries. When we expand out from gems and armaments to add in all extra-state industries, we are discussing a series of power grids that shape the fundamental economic-political dynamics of the world today.

Observations from Another Fieldsite[5]

War zones are defined by contradictions: the immense suffering and impoverishment of people fleeing ruined towns exist side by side with the immense profits of business people manipulating war economies. An example from my own field data can help introduce the latter. I often fly with emergency relief cargo planes when I am at the epicenters of conflict. These emergency airlifts are quintessentially international enterprises. They receive aid money, both from governments and large international nongovernmental organizations (INGOs). They require international alliances: airlifts are very expensive and cross a host of political, legal and technical jurisdictions. On a few occasions when I was preparing to ride with these cargo planes, I found the flights abruptly canceled with no explanation; but the planes departed at dawn, destination unknown. This in itself is unusual in airlift culture. Flight plans may not exist, pilots may give researchers unauthorized rides, but among colleagues (and this can extend to itinerant researchers) information is a commodity freely exchanged: staying safe in war zones depends on this.

I began to research these flight cancellations, and the facts turned out to be a study in power. A group of business people had requisitioned the plane (that means canceling not one, but five or six airlifts per day) to fly goods across the country: business goods, telecommunications equipment, war-related supplies, (stolen) motor vehicles, VCRs, luxury items, precious resources – the 'hard currency' of war zones. These people not only had the money to 'requisition' an airlift plane for personal use, they had the power to make sure the entire machinery that supported the airlift – from governmental to intergovernmental aid organizations and personnel (in this case, USAID among others was providing monetary support in the millions of dollars, though I doubt they were aware of the non-aid uses the plane was being put to) – was kept uninformed or unconcerned. Under cover of dark, planes were sometimes 'requisioned' to cross international borders surreptitiously, collect state-of-the-art computers and military supplies (with planes, we are talking not pounds, but tons of cargo) and fly them back into the country to top military bases.[6]

These aspects of 'business as usual' raise the larger analytical issue of currency markets. In war zones, currencies often collapse, and black market (or 'street') currency exchanges are the norm. Those who control the black market money exchanges also control the exchange rates. These are, in effect, more powerful than formal institutions: they set the 'true' currency prices for an entire nation. The rates change daily, the product of complex monetary calculations. This itself represents an interesting study in power: in the midst of a war zone where all telecommunications and electricity were knocked out with frequency, business people at various ends of the country would work in unison, along with many others in a world economy, to calculate and set daily currency prices countrywide. These are extra-state calculations, they do not run through the banks and the government institutions of the country. These currency markets are very international: business people are calculating money indices based not only on internal conditions, but on a host of global market factors that range from the accessibility of goods and their worth to international exchange rates for hard currencies.

These fundamental financial systems can be found in many guises worldwide. Take, for example, the extra-state 'banking systems' in Asia. People often think of offshore financial interests and their relationship to money laundering when thinking of extra-state banking systems. But a far more mundane, yet powerful, 'informal' banking system is in place throughout the world. A customer, for example, chooses an informal 'bank' in one country in Asia and can send any amount of money to a receiving 'bank' in another country in Asia to hold for anyone the sender designates. Cash, goods and credit flow along these banking lines. This system may be non-formal, and the 'banks' little more than storefronts, but the system is both vast and powerful, transmitting untold fortunes through family and ethnic linkages, business partnerships and triad associations.

The Defining Characteristics and Cultures of Shadow Networks

One of the more interesting questions regarding these vast economic-political networks is how such massive amounts of goods and money, which follow such a complex set of exchange routes and political associations, flow as smoothly as they do. In plain words: Savimbi's gems get to Antwerp, Belgium and then on to rings on our global fingers without a great deal more, and sometimes less, murder and mayhem than state-based transactions do. The billions that flow through the informal banks of Asia function quite a bit like state-supported banks in that their customers do not usually lose their money. In a nutshell, the system works. But *how* is another matter. Many people I have spoken to about this respond that the system works because if it does not, people are simply killed. That may or may not be true: the fact is, it is an assumption, people have not collected representative data. We simply do not know how these vast billion- to trillion-dollar systems function on a day-to-day basis.[7]

Part of the answer lies in the fact that extra-state networks are not haphazard collections of people in ad hoc groups circling like moths around the light of profit. There is an explicit assumption in many analyses of state and non-state actors that states are somehow supra-communities, born of unique institutions of leadership that are not replicated outside the formal institutions of the state. No matter how successful or large a non-state collectivity, it will never approximate the moral community of the state. However true the existential answer to this is, practicalities demand a more nuanced assessment.

From diamonds to drugs, dominions exist that follow hierarchies of authority, rules of conduct, ways of punishing transgression and codes of behavior. Within these dominions, communities form, ideologies evolve and worldwide alliances and antagonisms are developed. These cannot be confused with states, but such inter-related transnational associations do have governing structures, law-like apparatuses and security forces. The people populating international extra-state networks forge trade agreements, foreign policy and currency exchanges. Susan Strange (1996: 112) discusses the 'transnational diplomacy between national mafias' that operates worldwide today. The people forging these networks set up the transport routes, communication linkages and banking systems to sustain their interactions.

Profiteers, smugglers and black/gray market merchants are not isolated actors loosely linked into a web of profit. Farmers who plant drug-related crops or miners who harvest gems have families and children they must provide for, in a variety of ways, from paying mortgages to celebrating birthdays. Truckers who transport illicit goods need tires and tune-ups for their trucks, and dental work for themselves and their families the same as if they were ferrying post-toasties cereals. Pilots trained at accredited airschools fly smuggled goods, often wearing professional pilot's emblems and uniforms. The banker that launders the money and the college student who buys a smuggled diamond-studded Rolex watch or deals a few drugs to pay his or her tuition may not fit the image of the dangerous drug lord, but they are as essential to the whole enterprise as the growers and the transporters. All of these people are deeply immersed in society and civil life.

I am not arguing an ethical point here, nor am I arguing that there is a moral equivalency between people who operate in the shadows and those who operate in formal state systems.[8] I am, instead, exploring the theoretical implications of the defining realities of shadow non-state systems. My goal is to challenge simplistic notions of non-state networks as 'merely' markets – devoid of social, cultural, political and legal ramifications. It is also to challenge 'mere' outlaw notions that non-state systems operate on the sheer violent rule of tooth and claw. Neither of these approaches can explain how these vast networks operate across up to a third of global transactional exchanges.

One of the answers to the question of how these vast international extra-state networks operate as coherently as they do is that people in these systems generally trust (and trust implies interpersonal and cultural definition) that the transaction will occur as predicted, and that they will remain safe (Gambetta, 1988a). The fact that large-scale massacres, wars and trails of dead bodies are found with far less regularity within these shadow networks than in and among the wars of states attests to the fact that the systems do work. This is no mean feat when we consider we are talking of millions of people exchanging billions of dollars' worth of goods and services.[9] Ernest Gellner (1988: 147) provides an interesting take:

> The Hobbesian problem arises from the assumption that anarchy, absence of enforcement, leads to distrust and social disintegration... but there is a certain amount of interesting empirical evidence which points the other way. The paradox is: it is precisely anarchy which engenders trust or, if you want to use another name, which engenders social cohesion.

In a powerful irony, even Hobbes recognized that networks of self-interest were grounded in cultural codes of trust (Gambetta, 1988b: 215). Right or wrong, Gellner asks us to understand how what is taken to be anarchy becomes imbued with pattern and value. Chingono (1996: 114), writing on the war in Mozambique, captures well the paradoxes that can describe the complex intersections of legality/illegality and the state:

> Although operating within these constraints, the grass-roots war economy was more predictable and rational in many respects than the official one. Illegal and unrecorded trade was not haphazard but institutionalized, operating according to a system of rules known to all participants. Examples included the standardized equivalences observed for barter transactions, the set rate for paying border guides, the arrangements set up for the terms of clientage, and the reciprocal obligations of other personal ties. The organization of a grass-roots war economy depended to a great extent on these reciprocal obligations of personal ties. The trust and confidence inspired by personal relations or common cultural background provided the reliability and predictability that were so conspicuously lacking in the official economy. To some extent, therefore, the grass-roots war economy generated alternative economic opportunities for people as well as an alternative society, with parallel religio-economic institutions alongside official ones.

How large, and how interrelated, are shadow networks; how many networks operate at any given time around the globe? Pat answers are, obviously, impossible. But several key observations are possible. Informal economies (small-scale subsistence), large-scale gray and black markets (from arms through luxury items to oil and freon), and state industries and personnel (from sanctions-breaking technology to corrupt customs officials) are more interrelated than neoclassical theories suggest. I have sought to show in the examples such as Angola and of the business people commandeering aid flights and setting international currency exchange rates how running gems, for example, links within larger international exchange networks ranging from armaments through high-tech computers and industrial equipment to basic foods and medicines. Strange (1996: 111) observes that 'what is new and of importance in the international political economy is the networks of links being forged between organized crime in different parts of the world.' The lines between state and extra-state power can easily blur here: 'At the heart of the system', writes Castells (1998: 167), 'there is money laundering by the hundreds of billions (maybe trillions) of dollars. Complex financial schemes and international trade networks link up the criminal economy to the formal economy.' As I have discussed, such wealth and influence – straddling licit/illicit lines – can translate into significant political authority.

At the same time these networks are not all-inclusive: the gem runners in Angola may have nothing to do with the drug runners in Colombia or the non-state banking ventures in Asia. Neoclassical theory tends to postulate non-state networks as quite discrete: there are smugglers, there is official corruption and there are informal subsistence economies and, essentially, never shall these three meet.

In fact, judging from my data, it would seem that integrating networks internationally is viewed as desirable in practice. A clear indication of this can be shown in exploring the question of why some drug smuggling networks based in Latin America and Southeast Asia send drugs to Europe via Africa. Any number of ports, from remote Namibia to urban Nigeria, broker drugs from these drug-producing regions on their way to western destinations. The logic of markets and rational analysis would assume the routes with the least number of stops and locations where illegal goods can be confiscated and the carriers arrested or executed would be the most desirable – in other words, a route straight from Latin America or Asia to Europe makes the best sense. No matter how easy it is to get illegal goods into an intermediate port, it is just as hard getting them into Europe from Asia, Latin America or Africa. Why, then, route through Africa? A part of the equation might be that the heavy flow of precious minerals and gems, ivory, weapons, mercenaries, food and medicines in and out of Africa provides more avenues for other types of goods to travel along, speaking to the interrelatedness of diverse networks. But this is only part of the answer, for such exchanges route worldwide. Another part of the answer is that in a different kind of market and political logic, associations of extra-state networks (and their state linkages) are more productive and powerful than smaller, isolated coalitions of people and profit. Routing drugs through Africa links Africa with the goods and power politics of Latin America and Asia, and provides the latter with the rich resources and human power of Africa. Each country and continent gains more by its association with others than it could hope to achieve alone – much like multinationals.[...]

Networks, like the markets and the politics that gird them, are constellations of economic, political, demographic, historical and cultural processes (Appadurai, 1996; Greif, 1996). As such, they are dynamic, not static, phenomena: as the patterns of the constellations of factors that define networks change over time and circumstance, so too do the defining characteristics of the networks. Perhaps the very extra-state flexibility and fluidity of these exchange systems are a factor in their success.

A Question of Sovereignty

There is a general tendency to postulate that the non-formal markets of eastern Europe, the former Soviet States, Africa and Asia are the result of a combination of changing political regimes, social transitions and economic opportunism. The belief is that as these countries settle down in the course of normal state development their economies will become increasingly defined by state-regulated formal economies. In this view, while illicit markets and mafias will always exist in the countries of the world, they comprise a marginal part of the world's real power structures and economy. My research suggests we need to rethink these assumptions. I can stand in the most remote war zones of the world and watch a veritable supermarket of goods move into and out of the country along extra-state lines. Tracing the supply routes of these goods takes one through both major and minor economic centers of the world. The sanctions-regulated laptop satellite-linked computers I see on the battlefields of Africa are made in major cosmopolitan centers of the world, and the precious resources and human labor that pay for these commodities move along the same channels back to those cosmopolitan centers. Tanks, watches, industrial components, VCRs, electronic equipment, books, covert information, pornography and uranium travel these same routes. At the bottom line, it would appear non-formal economies play a formidable role in countries like Japan, Germany and the USA as well as in areas of more rapid economic and political change and development.

Given the complex social, cultural, political and legal, as well as economic, characteristics defining the vast international networks I discussed in the last section, and the enduring global nature of these networks described in the paragraph above, the question of the very nature of the power adhering to shadow networks arises. Tilly (1985: 169) opens his article 'War Making and State Making as Organized Crime': 'If protection rackets represent organized crime at its smoothest, then war making and state making – quintessential protection rackets with the advantage of legitimacy – qualify as our largest examples of organized crime.'

Tilly argues that war-making, extraction and capital accumulation interacted in shaping the development of the European state, and asserts that 'banditry, piracy, gangland rivalry, policing, and war making all belong on the same continuum' in this state-making process (1985: 170; see also Gallant, 1999; Heyman, 1999). Distinctions of legitimate/illegitimate force are of little importance in this process. States seek to monopolize the use of force over all others – and what, Tilly (1985: 173) asks, distinguishes the violence employed by states from the violence produced by anyone else?

> Eventually, the personnel of states purveyed violence on a larger scale, more effectively, more efficiently, with wider assent from their subject populations, and with readier collaboration from neighboring authorities than did the personnel of other organizations. But it took a long time for that series of distinctions to become established.

Tilly is discussing the period of state-making in Europe, a time now relegated to the historical past. Yet vast networks continue to link war zones, banditry and extraction. Perhaps the links between war-making, banditry and extraction are necessary to the continued success of the state. But Tilly is clear about the fact that the state gains legitimacy because it ultimately wields force more effectively than competing systems. If Strange (1996) and Castells (1998) are correct in their observations that criminal organizations are forming an unprecedented set of developmental alliances that are producing global networks, then it becomes logical to ask if the ability of the state to maintain its legitimacy and sovereign status will be challenged. Both authors see the ultimate authority of the state being undermined by these transnational associations.

Such questions prompt inquiries into the ultimate definition of sovereignty and its relationship to power. Is it possible to speak of non-state sovereignty in any aspect? Do coherent shadow networks – as transnational social, cultural, political and economic systems – operate as distinct power configurations which have full, or sovereign, authority – over which no larger power has control? Robert Latham's (1997) concept of social sovereignty is useful in this context. His work on social sovereignty revitalizes dynamic definitions of sovereignty as complex domains of power and exchange that move the concept out from under a purely state-based focus. Latham asks: 'But if the sovereign nation-state is a particular form of state, why cannot the state be a particular form of sovereignty?' and goes on to question the supposed monopoly of sovereignty by the state and according to territoriality. Latham's concern in this analysis is with globalizing financial market systems and the 'social sovereignty' that can explain internationally based collectivities. But the definition he applies to sovereignty fits well the 'shadow' power grids I have been discussing. Latham (1997: 23) asks:

> When does the web of global financial markets – or any given domain for that matter – constitute a sovereignty? ... [T]here is one key marker of a sovereign domain or social sovereignty. The degree to which upon entering the domain an agent is assigned or feels compelled to occupy or resist a role or place within the webs of codes, practices, and significances that constitute the domain. Thus, constitutive capacities rest exactly on the capacity to mark and code phenomena – from bodies and materials, to communications and values – that enter a relevant domain.

Latham (1997: 29) concludes:

> Sovereignty, not just as an attribute of the state but as a basic dimension of modernity, serves as a compass for directing attention to questions about accountability towards, responsibility for, and authority over setting the terms of social existence.

As this study has pointed out, shadow networks forge economic policies, they operate within political realms, they fashion foreign policy. These networks have developed dispute resolution systems and systems of enforcement. They have codes of conduct and rules of behavior set in social and cultural systems. They are not states, but they share these attributes with states. And perhaps they share the status of sovereignty – a social sovereignty in this case – as well. Studies of states are abundant while studies of the shadows are underdeveloped: what theory lacks is an understanding of the ways in which shadow networks function in daily international life – *how*, for example, disputes are settled and judgments enforced; *who* wields authority in the junctures of state/non-state transactions; and *how* extra-state realities shape global markets and fashion political power.

States, Tilly reminds us, first forged power and the means to protect this power, and then fashioned legitimacy. Sovereignty was a product of this process, not a natural attribute of a natural political unit. The links of war-making, banditry, extraction and state-making continue. Who will be most effective at mobilizing economies and the force to protect them in the future is as yet an unanswered question. What is certain is that sovereignty, authority and power are shaped today by shadow systems. A better understanding of the shadows might provide us with the tools to understand the Asian market collapse, failed states and the dynamics of in/equality affecting the future potential of people globally.

NOTES

1   I have conducted extended fieldwork in Sri Lanka (1979, 1981, 1982–3, 1985, 1986, 1988, 1991), Mozambique (1988, 1989, 1990–1, 1994, 1995, 1996, 1997, 1998, 1999), South Africa (1995, 1996, 1997, 1998, 1999) and Angola (1997, 1998, 1999); shorter visits to countries in Southern Africa and Southeast Asia in the years 1979–91; and shorter visits to Southern Africa and Central Europe in the 1990s.

2   Personal communication, senior economists and resident representatives of UNDP and World Bank offices in Mozambique and Angola; and senior economists of UN offices at the European headquarters.

3   The implications of this are extensive. For example, researchers are well aware that rebel goups do not have access to state taxes for the purchase of their military supplies and governing costs, and must raise money outside formal state channels. Given the tendency to disaggregate extra-state activities into distinct ethical categories, researchers often find it difficult to investigate these money-raising and weapons-purchasing actions if they support the group in any way. Thus, researchers who view a rebel movement in a favorable light often do not discuss extra-state illicit transactions for weapons, while those less supportive of the movements they study point out the links between weapons, drugs and illicit goods in the political economy of the rebel group.

4   Few people are surprised today by the degree to which state actors can be embroiled in illegal or extra-state activities. From the popular culture of Mel Gibson's movie *Air America* to the politically charged problems defining US–Mexico relations on drug and drug enforcement issues concerning the degree of state involvement, the pull of high profits and power is well recognized. Another example is less widely recognized, but equally influential in shaping ground-level politics. UN peace-keepers have been praised for providing solutions to intractable wars, and their work is often exemplary. But the story is more complex than that. Sarajevo provides an apt example, where during the worst of the war when UN peace-keeping troops were stationed there, a large percentage of Sarajevo's economy was diverted into black marketeering through UN troops (Fetherston and Nordstrom, 1995). 'The UN soliders are making themselves and the Sarajevo mafia rich. The locals are the middlemen for a trade in cigarettes, alcohol, food, prostitution and heroin, worth millions of pounds' (O'Kane, 1993). Not only luxury items flowed along these channels. Tanks and weapons rumbled along these pathways, from states through peace-keepers to fighting forces, each nationality following the alliances of their states, or, more obscurely, the alliances of profiteering.

5   Given the sensitive nature of the information discussed in this section, I have intentionally left this location unnamed.

6   The story is sometimes much bigger: in one case a major emergency airlift run by an international organization and paid for by such donors as USAID (who, I am sure, was unaware of any untoward activities) was headed by a European man who was both an international smuggler and a profiteer. The planes actually did fly many tons of cargo to bombed-out townspeople for months on end, but a number of other less altruistic activities were taking place as well. This one airlift operation in this one war zone grossed consider-able sums of money, though few know how high those figures actually are.

7   I have done interviews with United Nations officials and lawyers alike asking what actual
    data they have on what rules of conduct define these systems and how they are 'enforced'.
    Each one – from the UNDP officers (Dr Aboagye, Dr Clements, Dierckx de Casterle) to
    academic economists (Professors Dutt and Melber) – said that the question was fascinat-
    ing, but the data non-existent. And, lawyers and UN staff alike assured me, lawyers and
    economists do not 'do' fieldwork; without primary data, theory cannot emerge.
8   For a discussion of the negative impact of illicit networks, see Nordstrom (1999).
9   Gambetta (1988b: 230) stresses a key consideration here in writing: 'What is at issue is
    not the importance of exploring in greater depth the causality of those forms of cooper-
    ation which are independent of trust, but the fact that economizing on trust is not as
    generalizable a strategy as might at first appear, and that, if it is risky to bank on trust, it is
    just as risky to fail to understand how it works, what forces other than successful cooper-
    ation bring it about, and how it relates to the conditions of cooperation. Considering the
    extremely limited literature on this crucial subject it seems that economizing on trust and
    economizing on understanding it have been unjustifiably conflated.'
    [...]

REFERENCES

Appadurai, Arjun (1996) *Modernity at Large: Cultural Dimensions of Globalization*. Minneap-
    olis: University of Minnesota Press.
Ayers, Ed (1996) 'The Expanding Shadow Economy', *World Watch* 9(4): 11–23.
Bureau for International Narcotics and Law Enforcement Affairs (1997) *International Nar-
    cotics Control Strategy Report 1996*. Bureau for International Narcotics and Law Enforce-
    ments Affairs, Washington, DC: US Department of State, March.
Castells, Manuel (1998) *End of Millennium*. London: Blackwell.
Chingono, Mark (1996) *The State, Violence and Development*. Brookfield: Avebury.
Fetherston, Betts and Carolyn Nordstrom (1995) 'Overcoming Conceptual Habitus in
    Conflict Management: UN Peacekeeping and Warzone Ethnography', *Peace and Change*
    20(1): 94–119.
Gallant, Thomas (1999) 'Brigandage, Piracy, Capitalism, and State-Formation: Trans-
    national Crime from a Historical World-Systems Perspective', pp. 25–61 in Josiah Heyman
    (ed.) *States and Illegal Practices*. Oxford: Berg.
Gambetta, Diego (ed.) (1988a) *Trust: Making and Breaking Cooperative Relations*. Oxford:
    Basil Blackwell.
Gambetta, Diego (1988b) 'Can We Trust?', pp. 213–37 in D. Gambetta (ed.) *Trust: Making
    and Breaking Cooperative Relations*. Oxford: Basil Blackwell.
Gellner, Ernest (1988) 'Trust, Cohesion, and Social Order', pp. 142–57 in D. Gambetta
    (ed.) *Trust: Making and Breaking Cooperative Relations*. Oxford: Basil Blackwell.
Grief, Avner (1996) 'Contracting, Enforcement, and Efficiency: Economics Beyond the
    Law', pp. 239–65 in M. Bruno and B. Pleskovic (eds) *Annual World Bank Conference on
    Development Economics 1996*. Washington, DC: World Bank.
Gupta, Suraj B. (1992) *Black Income in India*. New Delhi: Sage.
Heyman, Josiah (ed.) (1999) *States and Illegal Practices*. Oxford: Berg.
Human Rights Watch Arms Project and Human Rights Watch/Africa (1994) *Angola: Arms
    Trade and Violations of the Laws of War Since the 1992 Elections*. New York: Human Rights
    Watch.
Human Rights Watch Arms Project and Human Rights Watch/Africa (1999) *Angola Unravels*.
    London: Human Rights Watch.

Latham, Robert (1997) 'States, Global Markets, and Social Sovereignty', paper presented at the Social Science Research Council conference Sovereignty and Security, Notre Dame, 18–20 April.

Lawson, Tony (1997) *Economics and Reality*. London: Routledge.

Lopez, G. and D. Cortwright (1998) 'Making Targets "Smart" from Sanctions', paper delivered at the International Studies Association meetings, Minneapolis, 18–22 March.

Maier, Karl (1996) *Angola: Promises and Lies*. Rivonia: William Waterman.

Minter, William (1994) *Apartheid's Contras: An Inquiry into the Roots of War in Angola and Mozambique*. London: Zed Books.

Nordstrom, Carolyn (1995) 'Contested Identities/Essentially Contested Powers', in K. Rupesinghe (ed.) *Conflict Transformation*. London: Macmillan.

Nordstrom, Carolyn (1997) *A Different Kind of War Story*. Philadelphia: University of Pennsylvania Press.

Nordstrom, Carolyn (1998) 'Out of the Shadows: Post-War Transformations and Extra-State Realities', presentation at the European University Institute, Florence, Italy, 28–9 March.

Nordstrom, Carolyn (1999) 'Visible Wars and Invisible Girls: Shadow Industries and the Politics of Not-Knowing', *International Feminist Journal of Politics* 1(1): 14–33.

Nordstrom, Carolyn and Antonius Robben (eds) (1995) *Fieldwork Under Fire: Contemporary Studies of Violence and Survival*. Berkeley: University of California Press.

O'Kane, Maggie (1993) 'The Soldiers Are Out of Control: They Are Feasting on a Dying City', *The Guardian Weekly* 5 September.

Reno, William (1995) *Corruption and State Politics in Sierra Leone*. Cambridge: Cambridge University Press.

Reno, William (1998) *Warlord Politics and African States*. Boulder, CO: Lynne Rienner.

Richards, Paul (1996) *Fighting for the Rainforest: War, Youth and Resources in Sierra Leone*. Oxford: James Currey.

Sassen, Saskia (1998) *Globalization and its Discontents*. New York: The New Press.

Singapore Newsroom (1997) WWW posting +65 870 3571.

Strange, Susan (1996) *The Retreat of the State: The Diffusions of Power in the World Economy*. Cambridge: Cambridge University Press.

Tilly, Charles (1985) 'War Making and State Making as Organized Crime', in P.B. Evans, D. Rueschemeyer and T. Skocpol (eds) *Bring[ing] the State Back In*. Cambridge: Cambridge University Press.

Tyson, Rae (1995) 'Freon-Smuggling Latest Miami Vice', WWW reprint of 1995 *Detroit News* report.

United Nations Research Institute (1995) *States of Disarray: The Social Effects of Globalization*. London: UNRISD.

Subject Index

Specific page numbers (e.g. 31–3) indicate that the discussion continues over the relevant pages; non-specific page numbers indicate separate references on two (31f) or more (31ff) pages. The index is thematic so that entries sometimes refer to a relevant theme rather than an exact use of a given word, concept, or phrase.

NAFTA 119, 134, 177, 187, 232, 298
narrow approach to state 6–7
nation 65, 229, 234f
nation-building 296
nation-state 12, 14, 16, 65, 73, 101, 106, 118, 128, 229
    as tendency 21, 65–6, 106, 118, 182 n., 204 n., 311
nation-state system 63, 168
    crisis of 134, 141
national identity 266, 297, 311
    and cities 297
    crisis of 18
national liberation struggles 314
national money 63, 66, 105, 175
national scale 10, 12
    crisis of 18, 21
national self-determination 65
national territorial state 11, 108, 186
    crisis of 108
national unity 73
nationalism 11, 106, 230, 234, 248, 311
nationality 10, 234
    unity of 10, 65, 73
nationalization of class 10
nationalization of economy 10, 66, 68, 107, 229
    see also market, internal (national)
nationalization of state 10, 106f, 230
nationalization of territory 46, 63, 66, 68, 72
NATO 124ff, 128
naturalism 38
naturalization 1–2, 5–7, 10–11, 40, 43ff, 50, 84, 229, 311
navigation 32
navy 36
Neo-classical period 30
neo-Gramscianism 12f, 148f, 161
neo-liberalism 14, 17f, 111, 134, 147f, 149f, 150, 156f, 159, 176
    embedded neo-liberalism 13, 148, 156, 160
neo-medievalism 13
neo-mercantilism 147, 151, 153f, 156f, 159
Netherlands 36ff, 104, 154, 156, 232
    see also Holland; United Provinces
network 14, 19f
neutralization 36–8, 40, 46, 50
new constitutionalism 171
New Left 111
new localism 4–5, 14
new regionalism 4–5, 14, 17, 259ff
new right 111
new social movements 11, 16, 21, 111, 266, 281, 302f
    see also "users'" movements
Nicaragua 314
nomads 7, 319

non-formal economy 339
nuclear age 108, 121, 281f

OECD 125
offshore economy 13f, 167, 172–5, 180, 210, 328
    and state 14, 175
    see also tax haven
open door policy 213f
organized crime 328–31, 333
Ottoman empire 131

painting 36, 43
Pakistan 311
Palestine 240, 310, 313
Panama 174
parcellization 8f, 10, 74, 87, 90, 94
partnership 4
path-dependency 8, 17, 133, 136, 268
patriarchy 19, 313–14, 318
patrimonial state 29, 56
patriotism 46
peasantry 70f, 82, 88, 233
"people-nation" 10, 29, 44, 66, 72, 77, 105f, 296, 306
periodization 2, 21, 30–1, 56, 68–9
peripheral Fordism 245, 250f, 254 n.
petty bourgeoisie 82
Philippines 137, 139
place (matters) 297
planning 33, 41, 95
Poland 109, 119f
policy
    industrial 153f, 156, 158
    infrastructural 154
    regional 257–63
policy networks 190ff, 215f
polis 69
    see also ancient state
political arithmetic 37, 41f
    see also statistics
political geography 9, 11f
political imaginary 3, 12, 46, 124, 172, 306
polymorphous crystallization 12, 122f
popular-democratic 19
popular movements 305
Portugal 32, 26, 118, 136
positivism 67
post-colonialism 314–15
post-disciplinarity 4f
post-Fordism 246, 289f, 304
postmodern state 15, 128
post-national citizens 303f
post-national scale 122, 233, 236f, 287–8
    and cities 18, 287f, 303f
post-Westphalian state system 15, 186f, 203–4
power container 1, 2f, 8f, 102–4, 118

Name Index

Specific page numbers (e.g. 31–3) indicate that the discussion continues over the relevant pages; non-specific page numbers indicate separate references on two (31f) or more (31ff) pages.

Printed and bound by CPI Group (UK) Ltd, Croydon, CR0 4YY

13/06/2023

03226537-0002